Nazi Cinema as Enchantment

Studies in German Literature, Linguistics, and Culture

Edited by James Hardin
(South Carolina)

Nazi Cinema
as Enchantment

The Politics of Entertainment in the Third Reich

Mary-Elizabeth O'Brien

CAMDEN HOUSE

First published 2004 by Camden House
Reprinted in paperback 2006

Camden House is an imprint of Boydell & Brewer Inc.
668 Mt. Hope Avenue, Rochester, NY 14620, USA
and of Boydell & Brewer Limited
PO Box 9, Woodbridge, Suffolk IP12 3DF, UK

ISBN
Cloth 1–57113–283–X
Paperback 1–57113–334–8

Library of Congress Cataloging-in-Publication Data

O'Brien, Mary-Elizabeth, 1959–
 Nazi cinema as enchantment: the politics of entertainment in the
Third Reich / Mary-Elizabeth O'Brien
  p. cm. — (Studies in German Literature, Linguistics, and Culture)
Includes bibliographical references and index.
ISBN 1–57113–283–X (alk. paper)
 1. Motion pictures — Germany — History. 2. National socialism
and motion pictures. I. Title. II. Series: Studies in German literature,
linguistics, and culture (Unnumbered)

PN1995.9.N36O27 2003
791.43'658—dc22
                                                    2003017140

A catalogue record for this title is available from the British Library.

This publication is printed on acid-free paper.
Printed in the United States of America

For my husband, Joseph Chautard

Contents

Illustrations

All photographs are reproduced courtesy of the Bundesarchiv-Filmarchiv Berlin.

Acknowledgments

IN 1991 I participated in an NEH summer seminar on Weimar Cinema taught by Anton Kaes at the University of California, Berkeley that inspired me to pursue film studies and led me down the long and winding path to the completion of this book. I am deeply indebted to Anton Kaes for introducing me to the field and for his continued interest in my project over the years.

Many individuals and organizations have helped me complete this book. I have profited greatly from discussions with friends and colleagues, who have given me bibliographical leads, information, and food for thought. For their generosity of spirit and valuable insight, I would like to thank Ehrhard Bahr, Steve Brockmann, Grace Burton, Bruce Campbell, Ruth Cape, Mao Chen, Glenn Cuomo, Cindy Evans, Hédi Jaouad, Karen Koehler, Marcia Klotz, Reinhard Mayer, Vibs Petersen, Shirley Smith, Frauke von der Horst, and Marc-André Wiesmann. In 1996 I attended an NEH summer seminar on Nazi Cinema at Cornell University taught by David Bathrick. The lively debates and collective moviegoing experience helped to refine my arguments, and I am grateful to David Bathrick and all the participants for their keen observations and collegiality.

Robert Reimer and Richard Etlin edited my work for anthologies and provided helpful advice. Sabina Hake, Karl-Heinz Schoeps, and Marc Silberman read the manuscript in its entirety and offered constructive criticism that I have tried to follow. I owe a substantial debt of gratitude to Kristina Sazaki for reading the manuscript several times and always giving me an exacting evaluation and creative suggestions. I am grateful for the opportunity to work with General Editor Jim Hardin and Managing Editor Jim Walker at Camden House and appreciate their openness, skillful reading, and careful editing. Ralf-Dietmar Hegel and Karla Horstmann-Hegel opened up their home to me during my first summer of archival research in Berlin, and made it possible for me to work unfettered during the day and look forward to coming home at night. I am grateful to Barbara Gügold for sponsoring my Fulbright application and inviting me to lecture in her courses at the Humboldt Universität zu Berlin. I would also like to thank Martin H. Geyer for inviting me to lecture at the Ludwig Maximilian Universität Munich and providing the rare opportunity to share my research with such challenging and engaged graduate students.

Numerous individuals at the Bundesarchiv-Filmarchiv Berlin helped me find materials and made me feel welcome. Document librarians Ute Klawitter, M. Kiel, and Heinz-Joachim Preßler familiarized me with their vast collection and provided helpful tips. Librarian Frau Kuschke generously allowed me access to the film journals and rare books. Frau Teschner and Herr Berger tirelessly spooled hundreds of films for me. Most of all, I would like to thank researcher Evelyn Hampicke for always making sure I had what I needed, sharing her passion for film, and spending countless hours discussing Nazi cinema. All the illustrations for this book are reproduced with permission of the Bundesarchiv-Filmarchiv Berlin.

At the Hochschule für Film und Fernsehen Konrad Wolf in Babelsberg-Potsdam, I was granted access to original film scripts, rare manuscripts, and fragile materials. Newspaper Librarian Renate Göthe helped me locate numerous articles. Librarian Ursula Schneeweiß was undaunted by my enormous requests and always seemed to find some jewel I had overlooked.

Several extended stays in Berlin and at research libraries in the United States were necessary to complete this project. I am deeply grateful to the National Endowment for the Humanities, the German Academic Exchange Service (DAAD), and the Fulbright Commission for their generous support. Skidmore College provided substantial funding from a Faculty Research Initiative Grant, a yearlong sabbatical leave, and a semester leave of absence, which allowed me uninterrupted periods of time for research and writing. I greatly appreciate the support I received from the college, my department, chairs John Anzalone, Giuseppe Faustini, and Paty Rubio, and Dean of the Faculty Phyllis Roth, who recognized the considerable resources required and offered encouragement at every step. Finally, I would like to thank my family for their gentle prodding and constant faith in me.

M.-E. O
Saratoga Springs, New York
July 2003

Introduction

THE CINEMATIC EXPERIENCE has often been compared to a dream. As we sit in the dark and allow uncontrollable images, sounds, and sensations to waft over us, we submit ourselves to someone else's dream, someone else's vision of reality. Working perhaps best on the emotional, non-cognitive level, film can transport us in an oneiric state to a simpler world where we need not, indeed cannot, participate physically in the events taking place before our eyes. Bystanders yielding to a communal fantasy, the audience safely maneuvers the dangers and pleasures of the cinema, assured of returning to the light of day unscathed. Akin to the national obsession with ecstatic subordination, the cinematic experience in the Third Reich offered the masses submission through entertainment. The National Socialist regime considered film's power to persuade and placate crucial to its cause and went to extraordinary lengths in an attempt to control celluloid dreams.

Between 1933 and 1945, the German motion picture industry produced over a thousand entertainment films and a vibrant cinema culture, captivating audiences with penetrating images, compelling stories, and a glamorous star cult. Although the National Socialist government considered film a vital indoctrination tool and instituted measures to regulate all aspects of filmmaking, it also recognized that the most effective propaganda hides its intentions and appeals to the emotions. Feature films that catered to the needs of a mass audience and were promoted as ideology-free consumer products could function as political vehicles by teaching behavioral modes, nourishing the demand for a private realm, and granting subversive desire a measured release. Nazi entertainment films sought to influence viewers via the conventions of classical cinema: emotional involvement, identification with characters and stars, and well-worn genres. The Nazi regime did not merely terrorize its citizens into submission, it also used seduction and offered people many of the things they wanted: stability, a traditional value system, a sense of belonging, and the belief in a better standard of living. Much of Nazi cinema's popularity rested upon its ability to express positive social fantasies and promote the enchantment of reality, creating a place so delightful that one wanted to share in the dream at any price.

I use the term "the enchantment of reality" here to denote how a motion picture can attract and move spectators so deeply that it influences them without their conscious knowledge. In the Third Reich, this process was orchestrated to achieve concrete political goals. The propaganda ministry promoted stirring motion pictures because it believed that intense emotional involvement could alter the audience's *perception* of the world so radically that it *felt* as if reality had changed. Transported by ardent emotions that filtered reality and made it more appealing, the audience could be motivated to accept that whatever transpired in everyday life was irrelevant as long as they felt satisfied. Moreover, if roused to ecstasy, a state beyond reason and governed by profound feelings, viewers could be provoked to frenzied action.

The enchantment of reality operating in Nazi cinema and society fulfilled a profound hunger for emotional gratification and moral certitude, and should be examined within the context of the larger ideological debates surrounding the crisis of modernity. Already during the First World War, notable German philosophers observed that modernity had drained the world of spirituality, fervor, and ethical direction. Siegfried Kracauer, for example, lamented in his essay, "On Experiencing War" (1915), that the average German had recently enjoyed material gains but was suffocating in a sterile environment devoid of meaning. In the decade preceding the war, "there was," according to Kracauer, "precious little that bound people together, and not just bound them together, but also stirred their highest will. Politics often repelled, was petty, and taken care of by a minority; art satisfied only individual, isolated parts of the soul." Kracauer continued, "Above all, the most important needs of the soul, the religious, lay fallow: there was no living, universally binding belief corresponding to our essence that could have expressed it."[1] Without a stable belief system capable of unifying the community, the masses embraced war as a guiding principle. War liberated such pent-up sentiments as "the sense of duty, the joy of being in agreement with the community, the numbing rapture gleaned from the mood of the masses, the adventurous impulse, the pleasure in smashing things up, ambition, curiosity," and channeled these feelings into a meaningful framework that satisfied individual needs and guaranteed social cohesion. The sacrifices war demanded were inherently part of its appeal because: "it is the most natural condition for men to serve ecstatically the purpose of an ideal. Even the smallest action becomes sacred and the sense of life endlessly exalted."[2]

Kracauer's analysis corresponds to the prevalent view of modernity as a shattering of foundations, a soulless age bereft of meaning. While Kracauer saw modernity as one of the main forces behind the war, other theorists argued in broader terms. They suggested that modern science had a profound effect on the collective consciousness. Key among these distinguished thinkers was Max Weber, who delivered his celebrated lecture on "Science as a Vocation" on November 7, 1917, at the Munich University.[3] Weber stated: "The fate of our times is characterized by rationalization and intellectualization and, above all, by the 'disenchantment of the world.' Precisely the ultimate and most sublime values have retreated from public life either into the transcendental realm of mystic life or into the brotherliness of direct and personal human relations."[4] Weber maintained that in earlier times man believed that supernatural forces governed the world and human events, and made them meaningful. Life was informed by an overarching principle that ordered everything. As man applied instrumental reason to his environment and came to believe he could master everything by calculation, he experienced a progressive loss of wonder. Weber concludes: "As intellectualism suppresses belief in magic, the world's processes become disenchanted, lose their magical significance, and henceforth simply 'are' and 'happen' but no longer signify anything. As a consequence, there is a growing demand that the world and the total pattern of life be subject to an order that is significant and meaningful."[5] As Weber demonstrates, science can answer many questions about how things work, but it can never address the greater ontological and religious questions of why we exist or what is sacred. Confronted by conflicting and man-made value systems, the individual is left adrift in an ethically ambiguous universe.

The disenchantment Max Weber associated with modernity permeated much of German cultural life in the aftermath of the First World War. The Weimar Republic failed in the end not only as a political system but as an ideal because it did not offer the broad public a satisfying emotional life and moral anchor, neglecting to address the widespread need for security, pride in oneself and one's country, communal happiness, and a sense of belonging to something higher than the individual. Germany's first experiment with democracy and pluralism, while engendering an exhilarating culture capable of supporting such varied artists as Thomas Mann and Bertolt Brecht, Arnold Schönberg and Richard Strauss, Max Beckmann and Walter Gropius, never managed to foster a communal sense of well-being and quell the pervasive yearning for what Peter Gay has called "the hunger for wholeness."[6]

National Socialism promised to fill the void by re-enchanting the world, recapturing the sense of wonder, wholeness, and authenticity previously attained through religion and shattered by modernity. Although the Nazi regime tried to control its citizens through coercion and the threat of violence, it also appreciated that a frightened, unsatisfied public was a potential threat to the movement. Working from the premise that it would need both the carrot and the stick, the government spent considerable energy organizing cultural life and the entertainment industry. Providing its citizenry with amusement was fundamental to the regime, not just because it quieted discontent and distracted the masses from those things they did not want to see. Recreation served a political goal because it could rejuvenate workers and revive their energy for further labor. Most importantly, entertainment would allow viewers to express and experience emotions collectively through fantasies that infused life with the magic and sentiment long associated with religion and the pre-modern world. The film industry in particular seemed tailor-made to the National Socialist agenda. Motion pictures create a momentary world in fleeting images and sounds, but they have tenacious staying power, lingering in the heart and mind long after the screen fades to black.

Enchantment as practiced by National Socialism is heavily dependent on intense emotional involvement. Precisely because emotions are non-rational and subjective, they do not require explanation. One simply feels the rightness of an event or a relationship, and this sentiment functions as a moral compass to evaluate the world and establish a point of orientation. The underlying principles of classical cinema, identification with characters and stars, emotional attachment and affective involvement in narrative outcomes, and the ability to transform reality through a sense of magic and make-believe all contributed to the enchantment of reality essential to the success of National Socialism. In his groundbreaking study, *The Ministry of Illusion* (1996), Eric Rentschler aptly states, "Film theorists have often speculated about the ideological effects of the 'dominant cinema,' proposing that classical narratives seek to mesmerize and mystify viewers by means of imaginary seductions. The Nazi cinema offers a strikingly concrete example of such a theoretical construct put into practice."[7] Rentschler's analysis initiated a paradigm shift in the study of Nazi cinema by recognizing the complex web of connections between filmic conventions and political ideology. This shift in focus is well under way, but more research is warranted into the ideological underpinnings of classical cinema, which structures narratives and organizes the ways in which audiences come to understand not just the events unfolding up on the screen but also the world as a meaningful story. The primary aim of my book is to look at the ways in which genre cinema contributes to this project of enchanting the world, suffusing it with meaning and developing and reinforcing a value system that harmonizes with the totalitarian state's political program.

What most distinguishes this study from other recent works is that it analyzes the politics of entertainment through enchantment and focuses on genre rather than on individual films. It presents for the first time detailed archival research on five popular film genres that helped define a shared visual culture in Nazi Germany. Although the films examined in this book were blockbusters and significant historical artifacts, none are available in commercial release with English subtitles and four are only accessible to scholars in rare 35mm prints at German archives. Readers will be introduced to a variety of rare and remarkable motion pictures that reveal the spirit of their time and deserve closer critical attention.

Genre films draw on a system of conventions structured according to cultural values. Genres are recognizable formulas for talking about basic human experiences, and while they are open to almost limitless variation, they function because audiences already know the story. Working with time-worn plots that guarantee predictable results, genre films embody society's deep-rooted values in what Barry Keith Grant has called "secular myths."[8] Nazi cinema relied on such commonplace narratives as the adventure film about a hero who triumphs after countless struggles or the romantic comedy about starry-eyed youngsters who find true love, laying claim to the basic fairytale morality that the righteous will be rewarded and the wicked punished. German war films and melodramas likewise recount difficult moral lessons that are nonetheless appealing because they give meaning to loss in predictable ways. These genres reassure audiences that those who die a tragic death, like the soldier defending his country, or who suffer the cruel loneliness of unfulfilled love, like the mother who sacrifices her own happiness for her children's sake, achieve immortality because they remain true to universal, noble sentiments. Because genre films are based on familiar outlines shaped by collective memories and a common cultural heritage, they produce "a regulated variety of cinema, a contained and controlled heterogeneity" and are uniquely suited to an investigation of how ideology and social values interact in the realm of popular culture.[9] In this book, I examine five film genres — the historical musical, the foreign adventure film, the home-front film, the melodrama, and the problem film — because they enact shared stories that can tell us much about how the family, war, history, nation, and community were imagined in Nazi Germany.

Movie stars play a substantial role in perpetuating genre cinema because they bring society's secular myths to life and provide identification opportunities. Stars serve as "political and psychological models who demonstrate some quality that we collectively admire."[10] In the Third Reich, the major studios and the propaganda ministry abundantly supported the star system because they recognized the economic, psychological, and ideological value in the audience's propensity to identify with celebrities. Since the motion picture industry continued to be profit-driven despite the government's zealous oversight, stars were a necessary advertising tool to sell films and ideas. Popular actors like the steely hero Willy Birgel, the sophisticated Gustaf Gründgens, and fatherly Heinrich George, along with vamp Zarah Leander, self-reliant Brigitte Horney, and girl-next-door Ilse Werner fulfilled audience expectations by behaving in familiar ways and by possessing personality traits and physical attributes the audience sought to emulate.[11] I focus attention on the stars who populate genre films and investigate their image in fan magazines, because these popular types reflect a compelling, broad-based social fantasy and resolute value system.

My interest in genre films is not limited to their ability to develop and reinforce values and behavioral patterns; it is also predicated on how they operate within the totalitarian state. Although Adolf Hitler wanted to incite a revolution of mammoth proportions and radically alter German everyday life to conform to his vision of a racially pure Aryan community of physically fit, hardworking, and self-sacrificing citizens, he recognized that the masses wanted security and a sense that they could still enjoy a politically free zone of leisure and privacy.[12] As film historian Klaus Kreimeier has recently noted,

"Genre cinema functioned for twelve years as an advocate for the little people, their everyday worries and commonplace wishes, their security demands, their notion of happiness, their 'petty escapes' and, above all, their need for normality."[13] Continuing to go to the movies to watch familiar stories with expected outcomes helped sustain the totalitarian state because it contributed to the widespread belief that National Socialism would not intrude upon the individual's right to find leisure in his own way. The sense of certainty and permanence provided by genre films reassured audiences that a stable, ordinary, and secure world continued to exist outside the movie theater — despite all rational evidence to the contrary.

Scholars in Germany and the United States have generally studied German film texts as discrete units and have failed to situate them within a regulated discursive system that included studio advertisement campaigns, the trade press, fan magazines, and star promotions. In this book, I appraise these long-neglected Nazi-era artifacts, including articles from the propaganda ministry's official organ, *Der deutsche Film,* daily trade sheets *Licht-Bild-Bühne* and *Film-Kurier,* fan magazines *Filmwelt* and *Filmwoche,* and studio press packages for individual stars and motion pictures. These texts present a fascinating and largely unexplored aspect of cinema in the Third Reich and shed light on the limitations of censorship in the totalitarian state. Although Joseph Goebbels forbade film criticism (*Kritik*) in 1936 and required reviewers to provide mere descriptive reports (*Berichte*), one encounters a surprising array of conflicting opinions on specific films and lively debates on fundamental issues such as realism and audience identification.

As early as 1933, the National Socialist state began to institute measures to organize all aspects of the film industry — from finance, distribution, advertisement, and critique to the choice of material, cast, crew, and directors. The first step was the creation of the Reich Ministry for Popular Enlightenment and Propaganda on March 11, 1933. The writer Dr. Paul Joseph Goebbels was appointed propaganda minister by presidential decree and empowered to direct the entire cultural production of the nation. Joseph Goebbels quickly established a complex bureaucracy to oversee the film industry. Within the propaganda ministry, the film department censored and rated films, while a separate entity, the Reich Film Chamber, regulated economic issues and membership in the profession. The Reich Film Chamber, founded on July 14, 1933, and integrated into the Reich Culture Chamber on September 22, 1933, was a trade organization for everyone involved in filmmaking. It consisted of ten departments with Propaganda Minister Goebbels as president. Actors, cameramen, writers, directors, stage designers, and editors were all legally required to apply for membership in the Reich Film Chamber as a prerequisite for continued employment. Only racially "pure" Aryan applicants were granted membership; as of July 1, 1933, Jews had been expelled from the film industry.

Along with limiting access to the profession, the regime sought financial control of film projects. In the years 1933 to 1937, the Film Credit Bank played a substantial role in financing motion pictures in Germany. Legally established as a limited liability company on June 1, 1933, the Film Credit Bank was able to finance up to 70% of a film, and since it provided the majority of funds, it exercised considerable control over a film's production schedule and content. The Film Credit Bank was promptly incorporated into the Reich Culture Chamber, so that the government could supervise a film's economic and ideological development. With the gradual and mostly covert nationalization of the film industry between 1937 and 1942, the state took on a more rigorous role in managing the film industry. In 1937, under the direction of Max Winkler, the holding firm Cautio-Treuhandgesellschaft GmbH began secretly to purchase stocks in the four largest film companies: Ufa, Tobis, Terra, and Bavaria. By January 10, 1942, the entire film industry was consolidated into the Ufa-Film GmbH, better known as "Ufi," which was then incorporated into the Reich Culture Chamber. The Nazi regime thereby effectively governed film production, distribution, and exhibition.

The most far-reaching measure instituted to control film production was the Reich Cinema Law of February 16, 1934, which created a new rating system, expanded censorship, and inaugurated the office of the Reich Film Dramaturge within the film department of the propaganda ministry. The new rating system provided economic incentives to filmmakers who complied with National Socialist ideology, since films deemed "politically" and "artistically" valuable were progressively exempted from taxes. It also expanded the film examination board's power to exercise censorship. According to paragraph seven of the new Reich Cinema Law: "Approval is denied if the examination demonstrates that the film's presentation will endanger vital state interests or public order or security, offend the National Socialist, religious, moral or artistic sensibilities, have a brutalizing or demoralizing effect, endanger German prestige or the relationship between Germany and foreign states."[14]

The Reich Cinema Law was later amended on June 28, 1935, so that the propaganda minister could forbid any film independently of the decision made by the examination board. According to this newly amended law, Goebbels could act without restrictions, "if he considers it necessary based on the public well-being."[15] Goebbels exercised his authority to censor films at various stages in their development and, especially in the cases of *Staatsauftragsfilme* (films commissioned by the state), was often personally involved in script changes.

The Reich Film Dramaturge was empowered to pre-censor film projects: "A draft and the screenplay of feature films produced in Germany must be submitted for examination to the Reich Film Dramaturge before filming can begin" in order "to prevent in a timely fashion the treatment of material which runs counter to the spirit of the time."[16] Goebbels defined the role of the Film Dramaturge as essential:

[He] has the task of examining a film project according to the state's point of view, and namely not as a critic but as a patron. The Film Dramaturge's task is to prevent in a timely fashion any possible mistakes from appearing, so that the film's correction does not begin when the film is complete but rather when it begins. Thus from the outset, censorship is kept at a minimum after a film's completion, so that the state's collaboration on a film is raised to a maximum when the film is conceived and begun in the studio.[17]

These measures were so successful that during the twelve years of Nazi rule, only about two dozen films were completed and then censored, while some eighty to one hundred films were censored shortly after they premiered.[18]

Beyond the level of organizational control, Joseph Goebbels turned his attention to more theoretical concerns. Goebbels maintained that effective propaganda has to go beyond mere proselytizing; it must appeal to the emotions. "Art," he asserted, "is nothing more than a shaper of feelings. It comes from feeling and not from reason; the artist is nothing more than an interpreter of this feeling."[19] Film was considered one of the most powerful media in this regard, for as Reich Film Dramaturge Dr. Fritz Hippler insisted, "in contrast to the other arts, film has by virtue of its capacity to work primarily on the optical and emotional, thus non-intellectual, levels, an especially penetrating and lasting effect from a mass psychological and propagandistic standpoint. It does not influence the opinion of exclusive circles of connoisseurs, rather it seizes the broad masses."[20]

If the government could ascertain and satisfy the audience's emotional and psychological needs, then it could simultaneously influence them without much resistance. Like sugarcoating a sour pill, the Nazis hoped to present their ideas so pleasantly that they would be readily acceptable. Goebbels advocated "invisible" propaganda that educated the masses, appealed to the emotions, and stressed behavior and moral values over overt political ideology. He urged the motion picture industry to create films in which the fascist agenda was motivated by the story and characters, not a mere veneer applied to conform to the propaganda ministry's expectations. Goebbels reasoned:

I do not want an art that proves its National Socialist character merely by displaying National Socialist emblems and symbols, rather I want an art that expresses its attitude through National Socialist character and by addressing National Socialist problems energetically. . . . The moment that propaganda becomes conscious, it is ineffective. At the moment, however, when it remains in the background as propaganda, as tendency, as character, as attitude and only appears through action, through time, through events, through contrasts between people, it becomes effective in every respect.[21]

Fritz Hippler contended that film's capacity to inspire identification was a crucial factor in influencing the broad masses because "film produces, besides the personal connection of the spectator to the main character during the course of the film, the attempt to be like him."[22] Star identification along with emotional engagement were seen as the most important tools to agitate for current political goals, shape behavioral norms and social practices, and foster a collective identity. However, film commentators noted that the audience did not merely consume films and adopt role models uncritically. Writing for the government-sponsored film journal, *Der deutsche Film,* Frank Maraun conceded that "it is often said that film condemns the viewer to passivity and — in contrast to the novel — grants his fantasy no elbowroom, no opportunity for validation. . . . If film derails the viewer's fantasy, forcing him to accept the world of ready-made images flashing by up on the screen, then on the other hand it also demands an active effort from him, actually two — observation and interpretation."[23] It was the filmmaker's difficult task to enchant viewers and win them over to National Socialism, limiting their avenues for interpretation by appealing to their emotional needs and obstructing critical thought.

Of the 1,094 German feature films made between 1933 and 1945, only 153 are generally considered outright propaganda.[24] Until recently, most critical studies of Nazi cinema concentrated on overt propaganda films commissioned by the state as a means to understand National Socialist ideology.[25] While propaganda films are an important facet of Nazi cinema, to concentrate exclusively on these well-financed, highly publicized political vehicles presents an inaccurate picture of film offerings during the Third Reich. Entertainment films (*Unterhaltungsfilme*) dominated the market; of all the feature films produced in Nazi Germany, 523 or nearly one half were comedies and musicals, 295 were melodramas or serious dramas, and 123 were detective and adventure films.[26] These genre films catered to the needs and desires of a mass audience, providing orientation and an outlet for wish fulfillment, escapism, amusement, distraction, and thrills. Based on these characteristics, many scholars have viewed the entertainment film as "apolitical" and as manifesting merely indirect or latent propaganda value.[27] Beginning in the 1990s, scholars such as Eric Rentschler, Linda Schulte-Saase, and more recently Sabine Hake and Lutz Koepnick among others, have ushered in a new era in film studies by looking beyond state-commissioned propaganda films to investigate Nazi popular cinema. These important book-length studies offer a nuanced evaluation of entertainment in the Third Reich and provide original and alternative models for understanding how classical narratives operated in complex and often paradoxical ways in the fascist state.[28]

Nazi entertainment films cannot be separated completely from politics. Although these motion pictures provide the spectator with a release from everyday life, many also exhibit central tenets of Nazi ideology. Values such as obedience, self-sacrifice, order, and the leadership principle, for example, are often promoted in the context of amusing stories. Entertainment films subtly participate in the larger framework of everyday fascism, perhaps more effectively than overt propaganda precisely because their messages are less intrusive and more readily acceptable. Ironically, some of the most memorable motion pictures seem to be telling two stories at once; one that endorses the system and one that calls it into question. I suggest that both stories work to uphold the status quo. In this book I explore two avenues of inquiry; one charts the regime's success in structuring films with mechanisms to steer the audience toward a specific ideological agenda, the other sketches an alternative reading that appears to offer utopian possibilities but ultimately reaffirms fascist institutions. I focus on discursive strategies in Nazi cinema, which neutralize subversive energy and validate the prevailing order. Deviant behavior is repeatedly played out and then reigned in and overcome at the conclusion. Contradictions in National Socialist society are thus exposed, worked out, and deflected. The spectator's pleasure in deviance and transgression evolves safely within controlled parameters, while challenges to the system are rendered ineffectual and unjust. A second, different reading examines how the pervasive attention granted conflict and aberrant behavior, the sympathetic portrayal of abnormal characters, and filmic devices such as self-reflexivity all run counter to the sometimes stated, sometimes illusive objectives of the Nazi propaganda machine. I will argue that this potential sedition, whether openly acknowledged by the state or not, operates as a ventilator for social frustrations. Most importantly, it is in the tension between these disparate yet complementary readings that pleasure and persuasion merge.

Clearly, not all German films made during the Third Reich contain an overt fascist ideology or even subtle, covertly fascist messages. However, all feature films were politicized by their function within the fascist state. Framed within a collectivized, government-supported entertainment industry, the feature film provided the German populace with a type of dream world, a safe place where the spectator could reconstitute reality in a socially acceptable arena. Subversive thoughts, resistance to collectivization, and transgression of moral laws were allowed expression in organized leisure. Whether a farce about vagabonds and petty criminals or a melodrama of seduction and adultery, the feature film could transport the spectator to a psychological realm in which opposition to daily life in fascism was given an outlet.

The films I analyze in the following pages are among the most popular German films ever made and many of them still delight television audiences today. It is my contention that these films were so well loved and continue to fascinate viewers because they espouse values that speak to basic human needs. The melodramas with their appeal for stability in the family and security in the community, the home-front films calling for unity, the adventure films providing an encounter with the exotic without physical danger, or the musicals with their happy-go-lucky song and dance routines all satisfy widespread psychological needs.

My book is organized around five popular film genres in Nazi cinema. I have selected a variety of genres that range from the immensely fashionable melodrama to the less celebrated adventure film because they reflect the public's taste and also conform to Goebbel's orchestra principle. Goebbels maintained that the film industry resembles an orchestra, where each performer plays a different instrument, but they all play the same tune. Genre cinema would offer a multitude of stories, but they would all function within a coordinated system with the same basic goals. I have chosen individual films to represent each genre based on several considerations. First of all, I concentrate on motion pictures produced in the years between 1937 and 1945 because by this time the Nazi government was purchasing stock in all the major film studios and had considerable oversight of the film industry and trade press. Therefore, the films produced in this period are more likely to reveal an aesthetic and ideological stance influenced by National Socialism than films made during the transitional period of 1933 to 1936. Secondly, I have chosen some films that were box office hits and others that failed to garner critical or public approval, because this array indicates what succeeded and also what failed to resonate with the moviegoing public. Finally, I explore a group of films that are currently available only in German film archives and range in quality from B-films to masterpieces, because they deserve scrutiny in order to gauge the full capacity of the entertainment industry in the Third Reich.

Chapter 1, "Dancing on the Volcano: History, Utopia, and the Social Construction of Happiness," examines how the Nazi musical depicts history as a state governed by two types of happiness, ecstasy and *Schadenfreude* (finding happiness in other people's pain), both having a political function in maintaining the status quo. These historical musicals belong to a larger category of films that use the nineteenth century to recount a shared past as the basis on which to forge a personal and national identity in the present. This genre invited viewers to recall the familiar collective memory of a good society lost and momentarily regained in the world of cinema.

The foreign adventure film features explorers and treasure hunters who journey abroad to encounter other races, conquer unknown realms, and return home with astonishing riches. Chapter 2, "Mapping German Identity: The Foreign Adventure Film," focuses on how this genre teaches substantial political lessons for building the German empire: the need to invade foreign territory to secure material resources and the equally pressing need to protect oneself from the fatal attraction to the foreign. The adventure film extols the rewards of conquering foreign soil and promotes a pioneering spirit, population growth, and the sacrifice of one's life for the survival of the folk. It routinely indulges in the seductive entertainment of violated boundaries, an upsetting enchantment associated with voyeurism, interracial desire, and homoeroticism to illustrate how deviant pleasure is successfully channeled into procreation.

The home-front film explores the bond between the civilian populace and the front-line soldier in wartime love stories and family dramas, using culture and entertainment to package war for sale to the German people. Chapter 3, "The Celluloid War: The Home-Front Film," examines how this genre mobilizes audiences psychologically for war. As vehicles promoting the idea of a nation united against the enemy, Nazi home-front films reflect developments on the battlefield and the government's need to adjust its propaganda according to the vagaries of war. Like all successful entertainment films in the Third Reich, the home-front film trains spectators to insulate themselves from the upsetting aspects of reality, extricating troubling events, and replacing them with palatable alternatives. The mindset created in the movies is transferable to everyday life, so that the audience can imagine total war as tenable.

The cinematic melodrama of the Third Reich engaged the popular imagination with mesmerizing images of strong, tormented women and discontented family life. Boasting some of the most successful films produced in Nazi Germany, the melodrama exerted a fascination on audiences altogether incongruous with government propaganda championing the Aryan home as the bastion of social harmony. Chapter 4, "Discontented Domesticity: The Melodrama," explores how this genre advances a political agenda in the guise of harmless diversion, entertaining viewers with archetypal love stories, while educating them to instrumentalize sexuality in the service of the state, to maintain racial purity, and to enforce euthanasia. The Nazi melodrama aestheticizes female suffering and sacrificial death, satisfying the emotional need for romance while sublimating fantasies of domination to the level of beautiful art.

Propaganda Minister Joseph Goebbels repeatedly called for exemplary films about contemporary life in Nazi Germany and lamented that "problem films," serious works dealing with social issues, seldom graced the screen. It is surprising that Goebbels would argue so adamantly in favor of the problem film because the genre demands an honest discussion of society's ills in a way that National Socialism routinely rejected. Emphasizing how individuals confront social contradictions beyond their control, the problem film casts a critical look at the world as it is and explicitly calls for change. Thus Goebbels was forced to censor the problem films he originally endorsed, because they exposed social problems that National Socialism did not want to address openly or could not solve satisfactorily. A common feature of these films is that they reflect disenchantment with National Socialism and leave the viewer with haunting images of unfulfilled passions, senseless brutality, and dissatisfaction with the status quo. Chapter 5, "The Forbidden Desires of Everyday Life: The Problem Film," introduces readers to these rare and noteworthy films, which illustrate the aspirations and the limitations of cinema in the Third Reich.

National Socialism wanted to control the nation's dreams and tried to enchant audiences with a mindset advantageous to its immediate political goals. However, for all its efforts, the government could never be entirely successful at determining how the public received motion pictures. Once the dream comes into being, it cannot be controlled. The state tried to manage the production of dreams — what ideas were presented, what actors held the roles, when the films premiered, what messages were conveyed through the plot — but once the films were projected onto the screen, the audience took on the role of interpreter. Spectators brought their personal experience, familiarity with actors, genres, myths, and filmic traditions into the cinema, and these factors could not be regulated completely. Indeed, it is often the ambiguities, the multivalent images, and the indeterminate narratives that make films of lasting significance.

Notes

[1] "Es gab sonst nur wenig, was die Menschen verband, und nicht nur verband, sondern auch ihren höchsten Willen erregte. Die Politik stieß häufig ab, war kleinlich und wurde von einer Minderheit besorgt; die Kunst befriedigte nur einzelne, abgeschlossene Teile der Seele. Vor allen Dingen lagen die wichtigsten Gemütsbedürfnisse, die religiösen, brach; es gab keinen lebendigen allgemeinverpflichtenden Glauben, der unserem Wesen entsprach, in dem wir es hätten läutern können." Siegfried Kracauer, "Vom Erleben des Krieges," vol. 5.1 of *Schriften,* ed. Inka Mülder-Bach (Frankfurt a. M.: Suhrkamp, 1990), 15.

[2] "Es streiten hier um die Vorherrschaft das Pflichtgefühl, die Freude an der Übereinstimmung mit der Gemeinschaft, das dumpfe Hingerissensein von der Stimmung der Masse, der Abenteurertrieb, die Lust am Dreinschlagen, der Ehrgeiz, die Neugierde." "Es ist ja der natürlichste Zustand der Menschen, im Rausch des Zieles dem Ideal zu dienen. Auch die kleinste Handlung wird dann geheiligt und das Lebensgefühl unendlich erhöht." Kracauer, "Vom Erleben des Krieges," 14 and 16.

[3] Wolfgang Schluchter discusses the controversial dating of Weber's lecture "Science as Vocation" in *Paradoxes of Modernity: Culture and Conduct in the Theory of Max Weber,* trans. Neil Solomon (Stanford: Stanford UP, 1996), 46–47.

[4] Max Weber, "Science as a Vocation," *From Max Weber: Essays in Sociology,* eds. and trans. H. H. Gerth and C. Wright Mills (London: Routledge & K. Paul, 1948), 155.

[5] Max Weber, *Economy and Society,* eds. Guenther Roth and Claus Wittich, trans. Ephraim Fischoff (Berkeley: U of California P, 1978), 506.

[6] See especially chapter four, "The Hunger for Wholeness: Trials of Modernity" in Peter Gay, *Weimar Culture: The Outsider as Insider* (New York: Harper & Row, 1968).

[7] Eric Rentschler, *The Ministry of Illusion: Nazi Cinema and Its Afterlife* (Cambridge, MA: Harvard UP, 1996), 16.

[8] Barry Keith Grant, "Experience and Meaning in Genre Films," *Film Genre Reader,* ed. Barry Keith Grant (Austin: U of Texas P, 1986), 114–28.

[9] Stephen Neale, *Genre* (London: British Film Institute, 1980), 63.

[10] James Monaco, *How To Read a Film* (Oxford: Oxford UP, 1981), 222.

[11] For a contemporaneous discussion of the star system in the Third Reich, see Hans Spielhofer, "Der Filmschauspieler: Eine typenkundliche Betrachtung," *Der deutsche Film* 2, no. 2 (June 1938): 326–28; Helmut Kindler, "Star als Genre," *Der deutsche Film* 3, no. 12 (June 1939): 340; and Hans Spielhofer, "Wunschtraum oder Wirklichkeit? Eine Betrachtung über Notwendigkeit und Problematik ihrer Abgrenzung," *Der deutsche Film* 3, no. 11 (May 1939): 317–22.

[12] In recent years, historians and cultural critics have explored the various ways in which National Socialism appealed to the German public. Scholars have been especially intrigued by Hans Dieter Schäfer's notion that Nazi Germany suffered from a "divided consciousness." On the one hand the government reigned through terror and enforced conformity, but on the other hand it also gave the public a thriving entertainment industry and the promise of a politically free zone filled with consumer products. See Hans Dieter Schäfer, *Das gespaltene Bewußtsein: Deutsche Kultur und Lebenswirklichkeit,* 3d ed. (Munich: Hanser, 1983); Detlev J. K. Peukert, *Inside Nazi Germany: Conformity, Opposition, and Racism in Everyday Life,* trans. Richard Deveson (New Haven: Yale UP, 1987); and Peter Reichel, *Der schöne Schein des Dritten Reiches: Faszination und Gewalt des Faschismus* (Munich: Hanser, 1991).

[13] "Das Genrekino funktionierte zwölf Jahre lang als Anwalt der kleinen Leute, ihrer Alltagssorgen und alltäglichen Wünsche, ihres Sicherheitsverlangen, ihrer Glücksvorstellungen, ihrer 'kleinen Fluchten' und, vor allem, ihrer Bedürfnisse nach Normalität." Klaus Kreimeier, "Von Henny Porten zu Zarah Leander: Filmgenres und Genrefilm in der Weimarer Republik und im Nationalsozialismus," *Montage/Av: Zeitschrift für Theorie & Geschichte audiovisueller Kommunikation* 3.2 (1994): 45.

[14] "Die Zulassung ist zu versagen, wenn die Prüfung ergibt, daß die Vorführung des Films geeignet ist, lebenswichtige Interessen des Staates oder die öffentliche Ordnung oder Sicherheit zu gefährden, das nationalsozialistische, religiöse, sittliche oder künstliche Empfinden zu verletzen, verrohend oder entsittlichend zu wirken, das deutsche Ansehen oder die Beziehungen Deutschlands zu auswärtigen Staaten zu gefährden." Qtd. in Gerd Albrecht, *Nationalsozialistische Filmpolitik: Eine soziologische Untersuchung über die Spielfilme des Dritten Reiches* (Stuttgart: Ferdinand Enke, 1969), 512.

[15] "Wenn er aus dringenden Gründen des öffentlichen Wohls für erforderlich hält." Qtd. in Albrecht, *Nationalsozialistische Filmpolitik,* 512.

[16] "Spielfilme, die in Deutschland hergestellt werden, müssen vor der Verfilmung dem Reichsfilmdramaturgen im Entwurf und im Drehbuch zur Begutachtung eingereicht werden," "[um] rechtzeitig zu verhindern, daß Stoffe behandelt werden, die dem Geist der Zeit zuwiderlaufen." Qtd. in Albrecht, *Nationalsozialistische Filmpolitik,* 510–11.

[17] "Diese Filmdramaturgie hat die Aufgabe, nach staatspolitischen Gesichtspunkten die Filmvorhaben zu überprüfen, und zwar nicht als Beckmesser, sondern als Förderer. Die Aufgabe des Filmdramaturgs besteht darin, auftauchende Fehlermöglichkeiten rechtzeitig schon zu verhindern, damit die Korrektur am Film nicht dann beginnt, wenn er fertig ist, sondern dann, wenn er angefangen wird, damit also von vornherein die große Zensuraufgabe nach Fertigstellung am Film auf ein Minimum

beschränkt wird, damit aber die Mitarbeit am Film von Seiten des Staates auf ein Maximum heraufgesetzt wird in dem Augenblick, in dem der Film im Begriff steht, im Atelier begonnen zu werden." Speech by Goebbels from February 15, 1941, qtd. in Albrecht, *Nationalsozialistische Filmpolitik,* 475.

[18] Kraft Wetzel and Peter Hagemann, *Zensur: Verbotene deutsche Filme 1933–1945* (Berlin: Volker Spiess, 1978), 7 and 44.

[19] "Die Kunst ist nichts anderes als Gestalter des Gefühls. Sie kommt vom Gefühl und nicht vom Verstand her; der Künstler ist nichts anderes als der Sinngeber dieses Gefühls." Speech by Joseph Goebbels from March 5, 1937, qtd. in Albrecht, *Nationalsozialistische Filmpolitik,* 447.

[20] "Im Vergleich zu den anderen Künsten ist der Film durch seine Eigenschaft, primär auf das Optische und Gefühlsmäßige, also Nichtintellektuelle einzuwirken, massenpsychologisch und propagandistisch von besonders eindringlicher und nachhaltiger Wirkung. Er beeinflußt nicht die Meinung exklusiver Kreise von Kunstkennern, sondern er erfaßt die breiten Massen." Fritz Hippler, *Betrachtungen zum Filmschaffen,* 5th rev. ed. (Berlin: Max Hesses Verlag, 1943), 14. Fritz Hippler later took over the newly inaugurated position of Reich Film Intendant on February 29, 1942.

[21] "Ich wünschte nicht etwa eine Kunst, die ihren nationalsozialistischen Charakter lediglich durch Zurschaustellung nationalsozialistischer Embleme und Symbole beweist, sondern eine Kunst, die ihre Haltung durch nationalsozialistischen Charakter und durch Aufraffen nationalsozialistischer Probleme zum Ausdruck bringt. . . . Im Augenblick, da eine Propaganda bewußt wird, ist sie unwirksam. Mit dem Augenblick aber, in dem sie als Propaganda, als Tendenz, als Charakter, als Haltung im Hintergrund bleibt und nur durch Handlung, durch Ablauf, durch Vorgänge, durch Kontrastierung von Menschen in Erscheinung tritt, wird sie in jeder Hinsicht wirksam." Qtd. in Albrecht, *Nationalsozialistische Filmpolitik,* 456.

[22] "Der Film erzeugt nämlich neben der persönlichen Verbindung des Zuschauers zum Hauptdarsteller während des Filmablaufs auch das Bestreben, diesem gleich zu sein." Hippler, *Betrachtungen zum Filmschaffen,* 95.

[23] "Man hat oft gesagt, daß der Film den Zuschauer zur Passivität verurteile und seiner Phantasie — etwa im Gegensatz zum Roman — keinen Spielraum, keine Bestätigungsmöglichkeit mehr lasse. . . . Wenn der Film die Phantasie des Zuschauers außer Kurs setzt, indem er ihn die auf der Leinwand vorüberziehende fertige Bilderwelt anzunehmen zwingt, so verlangt er auf der anderen Seite doch eine aktive Leistung von ihm, sogar zwei — Beobachtung und Sinndeutung." Frank Maraun, "Das Erlebnis entscheidet: Der abendfüllende Kulturfilm — von verschiedenen Seiten gesehen," *Der deutsche Film* 2, no. 7 (January 1938): 189.

[24] For a complete list of the films produced in Nazi Germany and a breakdown according to genre, see Albrecht, *Nationalsozialistische Filmpolitik,* 97–122. Albrecht categorizes films as "P-Filme" (propaganda films with manifest political content) or "nP-Filme" (non-propaganda films with latent political function), 103–8.

[25] Studies on propaganda films include Erwin Leiser, *"Deutschland, erwache!" Propaganda im Film des Dritten Reiches* (Reinbek bei Hamburg: Rowohlt, 1968); David Stewart Hull, *Film in the Third Reich* (Berkeley: U of California P, 1969); David Welch, *Propaganda and the German Cinema 1933–1945* (New York: Oxford UP,

1983); Hilmar Hoffmann, *"Und die Fahne führt uns in die Ewigkeit"*: *Propaganda im NS-Film* (Frankfurt a. M.: Fischer Verlag, 1988); and Klaus Kanzog, *"Staatspolitisch besonders wertvoll"*: *Ein Handbuch zu 30 deutschen Spielfilmen der Jahre 1934 bis 1945* (Munich: Diskurs Film Verlag, 1994). Broad-based surveys of Nazi cinema include Bogusław Drewniak, *Der deutsche Film 1938–1945: Ein Gesamtüberblick* (Düsseldorf: Droste, 1987); and Pierre Cadars and Francis Courtade, *Geschichte des Films im Dritten Reich,* trans. Florian Hopf (Munich: Hanser, 1975).

[26] Albrecht, *Nationalsozialistische Filmpolitik,* 97–123.

[27] Hull and Courtade and Caders view entertainment films as primarily escapist fare. By contrast, noted critic Siegfried Kracauer states: "To be sure, all Nazi films were more or less propaganda film — even the mere entertainment pictures which seem to be remote from politics." *From Caligari to Hitler: A Psychological History of the German Film* (Princeton: Princeton UP, 1947), 275. See also Wolfgang Becker, *Film und Herrschaft* (Berlin: Spiess, 1973), 119.

[28] See Stephen Lowry, *Pathos und Politik: Ideologie in Spielfilmen des Nationalsozialismus* (Tübingen: Max Niemeyer, 1991); Klaus Kreimeier, *Die Ufa-Story: Geschichte eines Filmkonzerns* (Munich: Carl Hanser Verlag, 1992); Dora Traudisch, *Mutterschaft mit Zuckerguß?: Frauenfeindliche Propaganda im NS-Spielfilm* (Pfaffenweiler: Centaurus, 1993); Linda Schulte-Sasse, *Entertaining the Third Reich: Illusions of Wholeness in Nazi Cinema* (Durham: Duke UP, 1996); Marcia Klotz, "Epistemological Ambiguity and the Fascist Text: *Jew Süss, Carl Peters,* and *Ohm Krüger*," *New German Critique* 74 (Spring-Summer 1998): 91–124; Sabine Hake, *Popular Cinema of the Third Reich* (Austin: U of Texas P, 2001); and Lutz Koepnick, *The Dark Mirror: German Cinema between Hitler and Hollywood* (Berkeley: U of California P, 2002).

1: History, Utopia, and the Social Construction of Happiness: The Historical Musical

THE MUSICAL IS often considered a frivolous and even trivial film genre, which audiences do not take seriously because it is unrealistic, promotes cheerfulness over substance, choreographs movement, and caters to escapist fantasies.[1] Yet it is precisely the musical's emphasis on nostalgia, gaiety, controlled energy, and collective release that makes it an excellent starting point for a study on the social construction of happiness in Nazi Germany. National Socialists recognized that the "low aesthetic tone" of popular culture could intoxicate the masses and fuel political action. The enthusiasm generated from such popular forms of entertainment as the musical could be channeled into the political realm. Adolf Hitler argued that widespread enthusiasm was essential to the Nazi revolution:

> Enthusiasm once scotched cannot be awakened at need. It is an intoxication and must be preserved in this state. And how, without this power of enthusiasm, should a country withstand a struggle, which in all likelihood would make the most enormous demands on the spiritual qualities of the nation? I knew the psyche of the broad masses too well not to be aware that a high "aesthetic" tone would not stir up the fire that was necessary to keep the iron hot.[2]

Exhilaration for the present can be wrapped up in nostalgia for a simpler time, one filled with music and a preordained happy ending. The feelings generated from such an encounter with the past are redeemable for the present with songs that linger in the audience's heart and mind after the screen fades to black. Several notable German musicals from the 1930s offer a utopian vision of history, where the turbulent political arena is subdued by light-hearted music and dance. Drawing on Richard Dyer's argument that the Hollywood musical offers a glimpse at "what utopia would feel like rather than how it would be organized,"[3] this chapter examines how the Nazi musical depicts history as a state driven by emotions with explicit parallels to the present. I will take as my point of departure the 1938 musical *Tanz auf dem Vulkan* (Dancing on the Volcano), directed by Hans Steinhoff and starring Gustaf Gründgens. What does this film about the July Revolution have to say about civil unrest and political dissent in general? Can an examination of the ways in which the musical treats the past tell us anything about the power of cinema to create a mind-set conducive to totalitarianism? And will such a venture in historiophoty, defined by Hayden White as "the representation of history and our thoughts about it in visual images and filmic discourse,"[4] help to broaden our understanding of the Nazi cultural sphere? The second half of this chapter examines Hans H. Zerlett's *Robert und Bertram*, Nazi Germany's only anti-Semitic musical based on a popular nineteenth-century stage production. What does this farce about two vagabonds cheating the Jews out of their property in 1839 Germany tell us about the cinema's use of the past to constitute an image of the national community and its enemies? And to what extent does the farce's basic premise of a cheerfully ridiculous world help accustom the viewer to a truly absurd reality outside the movie theater?

Politics as pathos: *Tanz auf dem Vulkan* (1938).

Ecstatic Revolution: *Tanz auf dem Vulkan* (1938)

Set in 1830 Paris on the verge of revolution, *Tanz auf dem Vulkan* is based very loosely on the life of celebrated nineteenth-century mime Jean-Baptiste-Gaspard Deburau.[5] In Steinhoff's film, Deburau is a revue singer who performs nightly to jubilant crowds in Théâtre des Funambules. By day he secretly writes satirical verses against King Charles X and in favor of the

Prince of Orléans, Louis Philippe. Debureau is the king's adversary in politics and in love, for they both desire Countess Cambouilly, a beautiful, married woman who enjoys the spotlight. Fueled by equal amounts of jealousy and political fervor, Debureau openly sings his satires against the king and is arrested. Sentenced to die by the guillotine, Debureau is saved by the revolting masses, while Charles is forced to flee the country leaving France in the hands of the beloved bourgeois king, Louis Philippe. The final scene features a triumphant Debureau held on his admirers' shoulders in front of the guillotine as he leads the ecstatic masses in a jubilant song celebrating the spiritual and emotional rewards of revolution.

Tanz auf dem Vulkan appears to be a cultural paradox, inviting more questions than answers. What inspired director Hans Steinhoff, best known to posterity for his overt propaganda films Hitlerjunge Quex (1933), Der alte und der junge König (1935), Robert Koch, der Bekämpfer des Todes (1939), and Ohm Krüger (1941), to direct a light-hearted musical about the July Revolution? Why would the highly respected classical actor Gustaf Gründgens star in this musical? Why did Steinhoff, co-authors Hans Rehberg and Peter Hagen,[6] all sympathetic to the NSDAP, write a story about political persecution, censorship of the arts, a police state, and totalitarianism? Finally, why would they take a prominent nineteenth-century French mime and turn him into a revue singer of political limericks?

Film historians, perhaps more than the viewing public in 1938, appear perplexed by this film and are often guided by false or misleading information. First of all, let us clarify the most basic facts. Tanz auf dem Vulkan passed the censor in Berlin on November 28, 1938.[7] It was never banned, as Curt Riess incorrectly asserts.[8] Indeed, it received the Propaganda Ministry's rating of "artistically valuable" and premiered on November 30, 1938, in Stuttgart. It was not held back from release until 1941 as Friedrich Luft and Heinrich Goertz falsely claim.[9] Finally, the Propaganda Ministry did not ban the film's main song, "Die Nacht ist nicht allein zum Schlafen da," as Volker Kühn, Christa Bandmann, and Joe Hembus erroneously maintain.[10] The Tobis studio provided movie theaters with a promotional recording and extensive publicity material tied to local radio stations and music stores where a commercial record would be available.[11] Grammophon also released a recording of the song in the summer of 1939.[12]

Three influential viewers, however, disliked the film, and their comments may have flavored subsequent readings. Adolf Hitler saw Tanz auf dem Vulkan before its premiere and criticized both Gründgens's performance and Steinhoff's direction.[13] Propaganda Minister Joseph Goebbels likewise berated the film in his diary: "Typical Gründgens. A bit too cerebral. It still needs to be edited a lot."[14] Gründgens was reportedly so disappointed with his own performance that he asked his colleagues whether he should have the film banned with Göring's help.[15] The broad public, however, apparently liked the film, because it had a successful run in the theaters.[16] The film's enduring popularity and the Propaganda Ministry's tacit approval are further demonstrated by the inclusion of a film clip from *Tanz auf dem Vulkan* in Werner Malbran's 1941 documentary of Tobis hit films, *Wir erinnern uns gern.*[17]

Hans Steinhoff's decision to make a historical musical is perhaps best understood if we review his career path. Steinhoff began his professional life as a singer and stage actor in Munich, Berlin, and Vienna but turned to screenwriting and film direction shortly after the First World War. During the Weimar Republic he worked in a wide variety of genres, ranging from comedies, musicals, and melodramas to literary adaptations, social commentaries, and historical dramas. Despite his versatility, Steinhoff was particularly drawn to two different film genres, the musical and the historical drama. Although most of his films can be delineated either as musicals providing exhilaration or as historical dramas affording political commentary, *Tanz auf dem Vulkan* represents a hybrid genre with its attendant viewer misapprehension.[18]

Audiences today will most likely recognize Gustaf Gründgens as the model for Klaus Mann's novel *Mephisto* (1936) and István Szabó's film adaptation of the same name (1981), in which the actor epitomizes the opportunistic, intellectual Nazi collaborator. During the Third Reich, Gründgens enjoyed a reputation as a distinguished stage actor playing such memorable roles as Hamlet and Mephisto. He was widely known as the talented managing director of the Schauspielhaus am Gendarmenmarkt, the general director of the Prussian state theaters, a cultural senator, and a Prussian state minister under Göring's patronage.[19] While Goebbels and Hitler apparently disliked Gründgens as an individual and an actor,[20] they recognized that his continued work in the cultural industry could lend respectability to National Socialism. Gründgens's achievements helped legitimize the Nazi regime and make it *salonfähig*.

Several contemporary critics have marveled at Gründgens's decision to work under the direction of the propagandist Steinhoff. Michael Töteberg, in his otherwise informative article, errs when he states, "*Dancing on the Volcano* (1938) was the name of a feature film by Hans Steinhoff, and Gründgens only took on the role of the politicizing actor Debureau in it because of the suggestive title."[21] This explanation is highly unlikely since the filmscript was given the working title *Wenn Debureau spielt,* and the trade papers first advertised the film under the titles *Debureau* and *Genie und Leidenschaft*. More plausible is the explanation Gründgens gave in an interview during the production of *Tanz auf dem Vulkan:* "The film has everything . . . love, politics and theater. Debureau is a tremendously passionate man whose life has a great adventurous tone. . . . I was tempted above all by the great romantic gesture of his life."[22] Indeed, Gründgens had already worked with the director, screenwriter, composer, cameraman, set designer, and many of the actors.[23] His choice of playing the historical figure Debureau in a musical was also consistent with his other film work in the 1930s and 1940s. While Gründgens was widely known for his adversarial roles in *M* (1931) and *Liebelei* (1933), his film career was characterized as much by his historical roles: Robespierre in *Danton* (1931), Metternich in *So endet die Liebe* (1934), Chamberlain in *Ohm Krüger* (1941), and Friedemann Bach in *Friedemann Bach (1941)*. He also made a name for himself in film, as he had done on the stage, through his work in comedies and musicals such as *Die Gräfin von Monte Christo* (1932), *Eine Stadt steht Kopf* (director, 1933), *Die Finanzen des Großherzogs* (director, 1934), *Pygmalion* (1935), and *Capriolen* (director/star, 1937).

Both Steinhoff and Gründgens favored historical dramas and musicals, especially biopics focusing on the life of a remarkable individual. Since stars bring to each new role their reputation and are recognized as a specific type based on their entire body of work, typecasting helps define audience expectations. The same can be said for directors. Audiences often attend a film based on their previous experiences with an actor or director. In a special issue of *Der deutsche Film* (May 1939) dedicated to audience expectations, surveys confirmed that most viewers chose a film based on the content and the star. Gustaf Gründgens was included among the ten most popular actors in Germany. Stars like Gründgens were seen as indispensable because, as one contemporary reporter remarked: "We all need to consider our dreams and wishes, looking up to the stars, to something higher, more beautiful, richer, to ideal and dream images, as anything but a mere waste of time or ineffective enervation."[24] The star was considered so significant that one critic suggested: "The name of the star reveals everything. It says whether it will be a burlesque film or a serious one, whether there will be singing and dancing, or whether there will be lots of good old-fashioned fun. In short, the name of the star designates a genre!"[25] Faced then with the "genre" of Gründgens and the historical-musical hybrid, what were audiences likely to expect? The trade papers emphasized the historical authenticity of this film, citing not only Gründgens's penchant for historical roles but also Steinhoff's exhaustive research into the life and times of Deburau.

During the production phase, *Tanz auf dem Vulkan* was promoted as an engaging historical drama with sensational musical pieces. Critics treated the film's historical setting as a serious attempt to portray authentic social and political conflicts. Felix Henseleit marveled at the attention to historical details, both in Rochus Gliese's set designs of nineteenth-century Paris and in the screenwriters' depiction of the revolution. Henseleit wrote: "And while the great actor of the July Revolution agitates more and more vigorously, we sense the historical meaning of the moment expressed so clearly under Hans Steinhoff's direction: Paris and thus France stood in those days at the turning-point of two ages." Henseleit was especially impressed with Gründgens's acting and "his power of transformation, which is so suggestive that we no longer believe we are experiencing a reenactment of events but rather the events themselves."[26]

Although *Tanz auf dem Vulkan* is clearly light-hearted, its presentation of history is not far from that of Steinhoff's serious and leaden historical films like *Der alte und der junge König*, *Rembrandt*, or *Ohm Krüger*. In all these films, it is the artist-leader who propels history. Erwin Leiser explains the importance of the leader figure in Nazi cinema: "The great poets, painters, sculptors, scientists, explorers, politicians and generals honoured in the Third Reich cinema were all projections of the Führer, himself exalted in propaganda as a great general, supreme politician, artist and architect of genius."[27] Just as the genius films create an enduring Führer myth resembling Adolf Hitler's own carefully fashioned self-image, we find here a great popular artist who is forced to become a rebel and politician to save the nation from a decadent and heartless rule. Debureau is featured as a charismatic leader who embodies the nation's utopian desires. He speaks on behalf of the masses, voicing their collective political will and acting as the conscience of society, because as one character remarks, "Debureau and Paris, that is the same thing."[28]

In Steinhoff's film Debureau is the primary force behind the revolution. He writes inflammatory political verses, organizes the underground movement, advises Louis Philippe to seize the throne, and preaches insurrection disguised as the Prince of Orléans. The masses revolt to save Debureau from the guillotine and not for any clear political agenda. Although this depiction of the July Revolution is obviously fictional by scholarly standards, the trade papers vouched for its historical validity. Critics argued that the film rendered nineteenth-century visual culture with amazing accuracy, reproducing on celluloid the popular images of artists like Daumier, Garvani, and Delacroix. Fan magazines repeatedly cited an old French encyclopedia to verify the factual nature of Debureau's film actions and to lend credibility to Steinhoff's rendering of the July Revolution.[29]

Although fan magazines aimed primarily at the broad movie-going public presented fiction as truth, more academic publications sought to define the precarious relationship between filmmakers and history. Reich Film Intendant Dr. Fritz Hippler, for example, maintained that filmmakers differ from historians because they do not attempt to recreate the past in all its verifiable details. Instead, filmmakers use historical events and persons to illuminate the present, "we make all films based on the necessities and for the demands of the present day. Therefore, contemporary audiences have to understand the historical film and be touched by it, in order to enjoy it or be inspired and enraptured."[30] In *Tanz auf dem Vulkan* the enthusiastic hero Debureau provides this much-needed emotional link to the present. The trade papers highlighted Gründgens's remarkable physical resemblance to Deburau and their shared passionate temperament.[31] Hans Hufszky called it "a fantastic duplicity of natures" and insisted: "It almost seems like fate's mysterious throw of the dice gave a second life to Debur[]au as Gründgens. . . . It is as if Gründgens managed to bridge this [hundred year] time difference and geographical separation."[32]

Propaganda Minister Joseph Goebbels argued that art, unlike science, uses history to validate a "higher" truth:

> One could not rightly demand of a historical performer that he confront history like a historian. The historian has the task to portray history factually based on the source material at his disposal. The artist is not limited exclusively to the sources. He has the right, I want to say, to penetrate intuitively into the historical events and shape them based on an intuitive judgement. And it has proven to be the case that in a higher sense great artists have always seen and depicted historical events more truthfully than historians.[33]

The "higher truth" of Steinhoff's film is that weak leaders and a decadent aristocracy fail to offer the broad masses a satisfying emotional life and must be replaced. Pathos lies at the center of Debureau's politics, and he preaches this creed in his song: "Become enchanted, friends, drink and love and laugh/ And live in the splendid moment./ Spending the night intoxicated/ Means happiness and bliss!"[34] He sings of men building bombs in the catacombs, but their revolution is not for a constitution, civil rights, or a new socio-political order. They are fighting for the right to pursue happiness and become intoxicated. Debureau calls for a mass revolution of feelings. While film reporter Martin Klockmann maintained that *Tanz auf dem Vulkan* was dedicated to the "fight for social rights," he accurately located the revolutionary drive in Debureau's "feeling of being slighted by the privileged classes. This feeling intensifies to passion and ignites the revolutionary flame in the Parisian masses."[35] History is driven not merely by the individual but by his feelings. Man's emotional needs fuel and even replace action. This idea is consistent with the National Socialist concept of emotion as the mainstay of propaganda and political conviction. Adolf Hitler consistently appealed to his followers' feelings and promised the masses an intense emotional bond in the utopian ideal of the *Volksgemeinschaft*. In *Mein Kampf*, Hitler clearly outlined his strategy and asserted that propaganda "must be aimed at the emotions and only to a very limited degree at the so-called intellect."[36] Goebbels in turn recognized that "art is nothing more than the shaper of feelings. It comes from feeling and not from reason. The artist is nothing more than an interpreter of this feeling."[37]

Social class differences are portrayed as more a matter of simple respect than economic or political stratification. The aristocracy has no consideration for the lower classes or fellow nobles. Count and Countess Cambouilly epitomize the heartless and vain aristocrats who use other people for their own amusement and political advancement. The count so desperately wants to be accepted at court that he condones and even promotes his wife's affair with the king. This laughable weakling displays no self-respect and repeatedly allows himself to be humiliated and emasculated. At home his wife beats him cruelly in a fencing match, and at court the king derides him for masquerading as his wife's lover, Debureau, just to get public attention. The countess is equally self-serving, collecting men as trophies and unable to overcome her inherent narcissism for true love. King Charles X, however, is the most egotistical and ridiculous figure at court, a petty tyrant who entertains himself with other men's wives and childish pranks. The king's conceited and absurd nature is poignantly revealed when his grand hunting expedition literally turns out to be child's play, with the king sitting in his palace shooting an air pistol at stuffed rabbits pulled on wheels by his servants.

The decadent aristocracy, amusing itself with frivolous games, masked balls, and adultery at court, is juxtaposed to an equally idle but hearty bourgeoisie whiling away the hours at the theater and street cafés. Indeed, the bourgeois audience seems less politically disaffected than merely entertained by the political lyrics. The actors who write, print, and distribute revolutionary pamphlets constitute the truly admirable class. Debureau, his helpers, and the actress Angele represent the most sympathetic characters, modeling the values of work, order, cleanliness, and family. When Debureau tries to become a bridge between the aristocracy and the artist class through his relationship to Countess Cambouilly, he is criticized. One character voices the general sentiment: "He should stay where he belongs," in the theater.[38]

The working class, by contrast, only appears at the film's conclusion when the masses take to the streets. Although the rebel Debureau argued throughout *Tanz auf dem Vulkan* for a new revolution of feeling, the final mass demonstration is choreographed to suggest that he was always really fighting for economic equality. The proletariat class functions as a primarily visual rather than narrative element, validating the call for revolution in more conventional economic terms. Characterized by their tattered clothing, work-worn faces, and piercing speech, the marching workers seem literally transported from leftist Weimar film classics to evoke a familiar cinematic history of the working class struggle. Steinhoff reverts to the Weimar tradition of depicting street demonstrations with extreme low-angle, close-up shots of running legs, a camera technique popularized in such films as *Mutter Krausens Fahrt ins Glück* (1929), *Kuhle Wampe* (1932), and Steinhoff's own *Hitlerjunge Quex* (1933). The director also uses a series of close-up facial shots superimposed over a flowing tattered flag to suggest the iconography of both Weimar cinema and nineteenth-century painting. With his proletarian figures staged in heroic poses on the barricades, Steinhoff evokes the visual memory of revolution captured in popular images ranging from Luis Trenker's film *Der Rebell* (1932) to Eugène Delacroix's famous painting, "Liberty Leading the People" (1830). The reliance on a shared visual vocabulary helps Steinhoff to align the Nazi concept of political pathos with an easily recognizable history of class struggle.

Tanz auf dem Vulkan repeatedly presents exhilaration as a political category. Indeed, the film propagates the notion that happiness is in itself the intended political action. In a state of near euphoria, Debureau recites his vision of Paris as an earthly paradise:

> Do you hear it, that is the music of the city! The melody of streets and squares, bells chiming and dishes clattering, trotting on the pavement and merchants screaming, whispers of girls and the heated debates of men. A rocking and waving, an endless gliding and striding. Noise! Noise! But noise that is like a song. A hell? A paradise? Paris! Be quiet! The city is at heart a lover. I want to hold her, I want to devote my existence to her. She should be happy, she should bloom. Joy should be in her. Joy and freedom! Passionate and glorious life, from day to day, season to season, from today through the centuries until eternity! An endless paradise: Paris![39]

This utopian vision of the modern metropolis lies outside the stratified social order of nineteenth-century France. Conceived in terms of an auditory, sentimental, and timeless state of being, Paris is far removed from the real life issues of social class and status, which determine Debureau's relationship to Countess Cambouilly and Charles X. Rather than imagining a world in which political rights and equality reign, Debureau imagines a place where the cacophony of urban sounds is a harmonious melody, time has no boundaries, and the emotions of joy and passion equal freedom.

By locating paradise outside society in a realm that transcends time and nurtures feelings rather than action, the "revolutionary" Debureau helps maintain the existing order. Nothing actually changes after the revolution except that the leader is now popular and the masses are happy. As Karl Mannheim aptly argued in 1936, societies "have always aimed to control those situationally transcendent ideas and interests which are not realizable within the bounds of the present order, and thereby render them socially impotent, so that such ideas would be confined to a world beyond history and society, where they could not affect the *status quo*."[40]

Debureau is an actor who feels most at home on stage, reigning in a world dedicated not just to magic and make-believe but also to powerful emotions. Although he complains about the constant demands put upon actors, he ultimately succumbs to the theater's charms:

> Because it is the greatest thing in the world for me to stand there as the curtain goes up and to know that all the people down there are waiting for you and what you have to say to them. You know their desires and dreams, and you can fulfill them. You know their happiness and misery, you can make them laugh and cry. Night after night you fight with

them to conquer their hearts! To enchant them enchants me. They let themselves be led by me and I lead them to where they will be happy: in the eternal realm of art.[41]

In Nazi Germany, a society so imbued with hero worship and ecstatic mass response, the cinematic vision of a popular entertainer battling the public to control its emotional life resonates with unique clarity the nation's dream image of itself. The eternal realm of art where everyone is happy, "das ewige Reich der Kunst," is the distorted mirror of the Third Reich. Just as Hitler stylized himself as an artist who sacrificed his personal desires for the nation, Debureau is rendered as an actor devoted to the theater but willing to sacrifice himself for politics. He not only writes and distributes political verses; he becomes, like Hitler, the drummer of revolution.[42]

The connection between theater and politics so central to National Socialist mass demonstrations and to the cinema of the Third Reich is made explicit in both the dialogue and the action. When asked the difference between life at the Théâtre des Funambules and King Charles's court, Debureau replies, "One puts on an act both here and there."[43] In order to achieve revolutionary change on the political stage, society needs the actor's visionary fervor. Indeed, it is the actor and entertainer who sees the inner landscape of the nation and expresses what the politician cannot formulate on his own. The historical mime Jean-Baptiste-Gaspard Debureau becomes the cinematic revue singer Debureau because he can voice the collective subjectivity of the nation. This conspicuous transformation of the historical mime into a cinematic singer may well facilitate the genre conventions of the musical, but it also reflects the National Socialist emphasis on inner-directed politics or *Lebensphilosophie*.[44] The mime is a potentially subversive presence because he can *act out* his grievances against the authorities. He does not rely on language; he simply *becomes* the thing he abhors. The singer, by contrast, gives voice to the burgher through the sentimental medium of music.

Debureau's song "Die Nacht ist nicht allein zum Schlafen da" is equal parts entertainment and dissent. When Debureau performs the song publicly, he targets the self-satisfied philistine and apolitical citizen in his sleeping cap, reminiscent of the German Michel popularized in nineteenth-century caricatures and poems. Composer Theo Mackeben acknowledged that Debureau's satire "aimed at the petty bourgeois" needed to appeal to the audience as both coarse amusement and lofty protest: "On the one hand, the song has to have a crude vulgar effect with a hint of the gutter, while it later has to sound like a rousing revolutionary song, almost like a hymn to freedom."[45] This dual function as a vulgar ditty and a solemn hymn is fitting because the melody is used outside the theater as an illegal protest song. Debureau secretly writes verses against the corrupt king and sets them to this same popular melody, so there is always a sense of the familiar in the new. These forbidden political limericks are thrown from "paradise" (as the Parisians named the cheap seats in the Théâtre des Funambules), posted on walls, and hidden in newspapers. While the music and the satirical tone remain constant, the lyrics and target of criticism constantly change. This shifting focus of discontent creates an ambiguity that allows the audience to read the song and the film in conflicting and subversive ways. The multiple layering of meaning inherent in satire, the critique of one thing that is really another, may well have appealed to contemporary viewers who could see the song as an indictment of National Socialism rather than King Charles's reign. If the cinematic depiction of a police state led by a petty tyrant who censored the arts and executed his political enemies seemed more like the present than the past, then the call for rebellion must have been a welcome release from a highly censored public sphere.

Tanz auf dem Vulkan offers the audience a lesson on how to read such satires and illustrates that a writer's intention and a reader's reception do not always correspond. King Charles X stages a satirical musical review at court in order to humiliate his popular cousin Prince Louis Philippe. The review plays off Louis Philippe's habit of carrying an umbrella and having a head shaped like a pear. Routinely lampooned in caricatures by artists like Honoré Daumier as "la poire," Louis Philippe's image was widely recognized and forms the crux of the satire. While a chanteuse sings of the king's desire to slice up and devour pears, dancers with umbrellas turn around to reveal the prince's pear-shaped face on their backsides. The king hopes to anger and embarrass the prince with this loosely disguised criticism. Louis Philippe, however, decides to read the performance as a compliment and thanks the disappointed king for the kind and original honor. The prince receives accolades while the king pouts, demonstrating that satire's very structure of half concealing dissatisfaction leaves the audience sufficient room to construct meaning on their own. Satire only hints at associations, it uses indirect comedy and skirts around the issues while winking, so that the audience can take pleasure in making the hidden connections visible on their own. The ambiguity and freedom of satire make it appealing but also unruly.

Because Debureau's own song relies on ambiguity and his audience must read between the lines for it to be effective, the actor yearns to voice his political agenda more directly. Ironically, Debureau must disguise himself in order to become a true agitator and speak directly to the masses. The masquerade is essential to the exercise of power because it allows communication of a truth that is otherwise socially or politically unacceptable. Even within this cautionary tale where the king is a ridiculous and petty figure unworthy of respect or the crown, an open assault on state authority is deemed inappropriate and must be cloaked in a more legitimate and hidden guise. When Debureau physically strikes King Charles and denounces him in a public forum, he goes beyond accepted social norms and must flee for his life. It is only by adopting the costume of a lawful representative of the state that Debureau can momentarily escape imprisonment and also convey his revolutionary goals to the masses.

Debureau disguises himself as Prince Louis Philippe, and in the mask of this legitimate power he openly preaches insurrection:

> Parisians, you have just asked me, when will we be ready? I ask you, aren't we ready now? Who among you is without hatred, without anxiety, without fear! You are no longer Frenchmen, you are mere subjects! . . . Where is your laughter, your happiness! Who is responsible for your fate? Perhaps the king? No! Frenchmen, you alone are responsible for your fate! . . . Do you really love the king so much that you do not dare to rise up against him and cast off your chains? . . . Every folk has the government it deserves! Do you want to wile away your life disheartened and groveling. You decide! What are you still waiting for! Our hour has come! The fatherland is calling you now! Frenchmen! Long live France![46]

Debureau uses the masses' emotional state as a measure of the nation's political health. If the king does not alleviate their hatred, anxiety, and fear, if he leaves them feeling disheartened and servile, they should simply replace him with a better leader, one more in tune with their emotional needs. Debureau argues that it is the leader's utmost task to guarantee the masses happiness and bliss.

Even as he is brought to the guillotine, Debureau questions the despondent crowds huddled together in the streets why they are not happy: "Parisians! I no longer recognize you. Where is the applause with which you usually greet me? Why are you crying? You have to laugh, when Debureau comes! Have you forgotten everything?"[47] In this climatic scene, Gründgens's performance is heightened to a feverish pitch and borders on hysteria. Although over-excitability is characteristic of his acting style, in the context of this film it takes on a different hue. As the leader of a revolutionary mass movement, Debureau tries to inflame "volcanic eruptions of human passions and emotional sentiments" in keeping with Hitler's own argument that "only a storm of hot passion can turn the destinies of people, and he alone can arouse passion who bears it within himself."[48] Debureau succeeds in whipping himself and the masses into a frenzy, and this violent unleashing of emotional energy forces King Charles to flee the country and saves Debureau from the executioner's blade. The actress Angele and the entire crowd wave at their leader in a trance-like rapture much like the throngs saluted the Führer in Leni Riefenstahl's *Triumph of the Will* (1935). In an eerie conclusion to Steinhoff's film, Debureau jumps onto the scaffold that holds the guillotine and turns the historic site of horrifying public executions into a stage for entertainment and communal happiness. The spectacle of political death is transformed into a musical production replete with a chorus chanting the refrain faithfully repeated throughout the entire film: "Become enchanted, friends, drink and love and laugh/ And live in the splendid moment./ Spending the night intoxicated/ Means happiness and bliss!"

Tanz auf dem Vulkan received mixed reviews. While Goebbels explicitly banned art criticism (*Kunstkritik*) in November 1936 and declared that only art reports (*Kunstberichte*) would appear in newspapers, some journalists like Werner Fiedler at the Berlin *Deutsche Allgemeine Zeitung* were able to publish negative reviews of state-sanctioned films. Fiedler argued that *Tanz auf dem Vulkan* did not strive to portray history accurately:

> The whole thing is too playfully structured for that. One would misunderstand the elegant, convincing satirist Gründgens, if one wanted to consider the harmless film action with its numerous improbabilities as serious history. . . . This film is full of original disguise scenes. It is not so much about historical-political tendencies; rather it wants to be an entertaining costume film, a political masquerade, which guarantees a famous actor lavish scenes.[49]

Fiedler contended that *Tanz auf dem Vulkan* was a costume drama that used historical artifice but did not engage historical issues. A similar review appeared in *Der deutsche Film,* where the film was criticized as unrealistic because it portrayed both the king and the prince as ridiculous and ineffective leaders unworthy of their opponent Debureau. The historical conflict is trivialized, because "the political, ideal moment lapses into the personal sphere, jealousy and offended vanity."[50] By contrast, the Tobis studio's official advertising campaign repeatedly advised theater owners "to avoid arousing in the audience the impression of a costume drama," because *Tanz auf dem Vulkan* "is much more than what the public expects from a costume drama."[51] Reviewers for the daily trade papers *Film-Kurier* and *Licht-Bild-Bühne* either accepted the film wholeheartedly as a convincing historical drama or merely criticized the portrayal of weak leaders as unrealistic.[52] Apparently none of the writers seemed to doubt the "higher historical truth" behind the film: that France's most celebrated mime incited the masses to revolution with a rousing nightclub act.

Whether audiences in 1938 Germany considered *Tanz auf dem Vulkan* a critique of National Socialism turns on questions that can never be answered with any certainty. Did viewers see the story as a reflection of history or the present? Did they recognize themselves and their own political circumstances in the events projected on the screen? Did they read the satire straight or against the grain? The more compelling and potentially more productive question to pose is why the concept of a mass emotional revolution continually dominated the public sphere in Nazi Germany. The notion of politics as pathos so well illustrated in this motion picture was doubtlessly in line with mainstream National Socialist discursive practices. In the political and cultural realm, German audiences were constantly reminded that communal well-being stems from the symbiosis between leader and folk, and the particulars of government are irrelevant as long as the leader fulfills the masses' emotional needs. Whether at the Nuremberg rallies where the Führer and the assembled ranks shared a highly emotional bond, where "even a paltry worm could feel like part of a great dragon,"[53] or in the movie theater where a charismatic leader joins the frenzied masses in communal bliss, the leader-folk symbiosis relied on the spectacle. The eye looking inward, the audience celebrating its own presence on stage, has no need to look beyond itself. If the masses are occupied with their own reflection, criticism of the political environment becomes unnecessary for happiness. The guarantee of communal bliss and shared emotional release replaces the need for action or political change.

Excursus on Jews and the Nazi Cultural Industry

The lack of empirical studies on the moviegoing public in Nazi Germany makes it difficult to gauge what viewers expected from a film like *Tanz auf dem Vulkan,* which social groups saw it, and how audiences reacted to its revolutionary and potentially subversive story. We can, however, determine one aspect of the audience composition with relative certainty. Jews did not attend the premiere run of *Tanz auf dem Vulkan* because they were officially banned from German cinemas.[54] In order to understand fully the Nazi concept of politics as pathos, the leadership principle, and the building of community illustrated in the cinema of the Third Reich, we need to remember that the *Volksgemeinschaft* (national community) defined itself in opposition to the Jews. It is no coincidence that the release of *Tanz auf dem Vulkan* in November 1938 coincides with heightened anti-Semitic measures. The veneration of a strong leader and an emotionally willing folk is inexorably linked to the vilification and exclusion of Jews from German society. The identity of a unified German nation was predicated on the notion that the Jews were the Aryan's natural enemy and had to be eliminated on both a physical and symbolic level. The leader in communion with his faithful followers was a core concept of National Socialist doctrine, but by November 1938 even the *image* of the leader was deemed sacred and the Jews were forbidden to gaze upon this image in a movie theater with Aryan spectators.

In the night between November 9–10, 1938, National Socialists unleashed their most violent attack on the Jews to date. Commonly known as the Night of Broken Glass (*Reichskristallnacht*), this pogrom marked a decisive shift toward more intense, systematically brutal, and public demonstrations of state-mandated anti-Semitism. The government used the assassination of diplomat Ernst vom Rath in Paris by the Jew Herschel Grünspan as grounds for a fierce strike against the Jewish community. The timing of Rath's death on November 8 was fortuitous for the NSDAP because party leaders were gathered in Munich for their yearly commemoration of Hitler's unsuccessful 1923 putsch attempt. Goebbels gave an impassioned speech to the assembled party leaders, who organized the pogrom and directed the SA throughout Germany to burn synagogues, destroy Jewish storefronts, and incarcerate some 30,000 Jews in Gestapo dungeons and concentration camps.[55]

Following the Night of Broken Glass, the Nazi regime instituted a new series of anti-Semitic measures aimed at excluding Jews completely from German cultural and economic life. On November 12, 1938, three days after the pogrom and two weeks before the premiere of *Tanz auf dem Vulkan,* Goebbels declared:

> Since for over five years now the National Socialist state has made it possible for the Jews to create and maintain their own cultural life in special Jewish organizations, it is no longer appropriate to allow them to participate in German cultural offerings. Therefore, as of now Jews are no longer permitted entrance to such events, especially theaters, cinemas, concerts, lectures, artistic undertakings (varieties, cabarets, circus events, etc.), dance performances, and exhibitions of a cultural nature.[56]

Although Jews had already been banned from employment in the film industry in 1933, they were now forbidden even to watch movies or participate at any level in communal forms of entertainment with Aryans. This total exclusion of Jews from social events, in the sense of both pleasurable and shared human experiences, marked a turning point in the persecution of the Jews and had far-reaching consequences for the social construction of happiness in Nazi Germany. The Nuremberg Laws of November 1935 had already isolated the Jews politically, socially, and emotionally. The Nuremberg Laws not only defined the Jews as a separate race lacking citizenship and political rights in Germany, they also forbade sexual intercourse and marriage between Jews and Aryans. Historians generally emphasize how these laws resulted in the Jew's political and social isolation, but they rarely give sufficient attention to how they structurally isolated the Jews in a separate emotional world. The government ban on physical and emotional intimacy between Jews and Aryans legally excluded Jews from the *Volksgemeinschaft* in the present and for future generations. As Hermann Graml rightly concludes, Jews became social lepers on the margins of German society:

> The most tender and strongest and also the most important social affection which can exist between human beings not related by family, if it joined "those of German blood" and Jews, was declared a crime punishable with a prison sentence. A minority ostracized to such an extent became literally and naturally also figuratively untouchable.[57]

Goebbels's decree of November 12, 1938 banning Jews from all cultural events went even further to isolate Jews in an invisible ghetto of untouchables. Jews were implicitly defined as sub-humans unfit to participate in everyday cultural events in public forums. With no legal right to enjoy

"German" entertainment, and by extension no right to "German" happiness, edification, and sublimation, Jews were effectively eliminated from the emotional life of the nation.

Hermann Göring, in his capacity as deputy of the four-year plan, was largely responsible for designing the economic sanctions against the Jews. On November 12, 1938, he declared that Jewish property owners had to pay for the pogrom's damage, estimated at several hundred million reichsmarks, while the government was authorized to confiscate the money from insurance claims. Göring also levied a fine of a billion reichsmarks on the entire Jewish community. Further, he proclaimed that as of January 1, 1939, Jews could no longer own retail or mail-order businesses, practice trades as artisans, attend conventions or trade fairs, hold managerial positions, or be members of business associations.[58] Since the Nazi regime had already instituted countless restrictions on Jewish workers, Göring's new measures virtually barred Jews from free participation in the German economy.

Although the government had effectively dictated that Jews were unworthy of the same social participation and happiness afforded Aryans, it was left to the cultural industry to cast the law of the land as a rewarding and universal moral value. Motion pictures held great promise for the task of creating a sense of German community and validating anti-Semitism. The historical musical in particular offered an effective formula for generating both pleasant and nostalgic sentiments, the necessary components for the enchantment of reality.

"The Refreshing Bath of Schadenfreude": *Robert and Bertram* (1939)

Robert und Bertram was the first feature film made after the Night of Broken Glass to portray Jews as cultural and economic outsiders in great detail. Hans H. Zerlett, known for his vaudeville drama *Truxa* (1937) and backstage musical comedy *Es leuchten die Sterne* (1938), wrote and directed this musical based on Gustav Raeder's 1856 farce *Robert und Bertram*. Raeder's play had already enjoyed a long run on German stages and provided the material for two silent movies before Zerlett's film premiered in Hamburg on July 7, 1939.[59] The story of two likeable vagabonds cheating the Jews had a firm tradition in Germany long before it came to the screen in the Third Reich, but it was the only anti-Semitic musical comedy made under National Socialism. Starring popular actor Rudi Godden as the debonair poet and operetta star Kurt Seifert as the down-to-earth individualist, *Robert und Bertram* casts a humorous look at German history and constitutes an image of Germans and Jews that is both engaging and ambivalent.

Stealing from the Jews: *Robert und Bertram* (1939).

While *Tanz auf dem Vulkan* highlights the ecstatic symbiosis between leader and folk, *Robert und Bertram* explores the historical opposition between the German folk and its archenemy, the Jew. Again this musical promises the chosen few: "A merry life we lead and free, a life of endless bliss!"[60] With these emblematic words from Friedrich Schiller's *Die Räuber,* the vagabonds Robert and Bertram sing their way through 1839 Germany, stealing from the rich Jews and giving to the poor Aryans. Reminiscent of Robin Hood, Til Eulenspiegel, and a host of simple outsiders who fight for the downtrodden, Robert and Bertram break all the rules of society to serve the higher purpose of "true justice." The title characters exist on the margins of society while helping the German community to remain intact and distanced from the Jews both culturally and economically.

The elaborate film plot is filled with many twists and turns typical of the farce. Before joining the army, Michel carves a heart into a tree for his beloved Lenchen because he is too tongue-tied to profess his true feelings out loud. Meanwhile the vagabonds and old friends Robert and Bertram are reunited in prison and escape together. They wander upon the Lips's family inn, where they overhear Biedermeier trying to blackmail Lenchen into marrying him because her father, Mr. Lips, cannot repay his debts. The vagabonds decide to take matters into their own hands and help the family who acted kindly toward them. They learn that Biedermeier in turn owes money to the Jewish Berlin banker Ipelmeyer.[61] Disguised as the Count of Monte Cristo and his music teacher Professor Müller, the vagabonds make their way to Berlin, where they use their new identities to impress Ipelmeyer, who invites them to his home for an evening of entertainment. The vagabonds then steal the Ipelmeyer family jewels and send them to Lips so he can repay Biedermeier. If Biedermeier returns the jewels to Ipelmeyer, the Jew will be repaid with his own property and all debts will be settled. Michel returns home as a resolute soldier and man of action. He promptly takes Lenchen into his arms and pronounces them engaged. Disguised this time as women, Robert and Bertram enjoy the local festival until they are recognized and forced to escape in a hot air balloon. The vagabonds fly to heaven, where the angels greet them and all is forgiven because they have shown the greatest of all virtues: gratitude.

The title characters are fugitives from justice whose crimes include loitering, vagrancy, petty theft, grand larceny, making false statements to the police, and breaking out of prison. They are outlaws with no respect for police authority and no desire to lead an orderly life. Bertram defends their actions as those of exemplary individuals for whom normal rules do not apply: "You see, Robert, you are a washed-up genius, and I am a drop-out bourgeois, one who would rather be a tramp than a conformist."[62] As fun-loving individualists, they roam the countryside in search of adventure and the easy life. More pranksters than hardened criminals, Robert and Bertram have little interest in money, for as they sing, "If you always have courage, what do you need with money? As a slowpoke in training you go merrily through the world."[63] Typical of characters in a buddy film, Robert and Bertram reject widely accepted behavioral norms and commit a series of crimes against unworthy opponents while bonding together emotionally.

As tricksters and loafers on the margins of society, Robert and Bertram belong to a long literary tradition ranging from Til Eulenspiegel to Joseph von Eichendorff's *Aus dem Leben eines Taugenichts* (1826). While their crimes against the Jews plainly correspond to anti-Semitic Nazi ideology, their non-conventional lifestyle calls into question accepted social norms, especially in regards to asocial behavior. In the context of Nazi Germany, these outlaws represent an anomaly. The National Socialist *Volksgemeinschaft* or national community was an ideal based largely on the concepts of race, work, and shared feelings. Community members were identified not only by their racially pure, healthy Aryan bodies but also by their capacity to work for the nation. From the haunting wrought iron sign "Arbeit macht frei" at the entrance to concentration camps to the obligatory National Labor Service (*Reichsarbeitsdienst*),[64] work constituted an essential aspect of everyday life in the Third Reich.

Those individuals who refused to hold down a job on a regular basis were defined as "work-shy" (*arbeitsscheu*). In 1938 the government intensified its efforts to require all able-bodied men to fulfill their duty to the community by engaging in productive activity. In a plan ostensibly to combat crime but more likely to provide labor for the arms industry, Interior Minister Wilhelm Frick directed the police to detain in preventative custody (*Vorbeugungshaft*) professional criminals, men who had no identity papers or possessed false documents, and those individuals who endangered the community by their asocial behavior, specifically beggars and tramps.[65] Based on these instructions, the Gestapo arrested some 2,000 work-shy men between April 21 and April 30, 1938. These men were deemed asocial, marked with a black triangle, and confined to the concentration camp Buchenwald. The Criminal Police Bureau likewise issued a directive to arrest all able-bodied asocial men defined as follows: "Those to be considered asocial are persons who demonstrate through their adverse behavior toward the community, which may not in itself be criminal, that they will not adapt themselves to the community."[66] The directive specifically targeted the work-shy, vagrants, homeless, and men "who evade the duty to work." Between June 13–18, 1938, the police undertook a nationwide action against the sub-proletarian male class, which resulted in the arrest of more than 10,000 men. "Action Work-Shy Reich" netted the government a slave workforce for the newly founded SS business enterprise "Deutsche Erde- und Steinwerke GmbH" with its intended quarries, granite mines, and brickyards at concentration camps Buchenwald, Sachsenhausen, Flossenbürg, Mauthausen, and Neuengamme.[67]

Set against the backdrop of the Nazi campaign to penalize work-shy outsiders, it is not surprising that Zerlett's film goes to great lengths to qualify the title characters' identity and motivation. For example, before the police interrogate Robert and Bertram, Lips describes them as "two merry fellows" and is quick to add "but they aren't vagabonds, they have to be roving minstrels or something like that. They are earning their keep by washing dishes." The policemen confirm that these outsiders must be harmless because they are willing to wash dishes, and as they say, "that's honest work."[68] Lenchen thinks they are "wandering artists" and subject to a different code of behavior, one that allows more freedom based on the romantic notion of the artist as an exceptional individual. Even though Robert acknowledges "well, it's more accurate to say we're actually skilled wanderers,"[69] the community gathered at the Lips's inn grants them special status.

Although Robert and Bertram are thieves, they only use what they need and return Jewish property in the end to its "rightful" Aryan owners. Their theft is justified when Ipelmeyer is unmasked as a swindler whose opulent but tasteless lifestyle is financed by stolen money. When one guest speculates that Ipelmeyer's Berlin palace must have cost a fortune, another guest replies: "In fact it cost several fortunes, but not Mr. Ipelmeyer's own, rather those of the people he swindled."[70] Although the local police issue a warrant for Robert and Bertram's arrest, the officials recognize the inherent justice of their crimes against the Jews. The case goes before the president, the chief of police, the prime minister, and even the king because all representatives of state authority agree upon the selfless motivations and true nature of these two outsiders. The king compares the vagabonds' harmless pranks to the serious crimes of the Jewish banker, and concludes: "The thing is, that a big crook who evades capture can become a financial councilor, while these little crooks, if they are caught, will spend a long time locked up, although their deception was not carried out for their own gain. Something is wrong here."[71]

In the publicity campaign for *Robert und Bertram*, numerous critics stressed the vagabonds' special status as exceptional individuals who are not subject to normal social constraints: "Whoever wants to be fair with them, must measure them by their own standards and not with the yardstick of bourgeois virtues. After all, normal standards only apply when it is a question of normal circumstances."[72] Robert and Bertram's unlawful behavior was justified based on extenuating circumstances: "The basically harmless 'criminals' only steal from those people who themselves have stolen before, and they give away the spoils to the disadvantaged. They are not common but rather 'higher' thieves, to a certain extent, morally sanctioned thieves."[73] The "higher" moral propagated here is that the theft of Jewish property is not really theft at all. Since the Jews are themselves exposed as thieves, expropriating their assets is a just and socially acceptable action.

The Tobis film studio emphasized in its press package for *Robert und Bertram* that the audience takes pleasure in the vagabonds' lighthearted approach to work. In a surprisingly candid acknowledgment that work and regimented everyday life in Nazi Germany were emotionally debilitating, one writer observed: "Our joy in them is surely an unconscious protest against the daily drudgery of working, against the obligations that all too annoyingly regulate our existence."[74] Another writer in the same press package argued that despite the nineteenth-century setting, the vagabonds' work-shy attitude held an important lesson for the present. While the two loafers might have been able to get away with not working in the past, the current work ethic demanded that "Robert and Bertram would nowadays be introduced to *refreshing physical labor*." This euphemistic phrase makes the familiar reality of forced labor in concentration camps seem harmless or even beneficial to its victims.

Robert und Bertram was advertised as a didactic piece intended specifically for an audience of *workers* and able to address their emotional needs: "Many a person who gets tired from the uniformity of daily work, whom the monotony of his task threatens to undermine, who only sees the work but can no longer see past it, he will discover delightfully in the swindler the shortcomings of human nature." The worker needs to laugh at human failings, to relax, and to rebuild his emotional strength so he can continue to

work for the nation. "Everyone laughs at the pranks, the hilarious entangle-
ments, the coincidences and circumstances, but he finds his way back to
work." The lesson propagated in this cheerful, seemingly innocuous farce
frankly echoes the widely known and cynical motto "work makes you free"
etched on the gates to concentration camps: "Such a swindler drama has a
moral: There is no freedom without work, or, there has to be order, or else
misfortune is just around the corner."[75]

Although Robert and Bertram fail to integrate themselves into society by
settling down in a permanent home, starting a family, and engaging in regular
work, they do offer the community a necessary service. They provide entertainment and an outlet for sentimental emotions. At the wedding reception,
for example, Robert and Bertram sing a folk song and unleash a current of
intense romantic feelings. These vagabonds also provide a vicarious outlet for
pent-up frustrations in a highly restrictive society. They do what normal people cannot do, but often dream about doing: dropping out, neglecting responsibility, and taking what they want regardless of the consequences. Their
freedom of movement is literally coupled with the joy of song and dance, so
that these men exude the pleasure of life. Despite their criminal behavior,
Robert and Bertram are highly sympathetic figures because their disregard for
rules is tempered by a sense of humor and good will toward the Lips family.

The innkeeper Lips and his daughter Lenchen represent the most positive
aspects of the German community and do not develop throughout the film
narrative. Lips is and remains a loving father and an honest, hard-working small
businessman trying to get on his feet. His daughter Lenchen is kind and sentimental but also resolutely intent on marrying a man worthy of her. Michel, on
the other hand, undergoes a transformation preparing him for manhood and
marriage. With his shoulder-length hair, knickers, and striped socks, Michel
starts as a little boy in a man's body. The impression of a shy and romantic
weakling is confirmed when he stutters his beloved Lenchen's name and stammers on about finding a woodpecker in the forest. In the all-male setting of the
prison and army, Michel is equally childlike and inept. He stands out in the
rain, apologizes when someone bumps into him, cowers in fear of the prisoners, and whines about the rigors of army life.[76] Only during military training
when he finally realizes his physical strength, does his voice drop an octave and
his posture become erect. Unlike his historical namesake, the "German Michel" immortalized as the apolitical citizen in his sleeping cap in countless
revolutionary poems and caricatures especially around 1848, this Michel awakens from his sentimental dream world and becomes a disciplined, robust soldier. While Michel initially berates the army, he eventually recognizes "what
the Prussians can do with a man."[77] If one were to focus on his statements in
isolation, then his criticism of military life could be construed as subversive and
directed toward regimented life under the NSDAP. However, if one considers
that the disparaging comments stem from a ridiculous weakling, they tend to

carry less weight. Framed within Michel's transformation from a country bumpkin to a strapping soldier, his early criticism of the army seems unfounded. Only the initiation into a disciplined military life made it possible for this weakling to become a man and win his girl.

Set in 1839 at the height of the restoration period (1815–1848), Zerlett's film idealizes the *Volksgemeinschaft* as a harmonious rural community bound together by folk traditions and strong emotional ties. This idyllic view of the past locates *Heimat* at the Lips's family inn where the whole village comes together to celebrate a marriage. The villagers, dressed in their native costumes and dancing to traditional folk music at a wedding reception, present the picture of a simpler time when the folk was united by ritual, entertainment, and the promise of a happy future together.[78] While Raeder's original drama was set around 1856, Zerlett shifted the action to 1839, Germany's last pre-industrial period and separated by nearly a decade from the 1830 and 1848 revolutions. Zerlett thereby emphasized the stability of the restoration and disregarded its darker side: Metternich's system of secret police, denunciation, censorship, exile, and imprisonment. Rather than the infamous repressive government, Zerlett features two archetypal enemies who stand in the way of communal happiness: Biedermeier and the Jew. The character Biedermeier is named after the allegorical figure of the petty bourgeois philistine who had come to embody the entire restoration period. This smarmy, unsympathetic character wants to marry Lenchen and tries to use his financial superiority to force her consent. Biedermeier's blackmail attempt represents a sexual, social, and economic threat, but behind him stands the Jew whose corrupt business practices enable the intrigue in the first place and threaten the long-term stability of the *Volksgemeinschaft*.

Zerlett's portrayal of the Jews is based largely on stereotypes, beginning with the popular notion that Jews have hooked noses, hoofed feet, a Yiddish accent, and a crude libido.[79] Bertram, for instance, correctly identifies Ipelmeyer on the street, "judging by the profile." Ipelmeyer's wife immediately recognizes her lover at the masquerade ball "by his feet."[80] And Dr. Corduan recognizes Ipelmeyer despite his costume by his Yiddish accent and lecherous gaze at the lead ballerina. Although the Jew attempts to assimilate into German society by adopting upper-class clothes and mimicking sophisticated manners, his misshapen body ultimately reveals his true identity. What separates the Jew from the Aryan is also a different moral code. For instance, Ipelmeyer considers fraud a normal trade practice and values a good business deal more than love or marital happiness. He tells fellow Jew Forchheimer, "For the last three years you have been my authorized signatory. For two years you have been stealing from me left and right. For one year you have been cheating on me with my wife. Now if even the smallest thing happens, you are fired."[81] When the young bookkeeper Samuel professes his love for

Isidora, Ipelmeyer replies, "Are you meschugge? What does 'love' mean on 600 talers a year wages? My daughter will be the stepmother of a million."[82]

The cinematic depiction of the Jew is strewn with contradictions. How are viewers expected to "read" the Jewish body as a visible racial-behavioral marker when all the Jewish characters are played by Aryan actors? Various critics attempted to resolve this dilemma by stressing that the Aryan actors playing Jews were so talented they could transform themselves to an extraordinary degree. However, the conflict is never completely resolved because the Jews share an uncanny resemblance to the Aryans. Not only Ipelmeyer and his servant Jack have difficulty with language, so does Bertram. Ipelmeyer confuses *faché* (embarrassed) with *Faschiertes* (minced meat), and mistakenly calls his daughter *the medical Venus* (die medizinische Venus) instead of the Medici Venus from Botticelli's "The Birth of Venus" (1483). The Jewish servant Jack mixes up *Zionism* and *cynicism* as well as *overture* and *Ofentür* (oven door). The Aryan Bertram displays an equally inadequate mastery of foreign words and even his native German language. Bertram not only mistakes *sublatern* for *subaltern* and *au trottoir* for *au revoir,* he also stammers *selbstmurmelnd* (muttering to yourself) instead of *selbstredend* (naturally). He is not sure how to react when he is called a *Banause* (philistine) because he does not know what *Banausentum* (cultural illiteracy) means.

Most striking, however, is that the Aryan and Jew mirror each other visually and behave in a similar manner. In three complementary sequences, Robert and Bertram interrupt collective merriment, are recognized as dangerous outsiders, and are expelled from both the Aryan and Jewish communities. At the Lips's family inn they steal Biedermeier's wallet, disturb the reception, and are chased over tables and through windows by the entire wedding party, leaving the bride and groom oblivious to the commotion and only engrossed in each other. At the Ipelmeyer home the vagabonds steal the family jewels, interrupt the festivities, and are chased from the house by the screaming guests, while Ipelmeyer sleeps unbothered. Finally, at the fair the vagabonds are recognized as escaped prisoners, thwart the fun, and are pursued by a wild crowd, while the minstrels continue their song without interruption. The similar narratives, the focus on interrupted entertainment, and the play on movement and stasis connect the Aryan and the Jew cinematically. All three scenes are characterized by rapid editing (twelve to eighteen shots in quick succession), a mobile camera at the center of the crowd, and a narrow, contained mise en scène filled with many obstacles. Even the shot of a screaming Jewish girl followed by a close-up of a screeching parrot finds its complement in the shot of an irate Aryan crowd followed by a close-up of a frenzied monkey. It is difficult to read this juxtaposition of images visually equating the frantic Jew to an animal without coming to the same conclusion for the Aryan. The most significant difference in the portrayal of the two communities is the inclusion of a commentary following the scene at Ipelmeyer's home. The camera pans away from the crowd and towards Jack as he slowly descends the stairs and walks center stage. He looks directly into the camera and says "the final gallop with Jewish haste, no?"[83] This self-reflective moment coupled with a popular anti-Semitic adage on Jewish haste juxtaposes skepticism and knowledge. The merger of two opposing categories of thought is ambivalent and leaves the meaning open to interpretation. Should viewers accept the widespread notion that unruly behavior or haste is a typical Jewish trait? Or is the statement made ironic through the self-reflective stance, so that viewers question the idea that the Jewish community is inherently prone to disorder and pandemonium? Or is the theatricality of the scene emphasized so that the viewers can feel like they are in on the joke?

These unresolved contradictions are also manifest in the contrast between Aryan and Jewish culture. On the surface, the cultural events depicted at the Lips's inn and the Ipelmeyer home appear to demonstrate that the Aryans enjoy inherited folk music and dance, while the Jews put on airs by "borrowing" foreign classical music and ballet. However, Zerlett's use of parody makes it difficult to determine whether the ostensible differences between the two groups are real or illusionary. In a contemporary review published in *Film-Kurier,* Georg Herzberg summarized the dilemma aptly:

> [Zerlett] presents a Viennese song in such a way, as if he wants to make fun of the Danube singing kitsch. And then comes something that captivates the majority of moviegoers just as it does the villagers up on the screen. Or when Rudi Godden begins an aria parody and afterwards one does not quite know whether one should laugh or take it seriously. Or a ballet whizzes by and Ursula Deinert dances the lead so well, that it is a feast for the eyes, and then the whole thing ends with a kitschy pose, and one does not know what the director actually wanted. One will have to wait it out to see if the difficult problem of parody in films can be solved with such compromises.[84]

The Viennese song that Robert and Bertram sing, for example, is not a true folk song. The vagabonds make it up and con the wedding guests into believing it is real. Moreover, their performance completely changes the audience's mood from merriment to melancholy. The entire wedding party is happy until the vagabonds sing "Geh nicht wieder fort von mir," a maudlin song about a lover who begs his sweetheart not to leave him. The contrast between a happy reality and a sad art, the celebration of fulfilled love and a lament about lovers separating, creates a parody of folk traditions and kitschy notions of love. While the whole community is swept away by the sentimental pathos, Robert and Bertram use this emotional outpouring to con the guests out of their money. They acknowledge their motivation and even incorporate it into their song, singing the following lines to the same melody: "What we are singing touches you deeply. Afterwards with 'your humble servant' we'll go around collecting. Everyone will give a penny. Only when our plate is full will our happiness be complete."[85] With the audience weeping and literally paying for it, the vagabonds have in effect used cultural traditions to outwit the German folk.

Adolf Hitler claimed that the Jewish race "is without any true culture, and especially without any culture of its own. For what sham culture the Jew today possesses is the property of other peoples, and for the most part it is ruined in his hands."[86] The Jew's relationship to art and culture was, in Hitler's words, "intellectual theft." Zerlett's film illustrates the Jew's lack of native culture and his appropriation of a foreign culture that he does not understand or appreciate.

Ipelmeyer's home becomes "a true temple of art" and a public forum where Jews can consort with British nobility who find them pleasant and with Aryan business associates who must fulfill their social obligations. The Jews use culture to enter into privileged social circles, but they do not appreciate the true value of art. The evening's entertainment begins with an instrumental piece followed by Robert's aria of betrayed love. While beautiful, richly dressed women and one dreamy, effeminate man listen intently to the "high" art, a Jewish guest does not understand that the song is "about a guy who had a fit with his lover."[87] In contrast to the earlier Viennese song, the aria tells the story of a scorned lover who gets drunk and decides that he does not need his paramour after all. Robert made up both the folk song and the aria by merely adopting the style appropriate for each audience. Both songs are parodies but their sentiments and the audience's reaction to them seem to define the Aryan and Jewish communities as different entities. While the "folk song" expressed unrequited but enduring love and moved the Aryan audience to tears, the sophisticated "aria" voices a base sentiment and fails to unite the mixed public of Jews and Aryans in a shared emotional state. The ballet also seems to unleash more sexual energy than artistic interest among the Jews. During the dance performance, Forchheimer makes a pass at Mrs. Ipelmeyer, Samuel tries to seduce Isidora, and Dr. Corduan (alias Dr. Caftan) and Ipelmeyer both cast a lustful eye at the lead ballerina.[88] Finally, in contrast to the joyous and methodic folk dance performed at the Aryan wedding reception, the gallop dance at the Jew's party is a wild and chaotic release, the perfect setting for the crime that follows. The Jew's unrestrained merriment creates a fertile environment for Robert and Bertram to steal without notice.

Anti-Semitic rhetoric claims that assimilated Jews masquerade as Aryans to gain access to German society, but here it is the Aryans who disguise themselves in the trappings of aristocratic and academic authority to gain access to Jewish society. Robert and Bertram come to the Ipelmeyer home disguised as the Count of Monte Cristo and his music teacher Professor Müller. Are the Aryans outwitting the Jews at their own game or is this merely another example of how the Aryan and the Jew resemble each other? At the costume ball held later in the evening, the Ipelmeyers adopt costumes that illustrate their ridiculous desire to be powerful rulers of foreign cultures that they do not understand. Jack comments that Mr. Ipelmeyer masquerades as "Louis Quartose the fifteenth," his wife as Madame Pompadour, "but she looks like an old sack" and his daughter Isidora as "Queen Kleptomania," alias Cleopatra.[89] Samuel the Jewish bookkeeper likewise tries to adopt the identity of a powerful, honorable knight by donning a suit of armor, but he cannot walk in it, let alone fight or make love when the opportunities arise.

After Robert and Bertram have demonstrated that the Jews are guilty of intellectual and financial theft and therefore deserve to be expropriated, the vagabonds' narrative function becomes tenuous. Because they have rectified a perceived injustice and fulfilled their role as unlawful agents of a higher morality, their own status as outsiders is called into question. In a series of seemingly unconnected episodes, they are literally made unreal, extrapolated from the narrative, and eliminated from the picture.

While the king decides their legal fate, Robert and Bertram admire a sculpture garden behind a barred fence and exchange the following dialogue:

BERTRAM: You see, Robert, that's life. Everywhere bars, the only difference is that the one looks out through the bars and the other looks in. I'd rather look out.

ROBERT: Well, then just let 'em lock you up again.

BERTRAM: Oh, you just don't have any imagination.[90]

Bertram recognizes that life itself is a prison. Whether one looks out or in, everyone is confined by socially proscribed boundaries. The advantage to being locked up is that the view is better. This farcical view of incarceration as something inevitable and even desirable helps the viewer accept the vagabonds' fate, but it also trivializes the incarceration of asocials in concentration camps, a very real political action that was occurring on a daily basis in Nazi Germany. The viewer is explicitly encouraged to draw parallels between the past and present. In the same scene, the vagabonds read a newspaper, and the headlines characterize political events in the nineteenth century that bare a remarkable resemblance to those in the twentieth century. When 1839 looks like 1939, seeing a past where work-shy outsiders actually want to be locked up makes it easier for viewers to fantasize a harmless version of the present where asocials want to be put away for their own good.

Visually restrained by bars and reconciled or even happily awaiting imprisonment, Robert and Bertram fall asleep and are transformed into the mythical figures Bacchus and Mercury from the sculpture garden. The transition from reality to dream and myth helps to decontextualize the vagabonds from the narrative and remove them from a social environment in which they can no longer justifiably roam unrestricted. This transition also establishes a utopian bond between the vagabonds, but could just as easily describe the chimerical bond between the audience and the sympathetic anti-heroes. Robert and Bertram appear in each other's dreams and joyfully proclaim: "Hear us, you gods, through time and space, we are one soul, one heart, one dream."[91] Just as in *Tanz auf dem Vulkan, Robert and Bertram* reveals "what utopia would feel like rather than how it would be organized" (Dyer). Viewers again experience a utopian vision of the nineteenth century as a realm in which time and space have no meaning, normal boundaries are overcome, and feelings bind people together more than any social institutions ever could. The utopian goal of spiritual unity is possible in a shared dream world so very similar to the experience of watching a movie in a crowded cinema. In this nexus of dream, myth, and movie, the characters and the audience share a powerful collective fantasy and emotional life.

In a further transformation, Robert and Bertram disguise themselves as countrywomen and appear at the carnival. Even this place on the edge of society, where libidinous energy is given a controlled release, cannot contain them. Emasculated and now fully stripped of their last vestige of potential male productivity, the vagabonds need to be removed from the narrative. They escape capture in a hot air balloon and fly to heaven while still alive, but as Robert reassures Bertram: "Don't bother yourself about it, we couldn't have expected very much from earthly justice anyway."[92] The asocials who have nothing to contribute to the work of the nation are delivered to a place from which they can never leave. The cinematic treatment of asocials, their willing expulsion from the *Volksgemeinschaft* to a place of eternal happiness, trains the audience to translate a real-life horror into reassuring images of contentment and order. *Robert und Bertram* ends with the enormous solid metal gates of heaven closing, locking the vagabonds safely away and signaling to the audience both the film's conclusion and the inevitable final solution for outsiders. The last image of impenetrable borders covering the entire screen suggests a finality so complete that there is no escape, and both the characters and the audience are locked into this course of action to protect the community. The ridiculous idea of going to heaven while still alive is made to seem completely logical. The absurdity inherent in the farce as a genre allows the audience simultaneously to accept and deny the existence of death and imprisonment as the punishment for non-conformity.

Some confusion, however, exists over the film's conclusion. Both Dorothea Hollstein and Linda Schulte-Sasse have incorrectly argued that *Robert und Bertram* was reshot with a different ending during the Second World War. Schulte-Sasse maintains: "The vagabonds are forcibly reintegrated into the social order in 1942, when the film's ending was changed to show them entering military service under the command of Michel — a move justified by the need to sustain the public's military morale."[93] I could find no evidence that Zerlett's film was actually reshot and only one publicity brochure that describes this alternate ending. *Das Programm von heute* 385 claims: "The film's conclusion does not seem to us like retaliation: Robert and Bertram stand neatly in a row as strapping soldiers and Michel commands them to the front: 'Right shoulder arms! Company march!'"[94] By contrast, the brochures *Illustrierter Film-Kurier* and *Lockende Leinwand,* the extensive press package, the advertising guidebook for theater owners, and the censor cards from both 1939 and 1943 contain no mention of the reputed altered ending.[95] Since the brochure in question, *Das Programm von heute* 385, is printed with the copyright date of 1938, the alternative ending is most likely a pre-war suggestion never actualized despite its rather prophetic vision. And since star Rudi Godden died unexpectedly at the age of thirty-four on January 4, 1941, it is even more unlikely that the film was ever reshot with a new ending for a reprise in February of 1942.[96]

Robert und Bertram received mixed reviews. *Der deutsche Film* was notably harsh, stating that the story had "far too many mothballs" and that the film could "in no way be called completely successful."[97] The portrayal of the Jews was particularly controversial, and the different opinions hinged on whether the reviewers found the characters realistic or not. In a review published in *Film-Kurier,* Georg Herzberg applauded Zerlett's musical because "for the first time ever in a film Jewry becomes the target of a convincingly effective ridicule."[98] Writing for *Licht-Bild-Bühne,* Albert Schneider also praised actors Herbert Hübner, Inge van der Straaten, and Tatjana Sais for depicting so well "the Jewish milieu in all its ridiculousness." What Schneider wanted, however, was "a single visible piece of evidence showing how dangerous the typical stock market speculator is." Rather than criticize the film for its failure to show the Jewish threat in a realistic manner, Schneider suggested that the viewer "take the film for what it wants to be: a folk play with heart and soul, and sentimentality, with beautiful songs and lively performances."[99]

Several other reviewers considered the film a realistic portrayal of the historical Jewish threat to German society. Reiterating standard anti-Semitic fare that Jews are cultural parasites, one critic asserted: "the festival in [Ipelmeyer's] magnificent palace *crawling with the uncultured* contains tidbits of superior humor . . . and at the same time it paints a picture of the time and customs: the way in which the East-Galician even then tried to win the right of abode in Berlin and sought to confuse the souls with money and philanthropy."[100] In his review for *Licht-Bild-Bühne,* Mario Heil de Brentani voiced the most vehemently anti-Semitic rhetoric and drew from nineteenth-century fiction explicit parallels to the Nazi present: "Gustav Raeder depicted the unscrupulous profiteer Ipelmeyer as the model for thousands, and he foresaw therein our own violent reckoning a hundred years later with all those who put self-interest before the common good." The "violent reckoning" of *Kristallnacht,* the brutality of concentration camps, and the inhumane persecution of Jews on a daily basis finds its justification in a century-old musical farce. Brentani echoes the simplistic anti-Semitic discourse found on the pages of the notorious newspaper *Der Stürmer* and *Mein Kampf,* when he argues that the vagabonds help "liberate the community completely from the disguised parasites."[101]

Reporter H. J. Hahn had visited the studio during the filming of *Robert und Bertram* and predicted audiences would like the film because the Jews get their comeuppance. Hahn asserted: "We leave the 'Israeli' paradise and look forward to being able to see for ourselves in the finished film, how the two shrewd vagabonds manage to outwit completely the Ipelmeyer family who think they are so clever and infallible."[102] It was exactly the film's ability to fulfill the audience's need for *Schadenfreude* (finding joy in other people's pain) that was highlighted in the advertising campaign. The Tobis studio advised theater owners to broadcast that "we have here *Schadenfreude* in its most harmless form. And as the saying goes, *Schadenfreude* is a sheer delight that everyone enjoys gladly and without hesitation. So get into the refreshing bath of genuine cheerfulness, the great German film farce of Tobis, *Robert und Bertram.*"[103] According to this advertising campaign for a motion picture produced under a highly restrictive state censor, happiness in Nazi Germany proudly embraced the "harmless" fun of watching others suffer.

The musical farce is based on a light-hearted, cheerful worldview, in which nonsensical events take place and problems are resolved with no effort or by completely unbelievable circumstances. Happy and carefree people populate the silly and harmless world of the farce. This philosophy has serious consequences when applied to the absurd and unbelievable aspects of everyday life in Nazi Germany. *Robert und Bertram* frames the expropriation of Jewish property as socially just, fun, and within a historical tradition, and the studio publicly stated that it wanted viewers to draw parallels to the contemporary treatment of Jews in Germany. In a similar manner, the film shows how asocials are literally eliminated from the picture and imprisoned in a place imagined as paradise, while the publicity campaign spells out how central work is to the identity of the national community. This musical farce trains viewers to hum the pleasant tunes, adopt the carefree attitude, revisit the calming or funny images, and adjust one's mind to the notion that the absurd, no matter how unbelievable, is part of everyday reality in the Third Reich.

History via the Musical

History is constantly revised and retold, not just in conversations at the dinner table or in academic textbooks but also in motion pictures. Each of these venues lays varying claims to authenticity, but motion pictures hold a special place in the collective imagination due to their audio-visual component and narrative capacity to make viewers feel like they are "there" reliving the past. Following the adage "seeing is believing," films can seem real and truthful despite the fact that they are human constructs. The labels "historical drama," "based on a true story," or even "freely adapted" lend credibility and can raise a film to the status of historical truth, effacing the conscious acts of selection, arrangement, and control necessary for its production.

Film scholars have long recognized that serious historical films like *Der höhere Befehl* (1935), *Ohm Krüger* (1941), *Bismarck* (1940), *Die Entlassung* (1942), *Der unendliche Weg* (1943), and *Kolberg* (1945) sought to portray the historical struggle for national identity and sovereignty as a guidepost for a similar political agenda in Nazi Germany. As Klaus Kanzog has cogently argued: "The viewer was supposed to come to the conclusion that what was aspired to in the past and already accomplished, what was lost and had to be fought for again, has come true in the present. Furthermore, the historical analogy to the present was supposed to be found in positive examples."[104]

The past as a mirror to the present, cinematic history as a means to see the contemporary world more clearly, seems to be a dictum that scholars are most comfortable ascribing to the serious historical film. Although many critics maintain that propaganda films like *Kolberg* use the past to illustrate National Socialist fantasies of community, nation, and leader, few have considered the extent to which the historical musical contributed to the same discursive tradition. Despite the fact that many German operetta films and musicals made in the 1930s and 1940s prominently featured historical settings, most critics claim that these popular and "light" genres use the past as a form of escapism. This line of thinking stems in part from commonly held views on what audiences expect from different genres. Francesco Bono represents the prevailing critical stance when he states:

> The operetta and the historical film have this in common: both use history as the premise for a spectacle, in order to impress the public with the splendor and exoticism of the scenes; they attempt to conjure up on screen the atmosphere of an epoch. However, the historical film proposes to narrate a piece of history "faithfully" (and the viewer expects that it will be so), while the operetta film treats it freely. What it narrates does not have to be true. It neither presents itself as truth, nor does the public count on that. In the operetta film, history is pliable it takes the form that one gives it.[105]

Do audiences look to serious dramas like *Kolberg* for lessons in history? Do they anticipate that the musical will not deliver "real" history but rather only historical atmosphere? In general the tone of a film, whether it is earnest or light-hearted, may well determine audience expectations before they go to the box office. However, several factors can influence how viewers approach a film and how they regard drama as history and the musical as fiction. In the case of *Tanz auf dem Vulkan*, the Tobis studio launched a rigorous advertising campaign to convince audiences that this film contained equal amounts of history and music. The casting of respected actor and cultural dignitary Gustaf

Gründgens in the star role together with Hans Steinhoff, a director known for his propaganda films *Hitlerjunge Quex* and *Der alte und der junge König,* lent credibility to the film's depiction of history via music. The Tobis studio press package for *Robert und Bertram* likewise presented this musical farce as a hybrid genre that used a playful stance and musical interludes but nonetheless told an important historical truth.

One aspect of *Tanz auf dem Vulkan* and *Robert und Bertram* has long been overlooked; they belong to a larger category of films produced in Nazi Germany and set in the nineteenth century. Both filmmakers and audiences seem to have been captivated by this historical period because it forms the background for countless popular films spanning nearly all genres. Whether state-commissioned propaganda films, historical pageants, love stories, operettas, or historical musicals, German films used the nineteenth century to recount a shared past as the basis on which to forge a personal and national identity in the present. Many scholars, most notably Linda Schulte-Sasse, have explored how the eighteenth century came to embody in Nazi Germany the "notion of a social body whose harmony is impeded by modernity's alienation."[106] I suggest that motion pictures set in the nineteenth century have a different and equally noteworthy agenda. Whereas the eighteenth century is the locus of cultural myths attesting to German identity, the nineteenth century represents Germany's arduous political struggle for nationhood. Filmmakers turned to nineteenth-century history and literature for a familiar discursive tradition on which to model notions of community, nation, the enemy, and the leader.

Nineteenth-century writers such as Storm, Nestroy, Kleist, Fontane, Keller, and Pushkin delivered the material for the films *Der Schimmelreiter* (1934) and *Immensee* (1943), *Lumpacivagabundus* (1937), *Der zerbrochene Krug* (1937), *Der Schritt vom Wege* [*Effi Briest*] (1939), *Kleider machen Leute* (1940), and *Der Postmeister* (1940) respectively. The lives of nineteenth-century artists were also depicted with great frequency: Tchaikovsky in *Es war eine rauschende Ballnacht* (1939), the Strauß family in *Unsterbliche Walzer* (1939), operetta director Franz Jauner in *Operette* (1940), writer Hans Christian Andersen and singer Jenny Linden in *Die schwedische Nachtigall* (1941), dramatist Ferdinand Raimund in *Brüderlein fein* (1942), and composer Carl Michael Ziehrer in *Wiener Mädeln* (1945/1949). The operetta film (generally distinguished from the historical musical because it is most often set in nineteenth-century Vienna and employs well-known melodies) was especially popular with the movie-going public.[107] Numerous classic operettas were brought to the screen: Johann Strauß's *Eine Nacht in Venedig* (1934) and *Der Zigeunerbaron* (1935), Franz von Suppé's *Boccaccio* (1936), and Karl Millöcker's *Der Bettelstudent* (1936) and *Gasparone* (1937). Finally, the nineteenth century served as the backdrop for historical musicals ranging from the late Weimar film classic *Der Kongreß tanzt* (1931) to *Frauen sind doch bessere Diplomaten* (1941).[108]

Most German historical musicals, especially those featuring popular female stars, revolve around a love affair and emphasize marriage as the fulfillment of individual desire and the means to social harmony. In his seminal article "Visual Pleasure Inhibited," Karsten Witte argues that the 1930s Hollywood musical and the German revue film tell strikingly different stories that reflect their national self-image in crisis: "musicals deal with fantasies of social climbing while the revue film takes up wedding fantasies."[109] The musical evokes the deeply rooted American fear of unemployment in the aftermath of the Great Depression. By contrast, the revue film addresses the German fear of liberty as a reaction against the Weimar Republic's decadence. Both the Hollywood musical and the German revue film, as Witte has described them, are backstage musicals that share a contemporary urban setting in the theater or film studio. Although Witte does not discuss the German historical musical as a sub-genre, his thesis holds true for many films in this category such as *Frauen sind doch bessere Diplomaten* (1941), a marriage fantasy starring Marika Rökk and set in the late Biedermeier period. What separates *Tanz auf dem Vulkan* and *Robert und Bertram* from other historical musicals of the 1930s and 1940s is that they star male performers and center on the leader and community rather than the heterosexual couple.

Tanz auf dem Vulkan and *Robert und Bertram* share a utopian view of the nineteenth century as a realm where communal happiness was still a real possibility. Whether it is a tale of the artist who leads the nation in ecstatic bliss or one of carefree outsiders who unite the people by foiling their enemies, these stories use history to recapture a sense of longing and belonging lost in the present. This aspect of the musical illustrates particularly well the concept of *Ungleichzeitigkeit* (non-synchronicity) that Ernst Bloch developed in his monumental study on National Socialism, *Erbschaft dieser Zeit* (Heritage of Our Times, 1935). Bloch recognized that "we are not all in the same Now," and that "we carry with us much of earlier times which interferes" with the present.[110] Unlike Marxism, National Socialism embraced the continued existence of the past in the present or non-synchronicity as a political strategy because it satisfied "the undercurrent of very old dreams."[111] Bloch argued that National Socialism succeeded precisely because it faithfully conjured up past visions of utopian, primitive desires to fulfill the nation's current unsatisfied emotional needs. He asserted, "It is not the 'theory' of the National Socialists but rather their energy that is serious, the fanatical-religious strain that does not merely stem from despair and stupidity, the strangely roused strength of faith."[112]

Bloch was among the first observers to note that the NSDAP was not merely a band of thugs governing through terror and coercion; the party also gave the nation much of what it wanted. Products of pop culture like historical musicals unabashedly sought to fulfill the audience's desire for a simpler existence, one in which the individual is connected to others by shared values, a common cultural heritage, and mutual recognition as vital, passionate human beings. The historical musical in the Third Reich invited the audience to recall the familiar collective memory of a good society lost and momentarily regained in the world of cinema. *Tanz auf dem Vulkan* and *Robert und Bertram* form a cross-section of social aspirations, ranging from the promise of elegance in the great metropolis Paris to the security of small-town life in Biedermeier Germany.

Paris, the city of lights, represents a place of extraordinary architectural beauty permeated by the elusive atmosphere of refinement, ease, and enjoyment of the best things in life. The Paris of 1830 is especially attractive because it witnessed armed rebellion and the toppling of a regime while still retaining the monarchy in the hybrid form of a "Bourgeois King." This nonsynchronicity, when the ancien régime coexisted with the modern age after the French Revolution, speaks to the dream of a good society in which complex issues of political change are resolved by personality and *Lebensphilosophie*. The figures populating the world of 1830 Paris employ life strategies to deal successfully with a harsh political environment and offer important lessons for viewers in 1938. In many ways Debureau reflects the Nazi concept of the leader as a genius who voices the nation's inner needs and generates a contagious mass intoxication. His call to maintain nearly ecstatic levels of enthusiasm and to accept freedom of emotion and thought rather than action places his political platform in line with both the German tradition of *Gedankenfreiheit* and National Socialism. However, he uses the weapons of satire, underground pamphlets, and inner resistance to combat an oppressive police state, which makes him an appealing counterculture hero for viewers who opposed National Socialism and saw parallels between a brutal regime in 1830 Paris and 1938 Germany.

More than nineteenth-century France, nineteenth-century Germany connotes a period of continual political transformations and extremes; the end of the Holy Roman Empire German Nation (800–1806), the Napoleonic Wars, the creation of the German Union (Deutscher Bund, 1815–1871), the revolutions of 1830 and 1848, and the founding of the Second Empire (1871–1918). Nineteenth-century German history is generally read as a rocky but inevitable path to nationhood marked by the stations of feudalism, foreign sovereignty, and a patchwork of states in loose association but ending with the dream come true: the recovery of a lost empire. *Robert und Bertram* is situated in 1839, halfway between the first two empires and exactly a century from the original audience's present in the third empire. It thus evokes the memory of a lost paradise regained, a sense of communal wholeness and happiness, glimpses of which only really existed in the wishful thinking of Biedermeier fiction.

Germany in 1839, with its geographical coordinates between the Spree-wald village and metropolis Berlin, is the stage for a morality play pitting the heartless exploitation of capitalism against authentic, peaceful coexistence of feudalism. Commonly known as either the Age of Metternich (stressing the prime minister's use of dictatorial power to enforce conformity) or as the Biedermeier period (named after the allegorical figure of the German every-man who retreats into the private sphere), 1815–1848 was characterized by radical change. This period saw the construction of the first German railroad line from Nuremberg to Fürth (1835), the invention of the steamship and electric telegraph, and the shift from a largely agricultural economy to one of manufacture. Rather than celebrating modernity, urbanization, and tech-nology, the visual arts, literature, and fashion of the day turned inward, retreating into the family and domestic concerns. As much a reaction to the repressive political regime as the unsettling cultural changes, the early dec-ades of the nineteenth century venerated the small world of hearth and home and envisioned a stable, traditional, and secure world even as it van-ished. Germany in 1839, like Paris in 1830, was a period of contrasts in which the average citizen felt powerless against the oppressive political regime and withdrew into the private realm.

Tanz auf dem Vulkan and *Robert und Bertram* used the nineteenth century in two complementary ways, to construct nationhood and to pro-mote a mutually beneficial posture toward totalitarianism. The nineteenth century became a backdrop for National Socialist notions of the leader, national community, work, Aryan superiority, and the Jewish threat, but the historical analogy also served to promote tolerance of a tyrannical system in exchange for social happiness. In the historical musical, the nation was built upon community, which in turn was held together by a strong leader and collective happiness defined as both intoxication and *Schadenfreude*. The idea of a nation predicated on a dictatorial leader who eliminated all opposi-tion but guaranteed its citizens happiness could serve as a model for viewers in Nazi Germany. The musical's use of satire and parody allowed subversive readings but their inherently ambiguous structure required that protest remain on the level of thought. Humor could give individuals a release valve for frustration without actually threatening the status quo.

Not only historical documents but also popular forms of entertainment help to shape perceptions of the past. Whereas serious historical dramas often focus on the lives of famous public figures and great deeds, the musical can address a different type of history, the intangible realm of emotion and social values. It would be misguided to assume that the musical is pure escapism and that the propaganda ministry merely favored it because it would distract the audience from the hardship of everyday life. National Socialism repeat-edly harnessed for its political agenda the nostalgic view of the past as the "good old days." Nostalgia originally referred to the sorrow of being separated from a familiar but lost place rather than a time, and reflects the search for a spiritual *home* in the past, one that offers the emotional security missing in the present. In our nostalgia for a simpler time, we often seek an existence not too distant from our own, familiar but just out of reach. This need for distance and proximity may explain why audiences in 1938–39 were fascinated by the nineteenth century, an age Walter Benjamin characterized as "a time period (a time dream)" ["ein Zeitraum (ein Zeit-traum")].[113] The collective dream of the good old days is captured in the movies, and though the movie must end, the dream and the music remain a vivid reminder of utopia. As the popular song from *Der Kongreß tanzt* (1931) goes: "It only happens once, it'll never come again."[114] The historical musical's greatest appeal may be that it mourns the loss of the past even as it recreates it, beckoning the audience to imprint the sounds and images of the past in their mind to recapture a sense of communal happiness.

Notes

[1] Carla Rhode aptly summarizes the widely held view that the Nazi musical served a political purpose by distracting the viewer from everyday reality. The musical, she writes, "consciously avoided any realistic portrayal of reality, instead one escaped into the illusory world of artists and variety performers infused with a stereotypical propaganda value system." [Bewußt wurde die realistische Schilderung der Wirklichkeit vermieden, man flüchtete sich vielmehr in die illusionistisch gesehene Welt der Künstler und Artisten und versah sie reichlich mit Klischees der propagierten Wertvorstellungen.]. Carla Rhode, "Leuchtende Sterne?" in *Wir tanzen um die Welt: Deutsche Revuefilme 1933–1945*, ed. Helga Belach (Munich: Carl Hanser, 1979), 119. For a more nuanced assessment of the musical genre, see Rick Altman, *The American Film Musical* (Bloomington: Indiana UP, 1987); Jane Feuer, *The Hollywood Musical*, 2d ed. (Bloomington: Indiana UP, 1993); and Thomas H. Schatz, *Hollywood Genres: Formula, Film Making, and the Studio System* (New York: Random House, 1981).

[2] Adolf Hitler, *Mein Kampf*, trans. Ralph Manheim (Boston: Houghton Mifflin, 1971), 167. "[D]aß die Begeisterung, erst einmal geknickt, nicht mehr nach Bedarf zu erwecken ist. Sie ist ein Rausch und ist in diesem Zustande weiter zu erhalten. Wie aber sollte man ohne diese Macht der Begeisterung einen Kampf bestehen, der nach menschlichem Ermessen die ungeheuersten Anforderungen an die seelischen Eigenschaften der Nation stellen würde?" Adolf Hitler, *Mein Kampf* (Munich: Franz Eher, 1935), 2:183–84.

[3] Richard Dyer, *Only Entertainment* (New York: Routledge, 1992), 18.

[4] Hayden White, "Historiography and Historiophoty," *American Historical Review* 93.5 (December 1988): 1193.

[5] Born into a Bohemian family of acrobats, Jean-Baptiste-Gaspard Deburau (1796–1846, original name Jan Kaspar Dvořák) performed throughout Europe until he joined the troupe at Paris's Théâtre des Funambules. This theater was located on the Boulevard du Temple, a thoroughfare on Paris's right bank known for its numerous theaters catering to mostly lower class audiences and offering pantomime, acrobatics,

puppet shows, animals acts, and melodrama. Nicknamed the Boulevard of Crime because of all the crimes staged in the countless melodramas, "this original Boulevard was a barbarian purlieu, a foil to classical France, a subliminal zone where popular forms — forms outgrown and despised — survived unofficially," Frederick Brown, *Theater and Revolution: The Culture of the French Stage* (New York: Viking Press, 1980), 42. Deburau became famous as a white-faced mime dressed in a baggy white costume with a black skullcap and was the star attraction on the Boulevard of Crime from 1830 to 1840. He was immortalized as the optimistic and lovelorn Pierrot in the classic French film *Les Enfants du paradis* (premiere: March 9, 1945). The mime's name occurs with various spellings, but I will retain the name "Deburau" for the famous personality and "Debureau" for the cinematic figure in *Tanz auf dem Vulkan*.

[6] Hans Rehberg was well known for his Prussian dramas celebrating the life of Frederick the Great including *Der siebenjährige Krieg*, which premiered on April 7, 1938 at the Schauspielhaus and starred Gustaf Gründgens. Peter Hagen was the pen name of Willi Krause, the Reich Film Dramaturge from 1933 to 1936.

[7] See *Tanz auf dem Vulkan*, Censor-Card 49884, Bundesarchiv-Filmarchiv, Berlin. In this case, the censor cards include not only the censor's approval and rating but also the entire film dialogue. The original screenplay is available at the Hochschule für Film und Fernsehen "Konrad Wolf" Potsdam-Babelsberg library, see Hans Rehberg, Hans Steinhoff, and Peter Hagen, *Wenn Debureau spielt . . . Arbeitstitel* (Filmscript, Majestic Film: Berlin, n.d.).

[8] Compare Curt Riess, *Das gab's nur einmal: Das Buch der schönsten Filme unseres Lebens*, 2d rev. ed. (Hamburg: Verlag der Sternbücher, 1956), 716.

[9] Compare Heinrich Goertz, *Gustaf Gründgens* (Reinbek bei Hamburg: Rowohlt, 1982), 91; and Friedrich Luft, "Gründgens und der Film," in *Gründgens: Schauspieler, Regisseur, Theaterleiter,* ed. Henning Rischbieter (Velber bei Hannover: Erhard Friedrich, 1963), 32.

[10] Compare Volker Kühn, "'Man muß das Leben nehmen, wie es eben ist . . .' Anmerkungen zum Schlager und seiner Fähigkeit, mit der Zeit zu gehen," in *Musik und Musikpolitik im faschistischen Deutschland,* eds. Hanns Werner Heister and Hans-Günter Klein (Frankfurt a. M.: Fischer, 1984), 233; and Christa Bandmann and Joe Hembus, "Tanz auf dem Vulkan," in *Klassiker des deutschen Tonfilms, 1930–1960* (Munich: Goldmann, 1980), 118.

[11] "Sonderreklame — die notwendig ist! Werbung durch Musik!" *Tanz auf dem Vulkan: Reklame-Ratschläge* (Berlin: Tobis Filmkunst GmbH, n.d.), 19, *Tanz auf dem Vulkan,* Document file 16695, Bundesarchiv-Filmarchiv, Berlin.

[12] "Grammophon — Die Stimme seines Herrn bringt das faszinierende Schlagerlied von Mackeben 'Die Nacht ist nicht allein zum Schlafen da' aus dem Film *Tanz auf dem Vulkan,* gespielt von Egon Kaiser, Refraingesang: Heyn-Quartett aus," "Filmmusik auf Schallplatten," *Der deutsche Film* 3, no. 12 (June 1939): 360.

[13] Bogusław Drewniak, *Der deutsche Film 1938–1945: Ein Gesamtüberblick* (Düsseldorf: Droste, 1987), 201, 634.

[14] Goebbels's diary entry for November 18, 1938, reads: "Ein typischer Gründgens: Gehirnarbeit wird ein bißchen zuviel getan. Muß noch sehr geschnitten werden."

Joseph Goebbels, *Die Tagebücher von Joseph Goebbels,* ed. Elke Fröhlich, Part I: Aufzeichnungen 1924–1942, 9 vols. (Munich: K. G. Saur, 1998), I. 6: 191.

[15] Michael Töteberg, "Gustaf Gründgens," *Cinegraph: Lexikon zum deutschsprachigen Film,* ed. Hans Michael Bock (Munich: edition text + kritik, 1984ff.), E4.

[16] Gerd Albrecht reports that *Tanz auf dem Vulkan* cost 1,423,000 DM to produce and returned an estimated 1,100,000 DM at the box office, *Nationalsozialistische Filmpolitik: Eine soziologische Untersuchung über die Spielfilme des Dritten Reiches* (Stuttgart: Ferdinand Enke, 1969), 428. According to Albrecht, *Tanz auf dem Vulkan* was enthusiastically received by critics and audiences alike despite its poor financial showing (267–68). The estimated financial loss may reflect the excessively high cost of producing a costume drama with a star-studded cast rather than a box office failure. The trade papers advertised *Tanz auf dem Vulkan* as one of the three most successful Tobis films of 1938; see *Film-Kurier* 24 (January 28, 1939). *Tanz auf dem Vulkan* reportedly had a successful run at the box office in Berlin and Vienna, see *Film-Kurier* 28 (February 2, 1939). A survey six months after the premiere confirmed that *Tanz auf dem Vulkan* was considered one of the most impressive films in recent memory, *Film-Kurier* 147 (June 28, 1939).

[17] The film continues to find a popular audience in its video format. Gründgens's rendition of the film's main song "Die Nacht ist nicht allein zum Schlafen da" also appears in countless evergreen CDs on the market in Germany today.

[18] For an informative study of Hans Steinhoff's early musical career, see Horst Claus, "Von Gilbert zu Goebbels: Hans Steinhoff zwischen Operette und Tonfilm mit Musik," in *Als die Filme singen lernten: Innovation und Tradition im Musikfilm 1928–1938,* eds. Malte Hagener and Jan Hans (Munich: edition text + kritik, 1999), 105–20. Steinhoff reported that it took him fifteen years to bring the Debureau material to the screen, in part because he insisted that Gründgens play the title role. Hans Steinhoff, "Meine Filmarbeit mit Gustaf Gründgens," *Licht-Bild-Bühne* 188 (August 12, 1938).

[19] Between 1933 and 1941 Gustaf Gründgens had fourteen film roles and directed four films. In 1938 Terra studio created "Gründgens Production Group" with an agreement for him to make two films a year, one as director and one as the star. Gründgens was among the top six highest paid film actors and top seven directors, earning 80,000 RM for each film.

[20] Goebbels wrote in his diary on July 29, 1937, that Hitler "is of the opinion that Gründgens has to go away completely" (Ist der Meinung, daß Gründgens ganz weg muß). *Die Tagebücher von Joseph Goebbels,* I. 3: 216. Goebbels wrote on August 17, 1941: "The Führer does not like Gustaf Gründgens. He finds him too unmanly. He is of the opinion that one should not under any circumstances tolerate homosexuality in public life" [Der Führer mag Gustaf Gründgens nicht. Er ist ihm zu unmännlich. Seine Ansicht geht dahin, daß man im öffentlichen Leben unter keinen Umständen die Homosexualität dulden darf]. Joseph Goebbels, *Die Tagebücher von Joseph Goebbels,* ed. Elke Fröhlich, Part II: Diktate 1941–1945, 15 vols. (Munich: K. G. Saur, 1998), II. 1: 272.

[21] "TANZ AUF DEM VULKAN (1938) hieß ein Spielfilm von Hans Steinhoff, und nur wegen des beziehungsreichen Titels übernahm Gründgens in ihm die Rolle des politisierenden Schauspieler Debureau." Töteberg, "Gustaf Gründgens," E3.

[22] "In dem Film ist alles drin' . . . Liebe, Politik und Theater. Debureau ist ein ungeheuer leidenschaftlicher Mensch, dessen Leben einen großen abenteuerlichen Atem hat. . . . Mich reizte vor allem die große romantische Geste dieses Lebens." "Gründgens im Gespräch," *B.Z. am Mittag* (June 20, 1938).

[23] Gründgens worked with Steinhoff in *Eine Frau ohne Bedeutung* (1936); composer Theo Mackeben in *Die Finanzen des Großherzogs* (1934) and *Pygmalion* (1935); and cameraman Ewald Daub in *Die Finanzen des Großherzogs* and *Eine Frau ohne Bedeutung*. Set designer Rochus Gliese, screenwriter Hans Rehberg, actors Theo Lingen, Erich Ziegel, Franz Weber, and Walter Werner all belonged to the ensemble at Gründgens's Schauspielhaus am Gendarmenmarkt.

[24] "So brauchen wir also unsere Träume und Wünsche, das Hinaufschauen zu den Sternen, zu dem Höheren, Schöneren, Reicheren, zu Vor- und Traumbildern keineswegs nur als Zeitverschwendung, als erfolgfeindliche Entnervung zu betrachten." Hans Spielhofer, "Wunschtraum oder Wirklichkeit? Eine Betrachtung über Notwendigkeit und Problematik ihrer Abgrenzung," *Der deutsche Film* 3, no. 11 (May 1939): 320–21.

[25] "Der Name des Stars verrät alles. Er sagt aus, ob es sich um einen burlesken Film handelt oder um einen ernsten, ob getanzt und gesungen wird oder ob es gutbürgerlich lustig hergeht. Kurz: der Name des Stars stellt ein 'Genre' dar!" Helmut Kindler, "Star als Genre," *Der deutsche Film* 3, no. 12 (June 1939): 340.

[26] "Und während der große Akteur der Juli-Revolution sich immer stärker in Erregung spricht, spüren wir die geschichtliche Bedeutung des Augenblicks, die unter Hans Steinhoffs Regie klar zum Ausdruck kommt: Paris und damit Frankreich standen in jenen Tagen an der Wende zweier Zeitalter. . . . Diese eindrucksvolle Geschichtsepisode, die wir hier in einer Pariser alten Straße nächstens erlebten, erhält Charakter und Prägung durch das Spiel von Gustaf Gründgens, der gerade in dieser Szene in der er als Debureau den Prinzen von Orléan zu spielen hat, zeigt, welche Kraft der Verwandlung in seinem Spiel ist, eine Kraft der Verwandlung, die so suggestiv ist, daß wir nicht mehr ein Spiel der Ereignisse, sondern die Ereignisse selbst zu erleben glauben." Felix Henseleit, "Szene zwischen Zeitaltern: Nachtaufnahmen in Johannisthal für den Gründgens-Film *Tanz auf dem Vulkan*," *Licht-Bild-Bühne* 186 (August 10, 1938).

[27] Erwin Leiser, *Nazi Cinema*, trans. Gertrud Mander and David Wilson (New York: Collier, 1975), 106. By contrast, Julian Petley argues, "The particular construction of history represented by these [genius] films can more usefully be considered in relation to the conjuncture as a whole, to petty bourgeois ideology in general and to bourgeois historiography in particular, rather than in relation to *conscious* decisions springing from National Socialist film policy." Julian Petley, *Capital and Culture: German Cinema 1933–1945* (London: British Film Institute, 1979), 139.

[28] "Das ist eins, Paris und Debureau!" *Tanz auf dem Vulkan*, Censor-Card 49884.

[29] Hete Nebel, "Die Gräfin und der Komödiant: Zwei Szenen aus *Tanz auf dem Vulkan*," *Filmwelt* 27 (July 1, 1938); H. N. "Die Birne," *Filmwoche* 29 (July 15, 1938); Hans Hufszky, "Im Scheinwerfer: Gustaf Gründgens als Debureau," Beilage zur *Filmwelt* 50 (December 9, 1938); M. Harvester, "Wer war Debureau?" *Licht-Bild-Bühne* 296 (December 17, 1938). See also Rehberg, *Wenn Debureau spielt*, shots 5 and 259.

[30] "Wir [machen] andererseits alle Filme aus den Notwendigkeiten und für die Bedürfnisse der Gegenwart. Sie vor allem muß daher den historischen Film verstehen und von ihm angesprochen sein, um sich über ihn freuen oder von ihm erheben und begeistern lassen zu können." Fritz Hippler, *Betrachtungen zum Filmschaffen* (Berlin: Max Hesses, 1943), 53.

[31] ej, "Debureau spielt Louis Philippe: Nachtaufnahmen zu *Tanz auf dem Vulkan*," *Filmwelt* 35 (August 26, 1938).

[32] "Fast scheint es, als habe hier das geheimnisvolle Würfelspiel des Zufalls in Gründgens einen zweiten lebenden Debureau geboren. . . . Debureau und Gründgens-das ist eine phantastische Duplizität von Naturen. . . . es ist, als habe Gründgens es fertiggebracht, diese [hundertjährige] Pause und auch die geographische Trennung zu überbrücken." Hufszky, "Im Scheinwerfer: Gustaf Gründgens als Debureau."

[33] "Man wird füglich von einem geschichtlichen Darsteller nicht verlangen können, daß er der Geschichte gegenübertritt wie der Historiker. Der Historiker hat die Aufgabe, die Geschichte darzustellen, wie sie nach dem ihm zur Verfügung stehenden Quellenmaterial tatsächlich ist. Der Künstler ist nicht ausschließlich auf das Quellenmaterial angewiesen. Er hat das Recht, ich möchte sagen, intuitiv in geschichtliche Vorgänge einzudringen und sie aufgrund einer intuitiven Einsicht zu gestalten. Und es hat sich dann immer erwiesen, daß große Künstler geschichtliche Vorgänge *in einem höheren Sinne* wahrheitsgetreu gesehen und dargestellt haben, als die Historiker." Wilfried von Bredow and Rolf Zurek, eds., *Film und Gesellschaft in Deutschland: Dokumente und Materialien* (Hamburg: Hoffmann und Campe, 1975), 185–86.

[34] "Berauscht euch Freunde, trinkt und lacht/ Und liebt und lebt den schönsten Augenblick,/ Die Nacht, die man in einem Rausch verbracht,/ Bedeutet Seligkeit und Glück." See *Tanz auf dem Vulkan*, Censor-Card 49884; *Tanz auf dem Vulkan*, *Illustrierter Film Kurier* 2862 (Berlin: Franke & Co, 1938); and *Tanz auf dem Vulkan, Das Programm von heute* 298 (Berlin: Das Programm von heute: Zeitschrift für Film und Theater, GmbH, 1937).

[35] " . . . Das aus gesellschaftlicher Nichtachtung entstandene Gefühl der Zurücksetzung gegenüber den bevorrechteten Schichten. An diesem dann zur Leidenschaft gesteigerten Gefühl entzündet sich die revolutionäre Flamme in den Pariser Volksmassen." Martin Klockmann, "Kampf um gesellschaftliche Rechte: Zum Film *Tanz auf dem Vulkan*," (Typescript: n.p., n.d.), *Tanz auf dem Vulkan*, Document file 16695, Bundesarchiv-Filmarchiv, Berlin.

[36] Hitler, *Mein Kampf* (1971), 180. "[So] muß ihr Wirken auch immer mehr auf das Gefühl gerichtet sein und nur sehr bedingt auf den sogenannten Verstand." Hitler, *Mein Kampf* (1935), 1:197.

[37] "Die Kunst ist nicht anders als Gestalter des Gefühls. Sie kommt von Gefühl und nicht vom Verstand her; der Künstler ist nichts anderes als der Sinngeber dieses Gefühls." Speech by Joseph Goebbels from March 5, 1937, qtd. in Albrecht, *Nationalsozialistische Filmpolitik*, 447.

[38] "Er wäre unter Kollegen gewesen, wo er hingehört!" *Tanz auf dem Vulkan*, Censor-Card 49884.

[39] "Hörst du, das ist die Musik der Stadt! Die Melodie der Straßen und Plätze! Glokkenklänge und Tellernklappern, Flastertrab und Händlergeschrei, Flüstern der Mädchen und die erregten Debatten der Männer. Ein Wogen und Weh'n, ein ewiges Gleiten und Schreiten. Lärm! Lärm! Aber Lärm, der wie ein Lied ist. Eine Hölle? Ein Paradies? . . . Paris! Sei still! Wie eine Geliebte liegt mir die Stadt am Herzen. Ich will sie halten, ich werde ihr mein Dasein weihen. Sie soll glücklich sein, sie soll blühen. Freude soll in ihr sein. Freude und Freiheit! Brausendes und herrliches Leben, von Tag zu Tag, von Jahrzeit zu Jahrzeit, von heute durch die Jahrtausende bis in die Unsterblichkeit! Ein ewiges Paradies: Paris!" *Tanz auf dem Vulkan,* Censor-Card 49884.

[40] Karl Mannheim, *Ideology and Utopia: An Introduction to the Sociology of Knowledge,* trans. Louis Wirth and Edward Shils (New York: Harcourt, Brace, and Co., 1936), 193.

[41] "Weil es das Schönste ist, was es für mich auf dieser Welt gibt, dazustehen, wenn der Vorhang aufgeht und zu wissen, alle diese Menschen da unten, warten nur auf Dich und das, was Du ihnen zu sagen hast. Du kennst ihre Sehnsucht und ihre Träume und kannst sie ihnen erfüllen . . . Du kennst ihr Glück und ihre Trauer, Du kannst sie lachen und weinen machen! . . . Abend für Abend kämpfe ich mit ihnen, um Sieger zu sein über ihre Herzen! . . . Sie hinzureißen, reißt mich hin! Sie lassen sich von mir leiten und ich führe sie dahin, wo sie glücklich werden, in das ewige Reich der Kunst!" *Tanz auf dem Vulkan,* Censor-Card 49884.

[42] Hitler considered himself the drummer of the national movement ("Trommler der nationalen Bewegung"). See Hellmuth Auerbach, "Der Trommler," in *Das Dritte Reich: Ein Lesebuch zur deutschen Geschichte 1933–1945* (Munich: C. H. Beck, 1997), 16–18.

[43] "Theater gespielt wird hier und da!" *Tanz auf dem Vulkan,* Censor-Card 49884.

[44] Adherents to *Lebensphilosophie* (vitalism) held that sincerity and authentic experience rather than reason should determine politics. See J. P. Stern, *Hitler: The Führer and the People* (Berkeley: U of California P, 1975); and Jeffrey Herf, *Reactionary Modernism: Technology, Culture and Politics in Weimar and the Third Reich* (Cambridge: Cambridge UP, 1984).

[45] "Im Rahmen einer bunt durcheinander wirbelnden Bühnenrevue trägt Gründgens dieses Spottlied auf die Spießbürger (dessen Verse wieder von Otto Ernst Hesse stammen) vor, das einerseits derb-ordinär wirken muß, mit einem Hauch von Gosse, während es später als mitreissendes Revolutionslied fast wie eine Freiheitshymne klingen soll." Waldemar Lydor, "Gesprochene Tänze: Besuch bei Theo Mackeben" (Typescript: n.p., n.d.), *Tanz auf dem Vulkan,* Document file 16695, Bundesarchiv-Filmarchiv, Berlin.

[46] "Pariser, man fragte mich soeben, wann es soweit wäre? Ich frage Euch: Ist es noch nicht weit genug? Wer von Euch ist ohne Haß, ohne Angst, ohne Furcht! Ihr seid nicht mehr Franzosen, ihr seid nur noch Untertanen! . . . Wo ist Euer Lachen, Eure Fröhlichkeit! Wer ist schuld an Eurem Schicksal? Etwa der König? Nein! Franzosen, Ihr selber tragt die Schuld an Eurem Schicksal! . . . Dem König dürft Ihr keine Vorwürfe machen. Liebt Ihr denn den König so sehr, daß Ihr es nicht wagt, gegen ihn aufzustehen und die Ketten abzustreifen? . . . Jedes Volk hat die Regierung, die es verdient! Wollt Ihr weiter mutlos und gebeugt dahinleben, entscheidet Euch! Auf was wartet Ihr

noch! Unsere Stunde ist gekommen! Das Vaterland ruft Euch jetzt! Franzosen! Es lebe Frankreich!" *Tanz auf dem Vulkan,* Censor-Card 49884.

[47] "Pariser! Ich erkenne Euch nicht mehr? Wo ist der Beifall, mit dem Ihr mich sonst empfangen habt? Warum weint Ihr? Lachen müßt ihr, wenn Debureau kommt! Habt Ihr denn alles vergessen?" *Tanz auf dem Vulkan,* Censor-Card 49884.

[48] Hitler, *Mein Kampf* (1971), 107. " . . . Vulkanausbrüche menschlicher Leidenschaften und seelischer Empfindungen. Völkerschicksale vermag nur ein Sturm von heißer Leidenschaft zu wenden, Leidenschaft erwecken kann nur, wer sie selbst im Innern trägt." Hitler, *Mein Kampf* (1935), 1: 116.

[49] "Denn er will ja gar nicht ernst genommen werden, dazu ist das Ganze von vornherein zu verspielt angelegt. Man würde den eleganten überlegenen Ironiker Gründgens mißverstehen, wenn man das unbedenklich mit allerlei Unwahrscheinlichkeiten kokettierende Filmgeschehen als ernsthafte Historie werten wollte. . . . Dieser Film ist reich an originellen Verkleidungsszenen. Ihm geht es nicht so sehr um historisch-politische Tendenzen, sondern er will ein unterhaltsamer Kostümfilm, eine politische Maskerade sein, der einem berühmten Schauspieler große Auftritte sichert." Werner Fiedler, *Deutsche Allgemeine Zeitung,* Ausgabe Groß-Berlin (December 17, 1938).

[50] "So gleitet das politische, das ideale Moment ab in die Sphäre des Persönlichen, der Eifersucht und gekränkten Eitelkeit," Ilse Wehner, "Filme des Monats," *Der deutsche Film* 3, no. 7 (January 1939): 195.

[51] "Vermeiden Sie den Eindruck eines Kostümfilms beim Publikum zu erwecken!" and "Der Film ist viel mehr als das, was das Publikum von einem Kostümfilm erwartet." *Tanz auf dem Vulkan: Reklame-Ratschläge,* 2 and 25.

[52] See Günther Schwark, *"Tanz auf dem Vulkan." Film-Kurier* 295 (December 17, 1938); Albert Schneider, *"Tanz auf dem Vulkan," Licht-Bild-Bühne* 296 (December 17, 1938), and various reviews in *Tanz auf dem Vulkan: Presseheft* (Tobis: Berlin, n.d.), *Tanz auf dem Vulkan,* Document file 16695, Bundesarchiv-Filmarchiv, Berlin.

[53] Hitler, *Mein Kampf* (1971), 473. "[A]ls kleiner Wurm dennoch Glied eines großen Drachens zu sein." Hitler, *Mein Kampf* (1935), 2: 529.

[54] The Propaganda Ministry made one notable exception and allowed Jews to see a limited number of German films at the Jewish Cultural Union cinema in Berlin. This cinema opened on December 30, 1938, and showed *Tanz auf dem Vulkan* among its first German films to an exclusively Jewish audience. See Drewniak, *Der deutsche Film,* 635–36.

[55] For an in-depth look at the Night of Broken Glass, see Hermann Graml, *Reichskristallnacht: Antisemitismus und Judenverfolgung im Dritten Reich,* 3d ed. (Munich: dtv, 1998).

[56] "Nachdem der nationalsozialistische Staat es den Juden bereits seit über 5 Jahren ermöglicht hat, innerhalb besonderer jüdischer Organisationen ein eigenes Kulturleben zu schaffen und zu pflegen, ist es nicht mehr angängig, sie an Darbietungen der deutschen Kultur teilnehmen zu lassen. Den Juden ist daher der Zutritt zu solchen Veranstaltungen, insonderheit zu Theatern, Lichtspielunternehmen, Konzerten, Vorträgen, artistischen Unternehmen (Varietés, Kabaretts, Zirkusveranstaltungen

usw.) Tanzvorführungen und Ausstellungen kultureller Art mit sofortiger Wirkung nicht mehr zu gestatten." *Film-Kurier* 267 (November 14, 1938).

[57] "Die sowohl zarteste wie stärkste und zugleich gesellschaftlich wichtigste Zuneigung, die es zwischen nicht verwandtschaftlich verbundenen Menschen geben kann, war also nun, wenn sie "Deutschblutige" und Juden verband, zu einem mit Haftstrafen bedrohten Verbrechen erklärt worden. Eine Minderheit, die sich solchermaßen geächtet sieht, wird im Wortsinne und damit natürlich auch in übertragenem Sinne unberührbar." Graml, *Reichskristallnacht*, 156.

[58] See Walter Hofer, ed., *Der Nationalsozialismus: Dokumente 1933–1945* (Frankfurt a. M.: Fischer, 1959), 294–95.

[59] Gustav Raeder's farce *Robert und Bertram* premiered on February 6, 1856 in Dresden and served as the basis for numerous stage adaptations. The Staatsbibliothek Berlin alone has seventeen adaptations of his play published between 1897 and 1938. *Robert und Bertram oder die lustigen Vagabunden*, directed by Max Mack and starring Ernst Lubitsch, premiered on August 12, 1915; see Censor-Card 1337 dated February 17, 1921, Bundesarchiv-Filmarchiv, Berlin. *Robert und Bertram*, directed by Rudolf Walther Fein, passed the censor on August 28, 1928; see Censor-Card 19914, Bundesarchiv-Filmarchiv, Berlin. A shortened version of Zerlett's *Robert und Bertram* with a running time of 1 hour and 32 minutes in 1000 meter length passed the censor in Berlin on April 14, 1943; see Censor-Card 58867, Bundesarchiv-Filmarchiv, Berlin. Hans Deppe directed a completely new version of *Robert und Bertram* in 1961. Deppe made over thirty films during the Third Reich but is best known for his post-war *Heimatfilme* including *Grün ist die Heide* (1951). Deppe's adaptation of *Robert und Bertram* has the vagabonds wandering some 500 kilometers to test shoes as part of a shoe factory's advertising campaign.

[60] "Ein freies Leben führen wir, ein Leben voller Wonne," Friedrich Schiller, *Die Räuber*, act 5, scene 5.

[61] Linda Schulte-Sasse explores the signficance of the names Biedermeier and Ipelmeyer. She notes: "As implied by the homophonic quality in the names '-meier' and '-meyer,' Biedermeier and Ipelmeyer are gentile-Jewish counterparts in their representation of exploitation. Not only is 'meyer' the more common spelling for Jewish names, but 'Ipel' is a South-German variation of *übel*, meaning 'evil.'" See *Entertaining the Third Reich: Illusions of Wholeness in Nazi Cinema* (Durham: Duke UP, 1996), 237.

[62] "Siehste, Robert, Du bist nun ein verkommenes Genie, und ich bin ein weggelaufener Bourgois, einer, der lieber ein Strolch sein will, als ein Spießer." *Robert und Bertram*, Censor-Card 51648, Bundesarchiv-Filmarchiv, Berlin. In this case, the censor cards include not only the censor's approval but also the entire film dialogue.

[63] "Wenn man nur stets Courage hat, was braucht man da viel Geld? Man kommt als Bummlerkandidat ganz lustig durch die Welt." *Robert und Bertram*, Censor-Card 51648.

[64] By June 26, 1935, all men age 18 and older were obligated to work for six months in the National Labor Sevice (Reichsarbeitsdienst, RAD). Women were required to fulfill the same service as of January 1939.

[65] Interior Minister Wilhelm Frick's circular on "the preventative fight against crime by the police," issued on December 14, 1937, is quoted in Michael Burleigh and Wolfgang Wippermann, *The Racial State: Germany 1933–1945* (Cambridge: Cam-

bridge UP, 1991), 173. For a detailed analysis of "asocials" in Nazi Germany, see Burleigh, *The Racial State*, 167–82; and Wolfgang Ayaß, *"Asoziale" im National-sozialismus* (Stuttgart: Klett-Cotta, 1995).

[66] "Als asozial gilt, wer durch gemeinschaftswidriges, wenn auch nicht verbrecheri-sches, Verhalten zeigt, daß er sich nicht in die Gemeinschaft einfügen will." Qtd. in Ayaß, *"Asoziale,"* 147.

[67] Ayaß, *"Asoziale,"* 162.

[68] ". . . Zwei lustige Burschen. Aber das sind keine Vagabunden, müssen Bänkelsän-ger sein, oder sowas. Verdienen sich ihr Mittagbrot mit Abwaschen. Mit Abwa-schen? — 'ne ganz ehrliche Arbeit." "Das sind keine Gauner . . . Das sind Bänkelsänger oder sowas." *Robert und Bertram*, Censor-Card 51648.

[69] ". . . Wandernde Künstler . . . ja, genauer gesagt, sind wir eigentlich auch mehr kunstvoll Wandernde." *Robert und Bertram*, Censor-Card 51648.

[70] "Das Palais muß dem Ipelmeyer ein Vermögen gekostet haben. Es hat sogar mehrere Vermögen gekostet, aber nicht von Herrn Ipelmeyer, sondern von den Leuten, die er hereingelegt hat." *Robert und Bertram*, Censor-Card 51648.

[71] "Die Sache liegt also so, daß ein großer Gauner, der sich nicht erwischen läßt, Kommerzienrat werden kann, während diese beiden kleinen Gauner, wenn man sie erwischt, für lange Zeit eingesperrt werden, obschon sie ihre Gaunerei nicht zum eigenen Vorteil vollführt haben. . . . Da stimmt doch etwas nicht." *Robert und Bertram*, Censor-Card 51648.

[72] "Wer ihnen gerecht werden will, muß sie nur eben mit ihrem Maße messen und nicht mit dem Zollstock gutbürgerlicher Tugenden. Das Normalmaß paßt schließlich eben nur dort, wo es sich um Normalerscheinungen handelt." "Tauge-nichts und Tu-nicht-gut" (n.p., n.d.), *Robert und Bertram*, Document file 13931, Bundesarchiv-Filmarchiv, Berlin.

[73] "[D]ie im Grunde kindsharmlosen 'Verbrecher' beklauen nur den, der selber schon geklaut hat, und sie beschenken die Geschädigten. Sie sind also keine gewöhnlichen, sondern 'höhere' Diebe, gewissermaßen moralisch sanktionierte Diebe." Ha. Hu., "Hans H. Zerlett dreht die Geschichte von den zwei Vagabunden, die trotzdem in den Himmel kamen!," *Filmwelt* 3 (January 20, 1939).

[74] "Unsere Freude an ihnen ist wohl unbewußt ein Protest gegen die Arbeitsfron des Tages, gegen den Zwang, der unser Dasein allzu lästig regelt." "Inhalts-Über-blick," *Robert und Bertram: Tobis Presseheft* (Leipzig: Tobis Filmkunst GmbH Presse-dienst, n.d.), 3, *Robert und Bertram*, Document file 13931, Bundesarchiv-Filmarchiv, Berlin.

[75] "Die beiden Gauner Robert und Bertram würden heutzutage leiberfrischender Arbeit zugeführt werden. . . . So manch ein Mensch, der im Gleichschritt täglicher Arbeit müde wird, den das Einerlei seiner Aufgabe zu untergraben droht, der nur noch die Arbeit sieht, der aber nicht mehr darüber hinwegzuschauen vermag, der wird in dem Gauner zu seiner Freude die Unzulänglichkeit alles Menschlichen entdecken. . . . Und plötzlich ist aus der Posse ein erzieherisches Stück geworden. Jedermann lacht über die Streiche, über die urkomischen Verwicklungen, über die Zufälle und Umstände, aber er findet zu seiner Arbeit zurück. . . . So hat ein Gaunerstück auch seine Moral: Das ist keine Freiheit, wo die Arbeit fehlt; oder: Ordnung muß sein, sonst läuft das Unglück

einen geraden Weg." Dr. B. M., "Gauner in der Posse," *Robert und Bertram: Tobis Presseheft* (Leipzig: Tobis Filmkunst GmbH Pressedienst, n.d.), 7, *Robert und Bertram*, Document file 13931, Bundesarchiv-Filmarchiv, Berlin.

[76] When Robert and Bertram lock up Michel in jail the night before he has to join the army, his uncle replies, "Serves you right, now you get to go from one arrest to another" [Das geschieht Dir ganz recht. Jetzt kommst Du von einem Arrest in den anderen]. Michel complains when a soldier cut his hair too short only to learn: "We determine how you look" [Wie Du aussehen wirst, bestimmen wir!]. When Michel hurts himself in training, the corporal informs him: "Ouch doesn't exist, at least not in the military!" [Autsch gibt es nicht, jedenfalls nicht beim Militär!]. *Robert und Bertram*, Censor-Card 51648.

[77] "Was die Preussen so alles aus einem Menschen machen, was?" *Robert und Bertram*, Censor-Card 51648.

[78] *Robert und Bertram* resembles the "village tale" (*Dorfgeschichte*), a popular nineteenth-century narrative genre, which used the village as a synecdoche for the nation. Zerlett's film portrays the village as the quintessential German home, while Berlin is seen as a café and Jewish. In its juxtaposition of an idyllic countryside to the corrupt city, this film reiterates a crucial topos of nineteenth-century German literature. For a general discussion of the village tale, see Friedrich Sengle, "Wunschbild Land und Schreckbild Stadt: Zu einem zentralen Thema der neuen deutschen Literatur," *Studium-Generale* 16 (1963): 619–31.

[79] For an overview of stereotypes regarding the Jewish nose and feet, see Kirstin Breitenfellner, "Der 'jüdische Fuß' und die 'jüdische Nase': Physiognomik, Medizingeschichte und Antisemitismus im 19. und 20. Jahrhundert," in *Wie ein Monster entsteht: Zur Konstruktion des anderen in Rassismus und Antisemitismus,* ed. Kirsten Breitenfellner and Charlotte Kohn-Ley (Bodenheim: Philo, 1998), 103–20; and Sander Gilman, *The Jew's Body* (New York: Routledge, 1991).

[80] On seeing Ipelmeyer in the street, Bertram remarks: "Das muß er sein, dem Profil nach zu urteilen." Mrs. Ipelmeyer recognizes Forchheimer "an de Fieß!" *Robert und Bertram*, Censor-Card 51648.

[81] "Seit drei Jahren sind Sie mein Prokurist, seit zwei Jahren begaunern Sie mich hinten und vorne, seit einem Jahr betrügen Sie mich mit meiner Frau. Also wenn mir jetzt noch das geringste vorkommt, sind Sie entlassen." *Robert und Bertram*, Censor-Card 51648.

[82] "Sind Sie meschugge? Was heißt 'lieben' mit 600 Taler Jahresgehalt. Meine Tochter wird die Stiefmutter einer Million." *Robert und Bertram*, Censor-Card 51648.

[83] "Schlußgalopp mit der jüdischen Hast, -no?" *Robert und Bertram*, Censor-Card 51648.

[84] "Er läßt ein Wiener Lied singen und tut in der Einleitung so, als wolle er gegen den donaubesingenden Kitsch einen grimmen Streich führen. Und dann kommt etwas, was die Majorität im Parkett genau so ergreift wie die Dorfschönen auf der Leinwand. Oder Rudi Godden hebt an zu einer Gesangs-Parodie und nachher weiß man nicht recht, ob man lachen oder ernst nehmen soll. Oder ein Ballett kommt daher gebraust und tanzt mit Ursula Deinert an der Spitze so gut, daß es eine Augenweide ist, und dann endet das Ganze mit einer kitschigen Pose, und man weiß nicht, was die Regie denn nun eigentlich

wollte. Man wird abwarten müssen, ob man das schwierige Problem der Parodien im Film mit solchen Kompromissen lösen kann." Georg Herzberg, *"Robert und Bertram,"* Beiblatt zum *Filmkurier* 162 (July 15, 1939).

[85] "Was wir singen, rührt Euch sehr, Nachher mit 'ergebnem Diener,' Gehen sammelnd wir umher. Jeder spende einen Heller, Keiner weise uns zurück, Erst wenn voll ist unser Teller, Ist vollkommen unser Glück." *Robert und Bertram,* Censor-Card 51648.

[86] Hitler, *Mein Kampf* (1971), 302–3. "Daher ist das jüdische Volk bei allen scheinbaren intellektuellen Eigenschaften dennoch ohne jede wahre Kultur, besonders aber ohne jede eigene. Denn was der Jude heute an Scheinkultur besitzt, ist das unter seinen Händen meist schon verdorbene Gut der anderen Völker." Hitler, *Mein Kampf* (1935), 1:331.

[87] "Was hat er gesungen? Nu, er sagt, er hat Zores mit seiner Geliebten." *Robert und Bertram,* Censor-Card 51648.

[88] The depiction of the Jewish doctor as a dangerous charlatan corresponds to anti-Semitic rhetoric. In *Robert und Bertram* the Jewish doctor Cordaun mistreats his patient Ipelmeyer, giving him sleeping pills instead of medicine, so the doctor can seduce the ballerina without competition.

[89] "Der Herr Ipelmeyer ist gekommen als Louis quartorze der fünfzehnte. Die Frau Ipelmeyer ist gekommen als Pompadour, aber sie sieht aus, wie 'ne miese alte Markttasche. Das Fräulein Tochter ist gekommen als Königin Kleptomania." *Robert und Bertram,* Censor-Card 51648.

[90] "Siehste, Robert, so ist das Leben. Ein Gitter ist überall, nur, daß die einen durch das Gitter rausschauen, und die anderen durch das Gitter reinschauen. — Ich möchte lieber rausschauen." "— Na, dann laß Dich doch wieder einsperren. Ach, Du hast eben keine Phantasie." *Robert und Bertram,* Censor-Card 51648.

[91] "Ach, Junge, wir träumen sogar dasselbe. Ja, -hört es, Ihr Götter, durch Zeit und durch Raum, Wir sind eine Seele, ein Herz und ein Traum." *Robert und Bertram,* Censor-Card 51648.

[92] "Was denn — jetzt schon, bei Lebzeiten? Laß man gut sein, von der irdischen Gerechtigkeit hätten wir sowieso nicht mehr viel zu erwarten gehabt." *Robert und Bertram,* Censor-Card 51648.

[93] See Schulte-Saase, *Entertaining the Third Reich,* 244; and Dorothea Hollstein, *"Jud Süß" und die Deutschen: Antisemitische Vorurteile im nationalsozialistischen Spielfilm* (Frankfurt a. M.: Ullstein, 1971), 52.

[94] "Das Schlußbild des Films erschient uns nicht als Vergeltungsmaßnahme: In Reih und Glied stehen Robert und Bertram als stramme Soldaten, und Michel kommandiert vor der Front: 'Das Gewehr über! Kompanie marsch!'" *Robert und Bertram: Das Programm von heute* 385 (Berlin: Das Programm von heute, Zeitschrift für Film und Theater GmbH, 1938).

[95] The following publicity materials and the censor cards do not advertise this alternative ending. Compare *Robert und Bertram: Illustrierter Film-Kurier* 2946 (Berlin: Franke & Co, n.d.); *Robert und Bertram: Lockende Leinwand* 23 (Berlin: Deutscher Verlag, July 31–August 3, [1939]); *Robert und Bertram: Tobis Presseheft; Robert und Bertram: Rekla-*

me-Ratschläge (Berlin: Tobis Filmkunst GmbH Werbedienst, n.d.); *Robert und Bertram,* Censor-Card 51648 (June 20, 1939); and Censor-Card 58867 (April 14, 1943).

[96] Compare Schulte-Saase, *Entertaining the Third Reich,* 244; and Hollstein, *"Jud Süß,"* 52, 321 nn. 71, 72.

[97] "Ein tiefer, allzutiefer Griff in die Mottenkiste" and "daß dieser Film keineswegs als völlig gelungen bezeichnet werden kann." "Film des Monats," *Der deutsche Film* 4, no. 2 (August 1939): 55.

[98] "Wird doch erstmalig in einem Film das Judentum zur Zielscheibe eines überlegenen wirkungssicheren Spottes gemacht." Herzberg, *"Robert und Bertram."*

[99] "So gut das jüdische Milieu dank der hervorragenden darstellerischen Leistungen von Herbert Hübner, Inge v. d. Straaten und Tatjana Sais in seiner Lächerlichkeit gezeichnet ist, so sehr vermißt man einen einzigen sichtbaren Beweis der Gefährlichkeit des typischen Börsenjobbers und so sehr könnte man an die Beziehungen und die Triebkräfte der Vertreter dieses Mileus und der handelnden Rahmenpersonen sehr kritische Fonden anlegen. Aber tun wir es nicht! Nehmen wir den Film als das, was er sein will: ein Volksstück mit Lust, Liebe und Sentimentalität, mit schönen Liedern und lebendigen darstellerischen Leistungen." Albert Schneider, *"Robert und Bertram." Licht-Bild-Bühne* 162 (July 15, 1939).

[100] "Das Fest in seinem prunkvollen Schloß, *in dem es von Unkultur nur so strotzt,* birgt Köstlichkeiten überlegenen Humors auf Seiten unserer beiden Tischler-Brüder, und es malt gleichzeitig das Zeit- und Sittengemälde: auf welche Art der Ost-Galizier schon damals versuchte, in Berlin Heimatrechte zu gewinnen und durch Geld und Spendabilität die Gemüter zu verwirren suchte." Iris, "Das Lokalstück: Die menschliche Komödie" (n.p., n.d.), *Robert und Bertram,* Document file 13931, Bundesarchiv-Filmarchiv, Berlin. Emphasis added.

[101] "Gustav Raeder hat den gesinnungslosen Geschäftemacher Ipelmeyer als Typus für Tausende gezeichnet, und er hat damit unsere eigene — hundert Jahre später erfolgte — gewaltige Abrechnung mit all denen, die Eigennutz über Gemeinutz stellen, vorausgeahnt." "[Die Gemeinschaft befreit] sich daraufhin erst richtig von ihren getarnten Schmarotzen." Mario Heil de Brentani, "Über den Volksfilm *Robert und Bertram," Licht-Bild-Bühne* 161 (July 14, 1939). The inclusion of Brentani's article in the Tobis press package suggests that his anti-Semitic diatribe received official approval and was intended for a wide audience. See also *Robert und Bertram: Tobis Presseheft,* 5.

[102] "Wir verlassen wieder das 'israelische' Paradies und freuen uns schon sehr darauf, nochher im fertigen Film miterleben zu können, wie die beiden gewizten Vagabunden der sich so schlau und unfehlbar dünkenden Familie Ipelmeyer ein anständiges Schnippchen schlagen." H. J. Hahn, "Auf die Feinheit kommt es an: Kleinigkeit um eine Filmszene," *Filmwoche* 6 (February 8, 1939): 174.

[103] "Hier herrscht Schadenfreude in der harmlosesten Form und ein Sprichwort sagt ja: Schadenfreude ist die reinste Freude, die jeder gern und unbedenklich genießt. Also hinein in das Erquickungsbad echten Frohsinns, hinein in die große deutsche Filmposse der Tobis *Robert und Bertram." Robert und Bertram: Reklame-Ratschläge,* 7.

[104] "Der Zuschauer sollte zu dem Schluß kommen, daß sich in der Gegenwart erfüllt, was in der Vergangenheit angestrebt wurde oder schon erreicht war, wieder verlorenging und neu erkämpft werden mußte. Im übrigen sollte in positiven Beispielen

jeweils das historische Analogon zur Gegenwart gefunden werden." Klaus Kanzog, *"Staatspolitisch besonders wertvoll": Ein Handbuch zu 30 deutschen Spielfilmen der Jahre 1934 bis 1945* (Munich: diskurs film, 1994), 31.

[105] "Das hat der Operetten- mit dem Historienfilm gemein: Beide benutzen die Geschichte als Anlaß für ein Spektakel, um das Publikum mit dem Prunk und der Exotik der Szenen zu beeindrücken; sie bemühen sich, die Atmosphäre einer Epoche auf der Leinwand vorzuzaubern. Aber nimmt sich der Historienfilm vor, ein Stück Geschichte 'treu' zu erzählen (und der Zuschauer erwartet, daß es so sei), geht der Operettenfilm frei damit um. Was er erzählt, muß nicht wahr sein. Er stellt es weder als wahr vor, noch rechnet das Publikum damit. Im Operettenfilm wird die Historie mürbe, nimmt die Form an, die man ihr gibt." Francesco Bono, "Glücklich ist, wer vergißt . . . Operette und Film: Analyse einer Beziehung," in *Musik Spektakel Film: Musiktheater und Tanzkultur im deutschen Film 1922–1937,* ed. Katja Uhlenbrok (Munich: edition text + kritik, 1998), 37–38.

[106] Schulte-Saase, *Entertaining the Third Reich,* 9.

[107] In the prologue to *Wiener Blut* (1942), an alchemist mixes together the perfect recipe for the operetta. Reaching for various bottles labeled "humor," "carelessness," and "heart," he adds the precious essences together in a phial, then pours generous amounts of "music" into the mixture, but before he is finished, he adds a few drops of "history" to spice it up.

[108] *So endet die Liebe* (1934), *Die Hochzeitsreise* (1939), *Das leichte Mädchen* (1941), and *Hochzeit auf Bärenhof* (1942) are also set in the nineteenth century. For a discussion of literary adaptations, see Richard J. Rundell, "Literary Nazis? Adapting Nineteenth-Century German Novellas for the Screen: *Der Schimmelreiter, Kleider machen Leute,* and *Immensee,*" in *Cultural History through a National Socialist Lens: Essays on the Cinema of the Third Reich,* ed. Robert C. Reimer (Rochester, NY: Camden House, 2000), 176–96.

[109] Karsten Witte, "Visual Pleasure Inhibited: Aspects of the German Revue Film," trans. J. D. Steakley and Gabriele Hoover, *New German Critique* 24–25 (Fall/Winter 1981–82): 251.

[110] "Nicht alle sind im selben Jetzt da. . . . Sie tragen vielmehr Früheres mit, das mischt sich ein." Ernst Bloch, *Erbschaft dieser Zeit,* vol. 4 of *Werkausgabe* (Frankurt a. M.: Suhrkamp, 1992), 104.

[111] Ernst Bloch, *Heritage of Our Times,* trans. Neville and Stephen Plaice (Berkeley: U of California P, 1991), 57. "[L]aufen auch sehr alte Träume mit unter." Bloch, *Erbschaft,* 63.

[112] Bloch, *Heritage of Our Times,* 60. "Nicht die 'Theorie' der Nationalsozialisten, wohl aber ihre Energie ist ernst, der fanatisch-religiöse Einschlag, der nicht nur aus Verzweiflung und Dummheit stammt, die seltsam aufgewühlte Glaubenskraft." Bloch, *Erbschaft,* 65–66.

[113] "Das XIX Jahrhundert ein Zeitraum (ein Zeit-traum)." Walter Benjamin, *Das Passagen-Werk,* vol. 5.1 of *Gesammelte Schriften,* ed. Rolf Tiedemann, 2d ed. (Frankfurt a. M.: Suhrkamp, 1998), 491.

[114] "Das gibt's nur einmal, das kommt nie wieder," *Der Kongreß tanzt* (1931), directed by Eric Charell and starring Lilian Harvey and Willy Fritsch.

2: Mapping German Identity: The Foreign Adventure Film

EXOTIC FAR-OFF LANDS, unexplored jungles, vast and timeless wastelands. Images of foreign realms have long captured the human imagination and have been a vital part of Western cinema since its inception. Travelogues and foreign adventure films bring viewers to places they would most likely never visit and allow them to share in the allure of exploration. The adventure film offers viewers the prospect of danger, intrigue, and conquest without ever leaving the safety of the movie theater. Both documentary expedition films and fictional travel adventures follow a similar narrative pattern: a Western European man travels to uncharted territory in Africa, Asia, or South America, where he conquers a wild land and captures its image and natural treasures. The explorer meets natives and distinguishes his own racial and cultural identity from that of a people he considers primitive. Traveling with the adventurer, viewers are given the opportunity to explore blank spaces on the map and experience the thrill of being in a strange new place where the unimaginable seems possible. In the encounter between the European traveler and the native, adventure films visualize popular notions of gender, race, and power surrounding national identity.

In Nazi Germany, the adventure film was a small but significant film genre. Comprising only 11.2 % of the entire film production between 1933 and 1945, the adventure film rarely delivered record-breaking success at the box office, but the German film industry supplied a steady fare of such films and supplemented its own production with Hollywood imports.[1] In 1938 and 1939 the adventure film reached its zenith, constituting 16.2% and 18.5% respectively of the yearly film production.[2] As the Third Reich expanded its borders, annexed Austria (March 13, 1938) and the Sudetenland (September 29, 1938), marched into Bohemia and Moravia (March 15, 1939), invaded the Memelland (March 23, 1939), and finally attacked Poland launching the Second World War (September 1, 1939), German cinemas featured more adventure films than ever before or after. These stories about explorers, treasure hunters, and colonists embarking on a perilous journey into the unknown belong to a larger discourse at home and abroad central to Nazi ideology and imperial conquest. Three adventure films in particular, *Kautschuk* (Caoutchouc, 1938), *Verklungene Melodie* (Faded Melody, 1938), and *Frauen für Golden Hill* (Wives for Golden Hill, 1938) exemplify the ways that Nazi popular culture imagined empire building. The questions that inform my study focus on the role cinematic geography played in mapping German national identity. In a society where race determined power, and difference often meant death, how did cinema codify the relationship between the white European and the racial Other? How does the adventurer's travel to foreign realms change him and his relation to *Heimat* (home)? And lastly, to what extent do these stories about treasure hunting and settlement in foreign countries conform to the Nazi quest for *Lebensraum* (living space)?

Imperial Conquest and the Fatal Attraction to the Foreign: *Kautschuk* (1938)

Kautschuk tells the story of how the British broke the Brazilian monopoly on natural rubber (caoutchouc) and contains many hallmarks of German adventure films made in the late 1930s. Filmed largely on location in the Amazon jungle and starring popular actors René Deltgen and Gustav Diessl, *Kautschuk* was marketed as a sensational and historically accurate portrayal of one man's heroic battle to win natural resources for his nation. The participation of several key figures in the making of *Kautschuk,* especially René Deltgen, Eduard von Borsody, and Ernst von Salomon, suggests a complex relation between adventure, military conquest, and imperialism in the popular imagination. These three men came from different backgrounds, but their combined experiences helped to shape "this manly film of determination and energy" into "a solemn hymn of selfless commitment to a lofty goal."[3]

By the time he starred in *Kautschuk,* René Deltgen had already established a name for himself playing "the vigorous daredevil," a maverick who went after whatever he wanted and teetered on the edge of death. Deltgen made a nearly seamless transition between roles calling for "a convincing spy who knew how to meet heroic death with a smile" in *Port Arthur* (1936, Farkas) and *Achtung, Feind hört mit* (1940, Rabenalt), a fortune hunter in *Kongo Express* (1939, Borsody) and *Brand im Ozean* (1939, Rittau), and a courageous soldier in *Urlaub auf Ehrenwort* (1938, Ritter), *Spähtrupp Halgarten* (1941, Fredersdorf), and *Fronttheater* (1942, Rabenalt).[4] Deltgen's roles called for a combination of strength, daring, and self-sacrifice, which made him a highly sympathetic and representative hero in the cinema of the Third Reich. Along with a growing popular following, Deltgen enjoyed official support. At the ceremonies surrounding Hitler's fiftieth birthday in 1939, the Führer honored Deltgen with the title of "National Actor" (*Staatsschauspieler*).

Director Eduard von Borsody and co-writer Ernst von Salomon worked on several projects together and became leading figures in the adventure film genre. Both Borsody and Salomon distanced themselves from the Nazi regime but continued to advance in the coordinated film industry of the

1930s and 1940s. Despite their detachment from National Socialist politics, Borsody and Salomon retained from their early military training a staunch patriotism and martial honor code that crystallizes in their adventure films. Both director and screenwriter had first-hand experience of the First World War, serving as officers in the Austrian and Prussian armies respectively. Ernst von Salomon was the far more controversial figure, known for his political autobiography *Die Geächteten* (The Outlaws, 1930), which traced his transformation from a Prussian cadet to a free corps officer involved in the assassination of Foreign Minister Walter Rathenau.[5] Eduard von Borsody specialized in action-packed adventure films set in foreign venues, but his greatest success was the blockbuster home-front film *Wunschkonzert* (1940).[6] Borsody's adventure and home-front films share many notable features, including sensational documentary footage, an exciting visual spectacle of male vigor and bravery, and a model hero who fights for the homeland.

Henry Wickham and José in *Kautschuk* (1938).

Film historian Klaus Kreimeier has suggested that Borsody was a conservative whose adventure films were nationalistic without ever becoming politically correct: "The director belonged to those (conservative) descendents of the Danube monarchy who cultivated the genre of patriotic adventure films at the Ufa studios without ascribing the 'political' implications. They formed a counterweight to the reactionary art-corporals like Karl Ritter and others."[7] While I agree with Kreimeier that Borsody's films do not tout the party line in the same way Karl Ritter's heavy-handed propaganda films do, I maintain that the conservative, patriotic story line of *Kautschuk* furthers National Socialist military and imperialist goals. This film about a lone wolf acting on behalf of his nation is a parable that preaches an honor code and a behavioral pattern consistent with the leadership principle and Nazi concepts of masculine identity. The fact that Borsody's film voices a pro-British sentiment is neither inconsistent with the regime's love-hate relationship with England in 1938 nor does it diminish the significance of its role models and mythic rendering of conquest. The patriotic adventure film that purports to be pure entertainment offers up exactly the type of excitement that makes the invasion of foreign territory and seizure of natural resources for the fatherland seem like a timeless and natural endeavor.

Kautschuk passed the censor in Berlin on October 31, 1938, and was awarded the distinction marks "artistically valuable" and "politically valuable."[8] Propaganda Minister Joseph Goebbels praised the film as "politically and artistically magnificent. A brilliant performance by Ufa."[9] *Kautschuk* premiered on November 1, 1938, at the Ufa-Palast in Hamburg, a marketing strategy motivated by the contemporary viewpoint that "Hamburg as a world trade center has always been interested in the treatment of colonial problems."[10] A week later *Kautschuk* premiered in Berlin at the Ufa-Palast am Zoo (the city's largest cinema with 2,325 seats), where it played for seventeen days and was heralded as the most successful film to premiere that month.[11] Despite *Kautschuk's* notoriety, surprisingly few film historians have examined Borsody's film as a cultural artifact that could help gauge the popular perception of colonial exploration in 1938 Germany.

The film is set in 1876. Brazil enjoys a worldwide monopoly on caoutchouc, the highest quality rubber, also known as "elastic gold." To safeguard its natural treasure, Brazil has imposed the death penalty on anyone caught exporting rubber seeds. The British Empire is especially hard hit by the monopoly. Without official support yet filled with patriotic zeal, the Englishman Henry Wickham (René Deltgen) sails to Brazil intent on stealing rubber seeds for British colonies in India, Ceylon, and Malacca. On the transatlantic journey, Wickham falls in love with Mary Waverley, the British Consul's daughter, who is all but betrothed to the Brazilian Don Alonzo de Ribeira (Gustav Diessl). Wickham and Don Alonzo battle for Mary's heart and for the precious seeds on Don Alonzo's rubber plantation near the Araguary River. Under the guise of a scientific expedition in search of a rare butterfly found only in the same area as the rubber, Wickham ventures into the Amazon jungle. Accompanied by the outlawed vaquero José, Wickham fights the elements, natives with poison darts, piranha, crocodiles, a giant anaconda, jungle fever, and a massive tidal wave. He succeeds in finding both caoutchouc seeds and the rare butterfly. However, transporting the seeds poses a problem, since the British survey ship Wellington will only take on the cargo in international waters. The police arrest Wickham and kill José but not before they have smuggled the caoutchouc seeds aboard the Wellington en route to England. Since there is no tangible proof that Wickham illegally exported the seeds, Don Alonzo tampers with evidence and accuses him of military espionage. Wickham cannot produce the rare butterfly as evidence of his "lawful" scientific objectives and is sentenced to death. When Mary intercedes, Don Alonzo admits stealing the butterfly and is arrested, while Wickham is set free. The British Empire has won the battle for autarchy.

Henry Wickham is an archetypal hero who possesses all the right characteristics to be either a great pirate or an honorable knight; he is a powerful and resourceful man who undertakes a dangerous journey to foreign realms in order to plunder treasures from the vanquished. The German trade press highlighted his steel-like character, describing him in admirable terms as "in control, restrained, alert, and brave." Central to Wickham's identity is "his willingness to sacrifice, his selflessness completely lacking any personal desire for advancement, employing everything for a cause he serves."[12] He displays not only all the qualities of a good citizen but also those essential to the soldierly male. Wickham's self-sacrifice for the fatherland was exactly the behavior German audiences were continually encouraged to adopt as part of their own self-image. Although Wickham is English and his actions are intended to benefit the British Empire, he is presented in such a favorable light that German viewers could easily identify with him as a European fighting against a foreign opponent. Wickham is an exceedingly sympathetic character played by a popular film star who specialized in heroes possessing a noble character, a good sense of humor, and a healthy disregard for rules. The British serve as a model for the German Empire in 1938 because as critic Hans Hömberg stated: "The film *Kautschuk* stands between report and fiction. It wants to give an impression of the suspense and elicit understanding for the battle between two countries over a trading monopoly. The story has a motto: responsibility and bravery belong to a man's adornments (*Schmuck*)."[13] The lessons garnered from this film corresponded to National Socialist expansion politics and indoctrination of the *Volksgemeinschaft*. In a review of *Kautschuk* published in *Licht-Bild-Bühne*, Adolf Hitler was prominently quoted to illustrate how this feature film displayed the prevalent notions of heroism and civic duty. Boldly outlined in a framed box at the center of the review, the Führer's words function as the film's emblem: "Offering one's own life for the existence of the community is the highest form of sacrifice. Precisely our German language possesses a word that describes marvelously the action in this sense: discharge of duty. This means not satisfying oneself but rather serving the general public."[14]

What separates *Kautschuk* most notably from the chauvinistic wartime propaganda films like *Feinde* (1940, Tourjansky), *Heimkehr* (1941, Ucicky), and *G.P.U.* (1942, Ritter), is that the foreign enemy is portrayed here as a man of dignity and honor. In Borsody's adventure film, Don Alonzo de Ribeira comes across as a worthy adversary. He is articulate and well mannered, at ease in the drawing rooms of power or socializing at a garden party, and a commanding presence as lord over his slaves. Most importantly, Don Alonzo is a patriot who loves his country enough to safeguard its natural resources whatever the costs. Like Wickham, who defies British international policy to secure his empire's future wealth, Don Alonzo breaks Brazilian law in order to protect his country's national interests. Don Alonzo steals evidence, falsely accuses Wickham of espionage, and perjures himself in a court of law to force the British to return the caoutchouc seeds. Despite his transgressions, Don Alonzo believes that his actions were justified because his country's economic security and sovereign domain were at stake. He wagers everything that Wickham will accept a deal for a stay of execution in return for the caoutchouc seeds, but he underestimates the Englishman's resolve. Don Alonzo loses the bet and pays with his own freedom; he is arrested and accepts his fate with resigned nobility: "The game is over, and I have lost."[15]

Much of Don Alonzo's appeal came from the actor who portrayed him. Gustav Diessl was a popular film star typecast as an adventurer hero. Diessl gained his first major success starring opposite Leni Riefenstahl in the mountain films *Die weiße Hölle vom Piz Palü* (1929, Fanck and Pabst) and *S.O.S. Eisberg* (1933, Fanck). Fan magazines promoted Diessl as a real-life patriot and thrill-seeker, who had fought in the Tyrolian mountain brigade in the First World War and was taken prisoner of war before traveling the globe making motion pictures. Diessl's wanderlust had taken him to Egypt, Paris, Hollywood, Africa, India, and Rome, where he made such action-adventure films as *The Big House* (1931, Fejos), *Der Dämon des Himalaya* (1935, Dyhrenfurth), and *Der Tiger von Eschnapur* and *Das indische Grabmal* (1937, Eichberg).[16] The casting of Diessl to play Don Alonzo as the foil to Deltgen's Henry Wickham ensured that the battle between Brazil and Britain would seem like a fair match fought between equals.

The British and Brazilians have much in common in the film. Both countries are empires with a rigid class system and governments based on a strict adherence to the law. The British Lord Chancellor and his Brazilian counterpart, the governor of Pará, insist that their citizens conform to all legal statutes and refuse to condone any violation of the law, even if it will further their national self-interest. The differences between the British and Brazilians are based largely on popular stereotypes. The British are represented as one racial and ethnic group, and white Englishmen like Consul Waverley, Henry Wickham, and Captain Murray are honorable, emotionally restrained, and adept at commerce, while the effeminate, over-civilized Lord Reginald and the absent-minded Professor Hickelberry are stock figures used for comic relief. What separates the Brazilians from the British are their passionate temperament and mix of races and ethnic groups. The European descendents who make up the Brazilian ruling class (Don Alonzo, the governor of Pará, the military court judge), display the wealth and regal bearing of their position, but their heritage is somewhat clouded. Don Alonzo de Ribeira, for example, is described in the film program notes as "a handsome, elegant *Spaniard,*" instead of the more logical Portuguese.[17] The Brazilian soldiers at Fort Ambé are somewhat unkempt and unruly, and their ranks include men of varied races. The blacks, *cafuzos,* mulattos, and indigenous people (the latter look like a Hollywood version of Indians in a typical Western) are depicted for the most part as wild and untamed.

In contrast to Don Alonzo, José embodies a different version of Brazilian national identity: the *cafuzo,* the offspring of a black and an Indian. José was played by the Brazilian actor José Alcantra and was described in the German press as "a truly unique figure, three-fourths Indian, one-fourth Negro, and brought back last year from the Amazon jungle by the returning film expedition." The filmmakers took "a mixed breed out of the jungle who acts as Wickham's servant and functions to a certain extent in individual scenes as the link between the jungle and studio shots."[18] As if reenacting the Golden Age explorers' gesture of bringing indigenous people back to Europe to validate their discoveries, the Ufa studios used José to authenticate the reality of *Kautschuk.* The cafuzo would serve as a visual and narrative bridge between two worlds, the savage and the civilized. Indeed, José is portrayed as both barbarian and noble savage, murdering his sexual rival in a fit of passion and faithfully serving his chosen white master in the pursuit of a lofty goal. Left to his own resources, José succumbs to primal urges and falls from grace. He kills the black man Raimundo and flees into the jungle, where he falls into a swamp and nearly drowns before being saved by Henry Wickham. José's plunge into the swamp signifies his descent into the primitive and his redemption by civilized man. Under the benevolent guardianship of the Englishman, José proves he can be gallant and brave. He devotes himself so completely to Wickham's cause that he sacrifices his own life to smuggle caoutchouc seeds aboard the Wellington. In much the same way as the British survey ship Wellington measures and maps uncharted territory, setting international standards and establishing borders, Wickham's so-called civilized behavior sets the standard for the "mixed breed out of the jungle."

The depiction of the black slaves relies on stereotypical notions of Africans as infantile savages who need the civilized white man to dominate and educate them. Black children play naked in muddy waters and a black man lies in a hammock, but when the master comes, the slaves engage in frantic activity. The women bathe the children and clean the porches while the men put on their shoes and comb their hair. The slaves come across as dirty and lazy comic figures: the children scream when bathed and a black man stares amazed at his mirror image when a comb breaks off in his bushy hair. The black maids working for Mary Waverley are equally childlike and ridiculous, giggling over her fancy new dresses, playing with a parasol, and throwing white dusting power on their black faces. Slavery is presented as a benevolent practice to safeguard primitive people from harming themselves. Don Alonzo de Ribeira owns slaves on the island of Marajá but he assures the Europeans that they are well treated: "You don't need to pity them. At this very moment my poor downtrodden slaves are celebrating a festival and are eagerly getting drunk on sugarcane liquor in honor of St. Anthony."[19]

A crosscut between the British garden party and the slave's festival shows the two cultures at different stages in human development. The British are genteel, dressed in their finery and drinking wine from crystal, dancing to a soothing waltz and engaging in polite conversation about science and business. In a series of dissolves, the civilized world of restraint is transformed into the untamed realm of desire; control literally dissolves into excess. In contrast to the British, the slaves are speechless and intoxicated from drinking rum, smoking, dancing to the loud rhythmic Latin beat, and giving themselves over to primal sexual drives. Linking the two cultures is an elementary human conflict: both scenes feature a love triangle and potential violence erupting from jealousy. Henry Wickham dances with Mary Waverley while her admirer Don Alonzo silently recognizes his rival but remains in control. Simultaneously, when the *mulata* Elizza dances with the vaquero José, her boyfriend Raimundo becomes enraged. In a series of voyeuristic close-ups, the camera moves ever closer to Raimundo's angry black face and Elizza's swinging hips, her smile, and then her undulating breasts. Jealousy turns into murder when José plunges a knife into Raimundo and kills him. This scene fulfills the prophetic words of the British Consul and sketches the film's further narrative development: "The Brazilians are nice people as far as it goes, but there are two things they don't like: when you pay too much attention to their women and when you try to penetrate territory where their riches come from."[20] The conquest of woman and the acquisition of wild territory are conflated in the cinematic imagination and personalized through the narrative when Wickham steals both Mary and the rubber seeds from his rival Don Alonzo. The equation of woman and land belongs to a broader political discourse that engenders imperialist conquest in order to make it appear natural. As Marianna Torgovnick has pointed out: "[Primitive] landscape is to be entered, conquered; its riches are to be reaped, enjoyed. The phallic semiology accompanies the imperialist topoi, a conjunction based on the assumption that if explorers (like Stanley and Tarzan) are 'manly,' then what they explore must be female."[21]

The Amazon jungle is significant in *Kautschuk* as a manifestation of primitivism, a site of mythic confrontation and transformation as well as a treasure trove to be plundered by the white man. Extraordinary care was given to render the Amazon jungle as true to life as possible. Noted documentary filmmakers Dr. Franz Eichhorn and his brother Edgar Eichhorn, along with Dr. O. A.

Bayer, undertook a Brazilian film expedition in 1936–37 to gather location footage for *Kautschuk*. The filmmakers' arduous journey became the subject of a popular book, and the trade press portrayed it as a heroic undertaking equal to Henry Wickham's historical adventure of 1876.[22]

The expedition film was a popular genre in the Weimar Republic and continued to draw audiences during the Third Reich.[23] Ostensibly a documentary film genre recording an authentic journey abroad to gain precious geographic and scientific information, these films have a formulaic structure similar to the fictional adventure film. Expedition films tell the familiar story of an explorer who ventures into unknown regions under great perils to find images never seen before and to bring them home to an eager audience. Explorers were routinely characterized as equal parts daredevil, scientist, and artist. Filmmakers like Hans Schomburgk, Otto Schulz-Kampfhenkel, and Martin Rikli delighted viewers with their footage of African deserts, Asian jungles, South American rain forests, exotic animals, and strange indigenous people.[24] They also published first-hand accounts of the expeditions to promote their films and propagate an image of the explorer as a modern-day hero.[25] Popular paperback books like *Adventure Tempts: Film Expeditions, Expedition Films* (1940) depict the documentary filmmaker as a lone wolf, often a pilot, who heroically battles countless dangers and often death to take pictures of extraordinary beauty and to record priceless scientific information. The expedition filmmaker exhibits the martial values of strength, determination, and self-sacrifice unto death. And like the conquering hero, he fights on foreign soil to bring home valuable treasures. Using the camera lens as his weapon, the filmmaker captures territory. A passage from *Adventure Tempts* illustrates that in Nazi Germany both critics and the public readily perceived the structural similarity between the goals of battle and expedition filmmaking: "On the pilot's mark, the companion now lifts himself over the fuselage, aims the small, mobile, hand-held camera, which almost looks like a large pistol, at the white flanks and with the lens touches the entire sparkling mountain world. Silently the film rolls away and swallows up the secrets of this world."[26] In an article published in *Der deutsche Film* in 1938, Frank Maraun valorized the heroic exploits of expedition filmmakers "as passionate and persistent hunters, rendering with lens and aperture the most exquisite feast for the eyes, snaring on celluloid a prey that often tastes better to us than the diet of feature films prepared in studios."[27] As film historian Klaus Kreimeier has recently noted, "in its heyday the documentary film genre, which specifically cast its eye and its cognitive interest on non-European scenery and non-European ethnic groups, was a project, if not to say, a projectile of colonial world acquisition and world conquest."[28]

Director Eduard von Borsody used extensive location footage from the Eichhorn-Bayer expedition in *Kautschuk*, and he also incorporated aspects of the mythic expedition filmmaker into the character of Wickham. Borsody capitalized on the public's interest in travelogues to promote *Kautschuk,* so that much of the publicity for this film described the 1936–37 Brazilian documentary expedition. In both the advertising campaign and the way in which Borsody blatantly spliced together documentary footage and studio shots, the borders between history and the present, fiction and documentary, hero and director, seem intentionally blurred. By drawing parallels not only between 1876 and 1937, but also between the historical British adventurer and the present-day German filmmakers, there are numerous points of slippage between the cinematic hero and the cinematographer. Since the historical figure Henry Wickham is obviously embedded into the documentary footage and resembles the contemporary Eichhorn-Bayer team, the filmmakers' accomplishments and perspectives seem to be grafted onto the character.

Franz Eichhorn described the Amazon jungle as a violent and fascinating place where the animals and natives posed an ever-present danger: "The battle for life is fought there step by step. We captured this battle on film: snakes, tiger cats, tarantulas, a praying mantis eating a butterfly, attacking jaguars, and, last but not least, the jungle people: the Jaculos, the Araras, the Ivaros, prowling Indians with poison darts. . . . This world is uncanny — and attractive time and time again due to its very incomprehensibility."[29] The European white man is drawn to this wild territory because it is so different from everything he knows at home. In the Amazon, strange animals seem to exist on the same biological plane as savage people, and the distanced observer who captures them on film conquers them by preserving their image. The documentary explorer is enchanted by the uncanny (*unheimlich*) foreign territory and risks falling prey to its lethal seduction. Only his ability to observe from afar and maintain a critical distance safeguards him from the jungle's deadly charms.

Kautschuk incorporates elements of the documentary expedition film and also relies on classical cinema's narrative conventions to establish a particular point of view and regulate the act of looking at bodies deemed inferior and territory inscribed as savage. The camera participates by steering and limiting voyeuristic pleasure of forbidden zones. Whereas the spectacle was an integral part of Nazi cinema and viewers were constantly given the opportunity to look at themselves, the adventure film offered a different type of spectacle, the unique prospect of looking at the Other, at alterity. In *Kautschuk,* the act of looking is thematized as both a sexualized, animalistic, deadly pleasure associated with the black man and also a distanced, scientific, and empowering tool used by the white explorer.

In *Kautschuk,* voyeurism is first steered through the fiction, so that the viewer watches Raimundo watching Elizza dancing with José, an act that ends in death. In this crucial sequence, the act of looking at an exotic body codifies the link between racial difference, sexuality, and death. In a series of close-ups showing Raimundo's dark black face with its distinctly Negroid racial features followed by close-ups of Elizza's fragmented, eroticized female body with its significantly lighter skin and more racially mixed features, the viewer is aligned with the black man's point of view. Raimundo gazes at the *mulata* with mounting lust and rage, reflected in the progressively tighter close-ups, until he must enter the scene and possess the object of his desire. The punishment for following his untamed sexual and violent drives is death. This sequence illustrates that the transgression of borders is lethal; only by maintaining the crucial line between spectator and spectacle as well as the racial divide between black, white, and Indian, can the violence be stemmed. The threat of miscegenation, the black who desires the *mulata* suggested on the visual and narrative levels, was also emphasized in the publicity materials that described José and Elizza as mixed breeds (*Mischlinge*). The use of this loaded term, which defined racial identity and legal status in Nazi Germany, together with the emotional and visceral experience of the subjective camera work, educated the German audience in 1938 to see the danger in looking at the racial Other.

When Wickham enters the Amazon, the camera captures amazing sights and becomes a participant in the story. The location shots taken by the Eichhorn-Bayer team are so closely woven into the fiction that the viewer associates the distanced, scientific camera perspective with the figure of Wickham. Reaching into the trees and dark recesses of the jungle, the camera finds numerous monkeys, jungle cats, and snakes hidden from the naked eye. It even ventures underwater to show the viewer the mysterious and deadly flesh-eating piranha that Wickham can see but José does not notice. The camera also pans across the water and encompasses hundreds of jacará, prehistoric-looking crocodiles that threaten to engulf all the space and destroy civilized man. The camera frames, limits, and fends off the relentless onslaught of crocodiles with its lens in much the same way as Wickham does with his pistol.

At first Wickham is able to fight off all the powers of nature: "With great courage and determination he penetrates the green hell and defeats all resistance from wild nature, her animals, white and colored men."[30] However, Wickham seems to have lingered too long in the jungle, because just as he finds the rare butterfly (laternaria phosphorea) he has been desperately seeking and reaches out to capture it, he is attacked by a giant anaconda. In this place of primal urges and antediluvian forms of existence, he falls prey to the ancient symbol of temptation and transformation. Suggesting the dangers of taking too much pleasure in looking at this forbidden zone, the snake twists its body around Wickham's neck and nearly crushes him to death. José rescues him, but immediately after this attack the Englishman suffers from jungle fever.

In a haunting montage of dissolves, Wickham hallucinates that the jungle is alive, taking over his space and appropriating his gaze. The sequence begins with a delirious, supine Wickham staring up at the cafuzo José who suddenly turns into a bizarre paper-maché snake. As the Englishman succumbs to the seductive power of wild territory, he loses control of his distanced, authoritative gaze and merges visually with the jungle. His face is covered with swirling water and fades into uncanny, ferocious animals staring out of the darkness. The enormous dark eyes of various jungle creatures fill the screen and threaten to engulf the white man and seize his identity. The sequence concludes with a dissolve from a monkey's face to that of a Brazilian soldier, so that the non-European man frames the entire hallucination. An extreme close-up of an unkempt Brazilian soldier laughing grotesquely acts as a segue from the jungle to civilization, as the camera slowly pulls back to reveal Wickham lying in a hammock at Fort Ambé. The camera work reiterates on the visual level that the borders between animal and mixed breed are fluid as shown in dissolves, while the borders between the mixed breed and the white man are sharper as rendered in cuts. The restoration of a distanced point of view coincides with Wickham's ability to restore his identity and authoritative gaze. Aided by a black man who acts as both facilitator and foil, Wickham stares into a mirror and reconfirms his status as *Mensch,* while the black barber Miguel gives him a shave and promises to make him feel like a human being again.

Even after the explorer's objective point of view is re-established, the act of image making continues to motivate the narrative. Wickham is tried for espionage because he cannot produce the laternaria phosphorea, and his drawing of this rare butterfly matches the map of Fort Ambé. Wickham argues that the ostensive link between image making and military objectives is mere coincidence. He denies any truth to the metonymic string equating the butterfly with art, geography, and military security, and tries to obscure the deeper affiliation between caoutchouc and scientific, economic, and military power. In the end, an image resolves the narrative conflict and proves Wickham's "lawful" intentions. By producing an intimate portrait of herself and Wickham, Mary proves that Don Alonzo perjured himself and stole the butterfly to harm his rival. Don Alonzo had sworn that he provided the court with all of Wickham's possessions, but since he gave Mary the portrait before the trial, it is clear that he tampered with evidence. Mary's possession of Wickham's domesticated image is seen as convincing proof, and he is exonerated of any wrongdoing.

Kautschuk ends with Wickham's acquittal and England's achievement of autarchy. Through his adventurous spirit and ingenuity, Wickham preserved his nation's dominance, an inevitable exploit according to the British Consul Waverley because "whenever the world needs a raw material, then it finds the means to obtain it."[31] Wickam's dream of rubber growing "in endless rows, tree next to tree" like soldiers on British colonial soil seems destined to come true, and the empire's consolidation of military power is confirmed in the film's final shot when the Wellington fires its cannons in a triumphant victory salute.[32]

Much of the publicity materials for *Kautschuk* asserted that Borsody's film was not really about Henry Wickham; instead it was about "how a country can gain independence from a certain foreign raw material."[33] Despite the historical setting, the press highlighted that the acquisition of natural resources continued to be a pressing issue in 1938. Writing for *Licht-Bild-Bühne*, critic Konrad Himmel summarized the impact of rubber on the global economy:

> Today Brazil's share of the world's supply of caoutchouc amounts to only about 16%, while England was able to establish its East Asian caoutchouc plantation industry because of Wickham's feat and in the course of time has seized the monopoly in the area of rubber production. The one thing Brazil has been able to prevent up to the present day is the export of the Uricury palm, which is only found in the jungles of the Amazonas and is extremely valuable for the quality of caoutchouc.[34]

Rubber was not merely an important economic resource used to make popular consumer products like raincoats and car tires. Along with other natural resources like fuel, rubber played a vital role in war. "A modern nation could not hope to defend itself without rubber. The construction of a military airplane used one-half ton of rubber; a tank needed about one ton and a battleship, 75 tons. Each person in the military required 32 pounds of rubber for footwear, clothing, and equipment. Tires were needed for all kinds of vehicles and aircraft."[35] From the start, the National Socialist government considered German self-sufficiency and complete independence from foreign natural resources a significant military goal. Beginning with the New Plan 1934–1935, the regime sought to regulate international trade, foreign currency, and the import of raw materials. The lack of natural rubber during the First World War had led German scientists at I. G. Farben to make pioneering discoveries in the production of synthetic rubber or Buna ("bu" for butadiene and "na" for natrium, the chemical symbol for sodium). The acquisition of synthetic rubber continued to be of utmost importance to German industries in the 1930s when I. G. Farben worked together with Standard Oil of New Jersey to develop Buna from petroleum. Rubber proved to be so important to Germany during the Second World War that the government followed Henry Wickham's historical deed and plundered foreign resources to maintain its position of autarchy. In 1942, I. G. Farben established a plant to produce synthetic rubber with foreign slave labor at the extermination camp Auschwitz III Monowitz.

Kautschuk presented audiences in 1938 an entertaining tale of exploration that contained substantial political lessons for building the future German empire: the need to protect oneself from the fatal attraction to the foreign and the equally pressing need to invade foreign territory to ensure autarchy. While *Kautschuk* may have provided audiences with a fictional model that helped prepare them for war, the film ironically proved to be a liability when the Second World War actually began. On September 13, 1939, the Ufa board of directors ordered *Kautschuk* withdrawn from commercial release: "Mr. Zimmermann reports about an order by the Reich Film Chamber, whereby all films which portray our enemies in a particularly favorable light will be withdrawn. From our films, the only one affected is *Kautschuk*, which glorifies the historical exploits of an Englishman. In consideration of this, the board of directors decides not to deliver the film *Kaut–schuk* for the time being."[36]

Barbara and Thomas in the desert: *Verklungene Melodie.*

At Home Abroad: *Verklungene Melodie* (1938)

Verklungene Melodie is a love story without a happy ending, a tale of missed opportunities and bad timing. Directed by Viktor Tourjansky and starring Brigitte Horney and Willy Birgel, the film traces the adventures, dreams, and disappointments of two people whose lives become intertwined in Algeria, Germany, and the United States. *Verklungene Melodie* passed the censor on February 22, 1938, and premiered three days later at the 1,200-seat Gloria Palast in Berlin, where it enjoyed a fairly successful run of twenty-eight days.[37] The film received mixed reviews and its box office performance ranged from a glowing success to a complete flop. The propaganda minis-try's official response was overwhelmingly positive; the film earned the rating of "artistically valuable" and also the propaganda minister's personal praise. Goebbels considered *Verklungene Melodie* "a sheer delight," even though he admitted, "the plot is sometimes extremely confusing and also illogical and not dramatic," adding: "But who demands everything from a film?"[38] Un-fortunately Tourjansky's film also earned a dubious reputation as the victim of "false laughter." In numerous cities throughout the Reich, *Verklungene Melodie* elicited a completely unexpected audience reaction; viewers inappro-priately laughed at serious or even tragic moments "based on the diminished suggestive power of the film image."[39] One commentator described false laughter as a serious problem because "an individual reaction which at the outset is without the general resonance of the public," eventually "interrupts and impedes the commonality of the mass psychic experience, the *experien-tial net,* which spins a web for all viewers."[40] What was it about this film that could elicit such varied responses?

Verklungene Melodie begins in 1932 at an Algerian airport in the Saharan desert where all commercial flights are canceled due to an impending sand-storm. German businessman Thomas Gront (Willy Birgel) decides to fly his own plane back to Berlin because the New York stock market crisis poses an even greater threat to his existence than the storm. A young German woman, Barbara Lorenz (Brigitte Horney), begs him to take her along because her child is sick and alone in Berlin. He reluctantly agrees, but soon after they take off, the sandstorm forces them to crash land in the desert. Barbara confesses that she lied about having a sick child because she wanted to go to Germany to become an actress. Alone in the desert with only minimal supplies, Barbara and Thomas cling to the hope of being rescued. Meanwhile in Berlin, Tho-mas's brother Werner (Carl Raddatz) tries to mount a search party but is unsuccessful because an unscrupulous reporter eager for headlines has invented a story that Thomas vanished with a mysterious woman to avoid paying his mounting debts. The officials refuse to search for Thomas if he willingly disap-peared, and his girlfriend Olga will not sell her valuable pearls to finance a private search party. Despite the intrigues, Thomas and Barbara are rescued and return to Berlin, where Barbara moves in with the wealthy Gront brothers and attends drama school. Werner tries to win Barbara's affection, but she is hope-lessly in love with Thomas, who lives for his work and does not want to settle down. After dancing to the Midnight Waltz, Barbara confesses her true feelings to Thomas, but he does not reciprocate her love and insists they remain just friends. Thomas only recognizes his mistake too late; Barbara has fled into the night, and his search for her the world over is to no avail. Years later he hap-pens to meet her by chance in New York City, where she is living with her husband and young son, Bobby. Now Barbara really does have a sick child, and her husband is out of town, so Thomas helps her care for the little boy. Taking on the role of the absent father and dancing again to the Midnight Waltz, Thomas falls in love with Barbara, and they make plans to run off together to Germany. However, at the last minute Barbara realizes that she cannot go with Thomas because her husband and child need her. The melody has faded and responsibility wins over passion.

Contemporary critics noted that *Verklungene Melodie* is set in three different countries and even partially shot on location in Africa, but it seems to operate in a never-never land beyond the here and now. Writing for *Licht-Bild-Bühne* Ludwig Eberlein argued that Tourjansky's travel adventure did not examine the foreign in a realistic manner: "Although these scenes were genuinely filmed on location in the Sahara, the director dwells on the cinematically fertile situation only as long as absolutely necessary for the development of the plot and the main characters. The remaining venues — Berlin and New York — never become part of the events. They always remain the backdrop for a tender chamber play carried by Brigitte Horney and Willy Birgel."[41] Indeed, the main characters travel to exotic locales, but the foreign functions more as a mirror to the inner self than as a reflection of the outer world. Following the adage: "The shortest path to the self leads around the world," Barbara's and Thomas's foreign adventures reveal their connections to *Heimat*.[42] Their travels conform to what Richard Phillips has identified as a typical aspect of the adventure genre: "Unknown, distant spaces of adventure are vehicles for reflecting upon and (re)defining domestic, 'civilized' places. . . . In the liminal geography of adventure, the hero encounters a topsy-turvy reflection of home, in which constructions of home and away are temporarily disrupted, before being reinscribed or reordered, in either case reconstituted."[43]

The vast Saharan desert becomes a blank canvas on which Barbara paints a picture of German national identity. The plane crash leaves the two travelers completely lost in the endless wasteland, and Thomas laments that his maps are useless because he cannot locate any landmark to orient himself. Barbara uses her internal map of German landscape and culture as a reference point to plot who she is rather than where. As the daughter of German colonists growing up in Maroua, Cameroon, Barbara diligently memorized an old city map of Berlin. She knows all the streets so well she can accurately describe the route from the Friedrichstrasse train station to the Staatstheater on Gendarmenmarkt and the Deutsches Theater in the Schumannstrasse. Although she has never been to Germany, she has internalized its geography and can conjure up her spiritual home from the sand dunes of North Africa. The former German colonist transforms the French colonial empire of Algeria into German soil and a fertile site to nurture Germany's glorious past. She fills the empty landscape with classical German culture when she recites Joan of Arc's final soliloquy from Friedrich Schiller's tragedy *The Maid of Orleans* (Die Jungfrau von Orleans, 1801). Kneeling before the roaring campfire, her eyes lifted toward the stars, Barbara assumes the identity of the legendary French female warrior who fought for her nation and died for her beliefs:

> Do you see the rainbow in the sky? Heaven has opened its golden gates. There she stands radiant in the choir of angels. She holds the eternal son at her breast. Laughingly she stretches her arms out to him. She waves to me. Soft clouds lift me. The heavy armor becomes a winged gown. Upward, upward, the earth flies back. Pain is brief, joy is eternal.[44]

Just as Barbara transformed French colonial soil into German territory through memory and dreams of a future empire, she now appropriates French history and redefines it as German by reciting the words of one of Germany's greatest playwrights. The German language overcomes the boundaries of time and space and can place universal heroic values in the immortal realm of eternity. Barbara's ability to appropriate foreign history and soil by asserting her German cultural identity in 1932 suggests that Germany's humiliating loss of colonies after its defeat in the First World War can be rectified in the near future when the national community regains a sense of self.

Thomas does not recognize that Barbara's soliloquy stems from Schiller, and his ignorance of the classical tradition is merely the first indication that he has not yet learned what it means to be German. Moreover, Thomas seems ill trained for the rigors of foreign adventure, in contrast to Barbara, whose African childhood and experience as a colonial settler have prepared her for the strenuous task of survival in the wilderness. Unlike Thomas, she can distinguish between an airplane engine and the mysterious winds that make the desert sound like it is singing, and while he drinks a whole cup of their precious water supply, she merely wets her lips. Wolfgang Struck has noted that in this barren landscape Barbara and Thomas are far from social roles that prescribe gender identity: "The plane crash in the North African desert becomes a plunge into overpowering emotions and above all an alterity that reverses the usual roles. . . . She, the woman with more African experience, strong nerves, and powerful feelings, displays a sovereignty that allows her to become the protector of Gront, who tends toward panic."[45] The reversal of traditional gender roles, however, must be seen within the context of cultural awareness, because it highlights the supremacy of Barbara's value system. The female warrior associated with the past, born in the Africa of Germany's lost colonial empire and nurtured on the homeland's cultural heritage, is endowed with a self-awareness and national pride lacking in her modern male counterpart. As a pilot, businessman, and world traveler, Thomas may have mastered technology and exterior space, but he has yet to understand the interior realm of national identity. Thomas must still learn to see the value of home, family, and a shared cultural legacy, lessons Barbara knows intuitively.

The foreign as a projection screen for thoughts and memories of home was not limited to the film's narrative. The advertising campaign also highlighted this process in articles about the making of *Verklungene Melodie*. Several fan magazines published accounts of Tourjansky's film expedition to Algeria for location shooting at the oasis Biskra, but these reports do not present Biskra as a unique city with its own cultural identity. Instead reporters describe the city as a mirror for the European and a place where *German* culture unfolds. According to one observer, wandering around the city of Biskra, the traveler quickly finds the "European quarter with broad streets, grand hotels, cinemas, stores, and administrative buildings, even the opera house where *The Ring of the Nibelung* is performed and neon lights comparable to those of any European metropolis." When the travelers pass the chotts (huge salt lakes), they have a heated conversation about the German adventure writer Karl May (1842–1912), and when they see the Medrasen, King Jugurtha's tomb, it conjures up memories of high school Latin classes in the Germany of their youth.[46] The North African culture and landscape is so foreign to the Northern European that he finds it difficult to compare it to anything he knows. Cameraman Günther Rittau described his travels through the Sahara as so far from anything he had ever experienced before that; he felt as if he had entered the hereafter: "I was no longer on earth. Everything that I had seen and felt until now was behind me in this world. It was as if the airplane had carried me out of my life without losing my life. . . . Just a few minutes outside Biskra one can escape from this world. One only has to have the eyes for it and understand how to carry the double burden as merely half."[47]

The German *Heimat* Barbara and Thomas return to is strangely interior. Whereas the African location shots helped to create a desert dreamscape, the Babelsberg studio shots leave much of the modern metropolis to the imagination. The Berlin that Barbara and Thomas inhabit consists of luxurious venues like Thomas's villa, Olga's apartment, and the elegant nightclub or nondescript locales like a newspaper office and airport. These interiors have no cultural specificity and could just as easily be in Paris, London, or Hollywood. The city of Berlin was already well known to moviegoers from such cross-section films as *Berlin, die Sinfonie der Großstadt* (1927, Ruttmann) and *Menschen am Sonntag* (1930, Siodmak) and would figure prominently in the feature films *Wunschkonzert* (1940, Borsody), *Großstadtmelodie* (1943, Liebeneiner), and even *Unter den Brücken* (1945, Käutner). Considering all the attention given to the African expedition, the narrative emphasis placed on the German homeland, and the technical possibilities open to a film crew in Berlin, why is the German capital missing from *Verklungene Melodie*? Tourjansky's film only ventures out of the studio once, for less than a minute, to show an aerial shot of Berlin juxtaposed to similar shots of London, a Middle Eastern city, and New York City. In a review for *Der deutsche Film*, Hans Spielhofer lamented that *Verklungene Melodie* simply did not live up to its promise: "The film starts out in grand style and suddenly the viewer is startled to see that we have landed back in a chamber play."[48] By contrast,

Georg Herzberg argued in *Film-Kurier* that Tourjansky was a talented filmmaker who used documentary footage to achieve both impressive images and powerful metaphors: "The original use of city shots [Berlin, London, a Middle Eastern city, New York City] should be mentioned. Here Tourjansky demonstrates his strong sense for images. The call for Barbara resounds over the sea of buildings in cosmopolitan cities and illustrates the hopelessness of the search."[49]

I suggest the lack of location shots in Berlin has more to do with time than place. *Verklungene Melodie* begins in 1932 and ends six years later, the time sequence being marked by an English language newspaper in Algeria, a German newspaper in Berlin, and a New Year's celebration in New York. What is striking about the time sequence is that it conflates world events in 1932 and implies that they are interrelated. At the airport in Algeria, Thomas reads a newspaper with the conspicuous headlines "Panic on Wall Street, crash of untoward dimensions, industrials slump by 80%" and the German titles "1932 Schwarzer Freitag in New York." The reference to the New York stock market crisis of Friday, July 8, 1932, when the Dow Jones industrial average hit an all time low and stocks had lost 89% of their value since 1929, situates Barbara's and Thomas's first meeting at the height of the Great Depression. The German newspaper reflecting the nearly simultaneous reaction in Berlin to Thomas Gront's disappearance, however, is dated Saturday, November 12, 1932. The United States financial crisis that sent ripples around the world is equated with a period in German history characterized not only by massive unemployment but also by the Nazi party's fluctuating electoral fortune. In 1932 Germany suffered from six million unemployed workers, its industry was at 50% of capacity, and its volume of foreign trade sank to two-thirds of the 1929 level. Adolf Hitler had run for the presidency in popular elections on March 13 and April 10, 1932, and while he lost to Hindenburg, he had won 37% of the popular vote and was gaining widespread acceptance. In July, when the United States stock market bottomed out, the NSDAP enjoyed its greatest gains with 37% of the vote in the new Reichstag elections. However, by November 1932, the NSDAP suffered a major setback with a loss of thirty-four seats in the Reichstag. By placing the stock market crash four months after it occurred and one week after the November 6th election defeat, the loss of popular support for the Nazi party in Germany now coincides with the economic failure in the United States.

The Berlin sequence begins two months before the Nazi seizure of power on January 30, 1933, and is painstakingly dated but nearly devoid of any location shots or photographic references to geography. The attention to time coupled with the notable absence of geographic realism seems to imply that 1932 Berlin was not the time or place that best defined the German homeland. Home, as Anton Kaes has aptly stated, resonates "with emotional connotations almost to the breaking point: Heimat means the site of one's lost childhood, of family, of identity. It also stands for the possibility of secure human relations, unalienated, precapitalist labor, and the romantic harmony between the country dweller and nature. Heimat refers to everything that is not distant and foreign."[50] Tourjansky's film highlights the fact that 1932 Berlin was not the harmonious, familiar, and safe place most contemporary viewers would have called home. The emphasis on interior space underscores the nation's inner crisis of decadence, and the distant setting allows the film to present clichéd figures from the hated *Systemzeit* without implying that they still define German identity in 1938.[51] The negative types associated with the "decadent" Weimar Republic, especially the vamp, the yellow-press reporter, the dandy, and the dilettante, were not the sort of characters the Nazi regime wanted to associate with *Heimat*. Even the two most sympathetic figures, Thomas and Werner Gront, start out as immature men who are products of an "unheroic" time.

Thomas emerges as a figure with great potential but presently undeveloped, a man of unequal talents who has not yet mastered himself. On the one hand, he is a sophisticated man-about-town and powerful business leader with a commanding presence. On the other hand, he is nervous in the face of danger, succumbs to meaningless sexual relationships, and displays a serious lack of commitment to family. In 1932 Thomas is a restless wanderer bereft of several notable values essential to heroism and, as such, a man who owns a beautiful house but has no spiritual home. Thomas sees himself as a lone wolf, free to roam and battle the world on his own terms, and he tries to convince Barbara that he must remain unattached: "You don't know me. I live for something completely different. I have to fight. I need change. I can't stay put anywhere. I have to be free. I am an immense egotist. I've never felt the urge to be together with someone for long, and I never will. I want you to be happy, and you'll never be happy if you commit yourself to me."[52]

"National Actor" (*Staatsschauspieler*) Willy Birgel brought to the character of Thomas Gront his own star image as a man of contrasts whose rigid exterior carefully held in check his rousing desires. In a publicity biography published in 1938, Birgel was described as a man endowed with "a disciplined, passionate nature. He is very well groomed and a cavalier in the good sense of the knightly, self-confident and courtly man. . . . He has always been the elegant, smart, courageous, iron-like, obliging, coldly passionate player."[53] It is worth noting that during the Second World War, Birgel's image was modified to emphasize his service record in the First World War and to align his acting style with a soldierly role model. In 1940, biographers recast Birgel's earlier image to reflect the wartime needs: "The word cavalier would hit the nail on the head if it were not a bit too superficial and blurred. Something else would have to be added: the atmosphere of a man who is always in control. He loves, suffers, and renounces with attitude. He does not appear with grand gestures and ambivalent words. Birgel's acting style can almost be called soldierly. . . . He expresses feelings by suppressing them."[54]

Whereas the character of Thomas Gront is initially too manly and must learn to cherish family values, his brother Werner represents the other extreme, an overly cultured man who must learn to assert himself and show resolve. Unlike Thomas, Werner is well versed in German music and theater and appreciates his rich cultural heritage. However, his knowledge of art and his national pride are marred by dilettantism because he lacks talent and merely dabbles in the arts. His relationships with women are equally unstable and frivolous; he is excessively sentimental and falls in love with every woman he meets. Werner suffers from "a weak artistic nature" and is initially too immature to be seen as a viable suitor for the self-assured Barbara Lorenz.[55] The publicity campaign for *Verklungene Melodie* drew parallels between the film's plot and real life by emphasizing that Carl Raddatz, the actor playing Werner Gront, was a young and inexperienced man who in time would follow in Willy Birgel's footsteps. Reporters were quick to point out that Raddatz not only looked like Birgel, he was also the older actor's protegee. Birgel had seen Raddatz on the stage and had convinced the studio to give him a screen test. Writing for *Der deutsche Film*, Hans Spielhofer argued that Raddatz could be a leading man in the near future: "if he is strong enough to assert his individuality, and if he is not consigned to the role of socialite, then he can become the best representative of the type we so eagerly seek: the 'He-man' who is not a lout."[56]

In contrast to Thomas and Werner Gront, Barbara Lorenz is a strong, self-assured adventurer. Unlike her irresolute male counterparts, she combines the practical and sentimental nature so often touted as "steely romanticism." As the daughter of German colonists in Africa, Barbara inherited a pioneering spirit and the courage to battle unknown perils abroad. Her appeal and believability as a character were due in large measure to the actress who played her: Brigitte Horney. A publicity biography published shortly after *Verklungene Melodie*'s premiere characterized Horney as a rare talent whose exterior exuded "strength and health paired with charm and reason." Moreover, Horney was a natural choice to play the sympathetic adventurer Barbara Lorenz because the actress was herself "inwardly a woman with the constant desire for and the constant determination to embark on a great experience. She gives herself over completely to an adventure, whether she triumphs or perishes."[57]

This strong female figure differed substantially from the typical traveler featured in Nazi cinema. As Eric Rentschler has noted:

> In Nazi fables about travelers, characters come undone in the topographies of alien cultures. Roaming about puts one's identity and person at risk. Films in the Hitler era, no matter how mobile they might appear, typically bind protagonists to constrained frameworks, to studiously choreographed and restlessly codified scenarios. Individuals who ramble and meander are usually suspicious or tragic figures in Nazi cin-

ema — unless they are explorers out to forge new empires and extend the Reich's domain.[58]

Barbara Lorenz has little in common with a wanderer like Astrée Sternhjelm, played by Zarah Leander in the blockbuster Ufa film *La Habanera* (1937, Sierck). While Astrée is seduced by the foreign and nearly languishes from the exotic and erotic appeal of Puerto Rico, Barbara's adventures abroad are difficult and necessary to fulfill her mission of disseminating German culture, first as an actress and then as the wife of a musician. Although Barbara travels to distant realms, she always retains a strong sense of self and never loses sight of home as the highest value. Barbara shares more with a character like Renate Brinkmann in *Kongo Express* (1939, Borsody), a woman who travels to Africa in order to help her fiancé get back on his feet. Renate fails to save this alcoholic Frenchman from his savage existence, but she does manage to fall in love with a German man and return home with him. She functions as a beacon, bringing the light of civilization to the African jungle and leading her countryman back to where he belongs. According to the *Illustrierter Film-Kurier,* the German man needed the German woman to travel abroad because "he finds *Heimat* in her and with her he will conquer a new life!"[59] Renate, like Barbara, represents Germany, and it is her fate to lead the restless male wanderer home.

Traveling in *Verklungene Melodie* is much less about the foreign's seductive power than about the male protagonist's search for self and the woman's role as facilitator. The hero's maturation process between 1932 and 1938 coincides with Germany's reemergence as a great imperial power. Barbara's and Thomas's voyage from Algeria to Germany and on to the United States can be read as plotting their nation's trajectory to greatness. Just as the African sequence charts how Germany can overcome its diminished political role by asserting its cultural heritage, the Berlin sequence illustrates that the decadent *Systemzeit* failed to produce self-sacrificing heroes with strong ties to hearth and home. The American sequence likewise maps German identity in 1938 by granting the protagonists their private fantasies, however short-lived, before reminding them of their civic duty. America gives Thomas the opportunity to envision himself in the role of devoted father and husband, and although he fails to find personal happiness, he finally recognizes the value of home. In the New World, the German travelers come to grips with their responsibilities to the larger community; Barbara remains a settler in the United States while Thomas returns alone to the National Socialist fatherland. The United States, like Algeria and Germany, is not a real country but an imaginary site based largely on well-worn myths about America as the land of unlimited possibilities. Coming to the New World, the adventurer embarks on a journey into the unknown and encounters utopian alternatives.

In Tourjansky's film, America holds up a mirror for the German to see what he is not and to discover what he could become.

In the Third Reich, America conjured up a set of images prevalent since its European discovery: the new frontier, a nearly magical place where wishes come true, a vast untouched empire waiting for the taking, and a country unfettered by an entrenched social system or antiquated ways of thinking. New York City, in particular, with its massive skyscrapers and expansive urban landscape, represented the most positive and the most negative aspects of modernity. America had successfully harnessed the machine and mastered industrial production, liberating vast amounts of energy, and manufacturing everything from Coca-Cola to automobiles with seemingly effortless efficiency. As such it stood for progress and innovation, but this haven for engineers and businessmen could just as easily be a living hell for the poor and alienated masses. America also symbolized the worst extremes of capitalism and the industrial age. It was a soulless concrete jungle, a nation without culture and tradition, governed by a materialistic consumer-driven economy and a seductive mass entertainment industry that would devour the German *Kulturnation* if not held at bay.[60]

Nazi Germany's infatuation with and antipathy toward America found vivid expression in its cinema. Luis Trenker's celebrated film *Der verlorene Sohn* (The Prodigal Son, 1934) featured New York City as a beguiling menace, promising fame and fortune but delivering only squalor and humiliation. This cautionary tale about Germany's native son adrift in an urban nightmare and reduced to an anonymous face in the crowd was a powerful narrative that warned against the deadly allure of America and modernity. By contrast, Paul Martin's *Glückskinder* (Lucky Kids, 1936) offered up the conflicting and yet equally compelling scenario of the modern American city as a place where dreams come true. New York City is a fast-paced, exciting metropolis open to all sorts of madcap adventures and ever-changing identities.[61]

Tourjansky situates his celluloid America somewhere between these extremes; it is a land where one can experience utopian possibilities but not necessarily a conventional happy ending. The director confirms New York City's legendary status as an immense and potentially overwhelming urban space through stock footage of the harbor, skyscrapers, and crowded streets, but this city does not pose any immediate threat to the German traveler. When Thomas Gront arrives in America, he is not diminished by the vast cityscape; instead he immediately assumes a commanding presence. Tourjansky literally places Thomas above the fray by superimposing his image onto the New York Stock Exchange. Towering over the bustling trading on Wall Street, Thomas nods his approval like a lord surveying his kingdom and dominating all he sees. Entering the city from this privileged point of view, Thomas's encounter with the New World bodes well.

In the midst of Manhattan Thomas finds a piece of *Heimat,* first by meeting Barbara on the street and then by walking into a restaurant where the waiter just happens to come from Köpenick outside Berlin. After reminiscing with the couple about the beautiful German countryside in a distinctly Berlin dialect, the waiter offers Thomas the one thing he desired most of all in Africa, a home-cooked meal of pig's knuckles and beer. Coming home to the lost sounds, smells, and tastes of Germany is made possible in the far-off land of America. By their mere presence and resilient memory, the Germans occupy America and are able to translate foreign territory into native space, just as they did so effectively in Africa. *Heimat* then is a frame of mind without respect for national borders and, as Eric Rentschler has aptly suggested, "a mutable force, both durable and flexible, reaffirming one's place no matter where one goes, no matter when (or with whom one travels)."[62]

America continues to grant Thomas his wish for home and intimacy via a surrogate family. When Barbara must care for her sick child alone, Thomas assumes the responsibilities of the absent father and is rewarded with the family's affection. He is briefly given the opportunity to enjoy domestic bliss with the woman he can imagine as his wife and the child he has come to view as "our son." Barbara suggests that wish-fulfillment is part of the American way of life and that if Thomas joins in the New Year's celebration he can redefine himself: "People just want to forget, all their troubles, everything difficult. They are crazy. It is one single intoxication, in order to be happy just once."[63] Drunk on America, Thomas and Barbara readily embrace the dream of being happily married. America becomes the catalyst for Barbara to live out her enduring romantic fantasy and for Thomas to see his domesticated self as the utopian alternative to a barren and restless existence. However, the dream of freedom and happiness is just that, a dream that can never come true. In the light of day Barbara convinces Thomas that they must forsake personal fulfillment and accept their duty to others.

Verklungene Melodie ends in 1938 with the German man returning to the fatherland and the German woman staying abroad. This scenario of departure and arrival, separation from loved ones, and the reconfiguration of romantic couples played out in numerous motion pictures made in Germany between 1937 and 1939. However, Thomas's and Barbara's parting on the New York docks differs substantially from departure scenes in contemporary movies like *La Habanera* and *Kongo Express.* In these two films, the female characters reject their foreign lovers and return home with a countryman who offers them a more conventional, if less satisfying, romantic relationship. While the couples travel back to Europe, at least one of the lovers is torn by ambivalent feelings, recognizing the necessity of going home while yearning for the foreign and a place that grants them freedom and difference. In *La Habanera* and *Kongo Express* the protagonists purge themselves of the foreign as best they can and are rededicated to the homeland via the most stabilizing social relationship:

marriage to a fellow countryman. *Verklungene Melodie* offers up a different national narrative that suggests that one can serve the community and guarantee its endurance through self-sacrifice and separation. Barbara is already married to a German and duty-bound to her role as a modern pioneer, dedicated to her family and to her husband's mission of disseminating Germany's musical tradition throughout the American cultural wasteland. Thomas returns alone to his native soil still longing for the absent woman who embodies the German spirit. This man, who admitted early on it was in his nature to fight, has finally abandoned his egotism and seems to have grown into the role of a self-sacrificing, disciplined man who can leave his loved ones when duty calls. Renouncing personal happiness for the greater good, he faces an uncertain future in which he may be called upon to sacrifice even more for the homeland. Thomas seems destined for the role of Germany's protector as implied by the final background music, the sentimental nineteenth-century folksong "Muß i denn, muß i denn zum Städtle hinaus," long associated with lovers parting and soldiers going off to war.

Unlike the early *Heim-ins-Reich* movies like *Flüchtlinge* (1933, Ucicky) or *Ein Mann will nach Deutschland* (1934, Wegener), in which patriots clearly battle their way home to join in a national rebirth or defend their country from imminent danger, *Verklungene Melodie* grants the German traveler no triumphant return. Thomas leaves alone, resigned to his duty and a loser in the love game, while Barbara pioneers a new life filled with opportunities but devoid of happiness. Instead of romantic closure, the film presents viewers with an emotionally less satisfying morality play. Thomas has finally learned the lessons that Barbara knew all along: to settle down and honor Germany as a spiritual home no matter where one roams. Perhaps German audiences reacted to *Verklungene Melodie* with "false laughter" because the film conformed more to genre expectations of the melodrama than the adventure. The male protagonist seems an unlikely candidate for the soldierly role his heroic departure suggests. Moreover, the female protagonist, first envisioned as a warrior, remains a significantly stronger character than her male counterpart. She remains abroad not as a rambling adventurer but with a clear objective to nurture the people and values associated with home, and thus it is the woman who undergoes a transformation typically reserved for the hero in Nazi cinema. In the late 1930s, German adventure films increasingly featured a male adventurer who gives up his wayward travels to become a settler abroad.

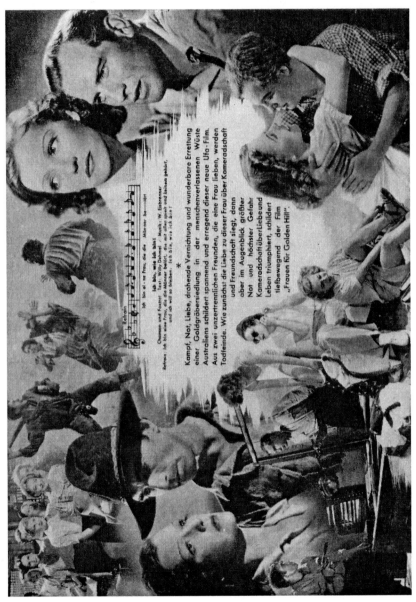

Program for *Frauen für Golden Hill* (1940).

The Quest for *Lebensraum:*
Frauen für Golden Hill (1938)

Erich Waschneck's *Frauen für Golden Hill* was neither a first-rate production nor a state-sponsored propaganda film, nor even a box-office blockbuster.[64] What makes this motion picture particularly interesting to scholars today is its commonplace function as a genre film in Nazi Germany's coordinated entertainment industry. *Frauen für Golden Hill* is a typical adventure film that uses well-worn character constellations and plot twists to advance a value system and behavioral patterns in keeping with National Socialist imperialist goals. This story about gold diggers in Australia extols the rewards of conquering foreign soil and promotes a pioneering spirit, population growth, exploitation of foreign resources, acquisition of *Lebensraum,* and the sacrifice of one's life for the survival of the folk. It likewise warns that the pursuit of individual desire endangers the entire community and represents a crime that can only be atoned with death.

The film passed the censor on December 21, 1938, and premiered nine days later in Frankfurt am Main at the Ufa-Theater im Schwan. On January 5, 1939, it premiered in Berlin at the Ufa-Tauentzien (1,025 seats) where it played for a mere twelve days.[65] Unlike *Kautschuk* and *Verklungene Melodie,* *Frauen für Golden Hill* was not budgeted for an expensive film expedition abroad. It was shot entirely in Germany at the Ufa studios in Babelsberg and on location in the Kurische Nehrung in East Prussia. Despite the lack of foreign location footage, *Frauen für Golden Hill* was promoted as a true-to-life adventure based on screenwriter Hans Bertram's own exploits. Bertram was a renowned pilot who had made several flights around the world and served as an air traffic advisor in China (1927–1933) before becoming a screenwriter and director. His autobiography *Flight into Hell,* detailing the harrowing experience of being stranded in the Australian desert after a plane crash in 1932–1933, was a thrilling bestseller that sold seven million copies.[66] Bertram's work in the adventure genre laid the foundation for his subsequent war films. Together with Wolf Neumeister, Bertram wrote the screenplay for *Frauen für Golden Hill* and for the fighter pilot adventure films *D III 88* (1939, Maisch) and its sequel *Kampfgeschwader Lützow* (Fighting Squadron Lützow, 1941, Bertram), which follow the lives of two young military pilots from their training days in the National Socialist Luftwaffe to combat in the Polish Campaign.

Frauen für Golden Hill follows the basic outlines of a typical Western. Thirteen gold diggers live in a makeshift village on Paradise River in the Australian outback and dream of one day hitting the mother lode. Tired of their wild and lonely existence, the men get drunk one night and write to Sydney for mail-order brides. All the men enlist except for Doug (Viktor Staal) and Stan (Karl Martell), two former air force officers who decide to go it alone, and

Cocky (pronounced Cookie), who abandoned his wife years ago and secretly signs up his reluctant friends as a joke. Officials in Sydney agree to send the women but insist that they marry the prospectors in absentia to avoid any squabbles. Since Doug and Stan did not sign their own names, Golden Hill's mayor (Otto Gebühr) is granted the right to conduct the wedding ceremony for the two remaining couples. The women arrive in covered wagons and are paired off with their new husbands. To Cocky's surprise, his wife Jenny (Grete Weise) is among the brides, so only one of the two remaining bachelors can lay claim to the beautiful chanteuse Violet (Kirsten Heiberg). Doug and Stan vow to forego marriage for the sake of their friendship, and Violet, a fortune hunter who intended all along to divorce her husband and leave with a treasure in gold, is happy with the situation but must wait until the rainy season to cross the desert. When a landslide forces the entire village to work together and unearth the water source, Violet and Stan pitch in but are quickly overcome by passion and make love on the mountain. Stan not only breaks his word of honor; he also shoots his best friend Doug in a drunken rage. The miners see no other solution but to banish Stan from Paradise River for violating the law of comradeship. Given six weeks worth of provisions, Stan leaves in disgrace with little hope of surviving the trek through the desert alone. Violet nurses Doug back to health, and after she reveals that she is pregnant with Stan's child, Doug promises to stand by her. When a landslide leaves the isolated village without water again, the prospectors and their families seem doomed to die of thirst. Miraculously, Stan, who reached the coast safely, hears that his friends are in danger and risks his life to save them. Flying through a blinding sandstorm, Stan uses his parachute to drop water to the villagers at Golden Hill and then radios their position just before his plane crashes. The miners arrive at the wreckage in time for Doug to forgive Stan and promise he will take care of both Violet and his friend's unborn child. Having redeemed himself through self-sacrifice and knowing he has fathered a child, Stan dies happily in his comrade's arms.

Waschneck's adventure film opens with idyllic images of male camp life that link it to Hans Steinhoff's *Hitlerjunge Quex* (1933), Leni Riefenstahl's *Triumph des Willens* (1935) and later war films, military newsreels, and soldiers' amateur movies where military life is akin to a weekend outing with the boy scouts. Steinhoff's propaganda film and Riefenstahl's infamous "documentary," two widely seen films in Nazi Germany, both depict campground scenes where young male party members happily fend for themselves and demonstrate their self-sufficiency and domestic skills as well as physical strength and male vigor.[67] The miners in Waschneck's adventure film resemble the party ranks, living in huts, toting water, bathing in a barrel, and cooking canned rations of corned beef. What binds both sets of men, the party ranks and the fictional miners, is camaraderie, cleanliness, and hard physical labor. The miners adhere to the basic tenets of the National Socialist

Männerbund; they form a union of men devoted to each other and a common cause, who are irreversibly shaped by a shared experience of combat.
Das Programm von heute singled out the former servicemen Doug and Stan
as paragons of virtue whose intimate relationship is laced with homoerotic
tension: "They are bound to each other for life and death by an old flying
comradeship; they also did not want any women."[68] The trope of two men
wed to each other for life because of their military commitment and their
subsequent battle over a woman are generic events common to German
adventure and war films of the 1930s and 1940s.[69] These stock figures and
dependable story lines conform to classical cinema's narrative conventions,
but they also reveal one of the Nazi regime's most persistent fears: homosexuality as a potential threat to the *Männerbund.* The party elite worried
that in this tightly bound fellowship where men worshiped power, virility,
and a strapping male body, homosexual desire would be a logical, if unwel-
come, outcome. While the National Socialists defined homosexuality primarily in terms of decadency, sickness, and pestilence, and rigorously
enforced Paragraph 175, punishing male homosexual intercourse with imprisonment in jails and concentration camps, their utmost concern was less
with the practice itself than its negative effect on population growth and
military dominance. In 1937 the director of the Reich Headquarters for
Combating Abortion and Homosexuality stated: "Since experience shows
that homosexuals are useless for normal sexual intercourse, homosexuality
also has an effect on the next generation and will inevitably lead to a drop in
the birth rate. The result of this is a weakening of the folk's general strength,
which endangers, not least of all, a folk's military significance."[70] Healthy
Aryan men were expected to reign in any carnal desires that proved to be
unproductive because their first duty to the state was to father children for
future military service. The motion picture *Frauen für Golden Hill* provides
a light-hearted story and appealing background to illustrate the important
lesson of how homoerotic pleasure is successfully channeled into procreation. In essence, the *Männerbund* evolves into the *Volksgemeinschaft.*

In the exclusively male environment of the mining camp, the prospectors
are starved for female attention and indulge in a form of entertainment that
affords voyeuristic pleasure, interracial desire, and homoeroticism. Crossing
sexual and racial boundaries, the black barkeeper Josua dons a skirt, swings
his hips, and tap dances to the syncopated rhythms of "Little Black Sweetheart" as the white male on-screen audience looks on in delight. Dancing in
drag but surrounded by pin-ups, advertisements, and magazine clippings
featuring women in provocative poses, the black man is the specular object
of desire and visually doubled. The camera cuts from a pin-up of a laughing
woman beckoning the viewer closer to a shot of Josua in a similar pose and
then to a portrait of the ever-smiling Mona Lisa. These enticing images drive
the men wild until the miner Bully shoots at Josua standing in front of the

images and stops the performance in a violent, explosive discharge. The miners quickly subdue Bully and confess that they are ashamed of their decadent lifestyle. Although they enjoy the collective delights of drinking, smoking, and gazing at exotic, erotic images, they see these forbidden pleasures as dangerous and admit that they need women to tame them. As one writer for *Filmwelt* described the situation at Golden Hill, the prospectors needed women because "the eternal feminine is the natural and necessary linchpin of masculine existence, the incentive and balance."[71]

Josua's nightly ritual reveals homoerotic tension in the *Männerbund* and also addresses the seductive entertainment of violated boundaries closely associated with Weimar Germany. His performance is reminiscent of the *Negerbälle* of the 1920s, where nightclub patrons would appear in blackface and dance the Charleston to American jazz, and also the gender-bending transvestite balls "that customarily marked Berlin Weimar's erotic vitalism, its taunting masquerade of tangled and flipped carnal lust."[72] African-American entertainers such as the Chocolate Kiddies and Josephine Baker performed to eager crowds in Berlin in the twenties, where they were seen as refreshingly savage creatures whose primitive sexuality, rhythmic music, and free-flowing dance could help to vitalize a petrified European culture.[73] Conversely, American blacks were vilified as a dangerously barbaric force that could destroy Europe if allowed to unleash their untamed libidinous drives.

Josephine Baker, in particular, seemed to fulfill disparate fantasies, embodying both savage sexuality and cosmopolitan modernity, a monstrous being without a stable identity, neither male nor female, animal or human. Upon seeing Baker perform *La Danse sauvage* in 1925, one Parisian commentator described her indeterminate nature in terms that border on horror: "Woman or man? Her lips are painted black, her skin is the color of bananas, her cropped hair sticks to her head like caviar, her voice squeaks. She is in constant motion, her body writhing like a snake or more precisely like a dripping saxophone. Music seems to pour from her body. She grimaces, crosses her eyes, puffs out her cheeks, wiggles disjointedly, does a split and finally crawls off the stage stiff-legged, her rump higher than her head, like a young giraffe."[74] The reaction to Baker was similar in Berlin, where she first appeared in *La Révue Négre* at the Nelson Theater in the winter of 1925–1926 and then performed in her notorious banana skirt at the Theater des Westens in 1928. Social critic Theodor Lessing was transfixed by Baker's ambiguity, declaring "she dances so primitively and genderless, that one doesn't know if one is watching a girl or a lovely boy."[75] White Europeans saw this black woman-man as the necessary actor in a colonial fantasy, where the foreign body rather than wild landscape is the territory to traverse and dominate. Explaining why African-American performers fascinated European audiences so intensely in the roaring twenties, one contemporary reviewer remarked:

Our romanticism is desperate for renewal and escape. But unknown lands are rare. Alas, we can no longer roam over maps of the world with unexplored corners. We have to appease our taste for the unknown by exploring within ourselves the lands we haven't penetrated. We lean on our own unconscious and our dreams. These blacks feed our double taste for exoticism and mystery. . . . We are charmed and upset by them, and most satisfied when they mix something upsetting in with their enchantments.[76]

Unable to explore unknown places, the modern urban adventurer seeks titillation in a troubling entertainment in which the borders between black and white, male and female, are blurred to allow a chimerical journey of self-exploration.

Josua's erotic dance number in *Frauen für Golden Hill* bears the imprint of an upsetting enchantment associated with Josephine Baker, African-American jazz performers, and the excesses of Weimar revue. This black transvestite dancer closely resembles Baker, whose image was widely circulated in German fashion magazines, on postcards, in stage parodies, and even as a doll in the late twenties. Although National Socialists and other conservatives denounced Baker as a depraved and dangerous racial inferior when she appeared in Berlin, Munich, and Vienna in 1928, her image circulated in burlesque form throughout the 1930s. Baker continued to be recognized in the visual culture of the Third Reich, parodied, for example, as a mysterious woman in blackface dressed only in a banana skirt in the 1937 musical revue *Maske in Blau*, which played at Berlin's Metropol Theater.[77] Despite official condemnation by the party elite, African-American music and dance steps had a profound and lasting effect on the German cultural scene. The propaganda ministry officially banned jazz from German radio in 1935 and mounted a rigorous campaign against "negerjazz" as insidious and pernicious anti-music, culminating in the May 1938 Degenerate Music exhibition in Dusseldorf. By conflating African-Americans with Jews to create a hybrid racial monster of mammoth proportions, advertised through an exaggerated caricature of a saxophone-playing Negro with a Star of David on his lapel, the regime hoped to persuade the German public that jazz was the cultural outgrowth of inferior races. However, despite the official disdain and numerous measures to ban jazz, the public demanded this musical idiom and so the cultural industry consistently made concessions to popular taste. German musicians routinely played milder versions of American dance music or merely changed the names of compositions by African-Americans or Jews. Isolated black performers such as trumpeter Herb Flemming played at Berlin's Sherbini Bar, and nightclubs like the Quartier Latin and the Ciro Bar offered "Negro jazz and dance" to an international clientele until the late 1930s.[78]

Although *Frauen für Golden Hill* is set in Australia, the character of Josua looks and dances like an African-American and is visually aligned with commodified sexual images associated with both Hollywood and Weimar girl culture.[79] The cross-dressing black man mirrors the white female pin-up, suggesting a similarity between deviant sexuality and commercially circulated media images of a bygone era and foreign realm. Nazi Germany's uneasy relationship with American (un)culture and its contempt for the lewd musical shows that swept its own theaters by storm just a decade earlier are employed in this motion picture as a critique of sex for sale. Marketing sexual pleasure is maligned as unnatural, but, as one character tells us, selling women for marriage and procreation is not only good business, it is morally right: "Finally the men out there have come up with a sensible idea [to buy wives]. . . . This is the most moral business deal the firm C. P. Barryman has ever made. Thirteen lonely men want to enter into the holy sacrament of matrimony."[80]

As a complement to Josua's dance and a further illustration of the deleterious effects of specularized eroticism, Violet (played by Kirsten Heiberg) appears in a sexually charged musical number. Her performance relies on prevalent notions of the vamp to identify her as a money-hungry spider woman intent on using her sexual power to steal a fortune from her unsuspecting prey. In an interview made during the filming of *Frauen für Golden Hill*, actress Kirsten Heiberg admitted it was delightful to play a real "vamp" and explained her character's simple moral transformation: "a selfish superficial woman turns into an upstanding, good comrade."[81] Imitating both Zarah Leander and Marlene Dietrich, Heiberg struts around stage in a revealing evening gown, a cigarette dangling from her mouth, while singing in the low-pitched voice and presentation style of her predecessors: "I am a woman, who beguiles men, who plays with them all and belongs to none." Her admission, "I have a smile that no one understands, that attracts men like a magnet," links her thematically to Josua's earlier performance in front of the Mona Lisa, but it also echoes Marlene Dietrich's famous line from *Der blaue Engel* (1930, Sternberg): "Men swarm around me like moths to the flame and if they burn up, I'm not to blame."[82] Equally obvious are the parallels to Zarah Leander in *Zu neuen Ufern* (1937, Sierck), where she starred as the singer Gloria Vane, who is banished to an Australian penal colony and released only when she agrees to marry the upstanding farmer Henry Hoyer.[83] Heiberg shared with Leander a Scandinavian heritage, a deep, almost masculine voice, and a similar stage persona as a sexual predator. Their characters undergo a comparable transformation from femme fatale to faithful wife and even end up with the same man, since actor Viktor Staal played both the farmer Henry and the miner Doug. Contemporary film critics argued that Heiberg functioned as a Leander stand-in. Writing for *Film-Kurier*, Günther Schwark acknowledged that "in her chansons [Heiberg] noticeably emulates Zarah Leander's performance style."[84] Most importantly, both female protagonists are purged of self-centered aspirations and conform to their future husbands' needs. Just as Gloria gives up her romantic dream and literally settles down as a pioneer wife, Violet concludes her song of seduction with a bitter note of things to come, "in this world it is planned that one quickly forgets his dreams. I imagined life quite differently, but I will take it as it is."[85] Pragmatism laced with resignation is a guiding principle in Nazi cinema, played out in numerous story lines that teach characters and viewers alike to mold their dreams to the contours of a harsh reality.

The mail-order brides have an immediate civilizing effect on the miners and shape more than just manners or the household routine. After the women arrive at Golden Hill, the rough and tough fortune hunters no longer dream of finding gold so that they can gamble, drive a Rolls Royce, and buy the favors of dancehall girls in Sydney. In their new roles as husbands and fathers, the miners reformulate their concept of utopia and begin to see that the greatest riches are to be found in family ties. Hard physical labor and a common cause continue to form the glue that binds the community together, and the women are expected to do their share. Rather than performing for men as specularized objects of desire or providing them with erotic pleasures, women's energy and sexuality must be put to practical purposes, first through work and then by producing children. As Jenny notes, the formula is clear-cut: "In a gold mining camp they need women, simple women, who also know how to work."[86] This community places little value on sentimentality. The one overly romantic woman who naïvely gushes, "I imagine it is marvelous to live out there in the boundless solitude with a man for whom you can be everything," suffers the greatest disappointment.[87] As if punished for imagining an idyllic love affair, she ends up married to the grandfatherly one-armed mayor who only wanted a mother for his adolescent son. A happy marriage, it seems, is not based on love or romance but on sharing hardships, because as the minister advises: "There are thousands of things that can break up a marriage. But it has been my experience that only one thing binds two people together closely and ardently: you have to have the opportunity to help one another."[88]

The prospectors and their brides are quickly given the opportunity to join forces when a landslide cuts off their water supply. The entire community goes out to the cliffs beyond the village, men and women marching up the mountain single file with their shovels to battle against nature. Waschneck utilized camera techniques often featured in Nazi era newsreels to conjure up the heroism and beauty of work. The villagers are shot in silhouette against the rolling hills and in extreme long shots as they trek through the barren but majestic landscape. These well-known characters are suddenly decontextualized, anonymous ranks in the distance reduced to their function as workers. When they reach the blocked water source and begin to lift the rocks, the scene is filmed in a rapid series of low angle shots magnifying the workers' size and strength and in close-ups of their enormous hands and arms with the muscles straining from the exertion. The sequence takes on further significance as a mythic event through the setting, since the rugged mountain terrain represents the ternary origins of life; it is the natural source of water, the sacred site of communal struggle, and the symbolic location of human desire. Just as water gushes from the rocks to satisfy the villagers' basic needs, Stan makes loves to Violet on the mountain and impregnates her.

Stan's unbridled behavior on the mountain of desire is not a sudden lapse in judgment but reflects his overall temperament and tragic flaw: his inability to control his base instincts. The miners respect Stan as "an upstanding fellow," a former air force captain, like Doug, who served on the front for two years and still upholds his commitment to martial values. Both men wear their service uniforms like a second skin and enjoy the gestures of military life, saluting each other, drinking to comradeship, and believing in the sanctity of a man's word of honor. When Stan swears to Doug that "Violet is a nice fellow but our comradeship is worth more to me" and agrees that "the woman has to be untouchable for us," his friend expects him to stand by his word.[89] What separates Stan from Doug is his unruly nature; he is a *Triebmensch*, a man who blindly follows his urges. While Doug is flawlessly dressed and squeaky clean, Stan is slightly unkempt, his oily hair falling in his face, constantly lighted a shade or two darker than Doug and wearing shirts that are darker, wrinkled, and never fully tucked in. And although Doug always remains sober and self-constrained, Stan loses self-control easily, drinking and smoking to excess, and quickly resorting to violence.

Stan commits the gravest crime when he breaks his word of honor and shoots his friend in a duel. Golden Hill's elderly mayor, played by actor Otto Gebühr, who starred in countless motion pictures as Germany's legendary leader Frederick the Great, speaks for the entire community and, by extension of his famous screen persona, for the German nation. Standing before the assembled miners, the mayor pronounces the collective verdict: "You have transgressed against our highest law. You raised a weapon against a comrade. We do not have the authority to sit in judgment of you, but we want nothing more to do with you."[90] As in so many feature films of the Nazi period, the characters in Waschneck's film maintain that there are unwritten laws and a basic honor code known to all members of the community. Adherence to this honor code outweighs any other moral or judicial authority, including the written law of the state. Expelled from Paradise River for breaking the commandment of comradeship, Stan has fallen from Grace and can only redeem himself through martyrdom.

The very definition of community (*Gemeinschaft*) in Nazi Germany was predicated on the notion that all members must be willing to sacrifice any personal desire and even their lives to ensure the survival of the whole. What better forum to preach this creed than in motion pictures personalizing basic beliefs in familiar stories that can easily be recognized as parables without destroying their value as entertainment. In 1940, film critic Felix Henseleit chronicled how important movies were in disseminating the idea that sacrifice is at the foundation of any community. Henseleit noted: "The idea of community is visible and recognizable in all those films in which a person fulfills his duty to the community by showing himself ready and willing to sacrifice himself totally. We always sense there the law that keeps a folk alive, the law of community, of unconditional comradeship."[91] In *Frauen für Golden Hill*, self-sacrifice and adherence to the law of comradeship result in two important outcomes: first, the community is saved from certain death, and second, the fallen sinner redeems himself. Stan's heroic flight to locate his friends at Paradise River, his selfless act of using his only parachute to drop water and thus not being able to jump to safety, means that the villagers will survive and that Stan is a worthy comrade in the end.

Stan's death is staged with all the clichés of Nazi cinema and its militarized Christian iconography. Surrounded by his comrades in a pieta of the dying savior, his crashed upright plane forming the cross of martyrdom on the mountain where he originally sinned, Stan dies a hero's death. The martial overtones outweigh the religious symbolism, when Doug looks up to the heavens suddenly filled with a squadron of six planes in formation and salutes his fallen comrade. The film program spelled out the hard but just consequences of Stan's actions: "Admittedly, [Stan] had to give up his life, but his act of rescuing the entire community wiped out his guilt to his friend."[92]

Along with the highly militarized heroes and themes that make this adventure film a typical product of the Third Reich, *Frauen für Golden Hill* relies heavily on the Hollywood Western for plot, character, and setting. American popular culture plays a significantly larger role in Waschneck's film than the vague Australian setting, but what both New World countries share is the myth of frontier life, a place where a lone man can live free and search for riches beyond his dreams in El Dorado. The gold rush and Western settings exerted an unusual fascination on German audiences in the 1930s, not merely in motion pictures such as *Der Kaiser von Kalifornien* (1936, Trenker), *Sergeant Berry* (1938, Selpin), *Gold in New Frisco* (1939, Verhoeven), and *Wasser für Canitoga* (1939, Selpin), but also on stage in Axel Iver's popular comedy *Wildwest-Lustspiel* and in various forms of popular entertainment. Berlin's gigantic pleasure palace "Haus Vaterland," for example, promised its patrons "a cheap vacation" in its Wild-West Bar, where cowboys in ten-gallon hats served American cocktails in a saloon surrounded by a cactus-lined prairie, cowgirls danced the Shimmy, and blackface minstrels performed American jazz.[93] A reviewer for *Filmwelt* noted that the wild-west adventure, "closely tied to danger, predicament, struggle, and ultimately victory, inspires a surprisingly enthusiastic response today. . . . And there are deeper reasons when we talk today about the exciting search for gold as the epitome of adventure, as the classic adventure per se."[94] While the reviewer left those deeper reasons unspoken, surely the gold rush's allure revolves around the notions of conquest, personal freedom, and adherence to a strict honor code. Gold prospecting represents man's universal struggle against nature and his ability to extract wealth directly from the earth through physical labor and enterprise. Panning for gold requires men with pioneering spirits and a combination of strength, flexibility, daring, and perseverance. Their rewards are not merely riches but also the personal freedom afforded by wide-open spaces and the promise of a new way of life. The western's philosophy of honor may have appealed to German audiences (and the propaganda ministry) in the late 1930s because it so closely resembled the value system espoused by National Socialism. The lone cowboy is endowed with a simple moral compass of polarized good and evil, believing in adherence to a higher law, gallantry among equals, the need to secure boundaries against a common enemy, and the white man's right to territorial expansion without respect to the interests of native inhabitants. Historian Hans Dieter Schäfer maintains that the Western film genre reflected the Nazi regime's expansionist goals particularly well: "The National Socialists felt their own dreams of being 'armed colonists' conquering new land in the East were substantiated by the Americans' 'daring thirst for action' and their conquest of the Golden West."[95]

The Western, like the *Heimatfilm,* is about conquering and defending land. Because man's relationship to the natural world is more obvious in the Western than in many other genres, it provides an exemplary setting to act out the Nazi concept of *Lebensraum* (living space). In German films of the late 1930s, adventurers increasingly become settlers. While they begin their journey in search of valuable ground for mining, they are typically rewarded with fertile soil for farming. The gold digger settles down to run a sawmill (*Gold in New Frisco*), the prospector becomes a farmer (*Frauen für Golden Hill*), the oil-rigger leaves the sea to manage a hacienda (*Brand im Ozean*). As one commentator for *Filmwelt* concluded, the German adventurer "never gives up hope of one day having earned enough to return home where he came from. Because to a real fellow it is a matter of not losing his home, if destiny should detain him as a pioneer in a foreign country."[96]

In the course of Waschneck's film, the miners learn the value of home and come to realize that their quest for material wealth is meaningless when compared to protecting what really counts: family and friends, self-respect and honor. These fortune hunters first thought only about finding gold and spending their wealth on decadent pleasures. Then they thought about finding wives and settling down to raise children. What they should have thought about was the need to secure their borders and obtain sufficient natural resources for survival. Whereas the first landslide helped the villagers to build a sense of identity as a community, the second landslide destroyed their homes and nearly killed them. In the aftermath of this catastrophe, the villagers demonstrate that they understand the crucial link between blood and soil and that their identity and survival are closely bound to the land they inhabit. In a remarkable scene that makes concrete the concept of *Blut und Boden,* the men and women of Golden Hill lie down on the ground and use their bodies to spell out the word "water" for the airplane flying overhead. Literally inscribing their needs onto their bodies and their bodies onto the soil, the villagers have found the formula that will ultimately save them. Along with redefining their relationship to land, they learn that they need to protect themselves against exterior threats. Although natural forces devastated the mining village, since the storm came immediately after Stan's betrayal, it seems to indicate that a weak community without honor and cohesion is doomed to failure. Another significant obstacle facing the group is that they do not have a strong enough leader to take the problem in hand. The one-armed mayor is a respected authority figure but simply too old and too weak to protect the community from its own interior weakness of unbridled passions or prepare it to fight against exterior perils. Men like Bully and Stan are strong but undisciplined, governed by their momentary impulses and unfit to lead. Doug alone seems to have the potential to step forward in the end and take the reigns of power. The important lessons on building a successful community are not lost on the villagers, and their plans for the future are clear: "There is enough water to start out tomorrow on the march to the coast, the march with wife and child to a country where there are fields and meadows, fountains and ponds."[97] The men and women of Golden Hill recognize that the true treasure is not gold but home. Having reconstructed their collective utopian dream and armed with the knowledge of how to survive as a community, they seem destined to find, occupy, and defend the living space they need.

The formulaic structure, predictable plot twists, model characters, and obvious ideological lessons found in *Frauen für Golden Hill* failed to win the approval of a mass audience through abundant ticket sales or the full endorsement of the state-coordinated critical community. Some observers like Felix Henseleit praised the film for its gripping realism, arguing that "although adventurous and unusual things happen here, the viewer always has the feeling that he is not standing *outside* the events, that they do not remain foreign to him, yes, that he too could in the end experience them *himself*."[98] Others like Ilse Wehner in a scathing review for *Der deutsche Film,* the official journal of the propaganda ministry, argued that making motion pictures with a conspicuous lack of imagination and such obvious ideological intentions was a recipe for disaster:

> Mix together: one of the first sound films *Braut Nr. 68* with *Zu neuen Ufern* and what you get is called *Frauen für Golden Hill.* There are numerous improbabilities here. Thirteen pretty girls, elegantly dressed for the most part, are happy to follow the rough, drunken, gold diggers in their primitive existence as wives. That is, not to follow, because they marry them, without ever having seen them! And what a miracle! It works out. Everyone is happy. Add to the mix a woman between two men, a

vamp who is purified in the end and sings like Leander similar chansons in a similar, if not as well-trained, voice. And garnish it all with sand-storms, lack of water, and other catastrophes. And don't forget: loyalty to friends right up to self-sacrifice. By hell or high water it'll have to be a box office hit (at least the producers must have thought so).[99]

Wehner's remarks echo Goebbels's mandate that popular cinema must instruct without making the audience consciously aware of its intentions. When a motion picture relies too heavily on beloved formulas and its political message is too obvious, it fails as entertainment and as propaganda.

The Voyage Home

Johann Wolfgang von Goethe, who never traveled past Italy and remained most of his adult life in the city of Weimar, wrote in *The Elective Affinities* that one was occasionally filled with wanderlust and yearned to visit far-off lands. "Sometimes," he observed, "when a curious longing for such adventurous things seizes me, I have envied the traveler who sees such wonders in living connection with other wonders. But he too becomes another person. No one wanders unpunished among the palm trees, and attitudes surely change in a land where elephants and tigers are at home."[100] Goethe's cautionary remarks on the transformative power of travel hold true for the characters in German adventure films of the Nazi era; after embarking on a journey abroad, no one remains the same. To varying degrees, these adventurers change during their travels, discovering within themselves the strength to forsake personal aspirations and devote themselves completely to the greater good. The protagonists in adventure films serve as identification figures to train viewers in behavioral models that promote the value of imperialism.

Explorer Henry Wickham knows from the onset what he wants. His sole aim is to obtain a vital natural resource for his empire, and he is willing to do whatever it takes, even sacrificing his own life and freedom, to ensure that his country retains its position of economic and military dominance. Wickham readily understands that he is part of a larger community and that it is the average citizen's duty to protect his nation's interests. His conversion, therefore, does not encompass his relationship to others; instead it takes the form of a psychic journey to purge him of the dangerous attraction to wild territory. Literally sweating out his feverish desire for adventure, Wickham is restored to the healthy state of selflessness. Thomas Gront, by contrast, starts out as a restless wanderer who travels the globe to satisfy his own need for action but without a deeper sense of purpose. Enchanted by the ever-changing scenery and the sheer exhilaration of motion, Thomas fails to see himself as connected to other people or a special place. It is only with the

help of a deeply patriotic woman that Thomas can finally gain an appreciation of home and willingly sacrifice personal happiness for the welfare of
others. In a similar manner, the prospectors at Golden Hill begin as undisciplined men in the wilderness, intent on making a fortune so that they can
buy material and sexual gratification. With the arrival of wives and children,
the men tame their urges and recognize that they are united in a fellowship
of kindred spirits. Survival of the whole is only possible when individuals feel
connected and are willing to give up everything, including their lives, to
realize a collective dream. The rewards are worth the sacrifices because in the
end they share the greatest treasure of all: a secure and lasting home.

In *Kautschuk, Verklungene Melodie,* and *Frauen für Golden Hill,* home
does not necessarily mean the place of one's birth or childhood, or even land
within the shifting borders of the German Reich. Instead, home is a con-
ceptual place where one feels like one belongs, an emotional state where one
develops a sense of communal identity and forms a set of values that sustains
the collective. Because the adventurer perceives home as a belief that he
carries with him wherever he goes, home is de-territorialized, separated from
a fixed terrain, and possible everywhere. The age-old idea that home is where
the heart is has surprising political implications. The adventurer, who feels
he is part of something bigger than himself, something pure and essential
that transcends national borders and the physical limitations of space, believes that he has the right, if not the mission, to possess the soil he occupies.
As Jamie Owen Daniel has articulated so well, "The call 'Heim ins Reich'
was thus not intended to induce ethnic Germans who had been living for
generations in Poland or the Soviet Union to come 'home' to Germany
proper, but to restore any soil upon which Germans had lived in communities to its 'proper' place *as* Germany. Heimat thus understood and lived,
allowed Germans to figure utopia not as 'no place on earth,' but rather as
'any place on earth' where Germans had established communities."[101]

The Nazi concept of being rooted in the soil (*Bodenständigkeit*) did not
necessarily contradict the idea that home can be anywhere. What it meant
according to party ideologues was that Germans have a special relationship to
the soil they inhabit, an emotional connection that is so strong it becomes
physical. The Germans literally are Germany; the people do not merely occupy
the landscape, they are one with it. Gustav Ucicky's prized "film of the nation"
Heimkehr (Homecoming, 1941) about the Polish persecution of Volhynian
Germans in 1939 justified Hitler's invasion of Poland as a necessary measure
to stop the brutal treatment of German settlers abroad. It also presented one
of the most emotionally stirring depictions of blood and soil ideology in Nazi
cinema. Huddled together in a dark and dank Polish prison shortly before they
are to be massacred, the Germans lose hope of being rescued and fear that their
lives have been meaningless. The school teacher Maria Thomas, played by
National Actress (*Staatsschauspielerin*) Paula Wessely, who projected a trust-

worthy, capable, and sisterly screen persona, tries to rally their spirits by conjuring up a utopian vision of Germany and promising them a homecoming, if not in life, than certainly in death:

> Just think people, how it will be, just think, when all around us there will be nothing but Germans — and not, when you enter a store that someone is speaking Yiddish or Polish, but only German. And not just the whole village will be German, but everyone all around and far and wide will be German. And we, we will be in the middle, inside, in the heart of Germany. Just think, people, how that will be. And why shouldn't it be so? We will once again live on the good old warm earth of Germany. Back home and at home. And at night in our beds, when we wake up from sleep, suddenly in our hearts we will know with a sweet shock we are sleeping right in the middle of Germany, back home and at home, and all around is the comforting night, and all around a million German hearts beat as one and softly pound: Man, you are home, home, back home with your own. Then we will feel quite wondrous at heart, that the crumb of the field and the piece of clay and the fieldstone and the tall grass and the swaying stalk, the hazelnut branch and the trees, will all be German, just like us, belonging to us, because they have grown from millions of German hearts that have gone into the earth and become German earth. Then we will not only live a German life, we will die a German death. And even dead we remain German and a whole piece of Germany, a crumb of the field for our grandchildren's seeds, and out of our hearts the vine grows upward in the sun — in the sun, people, that does not hurt and scorch without at the same time granting its sweetness, and all around the birds sing, and everything is German, all the children, like our song. Don't you want to sing our song, especially now? [A chorus strikes up the sentimental folksong, "I want to go home again."][102]

While Maria recites her bittersweet bedtime story, the screen fills with close-ups of the melancholy but starry-eyed Germans who share her vision of home as a place of absolute homogeneity and social cohesion. Gathered together in the dark cavity of their underground prison and collectively dreaming about being buried on native soil, the Germans imagine that they can transcend the borders between birth and death, soil and folk, past and future to become one. The price for eternal sameness and security in Germania's womb is death.

The homecoming is an inevitable conclusion to travel, and an archetypal event celebrated in the Western literary tradition since Odysseus found his way home to Penelope. The German adventure film of the late 1930s also leads the protagonist home so that his travels are momentary excursions into the unknown. Framed by the familiar, the experience abroad takes on significance as an exciting exploit, but it is marked off from normal everyday life and self-contained. Viewers too are brought home, returned to their own reality after a few hours on a cinematic voyage. But as Goethe suggested, travel to foreign realms leaves an indelible print on the mind, so if it affects the protagonists it should also influence the viewers. Although adventure films conclude with narrative closure and a return to the familiar, they focus the vast majority of the time on an encounter with difference. How did these movies function in a society where ethnic uniformity was considered sacred, sameness was espoused as the highest social virtue, and marking difference was a national preoccupation?

Kautschuk, Verklungene Melodie, and *Frauen für Golden Hill* granted German audiences in 1938 and 1939 an unusual opportunity to experience freedom of movement and the thrill of encountering people and places normally considered inferior or off-limits. For the length of the movie, one could dwell in and on the foreign without fear of reprisal. *Verklungene Melodie* visits exciting and exotic locales, but with its sad story of Germans leaving loved ones in 1938, it also resonates at this historical juncture with the pain of exile. In a nation where family, friends, and neighbors were increasingly faced with the prospect of permanent separation, Schiller's sentiment "pain is brief, joy is eternal" could offer solace or cynical reflection. *Kautschuk* and *Frauen für Golden Hill,* on the other hand, present the exploration of foreign territory and foreign bodies as a highly seductive but generally lethal undertaking. In scenes of stunning visual beauty and psychological insight, these films illustrate for viewers the myriad of pleasures inherent in watching a spectacle of difference, yet in each instance the act of looking at foreign bodies and space is inscribed with violence or death. Did actual moviegoers embrace the pleasure in looking at the Other without taking the moral imperative too close to heart, or did they continuously divert their attention from such pleasures due to the inherent threat of retribution, or did the prospect of violent seduction heighten titillation? Did the propaganda ministry create such films exactly because they provided a relatively safe outlet for pent-up emotions and the need for non-conformity? These questions cannot be answered with certainty, but it is clear that adventure films in the Third Reich did contain potential channels for resistance. The strong social taboos against homoerotic, interracial, and xenophilic desire, while not entirely lifted, are momentarily suspended, so that one could safely indulge in forbidden pleasures. The adventure film requires the observer to locate difference; one must constantly compare the known to the unknown, home to abroad, the forest to the jungle, familiar animals to strange ones, Germans to natives. It is in this tension, stories preaching homogeneity yet filled with the spectacle of difference, that the adventure film uniquely addressed its audience's needs.

Notes

[1] Hollywood Westerns and action adventures starring Wallace Beery, Clark Gable, and Gary Cooper were especially popular in Nazi Germany. For an overview of American films in the Third Reich, see Markus Spieker, *Hollywood unterm Hakenkreuz: Der amerikanische Spielfilm im Dritten Reich* (Trier: Wissenschaftlicher Verlag, 1999).

[2] Gerd Albrecht, *Nationalsozialistische Filmpolitik: Eine soziologische Untersuchung über die Spielfilme des Dritten Reiches* (Stuttgart: Ferdinand Enke, 1969), 110. *Der deutsche Film*, the official organ of the propaganda ministry, cited the adventure-criminal film as the third most popular genre in 1939, behind the contemporary drama (*Gegenwartsfilm*) and the serious drama (*Dialogfilm*). These conclusions were based on a survey reflecting a small sampling of primarily male (65%) moviegoers. See Frank Maraun, "Das Ergebnis: Wirklichkeitsnähe bevorzugt: Eine Untersuchung über den 'Publikumsgeschmack," *Der deutsche Film* 3, no. 11 (May 1939): 310; and Egon Gürtler, "Weshalb gehen Sie in einen Film?" *Der deutsche Film* 3, no. 11 (May 1939): 316.

[3] Reviewer Paul Otto referred to *Kautschuk* as "diese[r] männliche[] Film der Entschlossenheit und Energie," "Ein Monopol wird gebrochen: *Kautschuk* im Ufa-Palast am Zoo" (n.p., n.d.), *Kautschuk,* Document File 8701, Bundesarchiv-Filmarchiv, Berlin. *Kautschuk* was also called "ein starker, männlicher Stoff, ein hohes Lied selbstloser Einsatzbereitschaft für ein hohes Ziel," "Filme des Monats," *Der deutsche Film* 3, no. 6 (December 1938): 163.

[4] René Deltgen (1909–1979) was described as "der kraftstrotzende Draufgänger" in *Urlaub auf Ehrenwort* and "ein überlegener Spion, der noch im heroischen Tod zu lächeln verstand" in *Port Arthur.* H. W., "Im Scheinwerfer: René Deltgen," Beilage zur *Filmwelt* 55 (n.d.), *Kautschuk,* Document File 8701, Bundesarchiv-Filmarchiv, Berlin. By contrast, in a biographical piece published shortly before the premiere of *Kautschuk,* Deltgen was portrayed as a happily married man and young father who bears little resemblence to his on-screen persona. The one personality trait the star shared with his adventurer roles was a mischievous nature, see "René Deltgen: Weg von der Landarbeit zur Bühne und zum Film," *Filmwelt* 43 (October 21, 1938). After the Second World War, Deltgen continued to play bold adventurers, starring for example as the evil Prince Ramigani in *Der Tiger von Eschnapur* and *Das indische Grabmal* (1959, Lang).

[5] Ernst von Salomon (1902–1972) was sentenced in 1922 to five years imprisonment for his involvement in the Rathenau assassination. Today's readers may be more familiar with Salomon's post-war publication *Der Fragebogen* (The Questionnaire, 1951), in which he publicly answered the 131 questions posed by the Allied Forces in the denazification process. *Der Fragebogen* caused a lively debate and was a best seller in the Federal Republic of Germany. Salomon also wrote the screenplays for *Sensationsprozeß Cassila* (1939), *Kongo-Express* (1939), *Carl Peters* (1941), and *Liane: Mädchen aus dem Urwald* (1956).

[6] Eduard von Borsody (1898–1970) attended a military academy before serving in the First World War as a lieutenant in a heavy artillery unit. In 1916 he was wounded in action and decorated. Borsody began his career as a cameraman in 1919 and

worked on such notable films as *Polizeibericht Überfall* (1929, cameraman for Ernö Metzner) and *Flüchtlinge* (1933, editor for Gustav Ucicky), starring Hans Albers as a German persecuted abroad who returns triumphantly to the fatherland. Borsody directed the adventure films *Brillanten* (1937), *Kongo-Express* (1939), and *Sensationsprozess Casilla* (1939) and also the home-front film *Wunschkonzert* (1940). After the Second World War, Borsody continued to make adventure films including *Sensation im Savoy* (1950) and the cult-classic *Liane: Mädchen aus dem Urwald* (1956). For a contemporaneous assessment of Borsody, see Hans-Ottmar Fiedler, "Tempo, Spannung, Atmosphäre: Der Spielleiter Eduard v. Borsody und seine Filme," *Filmwelt* 34 (August 23, 1940).

[7] "Mit Karl Hartl gehörte der Regisseur zu jenen (konservativen) Abkömmlingen der Donaumonarchie, die bei der Ufa das Genre des patriotischen Abenteuerfilms pflegten, ohne den 'staatspolitischen' Implikationen beizumessen. Sie bildeten ein Gegengewicht zu den reaktionären Kunst-Korporalen vom Schlage Karl Ritters und anderer." Klaus Kreimeier, *Die Ufa-Story: Geschichte eines Filmkonzerns* (Munich: Hanser, 1992), 332.

[8] *Kautschuk*, Censor-Card 49615, Bundesarchiv-Filmarchiv, Berlin. The censor cards provide a narrative description of the action but not the dialogues. All dialogues are taken from the videocassette copy of *Kautschuk* available in commercial release.

[9] "1. November 1938: Filme geprüft: "Kautschuk," Regie Borsody, mit Deltgen, v. Langen, Hübner und Dießl. Großartig politisch und künstlerisch. Eine Glanzleistung der Ufa." Joseph Goebbels, *Die Tagebüücher von Joseph Goebbels*, ed. Elke Fröhlich, Part I: Aufzeichnungen 1924–1942, 9 vols. (Munich: K. G. Saur, 1998), I. 6: 169.

[10] "Hamburg ist als Welthandelsplatz schon immer an der Behandlung kolonialer Probleme interessiert gewesen." Elisabeth Holz, "Festliche Hamburger Uraufführung von *Kautschuk*," *Licht-Bild-Bühne* 258 (November 2, 1938).

[11] "Berlins November Uraufführungen," *Licht-Bild-Bühne* 287 (December 7, 1938). *Kautschuk* cost 802,000 RM to make and brought in an estimated 1.8 million RM in box office receipts, see Albrecht, *Nationalsozialistische Filmpolitik*, 415 and 428.

[12] Henry Wickham is described as "beherrscht, verhalten, geistesgegenwärtig und tapfer." Hans Erasmus Fischer, "Filme, die wir sahen: *Kautschuk*," *Filmwelt* 48 (November 25, 1938). Wickham is characterized "von seinem Opfermut, von seiner Selbstlosigkeit, die persönlichen Eigennutz vollkommen ausschließt und alles für die Sache einsetzt, der er dient." Felix Henseleit, "*Kautschuk*," *Licht-Bild-Bühne* 264 (November 9, 1938).

[13] "Der Film *Kautschuk* steht zwischen Reportage und Fabel; er will einen spannungsvermittelnden und einen verständniserweckenden Eindruck vom Kampf zweier Länder um ein Handelsmonopol erwecken. . . . Die Fabel, die sich um die Urwald–szenen rankt, steht unter dem Motto: Verantwortung und Tapferkeit gehören zum Schmuck des Mannes." Hans Hömberg, "*Kautschuk* Premiere im Ufa-Palast am Zoo" (n.p., n.d.), *Kautschuk*, Document File 8701, Bundesarchiv-Filmarchiv, Berlin.

[14] "In der Hingabe des eigenen Lebens für die Existenz der Gemeinschaft liegt die Krönung allen Opfersinns. Gerade unsere deutsche Sprache besitzt ein Wort, das in herrlicher Weise das Handeln nach diesem Sinn bezeichnet: Pflichterfüllung. Das

heißt: Nicht sich selbst genügen, sondern der Allgemeinheit dienen." Adolf Hitler, qtd. in Konrad Himmel, "Eine Tat, die die Weltwirtschaft umformte," *Licht-Bild-Bühne* 207 (September 3, 1938).

[15] "Das Spiel ist aus und ich habe verloren." *Kautschuk* film dialogue.

[16] For a contemporaneous description of Gustav Diessl (1899–1948), see "Im Scheinwerfer: Das Künstlerehepaar Gustav Diessl-Maria Cebotari," Beilage zur *Filmwelt* 44 (Oktober 28, 1938).

[17] "Don Alonzo [ist] ein[] schöne[r], elegante[r] *Spanier.*" *Kautschuk, Illustrierter Film-Kurier* 2879 (Berlin: Vereinigte Verlagsgesellschaften Franke & Co., n.d.). Emphasis added.

[18] "[José ist] eine wirklich einzigartige Figur . . . zu drei Vierteln Indianer, zu einem Viertel Neger und von der aus den Urwäldern von Amazonas im vorigen Jahre zurück-gekehrten Filmexpedition mitgebracht wurde. . . . Dadurch soll der lebenswahre Charakter, der dem Film eigen ist, ausgiebigst betont werden." Konrad Himmel, "Eine Tat, die die Weltwirtschaft umformte," *Licht-Bild-Bühne* 207 (September 3, 1938). "[Man brachte] aus dem Urwald einen Mischling mit, der darstellerisch als der Diener Wickhams auftritt und in den einzelnen Szenen gewissermaßen das Bindeglied zwischen Urwald- und den Atelieraufnahmen ist." "Abenteurlicher Kampf um das 'elastische Gold': Zu dem Film *Kautschuk,*" *Filmwelt* 45 (November 4, 1938).

[19] "Aber Sie brauchen sie nicht zu bedauern. Im Augenblick feiern meine armen getretenen Sklaven gerade ein Fest und sind eifrig dabei, sich zu Ehren des heiligen Antonios mit Zuckerrohrschapps zu betrinken." *Kautschuk* film dialogue.

[20] "Die Brasilianer sind so weit ganz nette Leute, aber zwei Dinge sehen sie nicht gern: wenn man sich zuviel um ihre Frauen kümmert, und wenn man in Gebiete einzudringen versucht, aus dem ihr Reichtum stammt." *Kautschuk* film dialogue.

[21] Marianna Torgovnick, *Gone Primitive: Savage Intellects, Modern Lives* (Chicago: U of Chicago P, 1990), 61.

[22] The brothers Eichhorn had previously traveled to Brazil from 1930 to 1931 where they worked on the cultural documentary *Urwald Symphonie: Die grüne Hölle* (Brückner/Bauer-Adamara). In 1937 Franz Eichhorn published a vivid account of his Brazilian adventures, *In the Green Hell: Winding Journeys Through Brazil,* see Franz E. Anders [pseudonym for Franz Eichhorn], *In der grünen Hölle: Kurbelfahrten durch Brasilien* (Berlin: Scherl Verlag, 1937). This book continued to be popular after the war, being translated into French and reprinted in the Federal Republic of Germany in the 1950s by Bertelsmann Verlag.

[23] For a historical overview of the German expedition film, see *Trivale Tropen: Exotische Reise- und Abenteuerfilme aus Deutschland 1919–1939,* ed. Jörg Schöning (Munich: edition text + kritik, 1997). For a broader analysis of ethnology in Nazi Germany, see Thomas Hauschild, ed., *Lebenslust und Fremdenfurcht: Ethnologie im Dritten Reich* (Frankfurt a. M.: Suhrkamp, 1995).

[24] Expedition films include *Abessinien von heute: Blickpunkt der Welt* (1935, Rikli), *Die Wildnis stirbt* (1936, Schomburgk), and *Rätsel der Urwaldhölle* (1938, Schulz-Kampfenkel).

[25] See Hans Schomburgk, *Mein Afrika: Erlebtes und Erlauschtes aus dem Innern Afrikas,* 2d ed. (Leipzig: Deutsche Buchwerkstätten, 1930); Otto Schulz-Kampfhenkel, *Im afrikanischen Dschungel als Tierfänger und Urwaldjäger* (Berlin: Deutscher Verlag, 1937); and Martin Rikli, *Ich filmte für Millonen: Fahrten, Abenteuer und Erinnerungen eines Filmberichters* (Berlin: Schützen, 1942).

[26] "Jetzt auf Zeichen des Flugzeugführers hebt sich der Begleiter über den Rumpf, zielt mit dem kleinen, beweglichen Handkino, das fast aussieht wie eine große Pistole, nach den weißen Flanken und übertastet mit dem Objektiv die ganze glitzernde Bergwelt. Lautlos laufen die Filmrollen ab und schlucken das Geheimnis dieser Welt in sich hinein." Bernhard Krüger, *Das Abenteuer lockt: Filmexpeditionen, Expeditionsfilme, Ein Taschenbericht* (Berlin: Karl Curtis, 1940), 3.

[27] "Als leidenschaftliche und beharrliche Jäger, mit Objektiv und Blende edelstes Weidewerk übend, bringen sie auf dem Filmstreifen eine Beute zur Strecke, die uns oft besser mundet als die Spielfilmkost, die in den Ateliers zubereitet wird." Frank Maraun, "Das Erlebnis entscheidet: Der abendfüllende Kulturfilm — von verschiedenen Seiten gesehen," *Der deutsche Film* 2, no. 7 (January 1938): 188.

[28] "Das Dokumentarfilm-Genre, das seinen spezifischen Blick und sein Erkenntnisinteresse auf außereuropäische Szenerien und nicht-europäische Ethnien richtete, war in seiner Blütezeit ein Projekt, um nicht zu sagen: ein Projektil kolonialer Weltaneignung und Welteroberung." Klaus Kreimeier, "Mechanik, Waffen und Haudegen überall: Expeditionsfilme: das bewaffnete Auge des Ethnografen," in *Triviale Tropen: Exotische Reise- und Abenteuerfilme aus Deutschland 1919–1945, ed.* Jörg Schöning (Munich: edition text + kritik, 1997), 47. For an in-depth study of how the documentary travelogue inscribes notions of race, gender, and empire, see Fatimah Tobing Rony, *The Third Eye: Race, Cinema and Ethnographic Spectacle* (Durham: Duke UP, 1996).

[29] "Der Kampf um das Leben wird dort Schritt für Schritt gekämpft. Wir haben diesen Kampf auf unseren Filmstreifen festgehalten, Peitschenschlangen, Tigerkatzen, Vogelspinnen, eine 'Gottesanbieterin,' die einen Schmetterling frißt, angreifende Jaguare — und nicht zuletzt die Völker der Dschungel: die Jaculos, die Araras, die Ivaros, schleichende Indios mit Giftpfeilen. . . . Diese Welt ist unheimlich — und doch in ihrer Unergründlichkeit immer wieder anziehend." Franz Eichhorn, "Das große Abenteuer: Kamerabeute am Amazonas," *Licht-Bild-Bühne* 278 (November 26, 1938).

[30] "Mit großem Mut und Entschlossenheit dringt [Wickham] in die grüne Hölle ein und besiegt alle Widerstände der wilden Natur, ihrer Tiere, der weißen und der farbigen Menschen," Hanns Bornemann, "Der Kampf um *Kautschuk:* Gefahren und Abenteuer miterlebt im Ufa-Palast am Zoo" (n.p., n.d.), *Kautschuk,* Document File 8701, Bundesarchiv-Filmarchiv, Berlin. *Kautschuk* was praised for its "Bilder von urzeitlicher Wildheit," Günther Schwark, "*Kautschuk:* Ufa-Palast am Zoo," *Film-Kurier* 263 (November 9, 1938).

[31] "Wenn die Welt einen Rohstoff braucht, dann findet sie auch die Mittel, sich ihn zu verschaffen." *Kautschuk* film dialogue.

[32] "In endlosen Reihen, Baum bei Baum." *Kautschuk* film dialogue.

[33] *Kautschuk* was seen as an important historical film because it illustrated "wie die Unabhängigkeit eines Landes von gewissen ausländischen Rohstoffen zu erreichen

ist." EF, "Deutscher Film am Amazonas, Kampf mit Schlangen und Pyranhas, Abenteuer um die Gummimilch," *Licht-Bild-Bühne* 262 (November 7, 1938).

[34] "Denn heute beträgt der Anteil Brasiliens an der Weltversorgung mit Kautschuk nur etwa 16 Prozent, während England durch die Tat Wickhams seine ostasiatische Kautschuk-Plantagenindustrie begründen und im Laufe der Zeit die Monopolstellung auf dem Gebiet der Gummiproduktion an sich reißen konnte. Nur eines hat Brasilien bis heute verhindern können, nämlich die Ausfuhr der nur in den Urwäldern von Amazonas vorkommenden Uricury-Palme, deren Vorhandensein für die Qualität des Kauschuks von hohem Werte ist." Himmel, "Eine Tat, die die Weltwirtschaft umformte."

[35] These statistics refer to supplies used by the United States military force during the Second World War but indicate the importance of rubber for the war effort. See James A. Plambeck, "United States Synthetic Rubber Program, 1939–1945." Industrial Organic Chemistry, Synthetic Rubber. http://www.chem.ualberta.ca/~plambeck/che/p265/p06184.htm. U of Alberta, 1996.

[36] "Herr Zimmermann berichtet über eine Anordnung der Reichsfilmkammer, wonach alle Filme, die unsere Feindmächte in besonders günstigem Licht erscheinen lassen, zurückgezogen werden. Von unseren Filmen wird hierdurch allein der Film *Kautschuk* betroffen, der die geschichtliche Tat eines Engländers verherrlicht. Der Vorstand beschließt, mit Rücksicht hierauf den Film *Kautschuk* in der nächsten Zeit nicht auszuliefern." Qtd. in Hennig Harmssen, "Flucht in die Unterhaltung: Verbote und Unverbindliches bestimmten den deutschen Film im Zweiten Weltkrieg," *Filmspiegel* (June 2, 1985).

[37] *Verklungene Melodie*, Censor-Card 47669, Bundesarchiv-Filmarchiv, Berlin. The censor cards provide a narrative description of the action but not the dialogues. All dialogues are taken from the videocassette copy of *Verklungene Melodie* available in commercial release.

[38] "Die Handlung spielt manchmal reichlich durcheinander und ist auch unlogisch und undramaturgisch. Aber wer verlangt alles von einem Film?" "Der Film ist ein einziger Genuß." Goebbels, *Die Tagebücher von Joseph Goebbels,* I. 5: 139 and 162. Journalists complained that the film degraded their professional honor by depicting an unscrupulous reporter. Goebbels countered that "film has to show life, not theories or dreams." [Der Film muß das Leben zeigen, nicht Theorien oder Wunschträume.] The propaganda minister was incensed with journalists who did not notice the film's historical setting: "The press is protesting incessantly against the film *Verklungene Melodie* because it shows a fairly rotten journalist. Yet the film plays in 1932. I reject the protests with a cold shoulder" [Die Presse protestiert unentwegt gegen den Film "verklungene Melodie," weil da ein etwas mieser Journalist gezeigt wird. Dabei spielt der Film 1932. Ich lehne die Proteste kaltlächelnd ab]. Goebbels, *Die Tagebücher von Joseph Goebbels,* I. 5: 174 and 176.

[39] "Es beruht, massenpsychologisch gesehen, auf einem Nachlassen der Suggestivkraft des Filmbildes." W. P., "Der 'falsche Lacher': Betrachtungen über die Psychologie des Publikums," *Film-Kurier* 155 (July 6, 1938). See also "Veit Harlan zum Thema 'Falsche Lacher' Ein Regisseur tritt für das Publikum an," *Film-Kurier* 157 (July 8, 1938). For a discussion of false laughter in Nazi cinema, see Eric Rentschler, *The Ministry of Illusion: Nazi Cinema and its Afterlife* (Cambridge, MA: Harvard UP, 1996), 112–14.

[40] "Eine Einzelreaktion, der zunächst die allgemeine Resonanz des Publikums fehlt . . . durch ihn wird die Gemeinsamkeit des massenpsychischen Erlebens, wird das *Erlebnisnetz*, das alle Zuschauer umstrickt hält, unterbrochen und beeinträgtigt." W. P., "Der 'falsche Lacher.'"

[41] "Obwohl diese Szenen tatsächlich in der Sahara gedreht wurden, verweilt der Regisseur nur solange bei der filmisch gewiß ergiebigen Situation, als es die Entwicklung der Handlung und die Charakterisierung der beiden Hauptpersonen erfordert. Auch die übrigen Schauplätze — Berlin und New York — werden nie Bestandteil des Geschehens, sie bleiben immer Hintergrund für ein zartes Kammerspiel, das von Brigitte Horney und Willy Birgel getragen wird." Ludwig Eberlein, "Verklungene Melodie: Ein Tourjansky-Film im Gloria Palast," *Berliner Morgenpost* (n.d.), *Verklungene Melodie*, Document file 18268, Bundesarchiv-Filmarchiv. Albert Schneider also commented that the African location shots tended to present the desert as a combination of reality, emotion, and fantasy. See Albert Schneider, "*Verklungene Melodie:* Ein Ufa-Film, Gloria-Palast," *Licht-Bild-Bühne* 49 (February 26, 1938).

[42] "Der kürzeste Weg zu sich selbst führt um die Welt herum." Motto to Graf Hermann Keyserling, *Das Reisetagebuch eines Philosophen*, 8th ed. (Stuttgart: Deutsche Verlags-Anstalt, 1932).

[43] Richard Phillips, *Mapping Men and Empire: A Geography of Adventure* (New York: Routledge, 1997), 13.

[44] "Seht ihr den Regenbogen in der Luft? Der Himmel öffnet seine goldenen Tore. Im Chor der Engel steht sie glänzend da. Sie hält den ewigen Sohn an ihrer Brust. Die Arme streckt sie lächelnd ihm entgegen. Sie winkt mir. Leichte Wolken heben mich. Der schwere Panzer wird zum Flügelkleid. Hinauf, hinauf, die Erde flecht zurück. Kurz ist der Schmerz, ewig ist die Freude." *Verklungene Melodie* film dialogue.

[45] "Für Thomas Gront und Barbara Lorenz (Willy Birgel, Brigitte Horney) wird der Flugzeugabsturz in der nordafrikanischen Wüste zum Sturz in übermächtige Emotionen und vor allem eine Alterität, die die gewohnten Rollen vertauscht. . . . Sie, die afrikaerfahrene und ebenso nerven- wie gefühlsstarke Frau, [beweist] eine Souveränität, die sie gegenüber dem zur Panik neigenden Gront zur Beschützerin werden läßt." Wolfgang Struck, "'Afrika zu unsern Füßen': Kinematographische Lufthoheiten über einem dunklen Kontinent," in *Geschichte(n): NS-Film — NS-Spuren heute*, ed. Hans Krah (Kiel: Ludwig, 1999), 68.

[46] "So schnupperte man etwas in der Stadt herum, deren europäische Viertel breite Straßen, große Hotels, Kinos, Geschäfte und Verwaltungsgebäude zeigen, in deren Oper sogar der Ring des Nibelungen aufgeführt wurde und deren Lichtreklame sich mit jeder europäischen Großstadt vergleichen läßt. . . . Der Zug führte an den riesigen Salzseen, den Schotts, vorbei, die eine angeregte Karl-May-Unterhaltung zur Folge hatten. . . . Das Medrasen. Unter dem Namen verbirgt sich die Grabstätte des Königs Jugurtha — was wiederum Erinnerungen an gymnasiale Lateinstunden bei unserer heiteren Reisegesellschaft heraufbeschwor." G. H., "Mit dem Film *Mitternachtswalzer* am Rande der Sahara," *Filmwelt* 49 (December 5, 1937).

[47] "Ich war nicht mehr in dieser Welt. Alles, was ich bisher gesehen und gefühlt hatte, lag hinter mir in Diesseits. Als hätte mich das Flugzeug aus meinem Leben herausgetragen, ohne daß ich das Leben verloren hatte. . . . Man kann doch von Biskra aus in

wenigen Minuten dem Diesseits entfliehen. Man muß nur die Augen dafür haben und die doppelte Belastung als halbe zu tragen verstehen." é, "Begegnung mit dem Jenseits: Filmarbeit über der Wüste, das wunderbare Erlebnis des Kameramannes" (n.p., n.d.), *Verklungene Melodie*, Document file 18268, Bundesarchiv-Filmarchiv. Günther Rittau went on to direct seven films in the Third Reich, including the adventure film *Brand im Ozean* (1939) and the war film *U-Boote westwärts* (1941).

[48] "Man fängt den Film an im großen Stil und sieht plötzlich voller Erschrecken, daß man wieder im Kammerspiel gelandet ist." Hans Spielhofer, "Der wichtigste Film des Monats," *Der deutsche Film* 2, no. 10 (April 1938): 289.

[49] "Die originelle Verwendung einiger Städteaufnahmen sei besonders erwähnt. Hier zeigt sich auch das starke Bildgefühl Tourjanskis. Der Ruf nach Barbara hallt über den Häusermeeren der Weltstädte und veranschaulicht das Aussichtslose des Suchens." Georg Herzberg, "*Verklungene Melodie*/Gloria-Palast," *Film-Kurier* 48 (February 26, 1938).

[50] Anton Kaes, *From Hitler to Heimat: The Return of History as Film* (Cambridge, MA: Harvard UP, 1989), 165.

[51] *Systemzeit* (the time of the system) was a derogatory term commonly used by National Socialists to denote the decadence of the Weimar Republic (1918–1933).

[52] "Sie kennen mich nicht. Ich lebe für etwas ganz anders. Ich muß kämpfen. Ich brauche die Abwechselung. Ich kann nirgendwo bleiben. Ich muß frei sein. Ich bin ein großer Egoist. Ich habe nie das Bedürfnis, lange mit jemand zusammen zu sein und das werde ich auch nie tun. Ich will, daß Sie glücklich werden, und Sie werden nur unglücklich sein, wenn Sie sich an mich binden." *Verklungene Melodie* film dialogue.

[53] "Dieser Mann ist gemessen und von einer disziplinierten Leidenschaftlichkeit. Er ist sehr gepflegt und ein Kavalier in dem guten Sinn des ritterlichen, selbstbewußten und höflichen Mannes. . . . Aber er war immer auch der elegante, kluge, mutige, eiserne, verbindliche, von kalter Leidenschaft getragene Spieler." "Im Scheinwerfer: Staatsschauspieler Willy Birgel — der Künstler und Mensch," Beilage zur *Filmwelt* 52 (December 23, 1938).

[54] "Das Wort Kavalier würde den Nagel auf den Kopf treffen, wenn es nicht eine Spur zu seicht und verwischt wäre. Es müßte noch etwas anderes hinzukommen: die Atmosphäre eines Menschen, der sich stets in der Gewalt hat. Der mit Haltung liebt, leidet, verzichtet. Der nicht mit großen Gesten und schillernden Worten in Erscheinung tritt. Birgels Spielhaltung ist fast soldatisch zu nennen. . . . Er drückt Gefühle aus, in dem er sie unterdrückt." Theodor Riegler, "Im Scheinwerfer: Willy Birgel," Beilage zur *Filmwelt* 16 (April 19, 1940).

[55] Werner is described as "eine weiche Künstlernatur." *Verklungene Melodie, Illustrierter Film-Kurier* 2772 (Berlin: Vereinigte Verlagsgesellschaften Franke & Co., n.d.).

[56] "Wenn er stark genug ist, seine Individualität zu wahren und wenn man ihn nicht auf den Salonlöwen abstellt, dann kann er der erste Repräsentant des Typs werden, den wir so brennend suchen: der 'He-man,' der kein Flegel ist." Spielhofer, "Der wichtigste Film des Monats."

[57] Horney possessed "Kraft und Gesundheit, gepaart mit Charme und Verstand," and further: "*Innerlich* betrachtet, ist sie die Frau mit der ständigen Lust und dem

ständigen Willen zu einem großen Erlebnis, die sich dem Abenteuer stellt, mag sie in ihm siegen oder untergehen." Hans-Joachim Schlamp, *Brigitte Horney,* Künstler-Biographien 1 (Berlin: Verlag Robert Mölich, n.d.), 4. For a similar discription, see Ma, "Brigitte Horney," *Der deutsche Film* 3, no. 6 (December 1938): 156–59.

[58] Rentschler, *The Ministry of Illusion,* 141.

[59] Renate Brinkmann "weiß den Mann ihres Henzens neben sich — den Mann, der in ihr die Heimat fand und mit ihr ein neues Leben erobern wird!" *Kongo-Express, Illustrierter Film-Kurier* 3051 (Berlin: Vereinigte Verlagsgesellschaften Franke & Co., n.d.).

[60] The image of America in Nazi Germany was based largely on the critique of America and modernity from the Weimar Republic. See Anton Kaes, Martin Jay, and Edward Dimendberg, eds., "Imagining America: Fordism and Technology," in *The Weimar Republic Sourcebook* (Berkeley: U of California P, 1995), 393–411; Anton Kaes, "Mass Culture and Modernity: Notes Toward a Social History of Early American and German Cinema," in *America and the Germans: An Assessment of a Three-hundred-year History,* ed. Franz Trommler and Joseph McVeigh (Philadelphia: U of Pennsylvania P, 1985), 2: 317–32; and Hans Dieter Schäfer, *Das gespaltene Bewußtsein: Deutsche Kultur und Lebenswirklichkeit 1933–1945* (Munich: Carl Hanser Verlag, 1983).

[61] For an excellent study of *Der verlorene Sohn* and *Glückskinder,* see Rentschler, *The Ministry of Illusion,* 71–124. See also Franz A. Birgel, "Luis Trenker: A Rebel in the Third Reich?" in *Cultural History through a National Socialist Lens: Essays on the Cinema of the Third Reich,* Robert C. Reimer, ed. (Rochester, NY: Camden House, 2000), 37–64.

[62] Rentschler, *The Ministry of Illusion,* 86.

[63] "Die Leute wollen nur vergessen, alle Sorgen, alles Schwere. Die sind wie toll. Das ist ein einziger Rausch, nur um einmal glücklich zu sein." *Verklungene Melodie* film dialogue.

[64] Erich Waschneck (1887–1970) directed twenty-three feature films in the Third Reich including the musical *Die göttliche Jette* (1937) and the anti-Semitic propaganda film *Die Rothschilds* (1940).

[65] *Frauen für Golden Hill,* Censor-Card 50106, Bundesarchiv-Filmarchiv, Berlin. The censor cards include a description of the scenes but not the dialogues. All dialogues are taken from the 35-mm film print *Frauen für Golden Hill* available at the Bundesarchiv-Filmarchiv, Berlin. *Frauen für Golden Hill* did not do well at the box office and sustained an estimated loss of 69,000 RM, see Albrecht, *Nationalsozialistische Filmpolitik,* 428.

[66] Hans Bertram, *Flug in die Hölle: Bericht von der Bertram-Atlantis Expedition* (Berlin: Drei Masken, 1933). Bertram's book was not only a best seller in the Third Reich; it remains popular in Germany today in a recent reprint edition, see *Flug in die Hölle,* Ullstein Buch 22467 (Frankfurt a. M.: Ullstein, 1986 and 1991). In 1985/1986 ARD made a series on Bertram's aviation adventures for television.

[67] Both *Hitlerjunge Quex* and *Triumph des Willens* were reasonably successful at the box office. From its premiere in September 1933 to January 1934, *Hitlerjunge Quex* reached a million viewers. *Triumph des Willens* premiered in March 1935 at discounted prices in the first-run movie theaters of seventy German cities and enjoyed record-breaking crowds. Both films were routinely shown without cost but in obligatory sessions at schools, in the Hitler Youth Organized Film Hour, and at the

NSDAP district film exhibitions. See Martin Loiperdinger, *Rituale der Mobilmachung: Der Parteitagsfilm* Triumph des Willens *von Leni Riefenstahl* (Opladen: Leske & Budrich, 1987), 50; and Rentschler, *The Ministry of Illusion*, 56.

[68] "Nur zwei nehmen eine Sonderstellung ein. Sie sind durch eine alte Fliegerkameradschaft auf Leben und Tod mit einander verbunden; sie haben auch keine Frauen haben wollen." *Frauen für Golden Hill, Das Programm von heute* 326 (Berlin: Das Programm von heute: Zeitschrift für Film und Theater, GmbH, 1938).

[69] The love triangle as the tension between comradeship, family, and community is a staple of the adventure film and the war film. See for example *Brand im Ozean, Kongo Express, Wunschkonzert, Spähtrupp Hallgarten, Kampfgeschwader Lutzow,* and *Besatzung Dora.*

[70] "Da die Homosexuellen erfahrungsgemäß für den normalen Geschlechtsverkehr unbrauchbar werden, wirkt sich die Gleichgeschlechtlichkeit auch auf den Nachwuchs aus und wird zwangsläufig zu einem Geburtenrückgang führen. Die Folge davon ist eine Schwächung der allgemeinen Volkskraft, durch die nicht zuletzt die militärische Belange eines Volkes gefährdet werden." Qtd. in Stefan Maiwald and Gerd Mischler, *Sexualität unter dem Hakenkreuz: Manipulation und Vernichtung der Intimsphäre im NS-Staat* (Hamburg: Europa Verlag, 1999), 171. For studies on the persecution of homosexuals in Nazi Germany, see Michael Burleigh and Wolfgang Wippermann, *The Racial State: Germany 1933–1945* (Cambridge: Cambridge UP, 1991); and Richard Plant, *The Pink Triangle: The Nazi War against Homosexuals* (New York, 1986).

[71] "Das ewig Weibliche ist eben der natürliche und notwendige Angelpunkt des männlichen Daseins, der Ansporn und Ausgleich." "Frauen ziehen durch die Wüste: Anmerkungen zu dem Film *Frauen für Golden Hill,*" *Filmwelt* 43 (October 21, 1938).

[72] Mel Gordon, *Voluptuous Panic: The Erotic World of Weimar Berlin* (Venice, CA: Feral House, 2000), 121.

[73] The Chocolate Kiddies, an eleven-piece jazz band lead by Sam Wooding (1895–1985), played at the Admiralpalast in May 1925. For information on Josephine Baker as a European phenomenon, see Peter Jelavich, "The Americanization of Entertainment: Jazz and Black Performers," in *Berlin Cabaret* (Cambridge, MA: Harvard UP, 1993), 165–75; Anton Kaes, Martin Jay, Edward Dimendberg, eds., "The Roaring Twenties: Cabaret and Urban Environment," in *The Weimar Republic Sourcebook* (Berkeley: U of California P, 1994), 551–68; and Nancy Nenno, "Femininity, the Primitive, and Modern Urban Space: Josephine Baker in Berlin," in *Women in the Metropolis,* ed. Katharina von Ankum (Berkeley: U of California P, 1997), 145–61; and Rony, *The Third Eye,* 199–203.

[74] Josephine Baker and Jo Bouillon, "Candide," in *Josephine,* trans. Mariana Fitzpatrick (New York: Paragon House, 1988), 55.

[75] Qtd. in Nenno, "Femininity, the Primitive, and Modern Urban Space," 155.

[76] Qtd. in Phyllis Rose, *Jazz Cleopatra: Josephine Baker in Her Time* (New York: Doubleday, 1989), 23.

[77] See Nenno, "Femininity, the Primitive, and Modern Urban Space," 158.

[78] See Knud Wolffram, *Tanzdielen und Vergnügungspaläste: Berliner Nachtleben in den dreißiger und vierziger Jahren,* 3d ed. (Berlin: Edition Hentrich, 1992), 185–89.

[79] Josua is also marked as African-American when he plays on the harmonica the American folk song "Swanee River," written in 1851 by Stephen C. Foster for blackface minstrelsy. Foster's song was popularized in a series of motion pictures all called *Swanee River* (1925, Dave Flisher; 1931, Raymond Cannon; and the best known version starring Don Ameche, 1939, Sidney Lanfield). Josua's mail-order bride, a large black woman named Mammy, is likewise a stereotypical and exaggerated African-American character played by an actress credited with the name of Josephine Bachert.

[80] Alice: "Endlich kommen die Männer da draußen mal auf eine vernünftige Idee . . . Sie haben anscheinend wohl nicht gemerkt, daß es hier um das moralischste Geschäft geht, das die Firma C. P. Barryman jemals gemacht hat. Dreizehn einsame Männer wollen in den Stand der Ehe treten . . . in den heiligen Stand der Ehe." *Frauen für Golden Hill* film dialogue.

[81] "Sehe ich nicht richtig nach 'Vamp' aus? . . . aus einer eigennützigen, oberflächlichen Frau wird ein anständiger, guter Kamerade." "Kampf um die Frau in Australiens Wüste: Kirsten Heibergs erste Hauptrolle. *Frauen für Golden Hill* und Kameradentreue" (n.p., n.d.), *Frauen für Golden Hill*, Document File 5697, Bundesarchiv-Filmarchiv, Berlin.

[82] "Ich bin von Kopf bis Fuss auf Liebe eingestellt . . . Männer umschwärmen mich wie Motten um das Licht, und wenn sie verbrennen, dafür kann ich nichts." *Der blaue Engel* film dialogue.

[83] For an excellent analysis of *Zu neuen Ufern*, see Marc Silberman, *German Cinema: Texts in Context* (Detroit: Wayne State UP, 1995), 51–65.

[84] "In ihren Chansons lehnt sie sich spürbar an Zarah Leanders Vortragsstil an." Günther Schwark, *"Frauen für Golden Hill," Film-Kurier* 5 (January 6, 1939).

[85] "Ich bin eine Frau, die die Männer betört, die mit allen spielt und keinem gehört, und ich will so bleiben, wie ich bin, wie ich bin. Ich habe ein Lächeln, das niemand versteht, das die Männer anzieht wie ein Magnet. Und ich will so bleiben, wie ich bin, wie ich bin. Man wollte mich ändern und hat's oft probiert. Doch man hat mich dabei unterschätzt. Ich habe im Leben fast immer riskiert, alles auf eine Karte gesetzt. Es ist auf der Welt dazu gemacht, daß man schnell seine Träume vergißt. Ich hatte das Leben ganz anders gedacht. Doch ich nehme es, wie es ist." *Frauen für Golden Hill* film dialogue.

[86] "In einem Goldgräberlager braucht man Frauen, einfache Frauen, die auch arbeiten können." *Frauen für Golden Hill* film dialogue.

[87] "Ich stelle es mir herrlich vor, in der unendlichen Einsamkeit da draußen mit einem Mann zu leben, dem man alles sein kann." *Frauen für Golden Hill* film dialogue.

[88] "Es gibt tausende verschiedene Dinge eine Ehe auseinanderzubringen, aber es gibt meiner Erfahrung nach nur eins, was zwei Menschen fest und innig miteinander verbindet: Sie müssen Gelegenheit haben, sich gegenseitig zu helfen." *Frauen für Golden Hill* film dialogue.

[89] "Violet ist ein netter Kerl, aber unsere Kameradschaft ist mir mehr wert. Die Frau muß für uns unantastbar sein." *Frauen für Golden Hill* film dialogue.

[90] "Du hast gegen unser Oberstes Gesetz verstossen. Du hast die Waffe gegen einen Kameraden erhoben. Wir haben nicht die Befugnis über dich richten zu sitzen, aber wir wollen nichts mehr mit dir zu tun haben. Wir geben dir Proviant für sechs

Wochen. Wie du zur Küste kommst, ist deine Sache. Wir sind fertig mit dir!" *Frauen für Golden Hill* film dialogue.

[91] "Der Gemeinschaftsgedanke . . . ist deutlich spürbar und erkennbar z.b. in allen den Filmen, in denen ein Mensch seine Pflicht gegenüber der Gemeinschaft erfüllt, indem er sich zu einem großen Opfer fähig und bereit zeigt. . . . [I]mmer da spürten wir das Gesetz, das ein Volk am Leben erhält, das Gesetz der Gemeinschaft, der bedingungslosen Kamaderadschaft." Felix Henseleit, "Gemeinschaftserlebnis im Film," *Licht-Bild-Bühne* 14 (May 18, 1940).

[92] "Sein Freund hat zwar sein Leben lassen müssen, aber die Rettungstat an der ganzen Gemeinschaft tilgt seine Schuld an dem einen." *Frauen für Golden Hill, Das Programm von heute* 326 (Berlin: Das Programm von heute: Zeitschrift für Film und Theater, GmbH, 1937).

[93] "Haus Vaterland" billed itself as "Deutschlands größter Vergnügungspalast" offering "eine billige Erholungsreise." See Wolffram, *Tanzdielen und Vergnügungspaläste,* 16–19; and Gordon, *Voluptuous Panic,* 224–25.

[94] "Der Begriff des Abenteuerlichen, eng verbunden mit Gefahren, Not und Kampf und schließlich Sieg, erweckt auch heute . . . erstaunlich viel Widerhall . . . Und es hat tiefere Ursachen, wenn wir heute geradezu als Inbegriff des Abenteuerlichen, als das klassische Abenteuer schlechthin, jene Geschehnisse ansprechen, die mit der aufregenden Suche nach Gold verbunden sind." "Frauen ziehen durch die Wüste."

[95] "Nationalsozialisten fühlten sich zudem von dem 'wagemutigen Tatendrang' der Amerikaner und durch ihre Eroberung des 'Goldenen Westens' in ihren Träumen, als 'bewaffnete Kolonisten im Osten neues Land zu erobern, bestätigt." Schäfer, *Das gespaltene Bewußtsein,* 128. For studies on the German Western in Nazi Germany, see Jan-Christopher Horak, "Luis Trenker's *The Kaiser of California:* How the West was Won, Nazi Style," *Historical Journal of Film, Radio, and Television* 6.2 (1986): 181–88; and Lutz P. Koepnick, "Unsettling America: German Westerns and Modernity," *Modernism/Modernity* 2.3 (1995): 1–22.

[96] "[Die Goldgräber geben] die Hoffnnung nicht auf, eines Tages so viel erarbeitet zu haben, daß sie dahin heimkehren können, woher sie kamen. Denn einem rechten Kerl kommt es darauf an, seine Heimat nicht zu verlieren, sollte ihn auch das Schicksal als Pionier im fremden Land festhalten." "Frauen ziehen durch die Wüste."

[97] "Es ist genug Wasser, um morgen den Marsch an die Küste anzutreten, den Marsch mit Frau und Kind in ein Land, wo Felder und Wiesen, Brunnen und Teich sind." *Frauen für Golden Hill, Illustrierter Film-Kurier* 2907 (Berlin: Vereinigte Verlagsgesellschaften Franke & Co., 1938).

[98] "Trotzdem sich hier abenteuerliche und ungewöhnliche Dinge begeben, hat der Zuschauer immer das Gefühl, daß er nicht *außerhalb* der Ereignisse steht, daß sie ihm nicht fremd bleiben, — ja, daß er sie schließlich auch *selbst* erleben könnte." Felix Henseleit, "*Frauen für Golden Hill,*" *Licht-Bild-Bühne* 5 (January 6, 1939), emphasis in original.

[99] "Man mixe: einen der ersten Tonfilme *Braut Nr. 68* und *Zu neuen Ufern* und was daraus entsteht, nennt sich *Frauen für Golden Hill.* Hier wird des Unwahrscheinlichen reichlich viel getan. Dreizehn hübsche Mädchen, vorwiegend elegant gekleidet, fühlen sich glücklich, den rauhen, versoffenen Goldgräbern in ihr primitives Dasein als Ehefrau zu folgen, d.h. nicht zu folgen, denn sie heiraten sie ja, ohne sie gesehen zu haben! Und

welch ein Wunder! Es geht gut. Alle sind glücklich. Nimmt man nun noch dazu eine Frau zwischen zwei Männern, einen Vamp, der zum Schluß geläutert wird und der in Leander-Manier mit einer ähnlichen, wenn nicht so geschulten Stimme, ähnliche Chansons singt und verbrämt das ganze noch mit Sandstürmen, Wassermangel und anderen Katastrophen, nicht zu vergessen: Freundestreue bis zur Selbstopferung, so müßte das doch mit dem Teufel zugehen, wenn das kein Erfolgsfilm würde (-meinen die Hersteller, oder?)." Ilse Wehner, "Filme des Monats," *Der deutsche Film* 3, no. 8 (February 1939): 228–29.

[100] "Manchmal, wenn mich ein neugieriges Verlangen nach solchen abenteuerlichen Dingen anwandelt, habe ich den Reisenden beneidet, der solche Wunder mit andern Wundern in lebendiger Verbindung sieht. Aber auch er wird ein anderer Mensch. Es wandelt niemand ungestraft unter Palmen, und die Gesinnungen ändern sich gewiß in einem Lande, wo Elefanten und Tiger zu Hause sind." Johann Wolfgang von Goethe, *Wahlverwandtschaften,* ed. Hans-J. Weitz (Frankfurt a. M.: Insel, 1972), 173.

[101] Jamie Owen Daniel, "Reclaiming the 'Terrain of Fantasy': Speculations on Ernst Bloch, Memory, and the Resurgence of Nationalism," in *Not Yet: Reconsidering Ernst Bloch,* ed. Jamie Owen Daniel and Tom Moylan (London: Verso, 1997), 59.

[102] "Denkt doch bloß, Leute, wie das sein wird, denkt doch bloß, wenn so um uns rum lauter Deutsche sein werden — und nich, wenn du in einen Laden reinkommst, daß da einer jiddisch redet oder polnisch, sondern deutsch. Und nich nur das ganze Dorf wird deutsch sein, sondern ringsum und rundherum wird alles deutsch sein. Und wir, wir werden so mitten, innen sein, im Herzen von Deutschland. Denkt bloß, Leute, wie das sein wird. Und warum soll das nich sein? Auf der guten alten warmen Erde Deutschlands werden wir wieder wohnen. Daheim und zu Hause. Und in der Nacht, in unseren Betten, wenn wir da aufwachen aus'm Schlaf, da wird das Herz in 'nem süßen Schreck plötzlich wissen, wir schlafen ja mitten in Deutschland, daheim und zu Hause, und ringsum ist die tröstliche Nacht, und ringsum da schlagen Millionen deutsche Herzen und pochen in einem fort leise: Daheim bist du, Mensch, daheim, daheim bei den Deinen. Dann wird uns ganz wunderlich sein ums Herz, daß die Krume des Ackers und das Stück Lehm und der Feldstein und das Zittergras und der schwankende Halm, der Haselnußstrauch und die Bäume, daß das alles deutsch ist, wie wir selber, zugehörig zu uns, weil's ja gewachsen is aus den Millionen Herzen der Deutschen, die eingegangen sind in die Erde und zur deutschen Erde geworden sind. Denn wir leben nicht nur ein deutsches Leben, wir sterben auch einen deutschen Tod. Und tot bleiben wir auch deutsch und sind 'n ganzes Stück von Deutschland, eine Krume des Ackers für den Korn der Enkel, und aus unserem Herzen, da wächst der Rebstock empor, in die Sonne — in die Sonne, Leute, die nich wehtut und nicht sengt, ohne zugleich auch Süßigkeit zu spenden, und ringsum singen die Vögel, und alles ist deutsch, alles Kinder, wie unser Lied, wollen wir's nich singen, gerade jetzt, unser Lied? [A chorus strikes up the sentimental folksong "Nach der Heimat möcht' ich wieder."]" Dialogue from *Heimkehr* (1941, Ucicky) qtd. in Gerald Trimmel, *Heimkehr: Strategien eines nationalsozialistischen Films* (Vienna: Werner Eichbauer, 1998), 118–19.

"Film as a psychological weapon in war": *Der deutsche Film* (1941).

3: The Celluloid War:
The Home-Front Film

SHORTLY AFTER GERMANY invaded Poland in September 1939, leading Nazi film journals began to question the role film would play in the hostilities. Would the muses be silenced by the din of battle or could the power of cinema to construct an alternate reality, capture objects, transform people into images, and reorganize time and space all be harnessed for the military struggle? Critics asserted that film could function as a powerful ideological weapon since it shared essential properties with the military: "Film has become a part of the armed forces. Like the latter it realizes the decisive characteristics of technology: speed, precision, thrusting force into the distance."[1]

Despite the Nazi's fascination with war and cinema, they produced fewer than twenty feature films about the contemporary Second World War experience: the combat film gives expression to the myth of the hardened warrior as the quintessential Aryan male;[2] the furlough film situates the soldier in the homeland where he enjoys an adventure of the heart;[3] and finally, the home-front film explores the bond between the civilian populace and the front-line soldier in wartime love stories and family dramas.[4]

The home-front film is especially noteworthy because it uses culture and entertainment to package war for sale to the German people. In this chapter I will examine the manner in which three home-front films cloak their ideological message in entertaining stories, enchanting audiences while mobilizing them psychologically for war. As propaganda vehicles promoting the idea of a nation united against the enemy, Nazi home-front films reflected developments on the battlefield and can be divided into three phases. The first phase corresponded to the Blitzkrieg victories (1939–1940), the second phase to the intensified struggle against the Allies (1941–1942), and the third phase to the repeated military defeats (1943–1945). Three films in particular, *Wunschkonzert, Die große Liebe,* and *Die Degenhardts,* best typify the official discourse on war prevailing in each period.

Filmed against the backdrop of the swift French defeat in 1940, *Wunschkonzert* (Request Concert) exemplifies the first phase because it presented a cheerful homeland adapting to the dictates of war while exuding optimism and confidence in victory. Through popular culture and light musical entertainment, the film attempted to appeal to the audience emotionally and win it over to the war effort.

As the war continued with no final victory in sight, the state needed to convince the civilian population to sacrifice family members and a personal life for the promise of a brighter future. During this second phase, in 1942 when Allied Forces were carpet-bombing German cities with ever greater frequency, *Die große Liebe* (True Love) furnished the audience with upbeat songs, a sentimental love story, and role models to cope with war-related stress. By drawing structural parallels between musical and military spectacles, the film also depicted war as a type of theater that demanded participation from soldier and civilian alike.

In the third and final phase, after the disaster at Stalingrad, when defeat seemed inevitable, the home-front film tried to persuade civilians to endure death as a soothing end to earthly existence and a necessary measure to insure that German cultural traditions would carry on. In 1944 *Die Degenhardts* (The Degenhardts) presented German high culture, specifically classical music and architecture, as the glue that bound the folk together and guaranteed it immortality.

Propaganda Minister Joseph Goebbels was determined to direct the war like a staged event, catering to his audience's needs while simultaneously manipulating public opinion in accordance with the changing military situation. With the onset of war, Goebbels's immediate task was to convince the masses that the armed conflict was a just cause. The German populace greeted the news of war in September 1939 with skepticism. In contrast to the enthusiastic war fever at the onset of the First World War, most Germans were ambivalent about the hostilities and accepted their duty with guarded reservations.[5] During this early phase in the fighting, Goebbels needed to persuade the people to accept the war as a necessary challenge imposed on Germany but one that promised victory in the foreseeable future. The Polish were the aggressors, he argued; the Germans were defending themselves and their way of life; sacrifices were necessary but triumph was inevitable.[6]

The Propaganda Ministry was quick to assure the populace that the military conflict would not alter German cultural life. In contrast to the "aggressor" enemy states who were concerned with mere existence, Germany would continue to offer its citizens various forms of relaxation and edification.[7] Every effort was made to boost morale and ensure that civilian life remained as stable as possible. Going to the movies and listening to the radio could provide distraction from food and coal shortages or worries over family members in the service. Motion pictures could play an important role in raising everyone's spirits, and keeping movie theaters open would demonstrate the unbroken continuity and power of German culture even under duress. Goebbels promised, "The darker the streets are, the brighter our theaters and movie houses will shine in the splendor of lights."[8] Indeed, the motion-picture industry flourished during the war, providing Goebbels with a captive audience for his program of instruction through entertainment.[9]

National Socialism was a vastly popular movement precisely because it promised the masses stability and the guarantee of a private sphere in which one could enjoy popular consumer products such as those offered by the entertainment industry.[10] The regime successfully addressed the psychological needs of its clientele and balanced those needs with its own military objectives. The Propaganda Ministry attempted to allay dissatisfaction and mitigate hardships because, in Goebbels's words, "No war can be won without optimism; it is just as important as cannons and guns."[11]

The Mass Media Play Along: *Wunschkonzert* (1940)

In order to generate widespread optimism, Goebbels conceived the motion picture *Wunschkonzert* (Request Concert) based on an immensely popular radio show featuring soldiers' musical requests. Goebbels personally worked on the screenplay and chose much of the cast.[12] The film, directed by Eduard von Borsody, was an enormous box-office hit. From its premiere on December 30, 1940, to the war's end, it reached an audience of some 26.5 million viewers and ranked among the top grossing films of the Third Reich. Borsody's film has two stars: the Second World War and armed forces radio.

The bachelor trio in the request concert: *Wunschkonzert.*

In *Wunschkonzert* war takes place on the symbolic level of art and popular entertainment and is presented in terms of musical performance, sports, technology, comedy, and heroism. The violence of battle is replaced with a quest for superior speed, mobility, information retrieval, and detection made possible through new technologies. Combat becomes a competition to achieve the highest levels of perception rather than a collective act of aggression. Since war is divested of its most destructive aspects, it becomes harmless, enjoyable, or at worst a tolerable and temporary burden to endure for the sake of the nation.

Wunschkonzert visualizes armed forces' radio for moviegoers to illustrate how soldiers and civilians can form a single unified front. The film weaves together musical performances, documentary footage, and a multitude of fictional stories connecting home front and battle front.[13] Along with newsreel footage of the 1936 Berlin Olympic Games, the Polish Campaign, and the actual "Request Concert" radio show, there are comic and dramatic vignettes dealing with soldiers and their loved ones. Each wartime experience is narratively linked to a musical performance on the radio, which unites the folk in its support of the war and in its consumption of entertainment. The radio, rather than any single character or narrative strand, becomes the unifying principle in Borsody's film and the means to achieve the *Volksgemeinschaft*, a harmonious national community bound by blood and cultural traditions.

Radio was a powerful tool in the Nazi campaign to coordinate all cultural activities and the flow of information. Soon after his appointment as propaganda minister, Goebbels stressed the value of radio in disseminating ideas and declared it "the most modern and most important instrument for influencing the masses."[14] Already nationalized in 1932, the broadcasting industry came under the jurisdiction of the Reich Chamber of Culture as part of the *Gleichschaltung*. As early as March 1933, Goebbels called upon broadcasting directors to create radio programs that instilled political convictions in the masses without being openly instructive:

> Just don't become boring. Just no tedium. Just don't place convictions on a serving plate. Just don't believe one could best operate in the service of the national government if one played blaring marches evening after evening. . . . There has to be conviction, but conviction does not have to mean boredom. Fantasy has to take into consideration all means and methods in order to let the broad masses hear the new conviction in a modern, current and interesting way, interesting and informative, but not pedantic. Radio should never displease with words, one senses the intention and is put in a bad mood.[15]

In order to implement this propaganda campaign of instruction through entertainment, Goebbels ensured that the *Volksempfänger*, a cheap and mass-produced radio, was readily available to the populace.[16] By 1936 one half of all

German households owned a radio. With the onset of the Second World War, Goebbels began to attach even more importance to the wireless as a medium to convey authorized information while also providing safe distraction through entertainment. Immediately after Germany invaded Poland in September 1939, for example, Goebbels donated 1,500 radios to soldiers on the front.[17] Listening to foreign radio broadcasts, by contrast, was forbidden by the law on "extraordinary measures for the radio" from September 1, 1939. Violators were subject to imprisonment and, in rare cases, even death.[18]

National Socialists recognized that the capacity of radio to be unhampered by spatial dimensions or limitations lent the medium symbolic character as the transmitter of an unseen, inner reality. As Peter Reichel has noted, "Precisely its 'spatial freedom' seems to qualify the radio as medium of an 'imaginary realm' to convey the 'inner unity' of all Germans as a community."[19] In the context of the Second World War, radio also established a metaphoric linkage between the goals of battle (soldiers capturing and mastering territory) and the achievements of spatial conquest through technology (radio waves overcoming the distance between home front and war front).

Radio's symbolic potential reached its zenith in the "Wunschkonzert für die Wehrmacht" (Request Concert for the Armed Forces), which premiered on October 1, 1939, and was broadcast live every Sunday afternoon from the studios of the Berlin Broadcasting Center.[20] Radio announcer Heinz Goedecke would take requests from soldiers and relay personal messages in return for charitable donations. Through this shared radio program, the nation united behind the war effort. As if attached by some invisible umbilical cord, a factory worker, a mother mending socks, and a child playing with a toy could participate in the collective and sanitized war experience by simply listening to the wireless. The film program for *Wunschkonzert* summarizes the magical effect radio had on the nation:

> A voice vibrates through the air. "Here is the greater German Radio! We are beginning the Request Concert for the Armed Forces." A magical ribbon embraces front and homeland. In the dugout in France, in the submarine on an enemy mission, in the air base on the coast, in the quiet room of a mother, in thousands and hundreds of thousands of homes, everywhere the flood of word and song and music resounds and vibrates. . . . The sorrow and joy of the individual, the unknown, the nameless become the sorrow and joy of the entire nation. All hearts beat in the same rhythm of feelings.[21]

According to one contemporary critic, "Request Concert" was much more than just entertainment, it actually transmitted the nation's inner feelings and military goals:

> Whoever has heard such a "Request Concert for the Armed Forces" knows how in such hours folk and army feel connected like one single

large family. He understands the incredible meaning of the radio as the only medium today that is in the position to link eighty million people in a great communal experience. Thus the "Request Concert" also conveys to every German *the feeling of power and belonging.*[22]

Radio and film technologies radically changed how the masses perceived war. Radio brought up-to-date war reports into the home, work place, social club, and school. It connected villager and city dweller, worker and housewife, young and old, while making physical presence unnecessary for instantaneous participation in the military action. Radio also brought about a change in the sense of public and private space by transforming the traditionally private realm into a public forum. Film, and especially newsreels, brought scenes from the war front into every neighborhood cinema on a weekly basis. The intimate battle experiences of soldiers in distant regions were transmitted with great speed into formerly private environs of the home front.

The manner in which the motion picture *Wunschkonzert* utilizes the media of radio and film to capitalize on changes in perception caused by technological advances corresponds to Walter Benjamin's theory of the fascist aesthetic. In his essay "The Work of Art in the Age of Mechanical Reproduction," Benjamin notes that new technologies seek to fulfill "the desire of contemporary masses to bring things 'closer' spatially and humanly."[23] Borsody's film satisfies both longings. By incorporating into the medium of film a successful radio program that stresses audience participation and unites soldier and civilian, *Wunschkonzert* overcomes physical distance and emotional separation. Furthermore, by connecting each emotionally charged wartime experience with a sentimental musical performance, it also triumphs over the coldly impersonal aspect of the scientific age. Finally, *Wunschkonzert* brings things closer spatially and humanly by providing a visual image of famous personalities known only by sound in the radio program and by framing newsreel footage within the context of a fictional but very human story.

The *Wunschkonzert* radio program and motion picture are both direct artistic outgrowths of the Second World War and therefore correspond to Benjamin's seminal notion: "Fascism [. . .] expects war to supply the artistic gratification of a sense perception that has been changed by technology."[24] Benjamin asserts that the aestheticizing of politics so central to fascism is merely a prelude to the more dangerous and logical development: the aestheticizing of war. *Wunschkonzert* participates in this discourse by depicting war as more than just a scenario against which the story unfolds. War becomes the key organizing principle of life, determining work, love, friendship, birth, and death. It also allows the individual members of the community to become strong, courageous, honorable, and charitable. Equally important, war entertains the German community in the sense that it creates extreme situations such as separation, economic hardship, and death, which are then sublimated through music. *Wunschkonzert* provides a musical response to every wartime experience, shifting war from the political to the aesthetic realm.

Wunschkonzert opens to the backdrop of the 1936 Olympic Games. Immortalized in Leni Riefenstahl's film *Olympia*, the Berlin Games were not merely a tribute to the highest physical achievements of mankind but also a media event of unparalleled propaganda value. They were the first Games ever to be broadcast over short-wave radio to some forty countries and to be televised; twenty-five TV halls were set up in Berlin and Leipzig. Berlin was transformed to represent Germany as a strong, harmonious, and, above all, peace-loving nation. The streets were decorated with Olympic flags and swastikas while anti-Semitic signs were taken down and publication of the inflammatory newspaper *Der Stürmer* was temporarily suspended. Hitler allocated over 100 million Reichsmarks to stage what were the most spectacular Games to date. Government-sponsored entertainment included fireworks, special concerts, operas, exhibitions, and lavish parties for thousands.[25]

Hitler saw in the Olympics a chance to show the world a peace-minded Germany, although he was planning military conquest.[26] Just a few months before the Games, on March 7, 1936, Hitler sent troops into the demilitarized Rhineland, an act in breach of the Locarno Treaty. On August 2, one day after the opening ceremonies, Hitler deployed the Condor Legion to participate in the Spanish Civil War. During the Games, Hitler secretly ordered German industry to convert to a war economy within the next four years and also instructed the military to prepare for an offensive war in the East.[27] The Olympics were thus transported from the realm of sports to the political arena, effectively depicting Germany's goodwill to all nations of the world as it secretly set its course on war.

The mainstay of the Olympic Games — athletic competition — is all but missing from *Wunschkonzert*. Despite the abundance of available sports footage from newsreels and *Olympia,* Borsody chose to concentrate on the opening ceremonies of August 1, 1936. Athletic performance denotes physical strength, agility, and beauty of the human form, yet it is never depicted in the film. Thus, the emphasis on theatrical ritual suggests Germany's desire for peace rather than military expansion, which the display of physical strength might imply.

The opening sequence of the film illustrates the glory of a New Germany in harmony with the nations of the world. A series of dissolves visually links Olympic symbols, the heavens, the German Stadium, the flags of the nations, and finally the crowd. This montage suggests that Germany will herald in a triumphant age of both peace and pageantry. Representatives from Sweden, Japan, Italy, and Germany parade around the stadium. The selection of athletes from a neutral country and the Axis powers politicizes the otherwise apolitical ceremony. Dressed all in white, their arms raised in the Nazi salute and preceded by the swastika flag, the Germans athletes resemble soldiers more than competitors. German uniqueness is cinematically demonstrated by a musical variation of the Olympic fanfare upon the athletes' arrival and by an aerial shot of their marching columns. Since Germany has the largest contingency and the only one framed in an extreme long shot, German superiority is confirmed in visual terms.

The ceremonies end with a ritual that seems to celebrate both war and peace; the stadium is filled with the sound of trumpets, bells, and canons while thousands of doves (resembling airplanes) fill the sky. The film then makes a fluid transition from the Olympic Games to the Polish campaign, thus conflating athletic competition, pageantry, and war. The nationalism, pride in German achievements, love for the Führer, and community spirit associated with the Olympics are mobilized in Borsody's film to solicit support for the war effort.

The characterization of Inge Wagner (Ilse Werner) and Herbert Koch (Carl Raddatz) also serves a didactic purpose. The young lovers stand in for the entire populace and set an example to which the audience should aspire. Their whirlwind romance is portrayed as representative of the exciting and troubled times. Their first encounter at the spectacular Olympic ceremonies is followed by a wedding proposal on their first date, an idyllic sailing trip on the Wannsee, and an abrupt, dramatic parting mandated by political circumstances. When Herbert is suddenly called to service in the Condor Legion and sworn to secrecy, Inge accepts her patriotic duty to endure separation stoically without knowing its purpose. Indeed, she demonstrates her unconditional loyalty by waiting three years for Herbert without hearing from him once. Inge also shows she knows how to "read" the signs of military authority.[28] She immediately recognizes that her childhood friend Helmut Winkler has been promoted to the rank of lieutenant by simply looking at his uniform. Inge's knowledge of military rites coupled with her submission to military standards define her as a model officer's wife. Herbert also exhibits conduct becoming a German officer. He exudes strength and discipline and immediately accepts that service must come first. Inge and Herbert assume roles that will become standard for men and women during the war. The woman patiently waits for her man and remains loyal to him, while the man puts his military duty and honor above all personal desires.

War is represented as inseparable from the fate of the young couple and the nation. The personalization of the war experience contributed widely to the film's popularity, but audiences were equally impressed by *Wunschkonzert's* presentation of the contemporary, real-life crisis of war through newsreel footage. Despite its documentary techniques, which create the illusion of reality, *Wunschkonzert* does not portray war in a realistic manner. War is the symbolic victory of man over machine, the mythic display of heroic ideals, or a light-hearted comedy, but never violent aggression against a political enemy. Borsody uses actual newsreel footage of the Condor Legion and the Polish campaign sparsely but effectively to portray the German armed forces as an invincible fighting machine. Whereas the true-to-life quality of this footage lends the combat sequences an air of reality, the extreme condensation of time and space situates the battle in the realm of the imaginary. The Spanish Civil War, for example, lasts only thirty-seven seconds in cinematic time. A map of Spain is followed by some fifteen shots in rapid succession depicting the Condor Legion in action. Images of a tank smashing down a wall, soldiers running alongside a tank carrying the Spanish flag, and airplanes flying through the sky bombing the mountains from a safe distance are underscored by uplifting march music. The Condor Legion consists of German soldiers discharged from the Wehrmacht and wearing civilian clothing. Defined in image and dialogue as a non-military unit, their victory is all the more sensational. The Condor Legion encounters no resistance. Indeed, there is no enemy in sight, no counterattack, no death; by their sheer presence the Germans seem to win a one-sided battle in a nondescript landscape. War becomes a fictional event despite its staging as documented fact.

The cinematic transition from Spain to Poland, from civil war to the Second World War, is nearly seamless. In a split second German pilots travel across the continent and three years time. After the date "September 6, 1939" flashes across the screen, shots of airplanes dropping bombs alternate with shots taken from within the airplane itself, positioning the spectator alongside the victorious German pilots. Like the Spanish Civil War, the Polish Campaign is condensed into a mere thirty-seven seconds.

With the incorporation of newsreel footage, Borsody adopts several essential properties of contemporary Nazi feature-length campaign films. These films accentuate the speed and mobility of the German army, giving the impression that it is an invulnerable, moving force.[29] For example, *Feuertaufe* (1940) and *Sieg im Westen* (1941) employ flash-cutting and numerous aerial shots to depict the Blitzkrieg. "Continual motion," Siegfried Kracauer argues, "works upon the motor nerves, deepening in the spectator the conviction of the Nazis' dynamic power; movement around and above a field implies complete control of that field."[30] Borsody uses the same techniques to demonstrate how German military power overcomes geographic and temporal distance effortlessly. In *Wunschkonzert,* the speed with which German "civilians" defeat the anti-fascists in Spain is eclipsed only by the near instantaneousness with which German "soldiers" triumph over Polish "aggressors." With the help of the cinematic apparatus, the military negates space and time. What Kracauer identifies as a lack of geographic specificity in the campaign films applies equally to *Wunschkonzert,* so that "whole battles develop in a never-never land where the Germans rule over time and space."[31]

Wunschkonzert portrays the Western Campaign primarily through dramatizations and only a few shots of newsreel footage. Again, the film does not stage war as violent aggression of one nation against another. War is instead waged on the symbolic level, specifically in the realm of perception. War and cinema, as Paul Virilio has convincingly argued, share the same structural framework in their common employment of technology to heighten perception. Indeed, "the history of battle is primarily the history of radically changing fields of perception."[32] Accordingly, the dramatic enactment of combat in *Wunschkonzert* can be seen as an attempt to rewrite the history of the First World War by winning a cinematic Second World War. The historical obstacles German soldiers encountered in battle between 1914 and 1918 are now symbolically reenacted and victoriously resolved. War, Virilio argues, "consists not so much in scoring territorial, economic, or other material victories as in appropriating the 'immateriality' of perceptual fields."[33] This immateriality of perception, specifically the ability to see, hear, and move, is secured in *Wunschkonzert* with the aid of technology and the "superior" Aryan body. Rather than actually killing a human adversary, the Germans win symbolic battles in which they conquer a nearly invisible enemy, master detection, and establish presence.

During the First World War, technological advances in weaponry limited hand-to-hand combat. The "invisible" and ever-changing battlefield of aircraft and submarine surveillance stood in stark contrast to the blind, static conflict of trench warfare. Deprived of sight and mobility in the grave-like trenches of the First World War, "the soldier had the feeling of being not so much destroyed as derealized or dematerialized."[34] Borsody's celluloid Second World War infantrymen transcend the historical obstacles of trench warfare. On a foggy night in France, the German infantrymen now cut through barbed wire, attack the enemy position in the trenches, and return to their base of operations with only one officer wounded and one foot-soldier, a young music student called Schwarzkopf, sacrificed in heroic death. By storming the enemy trenches, the German soldiers triumph over immobility in a military struggle devoid of any visible, physical confrontation; the audience does not see them actually killing the enemy. Equally significant, the soldiers overcome their loss of sight, ostensibly due to the thick fog but symbolically linked to trench fighting, by relying on their superior sense of hearing. They follow the sound of organ music to maneuver around a minefield and reach the safety of the church. The humiliating military losses in the trenches of the First World War are thus rectified cinematically.

Wunschkonzert highlights the machinery employed in all branches of the armed services to deploy soldiers and transmit information: tanks, airplanes, trains, submarines, cars, telegraph, telephone, radio. The Luftwaffe pilot, however, seems to epitomize the modern warrior best, for he controls the machine, harnesses its dynamic energy, and enjoys the freedom of flight. The pilot also possesses a bird's-eye view, a privileged vantage point from which he can observe the enemy. If the eye is the ultimate weapon, then the pilot will ensure victory.

Parallel to the infantrymen, who rely on their heightened sense of hearing to complete their mission, the Luftwaffe pilots overcome visual limitations by "appropriating the 'immateriality' of perceptual fields" (Virilio). Captain Koch and Lieutenant Winkler are sent on a reconnaissance mission, but like the foot soldiers, they are caught in the fog. Under heavy artillery fire, Koch locates the position of enemy ships with his naked eyes, so that the human body is inscribed into the war machine. His crew radios its sighting to headquarters seconds before Winkler is wounded and the plane is shot down. A German submarine intercepts their distress signal and rescues the crew as the Luftwaffe flies overhead on its way to engage the enemy. Aided by a discerning sense of sight in tandem with superior technology (airplane, submarine, radio), the German armed forces detect the enemy position, transmit the information, and begin an invisible (off-screen) attack.

Borsody focuses considerable attention on the soldiers' daily life, which is more akin to a camping trip than the regimented and deadly experience of war. Infantrymen march in columns and sing to the approval of the civilian populace as they leave for the front. The heroic Luftwaffe pilots Koch and Winkler find time between missions to lounge on the beach and talk about their girlfriends at home. The submarine crew, when it is not rescuing fighter pilots, gathers together to sing about the sailor's undying love for the sea. In their barracks the infantrymen shave, clean their weapons, play cards, and drink coffee. But most of all, servicemen from every branch of the military listen to the radio. With its emphasis on a cheerful, harmonious community of men who occupy themselves with mundane, everyday tasks or bask in leisure, *Wunschkonzert* romanticizes military life.

The war even engenders comical situations. The butcher Kramer and the baker Hammer, for instance, find five abandoned French pigs in the countryside but no French soldiers — unless the pigs are a comment on the French enemy. Ordered to deliver the pigs as a donation to the *Wunschkonzert,* the two enlisted men take the train to Berlin, compose a ridiculous song on the way, and appear on the radio program. Kramer and Hammer experience humorous adventures rather than the perils of armed struggle. Their comic exploits are presented with such levity that they trivialize the serious situation and make the war seem harmless.

Grim reality, bloodshed, and destruction are nonexistent in this film. Everyday life on the battlefield, in the trenches, in the submarine, and in the air is generally reduced to the domestic and work activities of peacetime. This mundane image of military service works to relieve the spectator's anxiety over the concrete dangers of war. It also sustains the myth widely spread in late 1940 that the war would end quickly. After the lightning victories over Poland, Denmark, Norway, Holland, Belgium, and France in 1939 and 1940, the majority of Germans basked in the euphoria of conquest. While there were numerous swings in public opinion and morale during the first year of war, the swift defeat of France marked a high point of public optimism never again met or surpassed. Notably encouraged by spectacular military successes in a war of movement and the reversal of the Versailles Treaty with France's defeat, the German populace expressed enthusiastic support for Adolf Hitler and his war effort.[35]

Rather than presenting war in terms of death and loss, *Wunschkonzert* stresses how war allows individuals to develop their inner potential to the fullest. Selected to speak on the *Wunschkonzert* radio program, for example, the shy and retiring baker Hammer becomes a forceful presence. On the home front, the war also provides opportunities for personal growth. Working women, pregnant wives, and grieving mothers all adapt to the necessities of war and seem to benefit from the sacrifices. The butcher's wife, a small and dependent woman, learns to run the business without her husband, while the baker's wife, a large and gruff woman, is able to demonstrate her hidden generosity and gentle spirit. Even the teacher's wife, a young woman in delicate health expecting her first child, seems better off having her baby alone. She expresses relief that her husband will be at the front and too busy to worry about her and the child. The German nuclear family, conceived in Nazi ideology as the bastion of Aryan virtues, is almost nonexistent in *Wunschkonzert*. Because of the military struggle, not one household remains intact. War dictates a new definition of kinship. Rather than extolling the individual family, Nazi war propaganda stressed the need for disparate groups to bind together into a large extended family, the *Volksgemeinschaft*.

Wunschkonzert depicts a war in which only one German soldier dies. The young music student Schwarzkopf sacrifices himself in an aestheticized, meaningful death accompanied by triumphant music on the church grounds. Schwarzkopf and his friend Friedrich are stationed as sentries at a church. From a window high in the choir loft, they look for their comrades who are lost in the thick fog. Schwarzkopf decides to play the church organ so that the soldiers can follow the music back to the church. Ironically, the soldier who does not fire a single shot saves his unit. Schwarzkopf's death is staged with religious iconography that exalts his sacrifice but shifts it from Christian to Nazi martyrdom. His death is set to organ music, a variation on Bach and the Olympic fanfare, which suggests a bridge between Germany's glorious past and the Nazi present. When bombs fall on the church and he becomes aware of his impending death, Schwarzkopf appears to be transfigured. His eyes glaze over and a strange, rapturous smile appears on his face while the fires rage in the background, symbolically consuming him on the sacrificial altar of the Reich. Like a martyr burned at the stake for his beliefs, Schwarzkopf is guaranteed eternal life after death in the mythic pantheon of Nazi heroes. An artistic soul whose life was devoted to his mother and his music, Schwarzkopf leaves behind no wife and no child. Because he neither furthers the race nor complies with the warrior image, his death is acceptable by fascist standards. Present at his death, however, is his friend, the school-teacher Friedrich, who has just become the father of a baby boy. Thus, death and birth are portrayed as complementary. When one man dies another takes his place so that the folk and the cycle of national life can continue in the male line. After Schwarzkopf's death, combat is over and entertainment takes precedence; the remainder of the film deals with the *Wunschkonzert* radio show and the resolution of the love story. The theater of operations is effectively replaced by musical theater.

In the Third Reich, radio technology allowed the regime to transmit to the entire nation simultaneously and orchestrate a common cultural experience for the masses. The Nazis were determined to tap into the nation's pride in a shared musical heritage and forge a collective national identity that would combine tradition with innovation. Well before it assumed power in 1933, the Nazi Party attempted to use cultural heroes like Ludwig van Beethoven to legitimize its political agenda. Beethoven was promoted as an artist who, like Adolf Hitler, embodied National Socialist heroic ideals. Music scholars drew explicit parallels between Beethoven and Hitler, emphasizing their artistry, patriotism, and leadership qualities. Critics portrayed Beethoven as not just a great composer but also a legendary spiritual leader who could unify the folk with his powerful art. The Nazis appropriated Beethoven's music for party rituals and sponsored concerts, festivals, and radio programs like the internationally renowned "Beethoven Cycle" broadcast in January 1934 on the *Deutschlandsender*, the national broadcasting station. By banning so-called degenerate music (jazz, swing, atonal music, and music by Jews, Negroes, and Bolsheviks) and cultivating "pure" German music by composers like Beethoven, Mozart, and Wagner, the Party could fashion itself as the legitimate heir, if not the savior, of Germany's rich cultural legacy. The alignment of National Socialism with German high culture was seen as an effective way to appeal to middle-class tastes and assure the educated burgher that the regime (and later the war) would not interfere with familiar leisure activities.[36]

This alignment of Beethoven and the Nazi war effort is given vivid expression in the film *Wunschkonzert*. Family and friends gather together in a neighbor's living room to listen to the young music student Schwarzkopf play Beethoven's *Pathétique* on the piano. In the movie, Beethoven's music acts as a social equalizer and creates a forum where all classes can freely mingle. Representatives from the educated bourgeoisie, petit bourgeoisie, and the artist class, each dressed in Wehrmacht uniform, find common ground in their shared cultural heritage and new military identity. Beethoven's music, like the war, allows this disparate group to come together in a common cause.

The connection between maintaining German cultural achievements and armed struggle is made apparent by the way this scene merges with the next. Beethoven's sonata is suddenly taken over by a soldier's marching song while the camera cuts to a shot from outside the apartment and pans over to columns of marching infantrymen. The nearly seamless transition of music and camera work establishes a bridge spanning the gulf between high and low art, classical and folk traditions, the intimate realm of neighbors and the wider social framework of nation. The fluidity of these scenes suggests that war is necessary to protect German culture. Indeed, the episode illustrates cinematically Goebbels's earlier declaration on why the nation was forced to fight, "We Germans are defending in this war against the hostile plutocratic powers not only our living space, our daily bread, and our machines, we are also defending our German culture."[37]

The "Request Concert" radio program staged in this motion picture plainly links war with the cultural industry. The show consists of ten performances ranging from classical to pop music and from comedy sketches to solemn tributes. Crowd pleasers include the Berlin Philharmonic performing the overture to Mozart's *Marriage of Figaro* and movie star Marika Rökk singing the hit song from her 1938 film *Eine Nacht in Mai*. Each performance functions like a microcosm of Nazi cultural policy and effective war propaganda since it provides a strategy on how to deal with the real-life hardships and emotional problems triggered by war.

In two numbers, a sense of humor is shown to be an important tactic for coping with war-related stress. First, Bavarian comedian Weiß-Ferdl sings a lighthearted salute to the anti-intellectualism so widely promoted by the Nazi regime: "I'm so happy I'm no intellectual, no enlightened fellow, no know-it-all, not quite a bright light! . . . Where you're better off not too educated, being a little bit dumb has often stood the test." Weiß-Ferdl also jokes about food rationing and regional differences, claiming Berlin can keep the "Request Concert" if Munich gets more butter. In another comic sketch, actors Heinz Rühmann, Josef Sieber, and Hans Brausewetter, known to contemporary audiences as the bachelor trio from the popular 1939 *Paradies der Junggesellen* (Bachelors' Paradise), sing the film's hit song "Can't Shake a Seaman." This song, reportedly the one most often requested by soldiers, relates to the fear of emotional involvement, but the sentiment can just as easily apply to the war: "And if the whole earth quakes, and the world becomes unhinged, that can't shake a seaman. No fear, no fear, Rosemarie! Ahoy!" By making fun of fear and turmoil, the song reassures the audience that everything will be okay.

Just as one needs an outlet for daily frustrations, one must also learn how to deal with such highly emotional events as birth and death suddenly decontextualized by war-related separation. The radio program offers the necessary support by reconstituting a sense of family and community with their familiar rituals. Instead of traditional Christian ceremonies like baptism and funeral rites, the Nazi cultural industry offers musical celebration and commemoration on the radio. For example, front-line soldiers first learn of their child's birth from radio announcer Heinz

Goedecke, who records the father's name and encourages the assembled audience to share in the joy of these separated families. While a children's choir sings the lullaby "Fall Asleep, My Little Prince," the camera cuts to a grandmother in an armchair reading to a little boy and girl, to an elderly woman adorned with the Mother's Cross sewing at the radio, to soldier Friedrich who learns he is the father of a baby boy, to his radiant wife holding the child, and finally to a tableau of soldiers who add their deep voices to establish the nuclear family acoustically. It is only with the aid of radio and cinema that the German family can remain intact. This montage sequence illustrates particularly well how National Socialism embraced modern technology while propagating the myth of the organic community.[38] In a similar manner, a soldier's death is memorialized in song, allowing the radio audience to mourn collectively in a performance that is simultaneously entertainment and sentimental ritual. The young music student Schwarzkopf, who heroically offered his life to save his regiment, represents a generation of fallen soldiers. His mother requests her son's favorite song, "Good Night, Mother." While the bittersweet song is played, the camera pans over Schwarzkopf's piano, his photograph, and a bust of Beethoven to the mother dressed in black at her usual place at the window. With her stoic grief and ability to share her loss with the community, Mrs. Schwarzkopf shows the nation how to cope with death. The performance sublimates the loss of a young man's life to the level of art (or kitsch).[39]

Wunschkonzert ends with a celebration of German strength and unity. The final sequence, edited out of most releases after 1945, begins in the broadcasting studios of the *Wunschkonzert* radio program. The on-screen audience demonstrates its support for the war effort when it spontaneously breaks into the song "Wir fahren gegen Engelland." The voices of the united home front flow into the next scene, a montage of airplanes, artillery launchers, speedboats, torpedo launchers, and battle ships. The flash-cut editing establishes German military speed, dominance, and omnipresence. A close-up of the billowing imperial war flag, the symbolic heir to the Olympic flag, closes the film and brings it full circle both structurally and thematically. This concluding montage, like the opening one, promotes a sense of belonging to a victorious nation fighting to maintain the newly gained pageantry, nationalism, and love for the Führer.

With its documentary footage and portrayal of current events, Borsody's film implicitly promises an authentic rendition of the war experience. What it delivers instead is an alternate reality, one in which war provides for every human need. *Wunschkonzert* fulfills the audience's request for war to entertain, instruct, grant an emotional release, and rectify history. Like all successful Nazi feature films, *Wunschkonzert* engages in a discourse of desire. It caters to the audience's emotional needs by integrating troubling aspects of everyday life into the more palatable reality of cinematic experience. For the duration of the film and its recasting in the mind's eye, one can imagine war as harmless or even beneficial to the national community.

Performing for soldiers on the Western Front: *Die große Liebe.*

The Spectacle of War: *Die große Liebe* (1942)

In the spring of 1942, the British government implemented a new military strategy of bombing civilian targets, especially working-class neighborhoods, hoping that it could destroy morale on the German home front. Shortly after midnight on May 31, 1942, the British Royal Air Force launched its first One Thousand Bomber Raid (code named "Millennium") with Cologne its target. Within an hour and a half the RAF dropped nearly half a million incendiaries on the city center. The fireball was visible from over one hundred miles away. Upon reaching the devastated city, one British pilot remarked, "It was suddenly silent on board. If what we were seeing was true, then Cologne had to have been destroyed. We looked at the Rhine, but it was no mistake: what we saw down there was reality."[40]

Less than two weeks after that bombing raid, on June 12, 1942, Rolf Hansen's home-front film *Die große Liebe* (True Love) premiered at Berlin's largest cinema, the Ufa-Palast am Zoo, and quickly became the most popular film of the year. In the first ten months of its release, *Die große Liebe* earned

8 million RM playing to an audience of some 27.2 million spectators.[41] The film's touching love story, sensational musical numbers, measured comic relief, and star-studded cast all contributed to its overwhelming popularity. The trade papers, however, praised *Die große Liebe* primarily for its timely subject and realism.[42] What kind of realism did the film offer the masses, especially in the weeks and months following the premiere and massive, persistent bombing raids? What drove audiences in the summer of 1942 to this love story about a revue singer and a Luftwaffe pilot repeatedly separated by the fighting in North Africa, France, and the Soviet Union?

I suggest we take our cue from the Nazi trade papers and examine the way in which this home-front film constructs the reality of war. The vast majority of German feature films made between 1939 and 1945 were set in either a distant, heroic past or a nondescript, seemingly peaceful present. *Die große Liebe,* a striking exception to this pattern, centers on daily life during the Second World War. With its contemporary setting, the film offered audiences a unique opportunity to identify and empathize with characters trying to balance the conflicting wartime demands of love and duty. *Die große Liebe* develops an entertaining and emotionally gripping model for dealing with air raids, rationing, separation, and suppression of desire for the sake of military victory. The film links the conflicts in the homeland and on the battlefield through highly sentimental episodes to illustrate how the nation forms a united front against the enemy. Hansen renders his fictional world with enough authentic details for the audience to see not just familiar characters and situations but also to see themselves in the events unfolding onscreen. Since the main characters are repeatedly depicted as spectators and performers, they hold up a mirror to moviegoers to look at themselves and imagine their own participation in the nation's real-life drama. By drawing structural parallels between musical and military spectacles, the film presents theater as a metaphor for the participatory role war demands of soldier and civilian alike.

Die große Liebe fashions reality so that war functions as a dominant and positive force in the lives of Hanna Holberg (Zarah Leander) and Paul Wendlandt (Viktor Staal). War works as a catalyst for the love story. Paul's battle report brings him to Berlin, while his knowledge of an imminent bombing raid allows him to gain access to Hanna's kitchen, cellar, and eventually her bedroom.[43] As the air raid warden comments about their budding love, "The siren will bring it to the light of day."[44]

For the soldier who knows nothing about blackouts and the singer who is not shaken by them, war changes ordinary experiences into a reality more beautiful than a fairy tale. As they look out over the darkened city in anticipation of a bombing raid, Paul and Hanna discuss how wartime reality, despite its dangers (or maybe because of its dangers) makes the city beautiful. When Hanna mentions that the city looks like a fairy tale, Paul disagrees, saying the city is "even more beautiful. Like reality."[45]

The dangers inherent in war give the everyday a dynamic quality that is both new and exciting. In this highly charged atmosphere of life and death, intense passion and true love can evolve. Despite the characters' disavowal of contemporary life as a fairy tale, the narrative continuously associates war with an imaginary kingdom where wishes come true. The film concludes with a song whose opening lyrics confirm the bond between war and fairy tales. Hanna sings: "I know, once upon a time a miracle will come to pass and then a thousand fairy tales will come true."[46] The song removes "once upon a time," the formulaic introduction of fairy tales, from the remote, make-believe past and situates it in a not too distant Nazi future as suggested by the lyrics "once upon a time it will come to pass." The film links the wish for a miraculous victory to an equally strong wish for a romantic happy ending, so that the former seems to be the only guarantee for the latter.

The battle between love and duty, rather than between Germany and the Allied nations, becomes the principal conflict of the film and, by extension, the times. With war so thoroughly intertwined with the love story, military victory seems predicated on whether or not the pilot and his girl can work out their problems.[47] Because the songs refer ambiguously to developments on the battlefield as well as in the love affair, they reinforce this idea. In the number "It's Not the End of the World," for example, Hanna sings of overcoming emotional heartaches to a hall filled with injured soldiers. While her song ostensibly deals with the ups and downs lovers suffer because of wartime separation, it could just as easily apply to the vicissitudes of combat. Hanna's lyrics, her gestures, and the soldiers' reactions aptly illustrate this ambiguity. She sings "sometimes things are up and sometimes down," while her hands mimic diving airplanes and the assembled Wehrmacht troops link arms to join in the rhythmic movements.[48] Whether a reference to war or to love, the song provides an outlet for frustration and generates an optimistic sense of camaraderie.[49]

The film addresses many of the emotional problems created by war, specifically how people waver between hope and desperation, deal with feelings of abandonment, endure loneliness, and successfully adapt to a curtailed domestic life. The main characters, who serve as models, anchor these psychological issues. Nazi film critics and officials maintained that feature films inherently encouraged viewers to identify with sympathetic characters and emulate their behavior. In his 1943 book *Betrachtungen zum Filmschaffen* (Considerations on Film Making), Reich Film Dramaturge Fritz Hippler asserted that if a film gratified viewers' emotional needs, it could also supply influential role models and an orientation in life. Hippler summarized how film could potentially define values and teach behavior:

> Besides the personal connection between the audience and the main character during the course of the movie, film also generates the ambition to be like the star. How he clears his throat and how he spits, how

he is dressed, how he behaves, if and what he drinks, what and how he smokes, whether he is a stuffed shirt or a man-about-town, that all has an effect not only in the film but also in the life of the audience. A powerful and victorious film releases a different public than a tragic or comic film. After an Albers film, an assistant barber is an Albers; nobody had better dare to get mixed up with him.[50]

Film critics in Nazi Germany praised home-front films like *Die große Liebe* because they evoked in viewers "an inner willingness to lose themselves completely and totally in the figures and the events surrounding them." They deemed the effect of these role models as substantial, "because everyone in the audience, whether soldier or civilian, man or woman, has someone 'present' and identifies the fate up on the screen with that of a friend, husband, brother or fiancée. In short, after the first images, every member of the audience sits in the auditorium with a trusting, open heart."[51]

Considering the significance attached to the characters, it is no surprise that Hansen chose Zarah Leander and Viktor Staal to play Hanna Holberg and Paul Wendlandt. Best known for her imposing stature, flaming red hair, and legendary contralto, Zarah Leander was by all accounts the diva of Nazi cinema. Directors most often cast the Swedish actress in melodramas where she played seemingly independent, sensual women who suffer unbearable anguish before being redeemed as proper and obedient wives. *Die große Liebe* capitalizes on Zarah Leander's star image to frame the character's education in appropriate wartime behavior within familiar and entertaining melodramatic conventions. As in nearly all her German films, Leander's character is a sensual entertainer who undergoes the painful process of being tamed by a man and disciplined for marriage. What distinguishes her role in this film is that her training directly relates to the contemporary military struggle. Hanna must learn what it takes to be an officer's wife: wait patiently and accept separation without question. She develops from a self-centered prima donna reluctant to sacrifice her own immediate gratification into a selfless wife/comrade committed to victory. Although she initially asserts "treat yourself to whatever you like" (erlaubt ist, was gefällt), she eventually comes to accept that separation is part of everyday life, each moment together is precious, and the postponement of pleasure serves a higher goal.

Although Viktor Staal did not possess the same star recognition as Leander, he had already established a solid reputation as a romantic leading man. Starring opposite such popular actresses as Leander in *Zu neuen Ufern* (1937, Sierck), Lilian Harvey in *Capriccio* (1938, Ritter), and Marika Rökk in *Eine Nacht in Mai* (1938, Jacoby), Staal specialized in roles of handsome and likeable (if somewhat wooden) bachelors who marry exciting, unpredictable women. Typecast as the strong and dependable suitor, Staal brings these qualities to his portrayal of Paul Wendlandt. A dedicated soldier, Paul must discover the value of attachment to a woman and the homeland. Whereas he starts as a daredevil without any emotional ties, he learns that a soldier needs someone special at home waiting just for him. Paul only recognizes how important love is for a man after he assumes the traditionally female role of waiting during war.[52] When Paul tries to visit Hanna unexpectedly, he discovers that she is entertaining the troops in France. Disappointed, he experiences first hand what it is like to wait for a loved one to return from the front. But one aspect of Paul's personality remains constant: he is an officer devoted to the strictest military code of honor. What we hear about Paul in the opening scene characterizes him throughout: "He won't leave his machine in the lurch."[53]

Like all melodramas, *Die große Liebe* needs to place obstacles in the path of the romantic leads to give the characters something to grow around and reach past. One serious obstacle to Paul and Hanna's romance is their different, yet equally valid understandings of *Glück* (luck). Paul thinks of luck as fortune. During the film, he repeats five times that he has "proverbial good luck" (ein sprichwörtliches Glück). Luck allows him to win Hanna's heart, succeed at games, avoid serious injury, and triumph over the enemy. Hanna, by contrast, talks about luck in terms of happiness. She pictures herself living contentedly with Paul in a cottage, gardening and washing diapers. Ultimately Hanna begins to recognize that personal happiness and the fortunes of war go hand in hand. She eventually develops a realistic attitude and accepts that an ideal married life must wait until after the war. In her final musical performance, Hanna acknowledges their common fate: "We both have the same star, and your fate is mine too."[54]

To reinforce the message, *Die große Liebe* mirrors the central plot in two romantic subplots. The first subplot, with Käthe and Albert, mirrors Hanna's search for an ideal relationship with Paul. By rendering the same story with minor characters in the tradition of the *Ständeklausel* (dramatic convention of social rank), the film ridicules unrealistic expectations for personal happiness and takes a humorous look at the ideal man. Käthe fools herself into thinking that the physically powerful acrobat Albert loves her. Only after she finds the ordinary soldier, Maxe, can Käthe have a realistic relationship and even find true love. Käthe, like Hanna, prefers a man who acts not on stage but in an arena that actually counts — the battlefield. In Käthe's words: "I'd rather have my Max in hand than Albert on the trapeze."[55]

The second subplot deals with Alexander's unsuccessful courtship of Hanna, which helps define the nature of a real man. "Hopeless but cheerful" (hoffnungslos aber heiter), Alexander serves more as a foil to Paul than as a viable suitor for Hanna. As the sensitive musician, Alexander's inability to be forceful and his tendency to be too nice make him both a comic and a tragic character. Both Alexander and Albert fall short of ideal masculinity. At one extreme stands Albert, seemingly desirable as the strong and silent type, but whose shyness and indecisiveness make him laughable. At the other extreme sits Alexander, an artistic type who is equally inappropriate because he is weak and overly sentimental. Paul forms the middle ground, a man who possesses the right mixture of strength, determination, and feeling. A fighter pilot with equal amounts of discipline and sentiment, Paul embodies the virtues Goebbels so often described as "romanticism tempered by steel."

In its presentation of the *Volksgemeinschaft* (national community) gathered together in the cellar during an air raid, the film also works out real-life tensions created by war. Elements of reality enter the scene through stereotypes: the high-strung, screeching old woman; the overzealously organized family patriarch; the humorless, intellectual complainer; and the hoarder who is generous with other people's property. Each stereotype represents a genuine problem on the home front: fear of bodily harm and death, need for a contingency plan in emergencies, and resentment of hardships, especially rationing. By poking fun at problems in a lighthearted manner, the film shows them to be either unfounded or easily remedied. A cup of real coffee and a good dose of humor seem enough to distract the home front from carpet-bombings and the conflicts of world war.

The images of a community spending an evening together, playing games, knitting, and chatting portray a sanitized version of life in the midst of Allied aerial strikes. The cellar with its comfortable furniture and friendly atmosphere looks more like a neighborhood social club than a bomb shelter. The film depicts shortages in consumer goods as minor inconveniences, which ultimately teach people to share with the community and forge a cooperative spirit. In contrast to this rather harmless depiction of civilian life, the situation on the German home front in 1942 was serious.[56] According to secret surveillance reports compiled by the *Sicherheitsdienst* (Security Service), food shortages in June 1942 were so severe that many workers complained of "a continuous feeling of hunger." The authorities voiced continued concern over the worsening food situation because "the atmosphere and attitude of the population is still determined by the difficulty in the food sector."[57]

Despite the discrepancy between the film's depiction of hardships and the state's assessment of them, especially in regard to the severity of the situation, *Die große Liebe* seems to have given audiences a reality compatible with their own. The cellar scene, for example, highlights everyday experiences of adversity, to which many viewers could relate. Moreover, the film offers a remedy by suggesting that humor can be an effective outlet for normal frustrations. When a character loses his sense of humor in the face of minor inconveniences, his attitude is depicted as inappropriate and somehow tied to more deeply rooted personal problems. For example, when Alexander yells at a waiter because he and Hanna cannot get dessert in a restaurant, his anger is plainly an overreaction to the situation. Alexander merely uses the food shortage as an excuse to vent his frustration; the underlying reason for his outburst is the news that Hanna loves another man. Just as the film associates passion with danger to illustrate the inherent connection between love and war, it also associates the frustrations of unrequited love with wartime food shortages to make the same connection.[58]

By constantly presenting contemporary hardships within the framework of the love story, the film obscures any direct correlation between war and bombing raids or food shortages. Wartime dangers and inconveniences, divorced from any geopolitical conflicts, function as catalysts for the love story or as signifiers of romantic intentions. While the film acknowledges wartime problems, it generally frames them as harmless in the short run and even beneficial in the long run. For example, the Allied bombing raid causes no apparent damage, but it allows Hanna to get to know Paul better. Furthermore, although a Soviet pilot shoots down Paul's plane, his minor injury gives him the opportunity to marry Hanna and enjoy a three-week honeymoon.

Die große Liebe provides a good example of how the home-front film forged the bonds between civilian and serviceman. Home-front films stressed the need for all members of the community to unite behind the soldiers and spoke to one of the more haunting myths of the First World War, namely that the German troops were stabbed in the back by the homeland.[59] *Die große Liebe* establishes this crucial link between the armed forces and the folk on the level of performance and spectatorship, uniting individuals through entertainment into a collective act that ultimately supports the war effort. Uniformed soldiers appear alternately as heroes performing a real-life display of martial skills for a captivated audience and as spectators attending an equally stimulating musical variety show. In a similar manner, the film depicts stage performers both as actors entertaining soldiers and as spectators mesmerized by newsreel footage of battle scenes. Since the characters and the scenes share the same properties, the film establishes a nexus whereby war and theater are structurally related. At four moments in particular, the spectacle of the theater merges with the spectacle of war.

The opening sequence blurs the distinction between reality, fiction, and documentary. Set in the skies over North Africa in 1941, familiar elements from contemporary wartime newsreels such as pulsating martial music, flash editing, and aerial shots of Stukas in flight fill the sequence. Into this newsreel-quality footage, the director Hansen intersperses the fictional story of Luftwaffe pilot Paul Wendlandt who is unable to engage his landing gear. The use of newsreel conventions heightens the drama of Paul's crash landing, giving the fiction an aura of reality. Because the opening sequence so obviously quotes a familiar newsreel style, it also draws attention to its own construction as a motion picture. This self-reflective narrative creates a decisive link between war and spectacle. Although the film renders Paul's crash landing as a real-life military action, it is also a visual sensation witnessed by onscreen viewers. The scene is presented in the same terms as theater, with Paul as an actor on display and his squadron as an onscreen audience who watches the scene intently but from afar. Watching the war thus resembles watching a cinematic or theatrical spectacle.

The second moment comes as Paul's real-life aerial show segues into Hanna's musical extravaganza, where she performs on stage as the object of desire, singing of unbridled passion to servicemen who need to renew themselves emotionally before returning to the front. Not only do structural similarities and visual thrills connect Paul and Hanna's shows, but so does the presence of an onscreen military audience. Paul and his friend Etzdorf, both dressed in Luftwaffe uniform, are prominently pictured as members of the audience watching Hanna's show "My Life for Love." A swift tracking shot from the back of the theater to the stage establishes the conventional distance between audience and actor, while numerous close-ups of Hanna and reaction shots of Paul work to redefine the theatrical relationship. The intimate camera work illustrates how emotional involvement can bridge the gap between viewer and actor, soldier and singer, war and entertainment.

The third time we encounter the theater of war, the roles are reversed. Unexpectedly, shots of a dogfight fill the screen, accompanied by the sounds of diving Stukas and dramatic, upbeat music. It appears as if we are watching a newsreel woven directly into the feature film when an announcer reports that Luftwaffe pilots continue to engage the British in a dramatic air battle. Suddenly the camera tracks backward to reveal a movie screen, theater, and audience including Hanna. War is rendered as cinema so that Hanna can watch it in the *Wochenschau* (weekly newsreel). The air show unfolding on the screen for Hanna resembles her own performance. Now she is the embedded spectator entranced by the sights and sounds of the Stukas, filled with desire for her fighter pilot conjured up in the newsreel. The military replicates the entertainment Hanna offered the soldiers so that she can enjoy the captivating pleasures of war.

Finally, Hanna becomes a bridge between war and spectacle when she entertains the troops on the Western front. Like the radio in *Wunschkonzert,* Hanna overcomes the distance between homeland and front by bringing her musical performance to the soldiers. Whereas she moved Paul emotionally and sexually in her first performance, she now literally moves the servicemen to sway in response to her song, "Davon geht die Welt nicht unter." Both performances send the same message: women are essential to the war effort because they motivate men into action. As long as women fight in concert with men, victory is inevitable. Hansen uses Hanna's participation in a cultural event organized by the *Sonderreferat Truppenbetreuung* (the Propaganda Ministry's special unit for troop entertainment) to help fulfill the state's mission of uniting war and art. As Hans Hinkel, the director of troop entertainment, remarked: "The connection between sword and lyre — as has been validated in troop entertainment for our soldiers — represents the most glorious symbol of German victory over the outdated plutocratic world hostile to us."[60] Maintaining the link between war and theater is portrayed as crucial to military victory and survival. For example, only after Paul and Hanna break up, after they sever the ties between home and war fronts, do the Soviets shoot down Paul's plane. The deadly consequences of autonomy are also apparent when the film cuts to Hanna walking along the Via Appia, where she contemplates the beauty of death and confesses: "Sometimes I too wish I were dead."[61] The symbiosis between Paul and Hanna demands that she understand what it is like to be surrounded by death and experience its fatal attraction so she can accept its seductive power.

When Paul and Hanna finally meet in the mountain hospital and look together toward the planes flying by, they are united in their role as spectators and in their dedication to the war effort. Again the film structures the scene to have an onscreen military audience. Two servicemen watch Hanna's arrival, nod to each other, and retreat. The camera takes over the servicemen's point of view and allows the film audience to watch the lovers watching the war. The self-reflective narrative provides a point of identification for the film's actual audience, allowing the viewer to participate in the love affair, entertainment, and war.[62]

Self-reflective moments in *Die große Liebe* do not call the film's ontological status or social reality into question. Instead, questions are directed towards the identity of the main characters who masquerade in illusory roles and must find their true selves. At the outset Paul and Hanna confuse the notions of "role" and "self" in respect to both their own identity and the identity of the other. In her first stage appearance, which is also her first appearance onscreen, Hanna plays the role of *femme fatale*. Costumed in a revealing gown and blond wig, she acts the part of an alluring, frivolous woman. Paul mistakes Hanna for her stage role, pursuing her relentlessly half the night. Only after the two share the role of parents in the bomb shelter does Paul see Hanna's hidden potential as a wife and mother.[63] Through the narrative, Hanna travels toward her authentic self, an officer's wife who subordinates her desire (read individuality) to the nation's wartime needs. National Socialism valorized a woman's sublimation of her own interests for the sake of her family and the national family, the *Volksgemeinschaft*. The prevailing view in the Third Reich held that women could only achieve the status of human beings when they accepted the role of motherhood as the genuine self and ceased to exist as an individual:

> If she is a real mother, she loses herself in her familial duties. But wonderfully: exactly therein, she becomes a woman and human being in the deepest sense. The more obvious her surrender, the more so. In losing her life she finds herself, her true dignity, her inherent humanity. . . . She becomes a mother and thus a whole human being by means of self-abnegation, not by self-assertion.[64]

Reduced to her function as potential mother and deprived of desire and even identity through self-denial, the individual woman vanishes. *Die große Liebe* illustrates this process of self-abnegation in the Via Appia scene, which ruptures the nearly seamless narrative fabric. Hanna walks as if in a trance along the deserted road in a landscape she calls "so endlessly cheerful despite the many gravestones" (so unendlich heiter trotz der vielen Grabdenkmäler). Her comfort among the graves and her desperate wish to be dead signal her symbolic death, one in which her ego and subjective desires perish. Only after purging herself of all vestiges of individuality does Hanna become reconciled with Paul and worthy of marriage.

Paul also masquerades when he adopts the persona of an adventurous and ardent man about town. Before he meets Hanna, Paul changes out of his military uniform into civilian clothing, disguising his true soldierly self. Paul's protective behavior in the bomb shelter, his concern for the community's well-being, and his ability to distract them from the bombs by organizing a group activity all reveal his potential role as father. Despite these demonstrated masculine qualities, Paul's identity is still unresolved. When Hanna asks him twice who he is, Paul only gives his name and describes himself in mysterious terms as a prophet and a traveler. Weeks later, when she reads his letters from the front, she finally learns his true identity as a Luftwaffe pilot. Still, she does not confirm his identity out loud. She merely says to him, "You are" (du bist), as if to imply that Paul's profession is so integral to his being that he simply "is."

The constant references in *Die große Liebe* to adopting roles, going to the theater and the movies, performing for others, and acting as spectators accentuate the pleasures inherent in the communal ritualized act of moviegoing. *Die große Liebe* creates an emotionally fulfilling experience of communion with others not only in the fictional narrative but also through the ritual of moviegoing itself. Both the fictional and the actual audience can enjoy the collective experience of being transported to a different time and space, a place where magic and make-believe govern the course of events. Günter Berghaus argues that fascist regimes throughout Europe "sought to translate their political creeds into theatrical language that drew heavily on the traditions of ritual and mysticism" to create a belief in the charismatic national community. Berghaus maintains that fascist theater, "like all ritual theatre, had the function of offering a healing power, or *katharsis,* in a moment of crisis and to communicate a binding belief system to the participants."[65] In the crisis of war, *Die große Liebe* offered the home and war fronts a group identity based on a shared emotional release, intimacy, physical closeness, and consumption of entertainment. It also provided a fictional model of viewers united in their consumption of entertainment and participation in war.

But the theater in *Die große Liebe* does not function merely as an escapist illusion or as a means to forge a collective identity. It also becomes a way to control the masses. Since war is defined in terms of participatory theater, civilians and soldiers alike become actors on display, constantly exposed to the policing gaze of their fellow actors. Confined in a perfect spectacle or panopticon as both actor and spectator, the individual is under constant surveillance with the implicit warning to behave. In his celebrated discussion of Bentham's panopticon, Michel Foucault writes, "visibility is a trap" and concludes:

> He who is subjected to a field of visibility, and who knows it, assumes responsibility for the constraints of power; he makes them play spontaneously upon himself; he inscribes in himself the power relation in which he simultaneously plays both roles; he becomes the principle of his own subjection.[66]

Die große Liebe presents this system of constant surveillance as a desirable condition. For instance, as an entertainer Hanna is constantly watched on stage. However, when she leaves the theater, she continues to be the object of the omnipresent gaze. The streetcar conductor observes her movements every night and reports on them to a group of men who continuously stare at her. Although Hanna seems mildly irritated by this scrutiny, it ultimately proves to be beneficial because it allows her love affair with Paul to develop. Only after Paul receives information from the conductor can he follow Hanna into the subway and find a way into her heart.

In a nation permeated by a state-sponsored surveillance apparatus, in a "terrifying social landscape . . . in which ordinary people eagerly helped to police one another," it is fitting that fantasies of an omnipresent gaze would penetrate the cinema.[67] As recent historical studies have demonstrated, the enthusiastic participation of ordinary citizens and not merely the watchful eye of Gestapo officials "kept the machinery of terror going and constituted a central component of the internal 'constitution' of the Third Reich."[68]

Die große Liebe contributes to the Nazi cinema of enchantment, creating a place so delightful one wants to share in the illusion at any price. Seen through the prism of cinema, constant surveillance of the civilian populace guarantees personal happiness. More importantly, total war becomes thinkable, tolerable, doable, when one keeps in mind that the world won't come to an end and perhaps a miracle will make fairy tales come true.

The Dance of Death: *Die Degenhardts* (1944)

By the summer of 1944, the Propaganda Ministry could hardly expect the home-front film to distract the audience from the fighting so close at hand. The German military situation was grim. The British-American forces had invaded the continent on D-Day, June 6, and were pushing eastward. On June 22, the Soviets successfully launched their summer campaign and were pushing westward with great speed. German cities were being reduced to ashes and rubble through continuous Allied aerial bombardment. Since civilians were forced to bear more and more hardships, Goebbels tried to boost morale with escapist fare. Of the sixty-two feature films that premiered in Germany in 1944, there were thirty-three comedies, eighteen dramas, six action adventures, and only five propaganda films.[69] Considering the general trend toward light distraction at this stage in the war, why did Werner Klingler's melancholy home-front film *Die Degenhardts* premiere in Lübeck on July 6, 1944?[70]

Die Degenhardts attempts not only to trigger anti-British sentiment by portraying Allied bombing strikes against German cultural monuments; it also tries to prepare the German people to cope with mass destruction and death.[71] This home-front film resonates with the pending doom perceived by the German populace at large. After the crushing defeat at Stalingrad and Goebbels's infamous call for total war, death is presented as a natural phenomenon. The war is no longer fought for individuals or the assurance of personal happiness but for the protection of future generations and German culture. The devastating bombing raids only alluded to in *Die große Liebe* become a palpable reality in *Die Degenhardts*. The city center is destroyed; the home front becomes the battlefield and soldiers are rendered as fleeting images in the collective memory. Emphasis is placed on rebuilding architectural milestones, preserving German classical music, and safeguarding the life of the Degenhardts's grandson.

Upholding cultural traditions: *Die Degenhardts*.

Klingler's film tells the story of an ordinary man's ambition, disappointment, and final triumph. On his sixty-fifth birthday, Karl Degenhardt (played by Heinrich George) receives a telegram from the mayor and believes he is to be promoted to Supervisor of City Parks. When he is given retirement instead, Degenhardt does not have the heart to tell his family. He pretends to go to work every day, but the truth is quickly revealed. After war breaks out and his hometown of Lübeck is bombed, Father Degenhardt volunteers for civil duty and is finally given the title he longed for: Supervisor.

German high culture plays a decisive role in the identity of the homeland, and the Degenhardt family nurtures this heritage in their daily lives. On their Sunday walk around town they admire the beauty of German architecture, represented by the Hanseatic Gothic brick houses, the city hall, the Holsten Gate, and St. Mary's Church. Their appreciation of German landscape is equally important. Father Degenhardt has a profound connection to the German soil; as a city official he is responsible for the planting and maintenance of city gardens and parks. In his free time, he tends his own private garden and potted plants or sends flowers to his loved ones.[72]

The Degenhardt men keep Germany's musical traditions alive with their evening concert performances. Neither mother nor daughter plays an instrument. Christine's only contribution is to turn the pages for her brother, while her mother provides the necessary audience. Son Jochen is an organ builder, pianist, and composer, who devotes himself completely to Germany's rich musical legacy. Like the past masters Dietrich Buxtehude and Johann Sebastian Bach, Jochen plays the magnificent organ in Lübeck's St. Mary's Church and maintains the continuity of German cultural life.

Finally, this middle class, nuclear family with five children (a rarity in Nazi cinema) seems intent on preserving a familiar domestic routine and social cohesion: the weekend family walks, music evenings, small circle of friends, solid bourgeois home, and sacrosanct patriarchal authority all contribute to communal stability and security.

Similar to *Wunschkonzert* and *Die große Liebe*, *Die Degenhardts* presents war as a national solution to personal problems. The conditions created by war allow for the fulfillment of individual desires and the resolution of domestic conflicts. As a price for the bounties of war, the individual must learn to deal with disappointment and accept duty stoically. Based on the example of the Degenhardt family, it becomes evident that every citizen needs to work for victory and pitch in for one another.

This home-front film also shows the audience how to cope with the omnipresence of death. Well before the war begins, Father Degenhardt contemplates the inevitability of dying and assures his family that death is a normal stage in the circle of life. The Degenhardt family is fascinated with the famous Lübeck *Totentanz* (Dance of Death), painted by Bernt Notke in 1463 for the Confessional Chapel in St. Mary's Church and destroyed in the Allied bombing raid on March 28, 1942.[73] Through its placement in the Confessional Chapel, its detailed depiction of the local cityscape, and its explicit references to typical Hanseatic civic figures and tradesmen, the Lübeck *Totentanz* invites the native observer into the narrative through personalization. One is compelled to envision oneself dancing with Death while reflecting upon one's own mortality and the Last Judgment.

The *Totentanz* functions in *Die Degenhardts* in the context of the Second World War much like the original frieze in the aftermath of the Black Plague. As a didactic art form in the tradition of the medieval *memento mori,* the *Totentanz* reminds the individual of his personal responsibility for the community's well-being and confirms God's divine will in the face of mass death. Despite its macabre subject, this work did not aim to instill fear in the viewer. Instead, it was meant to offer comfort and hope; it frames death in a meaningful order and gives sense to the position of powerlessness. It provides an anchor in a horror-filled existence while suggesting that eternal peace will be the just reward for the righteous.

The only human death actually depicted in the film is that of Degenhardt's boss, an unnamed character who laments how his life has been meaningless because he has no wife and no children. Degenhardt's boss is a lonely, sick, old man pictured in death with his hands gently crossed, covered in iridescent lighting, a peaceful end to a barren life. The heroic death of Degenhardt's oldest son Robert on the high seas, by contrast, is never depicted, nor is it even mentioned out loud. The viewer only learns about Robert's death by seeing Father Degenhardt's black armband as he silently hands a letter to a friend and receives condolences.

The destruction of cultural monuments, rather than the portrayal of a warrior's death, merits greater attention in this motion picture. The bombing of Lübeck is presented in a series of dissolves that link the organ built in 1516, a performance of Haydn's *Creation*, the German community gathered to celebrate its musical heritage in St. Mary's Church, the frieze depicting a community of death, and finally the bombed-out city. Accompanying the visual montage is a medley of the *Creation* swallowed up by a pulsating, sirene-like melody with the noise of airplanes dropping bombs. These sounds turn into a funeral march and are followed by a radio news report announcing the attack on German cultural monuments. In this unusual montage sequence the city becomes a surreal landscape of smoking ruins populated by throngs who walk in a daze through the rubble. The dissolves are particularly haunting, for in a strange way they seem to create and destroy the city through the camerawork and editing.

The character of Karl Degenhardt symbolizes German strength in adversity. He fought for his country in the First World War and spent twenty-nine years in military and civil service. When war breaks out again, Degenhardt overcomes his egoism and recognizes that the national good must come before personal ambitions. Together with the other old men in town, Degenhardt sustains the home front by planting victory gardens to supply the community with badly needed vegetables, and at home he now plays his cello alone. Robert's black-draped photograph rests on the piano while ephemeral images of Degenhardt's other children engaged in war duties are superimposed on the scene. Despite the absence of the children, the sounds of their instruments continue to accompany their father's cello. Combat is now rendered in a twenty-second overlay of images, in a sense bringing the remote war into one's home, in another sense banishing the reality of war to a half-image from a distant realm.

The final sequence reconstitutes the nuclear family, skipping the intermediate generation, to complete the triad of father, mother, and child. Robert's death is accepted as normal; since he has ensured his legacy by procreating, the cycle of life continues in both the smaller cell of the family and in the larger structure of the national family, the *Volksgemeinschaft*. Father Degenhardt reassures his wife (and by extension the audience) that a secure community continues to exist, one that provides each member with a sense of belonging to something larger than the self: "If someone goes away from us forever, then it's arranged that another will always grow up in his place. That's the way it should be in a big family, right? All the more so in the great big family, to which we all truly belong."[74]

Die Degenhardts received extremely mixed reviews. In Vienna it played to 93% capacity and was held over; in Gera the public found the film "too long-winded" (zu langatmig), and in Ulm the audience felt it was well-made, "but too realistic for the present time" (für die Zeit jedoch zu zeitnah). In Berlin, the press corps uniformly praised *Die Degenhardts* for its realism and accurate depiction of life in the immediate crisis of war. Commentators were especially impressed with Heinrich George's performance because it captured the emotional life of the typical German "for whom life is the realization of duty" and because it offered audiences coping strategies for living in "this state between hope and despair."[75] The film brought in a disappointing 3.5 million RM and was generally considered a flop. However, after Hitler's order to create the *Volkssturm* (militia) in September 1944, the Propaganda Ministry called for the revival of "great national films," including *Die Degenhardts*.[76]

The Limits of Enchantment

All three home-front films depict the struggle between duty and pleasure through characters who conquer their own personal desires and surrender themselves to the public's immediate needs. This narrative trope internalizes the geopolitical conflict in the way that the individual must first win a battle with himself before the nation can win the greater military battle.

The overwhelming success of *Wunschkonzert* and *Die große Liebe* was based in part on their use of popular culture to promote this story line. In these two films it is entertainment as much as war that unites the community. The romantic and humorous stories coupled with cheerful music generate an overall optimistic tone: suffering seems easily contained or sublimated through sentimental music. Both films present young lovers separated by war and end just short of a wedding ceremony. A brief lull in the fighting and a last shot of the couple together imply that offscreen the characters can finally marry and fulfill their long postponed emotional and sexual desires. The open-ended narratives encourage the audience to continue imagining the story long after they leave the cinema.

In *Die Degenhardts* German high culture is, like the times, somber and grave. Degenhardt's birthday serenade performed as a solo, Haydn's *Creation* interrupted by bombs, and the ruins of German architectural monuments hardly inspire optimism and confidence in victory. The story of an old man's personal success is a closed narrative with few possibilities for fantasizing after the curtain drops. Moreover, the cost of success is high: death and separation of loved ones become the price for status. In the end, *Die Degenhardts* has a message with little or no appeal: it promotes either a nuclear family of old people and babies bound by mutual dependencies or a community united in death.

The cinematic space for combat and for community grows smaller and smaller as the real war literally comes closer to the doorstep. The public buildings and institutions that offered excitement and frivolous low culture or a genuine sense of common experiences cease to exist. Unlike *Die große Liebe*, *Die Degenhardts* presents no theaters and no movie houses where one can escape the horrors of war for a few hours of illusion. In 1944 the radio even fails to entertain audiences as it did four years earlier in *Wunschkonzert;* in *Die Degenhardts* radio shows consist solely of war reports and martial music.

Since public buildings are completely destroyed in this final home-front film, the German family retreats to the privacy of the living room. This movement away from communal leisure space ironically mirrors the actual closure of theaters shortly after *Die Degenhardts* premiered. To free up the necessary resources for total war, Goebbels ordered all theaters, variety shows, cabarets, and acting schools closed as of September 1, 1944. Cinemas, by contrast, would stay open and continue to provide distraction and amusement. However, Nazi officials secretly acknowledged that the number of moviegoers had dropped substantially in late 1944, primarily because Allied bombs were increasingly destroying the movie theaters; and those still open and makeshift theaters lacked the necessary film prints to meet the demand.[77]

By stressing communal forms of popular entertainment, *Wunschkonzert* and *Die große Liebe* created explicit and highly pleasurable points of identification for the German audience from 1940 to 1942. These films present an exuberant onscreen audience and grant a behind-the-scenes look at the war-driven entertainment industry. The onscreen audience holds up a mirror to the moviegoer to look at himself and imagine his own participation in the nation's real-life drama. Like all successful entertainment films in the Third Reich, *Wunschkonzert* and *Die große Liebe* re-establish the contours of normality. They train the spectator to fantasize reality in such a way that war becomes a positive force in the end. War brings people together, transforms the ordinary into the spectacular, intensifies feelings, and helps the individual become stronger. Nazi entertainment films work in tandem to allow spectators to insulate themselves from the upsetting aspects of reality, extricating troubling events and replacing them with palatable alternatives. The mindset created in the movies is ultimately transferable to everyday life so that the audience can imagine total war as tenable.

The shift in 1944 to a more somber look at total war corresponded to the gravity of the military situation, but it also illustrates the limitations of fantasy. Without the necessary connections to reality, without belief in at least the possibility of victory, the story of a happy national community united through light entertainment simply does not ring true. *Die Degenhardts's* poor showing at the box office reflects more than just the closure of bombed-out movie theaters. The story of an ordinary family that must die to preserve German high culture was not the self-definition and national narrative the German home front wanted to buy as their world collapsed.

Notes

[1] "Der Film ist ein Teil der Wehrmacht geworden. Wie diese verwirklicht er die entscheidenden Eigenschaften der Technik: Schnelligkeit, Präzision, stoßhafte Wirkung in die Breiten." Frank Maraun, "Unsere Wehrmacht im Film," *Der deutsche Film* 4, no. 12 (June 1940): 227.

[2] The combat film enjoyed a brief high point in 1941 when five films premiered: *Kampfgeschwader Lützow* (Hans Bertram), *Über alles in der Welt* (Karl Ritter), *Spähtrupp Hallgarten* (Herbert B. Fredersdorf), *U-Boote westwärts* (Günther Rittau), and *Stukas* (Karl Ritter). In 1941 two other films with related subjects appeared: *Blutsbrüderschaft* (Philip Lothar Mayring) deals with the First World War, the interwar period, and the start of the Second World War, and *Auf Wiedersehen, Franziska* (Helmut Käutner) centers on a photo journalist in the interwar period who is later drafted into a propaganda company. By 1942, the combat film was out of favor with the Propaganda Ministry. *Der 5. Juni* (Fritz Kirchhoff) was banned in November 1942, but the reasons behind the ban remain unclear. Some film historians have argued that Goebbels disliked the overly didactic treatment of the French defeat and the Nazi government's relationship to Vichy-France. Other historians cite Goebbels's personal disputes with the Wehrmacht as possible grounds for the ban. *Besatzung Dora* (Karl Ritter) was banned in November 1943 and only given a closed screening to the Luftwaffe on February 2, 1945. *Besatzung Dora* was undoubtedly censored because the storyline of Luftwaffe pilots fighting in North Africa and

dreaming of settling in Russia after the war was completely unrealistic in November 1943, just months after Germany's crushing defeats at Stalingrad in February 1943 and in North Africa in May 1943. For further information on censorship, see Kraft Wetzel and Peter A. Hagemann, *Zensur: Verbotene deutsche Filme 1933–1945* (Berlin: Volker Spiess, 1978); and Felix Moeller, *Der Filmminister: Goebbels und der Film im Dritten Reich* (Berlin: Henschel, 1998), 313–46.

[3] Furlough films include *Sechs Tage Heimaturlaub* (1941, Jürgen von Alten), *Zwei in einer großen Stadt* (1942, Volker von Collande), and *Ein schöner Tag* (1944, Philip Lothar Mayring). *Eine kleine Sommermelodie,* directed by Volker von Collande, was censored in November 1944 and never premiered.

[4] The three most prominent home-front films are analyzed in this essay. Of interest is also *Fronttheater* (1942, Arthur Maria Rabenalt), which depicts a theater troop performing at the front during the Second World War.

[5] See Marlis G. Steinart, *Hitler's War and the Germans: Public Mood and Attitude during the Second World War,* trans. Thomas E. J. de Witt (Athens, Ohio: Ohio UP, 1977), 50–65.

[6] Jay Baird, *The Mythical World of Nazi Propaganda 1939–1945* (Minneapolis: U of Minnesota P, 1974), 41–56; and David Welch, *The Third Reich: Politics and Propaganda* (Routledge: New York, 1993), 90–97.

[7] According to editorials in the trade papers, the British and French governments had ordered the closing of all cinemas after declaring war on Germany, "Das deutsche Filmwesen während des Kriegszustandes," *Der deutsche Film* 4, no. 4 (October 1939): 94; and *Licht-Bild-Bühne* 206 (September 5, 1939). For articles on Germany's active role in promoting the cinema at home and on the front, see Hermann Gressieker, "Die Parole des deutschen Films," *Der deutsche Film* 4, no. 3 (September 1939): 63–67; "Der Film in Kriegszeiten: Neue Aufgaben und neue Pläne," *Licht-Bild-Bühne* 245 (October 20, 1939); and Curt Belling, "Der Film im Fronteinsatz," *Film-Illustrierte* (December 10, 1939).

[8] Joseph Goebbels, "Das Kulturleben im Kriege," speech from November 27, 1939, in *Die Zeit ohne Beispiel: Reden und Aufsätze aus den Jahren 1939/40/41* (Munich: Franz Eher Verlag, 1941), 220.

[9] In 1939 there were 6,667 cinemas with 2.4 million seats in the Reich, and the average German went to the movies 10.5 times a year. By 1942 there were 6,537 cinemas with 2.6 million seats, and the average German attended the movies 14.3 times a year. See Eric Rentschler, *The Ministry of Illusion: Nazi Cinema and Its Afterlife* (Cambridge, MA: Harvard UP, 1996), 247, 258; Bogusław Drewniak, *Der deutsche Film 1938–1945: Ein Gesamtüberblick* (Dusseldorf: Droste, 1987), 608, 623; and David Welch, *Propaganda and the German Cinema 1933–1945* (New York: Oxford UP, 1983), 35.

[10] Hans Dieter Schäfer, *Das gespaltene Bewußtsein: Deutsche Kultur und Lebenswirklichkeit 1933–1945* (Munich: Hanser, 1981), 114–62.

[11] Goebbels, "Das Kulturleben im Kriege," 219.

[12] According to Fritz Hippler, "This film was Goebbels's pet project; he even collaborated on the screenplay, wrote dialogues, and determined the particular singers

and musicians who were to perform in the big productions," *Die Verstrickung* (Düsseldorf: Mehr Wissen, 1981), 216. Goebbels wrote in his diary on December 31, 1940: "The premiere of 'Request Concert' in the Ufa-Palast am Zoo. Big hit. The film received stormy applause. I'm all the happier about it, since the idea came from me. Once again we did a good job. Above all the extraordinary popular character of the film was appealing. It will ignite the entire German folk," *Die Tagebücher von Joseph Goebbels: Sämtliche Fragmente*, ed. Elke Fröhlich, Part I: Auf–zeichnungen 1924–1942, 9 vols. (Munich: K. G. Saur, 1987), 1. 4: 451.

[13] Recent studies treating *Wunschkonzert* include Marc Silberman, *German Cinema: Texts in Context* (Detroit: Wayne State UP, 1995), 66–80; Linda Schulte-Sasse, *Entertaining the Third Reich: Illusions of Wholeness in Nazi Cinema* (Durham: Duke UP, 1996), 288–301; Mary-Elizabeth O'Brien, "Aestheticizing War: Eduard von Borsody's *Wunschkonzert* (1940)," *Seminar* 33, no. 1 (1997): 36–49; and David Bathrick, "Radio und Film für ein modernes Deutschland: Das NS-Wunschkonzert," in *Dschungel Großstadt: Kino und Modernisierung*, ed. Irmbert Schenk (Marburg: Schüren, 1999), 112–31.

[14] "Das allermodernste und das allerwichtigste Massenbeinflussungsinstrument." Joseph Goebbels, speech from March 25, 1933, in *Reden*, ed. Helmut Heiber (Düsseldorf: Droste, 1971), 1: 91.

[15] "Nur nicht langweilig werden. Nur keine Öde. Nur nicht die Gesinnung auf den Präsentierteller legen. Nur nicht glauben, man könne sich im Dienste der nationalen Regierung am besten betätigen, wenn man Abend für Abend schmetternde Märsche ertönen läßt. . . . Gesinnung muß sein, aber Gesinnung braucht nicht Langeweile zu bedeuten. Die Phantasie muß alle Mittel und Methoden in Anspruch nehmen, um die neue Gesinnung modern, aktuell und interessiert den breiten Massen zu Gehör zu bringen, interessant und lehrreich, aber nicht belehrend. Der Rundfunk soll niemals an dem Wort kränken, man merkt die Absicht und wird verstimmt." Goebbels, *Reden*, 1: 82–83.

[16] Detlev J. K. Peukert, *Inside Nazi Germany: Conformity, Opposition, and Racism in Everyday Life*, trans. Richard Deveson (New Haven: Yale UP, 1987), 78.

[17] Goebbels, *Die Tagebücher von Joseph Goebbels*, 1. 3: 611.

[18] Conrad F. Latour, "Goebbels 'Außerordentliche Rundfunkmaßnahmen' 1939–1942," *Vierteljahrshefte für Zeitgeschichte* 11 (1963): 418–35.

[19] "Gerade seine 'örtliche Ungebundenheit' schien den Rundfunk als Medium eines 'imaginären Raumes' besonders dafür zu qualifizieren, die 'innere Einheit aller Deutschen als 'Volksgemeinschaft' zu befördern." Peter Reichel, *Der schöne Schein des dritten Reiches: Faszination und Gewalt des Faschismus* (Munich: Hanser, 1991), 165.

[20] The last "Request Concert for the Armed Forces" was the seventy-fifth broadcast on May 25, 1941. For an analysis of this popular radio show, see Nanny Drechsler, *Die Funktion der Musik im deutschen Rundfunk 1933–1945* (Pfaffenweiler: Centaurus, 1988), 131–34, 153.

[21] "Eine Stimme schwingt durch den Äther. 'Hier ist der großdeutsche Rundfunk! Wir beginnen das Wunschkonzert für die Wehrmacht.' Ein magisches Band umschlingt Front und Heimat. Im Unterstand in Frankreich, im U-Boot auf Feindfahrt, im Fliegerhorst an der Küste, im stillen Zimmer einer Mutter, in Tausenden-Hunderttausenden von Woh-

nungen, überall klingt und schwingt der Strom von Wort und Lied und Musik. [. . .] Leid und Freude des einzelnen, Unbekannten, Namenlosen wird Leid und Freude der ganzen Nation. Alle Herzen schlagen im gleichen Rhythmus des Empfindens." *Wunschkonzert, Illustrierter Film-Kurier* 3166 (Berlin: Franke & Co, 1940).

[22] "Wer einmal ein solches Wunschkonzert hörte, weiß, wie in solchen Stunden Volk und Wehrmacht sich zu einer einzigen großen Familie verbunden fühlen. Er begreift die ungeheuere Bedeutung des Rundfunkes als des Mittels, das allein heute in der Lage ist, achtzig Millionen Menschen zu einem großen Gemeinschaftserlebnis zusammenzufassen. So vermitteln die Wunschkonzerte jedem Deutschen auch das Gefühl der Kraft und Zusammengehörigkeit." Alfred-Ingemar Berndt, foreword to *Wir beginnen das Wunschkonzert für die Wehrmacht,* by Heinz Goedecke and Wilhelm Krug (Berlin: Nibelungen, 1940), 8. Emphasis added.

[23] Walter Benjamin, "The Work of Art in the Age of Mechanical Reproduction," in *Illuminations: Essays and Reflections,* ed. Hannah Arendt, trans. Harry Zohn (New York: Schocken, 1968), 223. "Die Dinge sich räumlich und menschlich 'näherzubringen.'" Walter Benjamin, *Das Kunstwerk im Zeitalter seiner technischen Reproduzierbarkeit* (Frankfurt a. M.: Suhrkamp, 1963), 15.

[24] Benjamin, "The Work of Art," 242. "Faschismus [. . .] erwartet die künstlerische Befriedigung der von der Technik veränderten Sinneswahrnehmung [. . .] vom Kriege." Benjamin, *Das Kunstwerk,* 44.

[25] Cooper C. Graham, *Leni Riefenstahl and* Olympia (Metuchen, NJ: Scarecrow, 1986); Duff Hart-Davis, *Hitler's Games: The 1936 Olympics* (London: Century, 1986); and Richard Mandell, *The Nazi Olympics* (New York: Macmillian, 1971).

[26] Albert Speer, *Inside the Third Reich,* trans. Richard and Clara Winston (New York: Macmillan, 1970), 114.

[27] Hilmar Hoffmann, *"Und die Fahne führt uns in die Ewigkeit": Propaganda im NS-Film* (Frankfurt a. M.: Fischer, 1988), 152.

[28] Stephen Lowry, *Pathos und Politik: Ideologie im Spielfilm des Nationalsozialismus* (Tübingen: Niemeyer, 1991), 178.

[29] Siegfried Kracauer, *From Caligari to Hitler: A Psychological History of the German Film* (Princeton: Princeton UP, 1947), 279.

[30] Kracauer, *From Caligari to Hitler,* 279.

[31] Kracauer, *From Caligari to Hitler,* 280.

[32] Paul Virilio, *War and Cinema: The Logistics of Perception,* trans. Patrick Camiller (London: Verso, 1989), 7.

[33] Virilio, *War and Cinema,* 7.

[34] Virilio, *War and Cinema,* 15.

[35] Steinert, *Hitler's War and the Germans,* 65–72; and Heinz Boberach, ed., *Meldungen aus dem Reich: Auswahl geheimen Lageberichten des Sicherheitsdientes der SS 1939–1944,* 17 vols. (Berlin: Pawlak Verlag Herrsching, 1965).

[36] David B. Dennis, *Beethoven in German Politics 1870–1989* (New Haven: Yale UP, 1996), 142–74.

[37] Goebbels, "Das Kulturleben im Kriege," 223. Goebbels's reference to "plutocrats" was typical anti-British propaganda portraying the English as allied with the Jews in a conspiracy to dominate the world, see Baird, *The Mythical World of Nazi Propaganda*, 120–21.

[38] Jeffrey Herf explores the selective use of modern technology coupled with *völkisch* ideology in *Reactionary Modernism: Technology, Culture, and Politics in Weimar and the Third Reich* (Cambridge: Cambridge UP, 1984).

[39] Saul Friedländer defines the Nazi kitsch of death as "not real death in its everyday horror and tragic banality, but a ritualized, stylized, and aestheticized death. . . . Nazi death is a show, a production, a performance," *Reflections of Nazism: An Essay on Kitsch and Death,* trans. Thomas Weyr (New York: Harper & Row, 1984), 43–44.

[40] "[Es] war plötzlich still an Bord. Wenn das, was wir sahen, wahr war, dann müßte Köln zerstört sein. Wir blickten auf den Rhein, aber es war kein Irrtum: Was wir da unten sahen, war die Wirklichkeit." Qtd. in Wolfgang Paul, *Der Heimatkrieg 1939 bis 1945* (Esslingen am Neckar: Bechtle, 1980), 111. For a description of Operation Millennium and the Cologne bombing see Paul, *Der Heimatkrieg,* 105–17; Adolf Klein, *Köln im Dritten Reich: Stadtgeschichte der Jahre 1933–1945* (Cologne: Greven, 1983), 252–56; Wilber H. Morrison, *Fortress Without a Roof: The Allied Bombing of the Third Reich* (New York: St. Martin's Press, 1982), 24–31; Charles Messenger, *"Bomber" Harris and the Strategic Bombing Offensive, 1939–1945* (New York: St. Martin's Press, 1984), 74–78.

[41] Martin Loiperdinger and Klaus Schönekäs, *"Die große Liebe:* Propaganda im Unterhaltungsfilm," in *Bilder schreiben Geschichte: Der Historiker im Kino,* ed. Rainer Rother (Berlin: Wagenbach), 143. According to Stephen Lowry, the premiere run in Berlin lasted ninety-one days, while the average run was twenty-eight days, with the range from six to ninety-one days (*Pathos und Politik,* 20). Eric Rentschler notes that *Die große Liebe* registered an all-time record of over 400,000 admissions at the Berlin Ufa-Palast am Zoo for the period June 12 to August 29, 1942 (*The Ministry of Illusion,* 260). Klaus Kreimeier lists the film's gross at 9.2 million Reichmarks and the audience at nearly 28 million based on the period up to November 1944 (*Die Ufa-Story: Geschichte eines Filmkonzerns* [Munich: Hanser, 1992], 371).

[42] Typical is this review from Maria Waas: "The film takes its plot from our immediate present, the battle between love and duty grows out of the demands of the day and gives the film convincing true-to-life qualities" [Unmittelbar aus unserer Zeit nimmt der Film seine Handlung, der Kampf zwischen Liebe und Pflicht wächst aus den Forderungen unserer Tage und gibt dem Film überzeugende Lebensnähe] (n.t., n.p., n.d.), *Die große Liebe,* Document File 6214, Bundesarchiv-Filmarchiv, Berlin. See also *"Die große Liebe:* Zarah Leander und Paul Hörbiger in einem neuen Film," *Filmwelt* 47/48 (November 26, 1941); "Große Dekoration für Zarah Leander: Bei den Aufnahmen zu dem Ufa-Film *Die große Liebe," Film-Kurier* 30 (February 6, 1942); Wilhelm Hackbarth, "Das Lied der Hanna Holberg," *Filmwelt* 7/8 (February 18, 1942); and Hans Suchen, *"Die große Liebe," Filmwelt* 23/24 (June 24, 1942).

[43] At a dinner party Paul hears the announcement: "German National Radio will interrupt its program for a short period," and recognizes that radio silence means a pending Allied strike.

[44] "Die Sirene bringt es an den Tag." All dialogues are taken from the videocassette copy of *Die große Liebe* available in commercial release. The censor cards provide a narrative description of the action but not the dialogues. Compare *Die große Liebe*, Censor-Card 57295, Bundesarchiv-Filmarchiv, Berlin.

[45] Paul: "Donnerwetter! Schön, was? Hanna: "Mmm, wie ein Märchen." Paul: "Nein, viel schöner, wie die Wirklichkeit." *Die große Liebe* film dialogue.

[46] "Ich weiß, es wird einmal ein Wunder geschehen und dann werden tausend Märchen wahr." *Die große Liebe* film dialogue.

[47] I am grateful to Glenn Cuomo for bringing the following citation to my attention. Joseph Goebbels's diary entry from May 14, 1942, reads: "The new Leander film 'True Love' was shown. It attempts to incorporate a private story into the greater war experience, and it does so rather skillfully. The film can hardly lay claim to artistic merit, but it will certainly be a very effective crowd pleaser." *Goebbels Tagebücher*, Hoover Institute, Reel 3, frames 2750–51, pages 15–16 of typed manuscript.

[48] In the song "Davon geht die Welt nicht unter," Hanna sings, "Geht's mal drüber und mal drunter." *Die große Liebe* film dialogue.

[49] Micaela Jary relates the genesis of this song in her book, *Ich weiß, es wird einmal ein Wunder gescheh'n: Die große Liebe der Zarah Leander* (Berlin: edition q, 1993), 177–85. She writes that Leander, Jary's father the composer Michael Jary, and lyricist Bruno Balz (who wrote the text directly after his release from Gestapo arrest), considered the song openly subversive. They thought it would be obvious that the song did not refer to the end of the war or separation but to the end of the Nazi regime.

[50] "Der Film erzeugt nämlich neben der persönlichen Verbindung des Zuschauers zum Hauptdarsteller während des Filmablaufes zugleich auch das Bestreben, diesem gleich zu sein. Wie er sich räuspert und wie er spuckt, wie er gekleidet ist, wie er sich benimmt, ob und was er trinkt, was und wie er raucht, ob er ein Bieder- oder ein Lebemann ist, das alles hat nicht nur seine Wirkung im Film, sondern auch im Leben des Zuschauers. Ein kraftgeladener und sieghafter Film entläßt ein anderes Publikum als ein tragischer oder ein komischer Film. Nach einem Albers-Film ist auch der Hilfsfriseur ein Albers; niemand sollte es wagen, sich mit ihm einzulassen." Fritz Hippler, *Betrachtungen zum Filmschaffen*, 5th rev. ed. (Berlin: Max Hesses Verlag, 1943), 95.

[51] "[Der Heimatfrontfilm ruft] jene innere Bereitschaft wach, sich voll und ganz an die Figuren und das Geschehen um sie zu verlieren, das ist bei diesen Filmen selbstverständlich vorhanden, denn jeder Zuschauer, Soldat oder Zivilist, Mann oder Frau, hat einen Menschen 'dabei,' identifiziert augenblicks das Schicksal auf der Leinwand mit dem des Freundes oder Mannes, des Bruders oder Bräutigams, kurz, jeder Zuschauer sitzt nach den ersten Bildern mit gläubigem, aufgeschlossenem Herzen im Parkett." "Film und Zeitgeschehen: Zu dem Terra-Film Fronttheater," *Der deutsche Film* 7, no. 1 (July 1942): 8.

[52] In her analysis of the filmic love story, Mary Ann Doane notes, "the genre does seem to require that the male character undergo a process of feminization." (*The Desire to Desire: The Woman's Film of the 1940s* [Bloomington: Indiana UP, 1987], 116).

[53] "Er läßt seine Maschine nicht im Stich." *Die große Liebe* film dialogue.

[54] "Wir haben beide den selben Stern, und dein Schicksal ist auch meins." *Die große Liebe* film dialogue.

[55] "Mein Maxe in der Hand ist mir mehr wert als Albert auf der Trapeze." *Die große Liebe* film dialogue.

[56] As early as late autumn 1939, German consumers were complaining about the inadequate food supplies, coal shortages, and the lack of shoes; see Steinert, *Hitler's War and the Germans*, 59, 64–65. By the time *Die große Liebe* began filming in autumn 1941, Security Service reports compiled over the summer warned that the "catastrophic food situation" had triggered widespread resentment and low morale (Steinert, 121). Food shortages and deteriorating public mood only worsened in the winter of 1942, as filming of *Die große Liebe* concluded. The perceived threat posed by British bombing raids escalated in a similar manner. While RAF aerial strikes against the Reich in the summer of 1940 were largely symbolic gestures causing little damage, they nonetheless contributed to low morale on the German home front. The heavy bombing raid on Berlin in August 1940 left many citizens bewildered and discouraged. See Steinert, 77; and Baird, *The Mythical World of Nazi War Propaganda*, 127–30.

[57] Boberach, *Meldungen aus dem Reich*, 263–64, 266, 267.

[58] The strong man Albert also uses food to express his love for Hanna. He gives her coffee, a commodity in short supply, which Paul takes control of in a later scene, as if to illustrate the difference between requited and unrequited love.

[59] George Mosse discusses the centrality of the German First World War experience for the rise of National Socialism in his article, "Two World Wars and the Myth of the War Experience," *Journal of Contemporary History* 21 (October 1986): 491–514.

[60] "Die Gemeinschaft von Schwert und Leier — so wie sie sich im Betreuungswerk für unsere Soldaten bewährte — bedeutet das herrlichste Symbol des deutschen Sieges über die uns feindliche, gestrige plutokratische Welt." Hans Hinkel, "Der Einsatz unserer Kunst im Krieg," *Der deutsche Film* 6, no. 11/12 (May/June 1941): 217. SS Officer Hans Hinkel, appointed Secretary General of the Reichskulturkammer (Reich Chamber of Culture) in 1936 and Reichsfilmintendant (Reich Film Director) in 1944, was responsible for numerous projects, including the implementation of anti-Semitic cultural policy and the organization of troop entertainment during the war. According to Hinkel, 15,000 cultural events were staged for troops in the West in the winter 1939–1940.

[61] "Manchmal ist's mir selber, daß ich tot sein möchte." *Die große Liebe* film dialogue.

[62] Jane Feuer, "The Self-Reflexive Musical and the Myth of Entertainment," in *Film Genre Reader*, ed. Barry Keith Grant (Austin: U of Texas P), 329–43.

[63] Lowry discusses the centrality of the cellar scene for establishing Hanna and Paul as potential parents (*Pathos und Politik*, 164–70).

[64] "Ist sie eine rechte Mutter, so verliert sie sich selbst in ihrer Familienaufgabe. Aber wunderbar: gerade dadurch wird sie im tiefsten Sinn Frau und Mensch. Je selbstverständlicher sie sich aufgibt, desto mehr. Im Verlieren ihres Lebens findet sie sich, ihre wahre Würde, ihren eigensten Menschen. . . . Sie wird Mutter und damit Vollmensch auf dem Weg der Selbstverleugnung, nicht auf dem der Selbststbehaup-

tung." Guida Diehl, *Die deutsche Frau und der Nationalsozialismus* (Eisenach: Neulandverlag, 1933), 92.

[65] Günter Berghaus, ed., *Fascism and Theatre: Comparative Studies on the Aesthetics and Politics of Performance in Europe, 1925–1945* (Providence: Berghahn, 1996), 5.

[66] Michel Foucault, *Discipline and Punish: The Birth of the Prison*, trans. Alan Sheridan (New York: Vintage Books, 1979), 200, 202–3. I am indebted to Bruce Campbell for his careful reading of this essay at an early stage and suggestions on the controlling nature of participatory theater.

[67] David F. Crew, Introduction to Klaus-Michael Mallmann and Gerhard Paul, "Omniscient, Omnipotent, Omnipresent? Gestapo, Society and Resistance," in *Nazism and German Society, 1933–1945*, ed. David F. Crew (New York: Rutledge, 1994), 166. For an interesting study of the dream world in Nazi Germany, see Charlotte Beradt, *Das Dritte Reich des Traums* (Frankfurt a. M.: Suhrkamp, 1981).

[68] Klaus-Michael Mallmann and Gerhard Paul, "Omniscient, Omnipotent, Omnipresent? Gestapo, Society and Resistence," in *Nazism and German Society, 1933–1945*, ed. David Crew (New York: Rutledge, 1994), 173; see also Robert Gellately, *The Gestapo and German Society: Enforcing Racial Policy, 1933–1945* (New York: Oxford UP, 1990).

[69] Gerd Albrecht, *Nationalsozialistische Filmpolitik: Eine soziologische Untersuchung über die Spielfilme des Dritten Reichs* (Stuttgart: Ferdinand Enke, 1969), 110.

[70] *Die Degenhardts* passed the censor in Berlin on June 28, 1944, with the distinction marks "politically valuable" and "artistically valuable," *Die Degenhardts*, Censor-Card 60153, Bundesarchiv-Filmarchiv, Berlin. The censor cards contain no dialogues and no narrative description of the action. All dialogues are taken from the videocassette copy of *Die Degenhardts* available in commercial release.

[71] In retaliation for the Royal Air Force's bombing attacks on artistically significant buildings in German cities, including Lübeck on March 28, 1942, and Rostock on April 23, 1942, the Luftwaffe launched its own *Baedekerangriffe* (Baedeker bombing raids, named after the popular German tourist guidebooks) on the culturally rich but militarily insignificant English cities of Bath, Canterbury, Exeter, Norwich, and York between April and October of 1942. For a description of the Lübeck and Baedeker bombing raids, see Lothar Gruchmann, *Totaler Krieg: Vom Blitzkrieg zur bedingungsloser Kapitulation* (Munich: dtv, 1991), 158.

[72] For a study of the ideology of gardening and landscape design in Nazi Germany, see Joachim Wolschke-Bulmahn and Gert Gröning, "The National Socialist Garden and Landscape Ideal: Bodenständigkeit (Rootedness in the Soil)," in *Art, Culture, and Media under the Third Reich*, ed. Richard Etlin (Chicago: Chicago UP, 2002), 73–97.

[73] An excellent anthology on the Lübeck *Totentanz*, complete with extensive reproductions, can be found in Hartmut Freytag, ed., *Der Totentanz der Marienkirche in Lübeck und der Nikolaikirche in Reval (Tallinn)*, Niederdeutsche Studien 39 (Cologne: Böhlau, 1993).

[74] "Und wenn auch mal einer für immer von uns geht, dann ist es so eingerichtet, daß immer ein anderer nach wächst. So sollte es auch sein, nicht, in einer großen

Familie. So ist es erst recht in der ganz großen Familie, zu der wir ja alle gehören."
Die Degenhardts film dialogue.

[75] See Felix Henseleit, *"Die Degenhardts," Film-Kurier* (August 15, 1944); and Lothar Papke, "Familienroman von heute: *Die Degenhardts," Völkischer Beobachter,* Berlin edition (August 13, 1944). Wilhelm Westecker wrote that the film was characterized by "diesen Zustand zwischen Hoffnung und Entäuschung," Wilhelm Westecker, "Filmepos einer deutschen Familie: *Die Degenhardts* im Tauentzienpalast," *Berliner Börsen-Zeitung* (August 12, 1944). Theo Fürstenau admired the film for its portrayal of "die seelische Haltung des unkomplizierten grundanständigen Menschen, dem das Leben Verwirklichung der Pflichten ist." Theo Fürstenau, *"Die Degenhardts," Deutsche Allgemeine Zeitung* (August 13, 1944).

[76] Drewniak, *Der deutsche Film,* 400–401, 631, 647–48; and Albrecht, *Nationalsozialistische Filmpolitik,* 118.

[77] Drewniak, *Der deutsche Film,* 619, 625–27; and Albrecht, *Nationalsozialistische Filmpolitik,* 220–21.

The erotic woman: Zarah Leander in *Damals* (1940).

4: Discontented Domesticity: The Melodrama

THE CINEMATIC MELODRAMA of the Third Reich engaged the popular imagination with penetrating images of strong, tormented women and discontented family life. Boasting some of the most successful films produced in Nazi Germany, the melodrama was an immensely popular genre, especially in the waning years of the Second World War. The portrayal of unhappy, dysfunctional families exerted a fascination on audiences altogether incongruous with Nazi ideology concerning the Aryan home as the bastion of social harmony. This disparity between the rosy picture painted in propaganda posters and the pessimistic narratives of popular entertainment has yet to be scrutinized with sufficient vigor.[1]

The melodrama emphasizes family conflict, especially women's trials and tribulations, as well as the traditional sphere of the feminine (feelings, domesticity, personal relationships) and is, therefore, uniquely suited to an inquiry into the symbolic encoding of gender difference. In this chapter I will explore the ways in which the melodrama treats sexuality and gender roles within the context of the fascist state. The Nazi-controlled media did not engender a single universal image of woman, rather they presented an entertaining model of social justice whereby the "abnormal woman" is contained and eliminated while the "normal woman" is reintegrated into a joyless marriage. My interest in the fascist melodrama is grounded in the historical nexus of woman, pain, sacrifice, and self-negation coupled with man, taming, domestication, and self-identity as a means to validate the prevailing order. Two films exemplify complementary discursive strategies in Nazi cinema to neutralize subversive energy. *Opfergang* (Rite of Sacrifice, 1944) directed by Veit Harlan and *Damals* (Back Then, 1943) directed by Rolf Hansen employ the two most common and diametrically opposed narrative solutions to the disintegration of the family: the death of the erotic woman and her reintegration into the nuclear family respectively.

At the core of Nazi social policy lies the notion of a "natural" distinction between the sexes that requires the separation of male and female domains into clearly demarcated spheres of influence. Gertrud Scholtz-Klink, the Reich Leader of the National Socialist Womanhood organization, summarizes the official outlook:

From the beginning of time man and woman have been two different beings, with likewise different functions. Seen purely biologically, the role of the man in maintaining the human race is relatively short lived, that of woman is an unequally longer one full of sacrifices. She shelters for many months the future of a people in her womb — gives birth amid pain, protects and preserves the future with every fiber of her heart.[2]

The reproductive difference between men and women is conceived as a fundamental truth that determines the entire social structure of the nation: "This basic truth which cannot be suppressed . . . is the starting point for all further formations of collective life and work in every cultivated people."[3] The polarity between the sexes necessitates a division of labor that allows men to become creative agents and forces women to fulfill their role as guardians of cultural traditions. Gertrud Scholtz-Klink maintained: "The task of the man in a healthy people will always be primarily the creative act, that of the woman the shaping, protecting, maintaining, preserving. These natural characteristic features of woman include, beyond physical mother-hood, all instinctive tendencies to spiritual and mental motherliness."[4]

Motherhood, whether physical or spiritual, is based on a woman's ability to sublimate her own interests and needs for her family. Guida Diehl, leader of the Neuland movement, advances the prevailing notion that woman can only achieve the status of human being when she ceases to exist as an individual: "If she is a real mother, she loses herself in her familial duties. But wonderfully: exactly therein, she becomes a woman and human being in the deepest sense. The more obvious her surrender, the more so. In losing her life she finds herself, her true dignity, her inherent humanity."[5] The valorization of racially and socially "valuable" mothers epitomized in the elaborate Mother's Day festivities and the awarding of the Mother's Cross to women with four or more children shrouds the inherently misogynist aspects of National Socialism. Reduced to her biological function in the mother cult, deprived of desire and even identity through self-denial, the individual woman vanishes.

Recent film studies dealing with the Hollywood melodrama are predicated on a basic assumption about the American society that engenders images of discontented family life. At the most elementary level, the United States is seen as a culture "in which the choice of marriage partners is, in theory at least, completely free."[6] Nazi Germany, by contrast, was a society in which the individual's right to marry at will was so severely restricted as to be nearly non-existent. The National Socialist state regulated marriage according to racial, hereditary, health, and behavioral criteria. One of the first intrusions by the state into the "private" realm of the family was the Law for the Prevention of Progeny with Hereditary Diseases of July 14, 1933, which allowed for compulsory sterilization of those individuals deemed "unfit." The infamous Nuremberg Laws of September 15, 1935 went further to criminalize not only marriage but also sexual intercourse between an Aryan and a Jew. According to the Marriage Health Law issued in October 1935, the right to marry at all was contingent on a couple's racial and hereditary "fitness." Only after a medical examination proved their physical health could a couple obtain a certificate from the health department and marry.[7]

The National Socialist government instituted measures to promote marriages between partners who would produce "racially valuable" children. The Law for the Reduction of Unemployment from June 1, 1933, offered interest free loans of up to 1,000 RM to newlyweds on the condition that the wife gave up her paid employment. With the birth of each child the couple was given a 25% reduction of the marriage loan.[8] State intervention into the realm of procreation was not limited to incentives to encourage the birthrate of "valuable" offspring; it also included draconian measures to prevent the birth of racially "worthless" life and exterminate "hereditarily inferior" children. The Law for the Prevention of Progeny with Hereditary Diseases was amended on June 26, 1935, to allow for the termination of pregnancy based on eugenic grounds. Those who performed abortions on hereditarily healthy women, by contrast, were punished with imprisonment and, after the outbreak of war, with death.[9]

Individual self-fulfillment, personal happiness, passion, companionship, and affection played no role in Adolf Hitler's concept of marriage in the National Socialist state: "Furthermore, marriage cannot be an end in itself, rather it must serve the one greater goal, the propagation and maintenance of the species and race. This alone is its meaning and purpose."[10] The propaganda campaign directed at the broad masses, while highlighting the biological basis of "proper" marriages, made concessions to socially ingrained attitudes on free choice as illustrated in the "Ten Commandments for Choosing a Spouse":

> Remember that you are a German!
> You should keep your mind and soul pure!
> Keep your body pure!
> You should not remain single, if you are hereditarily healthy!
> Marry only for love!
> As a German, choose only a spouse of the same or related blood!
> When choosing a spouse, ask about his ancestors!
> Health is the prerequisite for external beauty!
> Choose a companion for marriage, not a playmate!
> You should wish for as many children as possible![11]

The government viewed marriage primarily as a social institution to maintain and perpetuate racial "purity," so it strenuously enforced the selection of spouses according to racial, hereditary, and health criteria with the explicit purpose of producing children. The centrality of love in this formulation, the fifth of Ten Commandments, does not attest to the importance of individual emotional needs in Nazi ideology. "The motive here," as Jill Stephenson rightly points out, "was that a loving couple would be more likely to provide a stable home, and so it was thought, many children."[12]

The German melodrama of the 1940s shares much with its Hollywood counterpart. Along with classic Hollywood cinema, Nazi film is firmly rooted in the discursive tradition that sets out to expose and contain the inconsistencies evident in patriarchy. "Ideological contradiction," Laura Mulvey argues, "is the overt mainspring and specific content of melodrama, not a hidden, unconscious thread to be picked up only by special critical processes. No ideology can even pretend to totality: it must provide an outlet for its own inconsistencies."[13] "As a safety valve for ideological contradictions centered on sex and the family,"[14] the melodrama questions patriarchy's overvaluation of masculinity in terms of virility, power, and conquest. Melodrama seeks compromise between the sexes in a renewed appreciation of femininity and domesticity.

These basic strategies informing the family narrative not only correspond to the project of Nazi melodramas but are also consistent with statements of early National Socialist women leaders. These party ideologues openly acknowledged the potential threat inherent in a society organized exclusively around male fellowship. Lydia Gottschewski, leader of the League of German Girls (*Bund Deutscher Mädel*) argued in her book *Male Union and the Women's Question* (1934) that an exaggerated valuation of masculinity could only lead to the destruction of the community: "The idea of male union (*Männerbund*) as a principle of order has saved our people from the chaos of Bolshevism. But the other must be said: the over exaggeration of this idea, its fixation as the exclusive measure of all things tears the community apart."[15]

The fascist melodrama articulates this problem in its construction of gender difference and social integration. Various tropes operate in these films to neutralize any threat to the stability of the nuclear family. In order to survive as a folk, men must make concessions to the domestic order. Men's transgressions revolve around their inappropriate use of masculine values in their relationships with women. Men threaten stability when they refuse to tame indiscriminate sexual drives and to redirect this energy toward their wives. Good husbands, the melodrama instructs, need to recognize the value of their wives' sacrifice and the inherent value of femininity, and, especially, motherliness. Women pose a danger to the domestic order when they assert their own female desire, subjectivity, and activity. Aberrant femininity, exemplified in a woman's mobility, self-interest, and eroticized motherhood is punished with illness, banishment, or death. Women are ultimately judged according to their ability to conform to the ideals of femininity with its apotheosis in motherhood. Good mothers, or potentially good mothers, are integrated into the family while bad mothers are eliminated.

Since it emphasizes paradox and discontent, the melodrama represents a potentially subversive text. Criticism and the call for change, however, are directed inward to the character and not outward to social institutions. In reference to the melodrama, David Bordwell notes that "the characters' volatility is a structural necessity for the genre's narrational processes and effects."[16] The characters adjust themselves to the system rather than look for ways to change society. Those who adapt are rewarded. Those who cannot or will not adapt to the system are conveniently eliminated from the picture. Melodramas, or weepies, as Molly Haskell likewise argues, "are founded on a mock-Aristotelian and politically conservative aesthetic whereby women spectators are moved, not by pity and fear but by self-pity and tears, to accept, rather than reject, their lot."[17] I would like to expand Haskell's idea to postulate that the melodrama addresses both men and women in order to maintain the status quo of the patriarchal family unit.

The predominantly female audience widely attributed to the Hollywood melodrama cannot be ascribed to the Nazi melodrama without raising serious problems. The question as to who actually attended the cinema during the Third Reich, more men or more women, and which genres each group favored, is exceedingly difficult to ascertain since the Propaganda Ministry published no statistical analyses of German audiences based on their sex. The few shreds of evidence we can garner from contemporary film journals show us more about prevalent stereotypes than actual audience composition and opinions. Writing in January 1938 for the Propaganda Ministry's official organ *Der deutsche Film,* Frank Maraun maintains:

> Recently we have determined that 70% of all moviegoers are women. Why women go to the movies is clear: they want to see love and have feelings. With one sparkling and one wet eye, feature films never tire of granting them both. Their thoughts also love to circle around human things and ponder psychological conflicts. Here film constantly gives them practice material for life. Moreover, they have naturally a better sense of the arts and a greater inclination to give themselves over to daydreaming. And here too film provides everything needed.[18]

Unfortunately, Maraun supplies no details on how the Propaganda Ministry came up with the figure of 70% for the female audience, whether it distributed questionnaires, conducted interviews, or measured ticket sales. In June 1938, the trade paper *Licht-Bild-Bühne* likewise cited that 70% of all moviegoers were women and attributed this statistic to a local study conducted in the city of Hamburg. While not commenting on the narrow scope of the study or whether it could be useful to generalize audience composition throughout Germany, the reviewer for *Licht-Bild-Bühne* disagreed with Maraun's conclusions and argued that "women and men concur in their demands for artistic, true-to-life films."[19] Indeed, two conflicting views were repeatedly voiced on the pages of film journals throughout 1938. In a series of articles addressing what women wanted from the motion picture industry, Ingrid Binné claimed that German women "today no longer watch with disinterest the political process in the Reich and in the world. They actively experience the central events of our time."[20] They do not want fairy tales of riches and ideal love affairs. Instead they want to see films that bring to life Adolf Hitler's vision of an ideal National Socialist womanhood. Quoting the Führer, Binné asserted that women went to the cinema to see "the eternal mother of our folk and man's life partner, fellow-worker, and comrade-in-arms."[21] Writing for the same trade paper, reviewer Christine Großmann argued along completely different lines. Großmann stated that women "have more imagination, if one understands that as having the ability to dream, the ability to go along with the events unfolding before them on the screen, and the ability to put themselves into these events."[22] Women go to the cinema because they want to fantasize about an exciting and carefree lifestyle and imagine that they could look, dress, and behave like their favorite stars Marlene Dietrich, Greta Garbo, and Joan Crawford up on the silver screen. This debate over what was more appealing and in demand — politically correct role models that reinforced Nazi ideology or amusing escapist fantasies that satisfied emotional needs — tells us less about what ordinary women wanted than about the film industry's difficulties in fulfilling Goebbels's mandate for instruction through entertainment. The propaganda ministry called for stirring motion pictures with equal parts ideology and distraction, which would enchant both male and female audiences and persuade them to filter the reality of gender roles in politically acceptable ways.

Recent scholarship on Nazi cinema has rarely addressed the question of audience composition with adequate results. For example, film historian David Welch makes a generalization about German film audiences during the Second World War that demands closer inspection. Welch concludes:

> One can reasonably assume that in wartime women and children would make up the majority of the audience. For ideological reasons, relatively few women were employed in Germany during the war compared to Britain and Russia. One reason for this was that the allowances paid to soldiers' wives were so generous that it was often more economical for them not to work. In times of rationing, hardship, and loneliness, sitting in a warm cinema was an obvious way for such women to spend their time and money.[23]

Welch's statement is misleading on several grounds. First, the assumption that the cinema audience was primarily female during the war years due to military conscription cannot be confirmed with any certitude, and, if we take Hollywood as our model, this assumption seems to work more on the stereotype of the bored housewife than on facts.[24] Second, the Propaganda Ministry took extreme measures to assure that soldiers at the front were provided with mobile cinemas and that feature films constituted an important source of entertainment and education in Nazi party organizations. Indeed, the need for mobile cinemas in rural areas and makeshift cinemas in bombed-out cities indicates that the filmic experience during the war did not universally take place in a warm theater. More importantly, Welch presents woman as a monolithic category not taking into account issues of social class, age, marital status, labor conscription, and volunteer labor. His female audience seems to consist largely of married, middle-class women with nothing better to do than go to the movies. Already before the outbreak of war, 12.7 million German women were gainfully employed outside the home comprising 37% of the workforce.[25] Women also performed a considerable amount of unpaid labor that is generally not calculated in standard employment statistics: volunteer work for Winter Relief, the NS-Womanhood, and the League of German Girls, not to mention housework and childcare. The National Socialist regime initiated legal measures to assure women's participation in the wartime labor force. The National Service Law of May 1935, for example, allowed for the wartime industrial conscription of all women ages 15 to 65 who were not pregnant or who did not have children under the age of 15. Likewise, the Women's Labor Service, compulsory as of September 4, 1939, called for unpaid female service to the state in domestic and agricultural economies for up to a year. While compulsory labor measures for Aryan women were never fully implemented in German society, it would be false to conclude that women as a social group were completely free from duties to the state and could devote themselves exclusively to the pursuit of leisure activities.

Various statements from leading political figures and entertainers suggest that the German melodrama was not conceived solely for a female audience. According to comments by Goebbels, the military high command, and members of the film community, the prevailing view was that the melodrama addressed both male and female spectators. Goebbels, for instance, voiced his concern over the effect that the melodrama *Opfergang* would have on soldiers at the front. He also complained that the High Command of the Armed Forces (OKW) created difficulties for him in his film work. In a diary entry for May 23, 1942, Goebbels depicts a widely publicized dispute between himself, the OKW, and Field Marshal Göring over the morality of a Luftwaffe officer who spends the night with a famous singer in the melodrama *Die große Liebe* (True Love).[26] The popular star Kristina Söderbaum also acknowledged the great impression her melodrama *Immensee* (1943) left on male spectators. She received numerous letters from soldiers at the front who had found consolation in this "hymn of a loyal wife."[27]

It seems surprising that the German film community would be concerned with images of men and the reactions of a male audience, since the melodrama focuses chiefly on the lives of women. These female protagonists, however, are portrayed much less as individuals than as family members. Wife, mother, daughter, lover: these are the primary roles for women. Gerd Albrecht has conducted extensive statistical research on main characters in Nazi films based on their sex and family status and concludes that women are significantly more likely to be defined by kinship than men.[28] A woman's place in the family, however, is most often determined by her relationship to a man rather than to another woman. Rarely are relationships between women — sisters, girlfriends or even mother and daughter — so well developed that they become the focal point of these narratives.[29] Nazi cinema is conceived on the premise that the audience not only identifies with the film characters but also tries to emulate their behavior. Fashioned by a patriarchal social order committed equally to the conflicting principles of polarity and harmony between the sexes, the Nazi melodrama instructs its audience on how women and men should relate to each other.

Male Conquest of the Female Continent: Veit Harlan's *Opfergang* (1944)

The only Nazi filmmaker ever brought to trial for crimes against humanity, Veit Harlan is best known for his virulently anti-semitic film *Jud Süß* (1940) and his ballad to total war *Kolberg* (1945). A star director in the Third Reich, Harlan was awarded the title "Professor," received some of the highest wages and most prestigious projects, and directed four of the first nine German full-length feature films in Agfa color. However, as Karsten Witte maintains, "Harlan's specific service to the Third Reich was his heavy melodramas . . . which together all seismographically reflect Nazi domestic and foreign policy developments."[30] Despite their exemplary nature, Harlan's melodramas have been largely overlooked by film historians. His melodrama *Opfergang* (Rite of Sacrifice, 1944) is a case in point and deserves more critical attention.[31]

The screenplay of *Opfergang*, written by Veit Harlan and Alfred Braun, is based loosely on Rudolf G. Binding's novella of the same name published in 1912. With its color film format and star cast including Kristina Söderbaum (Harlan's Swedish wife), Carl Raddatz, and Irene von Meyendorff, *Opfergang* was clearly conceived as a box office success but did not premiere until December 8, 1944, thirteen months after its completion. Harlan claimed that Propaganda Minister Joseph Goebbels held the film from the theaters for nearly a year because it mythologized adultery as sublime and emanated "Todeserotik."[32] The eventual release of the film and its rating of "artistically especially valuable," however, testify to its general adherence to the dictates of fascist propaganda. Films produced during the peak war years were endowed with two primary functions, entertainment and education, which Goebbels maintained could not be divorced from politics:

Moreover, we do not want to ignore the fact that film as a great and deeply penetrating mass art must also serve as entertainment. But at a time in which the entire nation is burdened with such difficult hardships and worries, entertainment is mainly valuable politically. . . . Additionally, film in its modern development is a first-class educational medium for the nation.[33]

Opfergang advances just such a political agenda in the guise of harmless diversion. This melodrama entertains the audience with an archetypal story of a love triangle, while educating the masses to maintain the sanctity of marriage and instrumentalize sexuality in the service of the state. Harlan's film charts the development of a married couple as they learn to overcome socially unacceptable behavior and adopt prescribed gender roles. This narrative development corresponds to a dominant strategy of Nazi entertainment films, whereby deviant behavior is played out only to be reigned in and overcome at the conclusion.[34] The pedagogical value of cinematic transgressions and their sublimation lies in their function as a cathartic release and redirection of desire cloaked in an innocuous vehicle, for as Goebbels argued, the best propaganda is invisible and conceals its true intentions.[35] Harlan's film conforms to Goebbels dictate by veiling its ideological stance in entertainment. *Opfergang* engages in a discourse about masculinity centered on territorial domination and about femininity that rewards sacrifice, self-effacement, and service while punishing mobility, self-interest, and passion with death.[36]

Typical of melodrama, the narrative is highly convoluted. Upon returning from a long sea voyage to his hometown of Hamburg, the world traveler Albrecht Froben (Carl Raddatz) marries his cousin Octavia (Irene von Meyendorff), a beautiful but extremely reserved young woman. Despite admonishments from his cousin Mathias (Franz Schafheitlin), Albrecht befriends his strange and adventurous neighbor Älskling Flodeen (Kristina Söderbaum), who rides with him daily through the countryside. In order to distance himself from Äls, Albrecht moves with his wife to Düsseldorf and tries to lose himself in business and parties. At the carnival ball, however, Octavia realizes that she cannot bear the wild, intoxicating festivities and longs for her quiet home on the Alster. The Frobens thus return to Hamburg and learn Äls is confined to her bed with the remnants of a tropical fever. Encouraged by Albrecht's daily greeting on horseback outside her window, Äls recovers and the two continue their rides together. Soon Äls admits: "My friend, we love each other, and it will end badly." She suffers a relapse just as typhus spreads through the harbor district, where her illegitimate daughter is staying with a governess. Albrecht saves the child but is infected himself. When Octavia hears Albrecht's feverish torment over Äls's deteriorating health, she resolves to don her husband's riding habit and perform the ritual greeting to his dying lover. Albrecht learns of Octavia's self-sacrifice after Äls's death and finally recognizes his wife's great love. Reconciled, the couple rides along the seashore and bids one last farewell to Äls, whose ashes have been scattered among the waves.

The opening sequence positions Albrecht Froben as an accomplished world traveler with Viking blood, a respected member of an all-male group defined by mobility. After Hamburg has been established as the venue with an aerial shot of the Elbe River followed by shots of the harbor, scenic buildings, and the Bismarck monument, the scene shifts to a large paneled room filled with maritime artifacts. At the head of a rectangular table, where nearly twenty members of the German Colonial Union[37] are seated, a man stands next to a large globe and reports on Albrecht's travels to former German colonies in Africa and on to Japan. As a sign of their esteem, the group awards Albrecht "the entire world," the globe.

The strategic placement of colonialism at the beginning of the film, our entrance into the filmic text, suggests that *Opfergang* participates in a discourse of domination. Rudolf Binding's novella of 1912 contains no references to the pre-First-World-War German ambition of a middle-African empire stretching from Togo and Cameroon to German East Africa. Embedded in Harlan's film in the form of the German Colonial Union (a slightly veiled reference to the Reich Colonial Union[38]) and transported into 1942–1944, colonialism carries striking significance. With its emphasis on geographical orientation and spatial conquest, the film seems to resonate anxieties aroused by the war and the quest for *Lebensraum*. Yet, despite its contemporary setting, *Opfergang* is devoid of any overt references to the war in North Africa, Europe, or Asia.[39] The lack of historical specificity invites an allegorical reading of colonialism. *Opfergang* conflates masculinity with exploration and conquest, and femininity with stability of the soil. Herein lies both a central metaphor of the film and a fundamental aspect of fascist mythology. Land and woman stand as interchangeable elements, objects to be subdued by male drives of domination and movement.

This reading is supported in the second sequence. As the camera focuses on the globe and the shot dissolves into the next scene, Albrecht points to the countries of his travels and displays to his cousin Mathias three treasures: a warrior statue, an eleven-headed Kuan-yin,[40] the Goddess of Mercy that Albrecht mistakes for a Buddha, and a kimono. While Mathias admires the Kuan-yin, Albrecht seductively dons the kimono and boasts of his sexual exploits until he rests upon a portrait of Octavia. At the same time Mathias protests: "Albrecht, Albrecht, you are now a famous, dignified man. You can no longer afford such stories. You are bound by your position."[41]

Albrecht's souvenirs and the geography of his travels can be read as the representative elements in the dangerous conquest of the "dark continent." These objects and spaces stand in for the three main characters and embody their essence, foreshadowing the conflicts ahead. The male warrior figure symbolizes Albrecht, a mighty conqueror who defies the boundaries of political division to re-capture the colonial ideal. The Kuan-yin, the unrecognized Goddess of Mercy, exemplifies Octavia, who patiently forgives her husband for his adultery while he fails to see her virtue and selfless love. The alluring kimono and unexplored regions of Asia and Africa represent Äls, the sexual threat inherent in the erotic realm of forbidden pleasure or, in Freudian terms, the dark continent of enigmatic female desire.[42]

In the masculine battle for the colonization of woman, virtue and desire stand for the oppositional feminine components of stability and dissolution. This dual vision of femininity is represented in the "heavenly" Octavia and the "earthly" Äls, who are never captured in the same frame.[43] Albrecht mediates between the two women and functions as a catalyst for change, compelling Octavia to integrate aspects of Als's personality into her own.

Octavia first appears as an objectified framed icon; she is, like her painted image, a constant ("She is what she always was.").[44] Timeless and motionless, Octavia's portrait retards Albrecht's movement and contains his sexual desires, defined by Mathias as socially unacceptable. When she appears before Albrecht descending the stairs in a flowing white gown to greet him, Octavia literally embodies the lofty realm of ideal femininity, which must descend from its pedestal to meet the rugged earthbound male. Indeed, the original visual stability of her portrait and the subsequent movement of her body mirror Octavia's development within the filmic narrative from an unapproachable angel to a corporeal wife. Initially staged as stationary, seated, or moving slowly, Octavia only begins to move quickly when her relationship with Albrecht is threatened by her physical passivity. Despite her inhibitions, for example, Octavia glides down the giant carnival slide, and when Albrecht cannot divert his attention from Äls, Octavia runs after her in search of the key to her rival's magnetism. In the ultimate self-sacrifice, she adopts Albrecht's persona and rides his horse past Äls's window to comfort her husband's dying mistress. Octavia's development is complete in the final scene, when she joins her husband on horseback along the seashore. Each movement brings her closer to a vital physicality that will satisfy her husband's desires.

Octavia is a beautiful, artistic, and somewhat fragile woman bound to her family's dimly lit drawing room, her gleaming white music room, or the garden of her family's estate. Playing the piano is her entire life, an activity that "signals harmony, cultural refinement and the restriction of women to the domestic sphere."[45] Octavia's artificial environment, and by analogy the homeland, is associated with extreme intellectualism and pending death. The Froben estate is filled with reminders of transitoriness and mortality. The grandfather clock, inscribed with the adage "One of these hours will be your last," dominates the scene.[46] Likewise, the table clock in Octavia's room holds a central position in the middle of the frame, suggesting the overwhelming sense of life's brevity.

This morbid preoccupation with death culminates at the Froben family gathering. The scene opens on a close-up of orchids on the drawing room table. These tropical flowers are later featured prominently in Äls and Albrecht's sick rooms, creating a link between the extremes of the mind and body. Octavia plays Chopin's nocturnes in a dark room filled with heavy furniture and filtered light, while her father recites Nietzsche's "Todesahnung" from the *Dionysos-Dithyramben* cycle, "The Sun Sinks." Albrecht is deeply disturbed by the changes in Hamburg since his departure three years earlier. Especially bothered by the emphasis on death, he opens the door to reveal the sunlight and thus asserts the life-affirming value of nature: "wind and waves, the glow and pleasure of the sun."[47] The parallels to Germany in the later stages of the war are clear. As a counter to the pervasive obsession with death resulting from crushing military defeats, the film offers sports and nature as a refuge.

Albrecht exhibits many of the attributes of the ideal fascist male: he is an explorer, active, mobile, and most at home outdoors. While his world travels function as an initiation rite, his road to manhood has just begun. He cannot remain an aimless, restless wanderer, and Octavia activates his return to *Heimat,* the family estate. Although Albrecht becomes anchored in the homeland, he never seems to have a space of his own. While the Froben coat of arms adorns the estate windows and model ship, confirming his membership in the family "empire," Albrecht is always in someone else's space. In contrast to both Octavia and Äls, who inherit large estates, Albrecht has no land of his own. Even his cousin Mathias has a study filled with the relics of the East and, ironically, Albrecht's globe. Far from being alienated, Albrecht dominates indoor space and makes it his own by his sheer presence. An energetic, strong man without his own clearly defined territory, Albrecht embodies the fascist male who needs *Lebensraum* and embraces the Nazi policy of territorial expansion. His situation also illustrates that when a man has no land (read woman) to control, he cannot control himself.

Like Octavia, who must learn to become more physical, sensuous, and active, Albrecht must also change the direction of his life. He must learn to tame his reckless behavior and carnal passions and redirect his libidinal energy toward his wife. His development within the film's narrative consists of recognizing Octavia's virtues and controlling his unproductive sexuality. Albrecht's journey towards social integration is endangered by the erotic woman.

Älskling Flodeen's initial appearance establishes her mythic identity as a water nixie; the audience only glimpses her hands, arms, legs, and blond hair as she grasps onto Albrecht's boat. With her fragmented physicality, Äls is the epitome of the mobile woman defined by a "free lifestyle." Without a definitive homeland (Octavia thinks Äls is from Finland) or even a real name (Älskling was a nickname given to her by her mother), Äls is described as a migratory bird, who travels south in the winter as far as Africa. Her unrestrained lifestyle is inimical to the ideal of the Aryan woman.

Äls negates several essential features of National Socialist ideology. She does not conform to Nazi standards on racial purity, the health of the national body, and the sanctity of motherhood. To begin with, although Äls is outwardly the model of the Aryan woman with her blond hair, blue eyes, and athletic body, she is marked a foreigner of uncertain origins. Her foreignness is emphasized by the fact that Albrecht, Octavia, and Mathias are cousins, blood relatives who share the same name, family estate, and homeland. The question of Äls's racial value in Nazi terms is ultimately linked to her state of health. As she swims, rides, and practices archery accompanied by nearly twenty hounds, Äls appears to be the picture of health. Likewise, her home, filled with plants, parrots, and hounds, reflects the external vitality so characteristic of her being. But Äls suffers from the remnants of a tropical fever and has inherited poor health from her mother, who spent her life in hospitals and vegetated long before she died. Äls shares a fatal connection with her mother.[48] Both women are described as "foolhardy," "frivolous," and especially "irrational." Moreover, their diseased bodies prevent them from being good mothers and caring for their daughters, and as the governess concludes: "A sick mother? . . . The child suffers the most from that."[49] The repeated comparisons between Äls and her deceased mother reflect Nazi concepts of racial hygiene and biological determinism. The diseased female body is passed down from generation to generation and threatens the health of the national body. Even Äls's daughter Susanne is a danger; although she is not infected with typhus, she passes the disease onto Albrecht.[50]

Along with her illness, Äls's mobility and self-interested desire to live to the fullest define her as a poor mother. In response to her pleas to let Susanne live with her, the governess replies: "There would be absolutely no sense in that. You are hardly here, then you close the house up again and move to the south or to the north and then the child has to leave again. That is not good for a child. Or do you want to drag it along everywhere? A child must have an ordered life."[51]

Although Äls's status as an unwed mother might suggest a violation of conventional morality, according to Nazi family policy her physical inability and reluctance to care for her child are a more formidable offense.[52] Äls's "abnormality" is again written on her body. The film draws a clear connection between femininity and pain in a scene with Äls and her doctor. The doctor characterizes pain and suffering as positive because, as a warning signal, they protect the body from serious injury. Äls, however, does not perceive pain. Herein lies her ultimate transgression against the fascist concept of femininity. Adolf Hitler's formulation of male and female duties can serve as an example of how National Socialism encodes woman:

> What a man sacrifices in the struggle of his people, a woman sacrifices in the struggle for the preservation of this people in the individual cases.

> What the man employs in heroic courage on the battlefield, the woman employs in eternal, patient devotion, in eternal, patient suffering and endurance. Every child that she brings into the world is a battle that she wins for the existence or nonexistence of her people.[53]

Defined in the metaphors of battle, woman's essential nature is to bear children, maintain the nuclear family, and suffer pain silently. Äls does not conform to these expectations; pain is alien to her being, and she fails to fulfill her maternal duties.

Whereas Äls and Albrecht are both associated with water — Harlan's recurring symbol of fluidity, passion, boundlessness, and mobility — they negotiate water differently. Äls is inscribed as a siren; a temptress who emerges from the sea and ultimately merges with it as her ashes are scattered among the waves. Äls relates to water physically, in that she becomes the sea itself on both a visual and narrative level.[54] Albrecht, by contrast, masters the seas as he sails across the globe, just as he masters land that does not belong to him. This dominion is endangered by his relationship to Äls, illustrated by the fact that sailing was his favorite sport until he met her. Thereafter, he no longer commands the waters.

The *Faschingsball* sequence in *Opfergang* provides the main characters with an opportunity to subvert fascist stereotypes, if only momentarily.[55] As a central metaphor in Weimar cinema for unlimited sensual and social possibilities, the carnival is a relatively rare event in Nazi films.[56] The carnival, as defined by Mikhail Bakhtin, is the freedom that comes from inverting the social hierarchy, suspending moral conventions, and masquerading in new roles. Unlike ritual, which is created and practiced by the elite, "Carnival is not a spectacle seen by the people; they live in it, and everyone participates because its very idea embraces all the people." Bakhtin continues: "It is the people as a whole, but organized in their own way . . . It is outside of and contrary to all existing forms of the coercive socioeconomic and political organization, which is suspended for the time of the festivity."[57] The carnival functions as a safety valve. It gives voice to an alternative conception of reality within a controlled framework. By allowing difference to be played out and affording potentially destructive desires a limited release, the carnival averts any real threat to the system.

In Harlan's film the subversive quality of the carnival is directed towards new sexual identities, which ultimately reaffirm the institution of marriage. Wearing a red mask and black cape lined in red reminiscent of his red kimono and situated in the realm of unacceptable eroticism, Albrecht pursues two blond women dressed like Äls in black riding habit, black top hat, mask and veil covering their faces. The erotic woman is doubled in an optical encoding of her underling enigma and then fetishized in the mask and veil, which function "to visualize (and hence stabilize) the instability, the precariousness of sexuality."[58]

True to the carnivalesque principle, however, this image of woman proves to be false. A fade-in of Äls seated at her desk, dressed in a modest white night-gown, writing in her diary of how she must remain silent about her love for Albrecht, calls the cinematic inscription of the erotic woman into question. Not only is Äls not present at the festivities, she is determined to uphold the sanctity of marriage and renounce her passion. In a similar manner, for the duration of the carnival Octavia seems willing to adopt a more sensual persona to match her golden mask and white dress. Indeed, at the carnival the two women begin to play with roles foreign to their character — in effect they exchange roles in the masquerade. Äls adopts the modesty, virtue, and corresponding physical passivity long associated with Octavia, while Octavia embraces Äls's vitality, sensuality, and movement.

In an attempt to assume Äls's energetic persona, Octavia agrees to go down the giant mouth slide with Albrecht but is soon upset by his public display of passion. When she is voted the winner in the Triumph of Beauty contest and captured by the throngs, Octavia screams, struggles free, and runs away. The scene denotes the symbolic rape of Octavia: alone in a taxi, her mask gone, tears streaming down her face, Octavia is engulfed in a dark red velvet cape covering her white dress resembling a wedding gown. Albrecht is titillated by his wife's pain and humiliation and gleefully reveals: "She screamed bloody murder."[59] The marriage has been consummated.

Female desire as sickness: *Opfergang*.

Whereas Octavia is associated with death on an intellectual level, Äls is preoccupied with her own death: "One is always near him — Death. And its really quite good, if one smiles a little once in a while and says: you are my friend. You come when I cannot go on any longer."[60] Äls's death scene reveals the nexus of excessive female physicality, unbridled passion, and erotic death. The audience witnesses Äls dying on her sumptuous bed in a medium shot. With her hair tousled, dressed in a negligee, her right shoulder and much of her chest exposed, Äls radiates the fever engulfing her life force. The filmic strategies in *Opfergang* correspond to the trope Mary Ann Doane has found in American women's films of the 1940s: uncontained female sexuality and desires are externalized as a fever that consumes the woman and leads to her death.[61] Äls's disease also resonates fascist ideas on female desire. Both Albrecht and Äls travel to the tropics, but he returns as the mighty conquering hero integrated into society through male bonding and marriage. She, by contrast, is punished with the remnants of a tropical fever for venturing into places culturally forbidden to woman. The fever that consumes Äls is gender specific. The disease inscribed on her body is related to her mother's ill health and becomes a hereditary trait transmitted from one infected female to the next. Although Albrecht also suffers a fever from typhus, he recovers in direct opposition to the conclusion of Binding's novella. According to Harlan, it was Goebbels who insisted on changing the end of the film: "The woman guilty of adultery has to die, not the husband. The marriage must remain intact. Besides, this would be better in a pedagogical sense not only for the front but also for the homeland."[62] In the fascist state, the erotic woman must die, so that the marriage can survive.

The focus on voyeurism, exhibitionism, and spectacle in Äls's death scene illuminates a characteristic function of the erotic woman in Nazi cinema. Äls's bed is moved to the window so that she can see Albrecht and be seen by him. Woman, encoded as the specular object of male desire, is ironically situated in the role of spectator but deprived of agency and control. Her body motivates the spectacle, but her entrance into the system likewise triggers the containment, physical punishment, and elimination of the female body. Without a body to act out her passion, Äls's look is disengaging; all that remains is the desire of the gaze.

The parallel montage, whereby both Albrecht and Äls lie in their separate beds engulfed by fever, illustrates the opposing consequences of male and female adultery in Nazi cinema. The soft lighting, choral music, and intimate camera work intent on highlighting the romantic aspects of death culminate in a close-up of Äls's disembodied face. Divested of the erotic, her body is literally eliminated by the clouds, waves, and lighting. She is contained in a collage composition, where her de-eroticized face is superimposed onto her garden gate and the roaring waves behind it, while Albrecht, in a medium shot (significantly capturing his torso), occupies the left corner of the frame. When the gate opens and the water rushes into the garden, her face disappears in a fade-out. Äls and the passion she represents are completely extinguished. She becomes the ocean, a flowing space for man to dominate.

The fascist melodrama, rather than directed exclusively at a female audience (Goebbels's insistence on script changes based on their presumed effect on soldiers at the front, should suffice to question this long-held premise), aestheticizes female sacrifice. As the restless embodiment of unbridled passion, the non-conforming woman poses a danger to the warrior male and is cinematically contained in the *image* of pain. Äls, the woman who cannot perceive pain internally, ironically becomes the vehicle for rendering pain visible. Female suffering, rather than portrayed as a "reality," is externalized as an image and becomes an overriding aesthetic principle.[63] The act of violence waged against a female body defined as inferior, her erasure from the picture, is rendered beautifully to elicit aesthetic pleasure rather than moral outrage.

The staging of female death in *Opfergang* is typical of how many fascist films deal with a woman whose sexuality is outside the confines of the nuclear family. Äls is condemned to death for her transgressive sexuality. More significant than her adultery is her role as an erotic mother, a mother who fails to raise her own child, who has no husband, and who risks her own health for sensual pleasures while endangering the life of her child. Äls shares much with the figure Hanna from *Ich klage an!* (I Accuse!, Wolfgang Liebeneiner, 1941), a film designed to gain approval for the "Aktion T-4" euthanasia program. Both films present an idealized version of female death from disease. By mapping the deterioration of two protagonists who begin as vibrant young women and turn into bedridden invalids, the filmmakers present death as a solution to suffering that is merciful and readily embraced. When Äls lies in Albrecht's arms, she purrs contentedly, "To die like this would be the most beautiful death!" Likewise, after Hanna's husband has given her poison instead of medicine, she sighs, "I feel so light, so happy, like never before. I wish it were death." What Karl Ludwig Rost writes of Hanna applies to Äls as well: "It is not the fear of death but the fear of dying alone without the beloved husband that appears to be the true horror."[64]

Although much has been written on the glorification of death and aestheticizing of violence in Nazi culture,[65] the gender issues involved in staging death remain relatively unexplored. Male death, epitomized in films ranging from *Hitlerjunge Quex* (Hitler Youth Quex, 1933) to *Wunschkonzert* (Request Concert, 1940), is most often a heroic act of sacrifice for the good of the community and the fatherland. Young Heini Völker in *Hitlerjunge Quex*, for example, is murdered by the Communists and dies in his comrades' arms with the words of the official Hitler Youth Song on his lips. Heini becomes immortalized as the swastika is superimposed on his dead body and replaced by columns of marching Hitler Youths. Romanticized male death is usually violent but quick and apparently painless (since the man is nearly anesthetized by visions of grandeur), often taking place offscreen. There are few examples of men dying from diseases, but when figures such as Fritz von Hartwig in *Robert Koch* (1939) and Professor Achenbach in *Germanin* (1943) die from tuberculosis and sleeping sickness, their deaths are meaningful because they help find cures for these deadly diseases.[66]

Saul Friedländer has noted that Nazism presents "not real death in its everyday horror and tragic banality, but a ritualized, stylized, and aestheticized death."[67] A contemporary critic of *Opfergang* recognized the "decorative" function of female death:

> The impetuosity of wanting to die young, to ride as an elegant bride of the wind on the waves and to hunt on the back of a horse, the unbridled, feverish, life addiction is expressed very effectively by Kristina Söderbaum. She knows how to die with decorative grace.[68]

Due to her diseased body and aberrant maternal role, Äls cannot contribute to society and her death therefore corresponds to the Nazi euthanasia measures prescribed for "inferior" people. Beyond this, Äls's demise also fulfills a significant propaganda function in the waning years of the war. Her personification of Death as a long awaited and helpful friend diminishes the horror of real death.

With the elimination of the femme fatale, the remaining femme fragile must be transformed into a vibrant woman for the picture to be complete.[69] Octavia, characterized by self-effacement and renunciation of her own desires, manifests many of the pivotal components of the model fascist woman. When Albrecht is disturbed by her family's bourgeois intellectualism, she consoles him: "But later we can do what we want, or rather what you want, Albrecht." In a similar vein, when Mathias asks how she is, Octavia replies: "I am as happy as Albrecht is."[70] Octavia's identity and sense of purpose are determined by her relation to her husband and thus she corresponds to Hitler's dictate: "The world of woman is man. She only thinks about other things now and then."[71] But Octavia, "in her cool, refined beauty, in her nobility, calmness, and inattentively measured deportment,"[72] is unapproachable. In order to adopt the masquerade of vitality initiated at the carnival and integrate it completely into her personality, Octavia must again disguise herself. She now dons Albrecht's riding habit and trots past Äls's window, participating for the first time in the ritual shared by her husband and his lover. Dressed in her husband's clothing and performing his ceremonial greeting, Octavia is vitalized in masculine terms or in the guise of masculinity. Octavia, who at the beginning of the film is characterized as distant and effete, successfully transforms herself by adopting Äls's sensuality and Albrecht's vigor. The emancipatory potential of the carnival is united with the stabilizing function of ritual to create a unified image of woman in Octavia.

In the final scene of the film, Octavia and Albrecht embody the ideal married couple as they slowly ride horses along the seashore. Both partners have had to sacrifice a part of their former selves. Octavia has abandoned her restraint and exhibits a new vigor. Albrecht has recovered from his sexual fever and shows self-constraint. Having gone from a gallop to a trot, Albrecht has literally bridled his passion. The couple has not only found a balanced pace on horseback, the arm's length between them has been overcome as they shake hands. Their acceptance of prescribed social roles is symbolized in their handshake, a pact to build a common future together.

Opfergang advances a concept of gender difference and social integration consistent with Nazi ideology in general. Any threat to the stability of the nuclear family is neutralized. Äls is eliminated from the picture because she poses a danger to the domestic order with her assertion of female desire and subjectivity. Octavia, by contrast, proves herself a good wife by conforming to her husband's desires and sacrificing self-identity. Albrecht in turn abandons his quest for forbidden pleasure, reaffirms his commitment to marriage, and conquers himself by taming his own drives. *Opfergang* inscribes gender identities that accommodate and propagate the government's stance regarding motherhood, the family, racial purity, euthanasia, sacrifice, and dominance.

Identity of the Mother Confirmed by the Language and Law of the Father in *Damals* (1943)

The Swedish actress Zarah Leander was brought to Germany in 1937 under contract with Ufa, Germany's largest film studio, in the hope that she could fill the gap in German film left by the departure of Greta Garbo and Marlene Dietrich.[73] In the grand tradition of the studio contract system, Ufa created a star image for Leander. Cast most often in the role of the ostensible femme fatale who suffers unbearable pain due to her subversive desires but in the end is vindicated as proper and respectable, Leander masquerades in dual roles. Her celluloid figure engages in non-domestic female occupations: she is a nightclub singer, revue star, or chanteuse, who has the liberty to be different and frequent the exotic and erotic. Featured as a foreigner from Great Britain, Sweden, Hungary, Russia, or Denmark who travels to all the corners of the world, she stands outside conventional norms. Her figure is marked not only by a deep, almost male voice, strong willed nature, and sexual activity, but also by her freedom of movement and function as spectacle. This independent, sensual woman is nearly always constituted as a deviance and danger to the moral order, but surprisingly is rewarded with a husband at the end of the film.[74]

The melodrama *Damals* (Back Then) best illustrates Zarah Leander's masquerade as the good girl everyone thinks is a bad girl. Her last film in the Third Reich, *Damals* was directed by Rolf Hansen and received the rating "artistically valuable." The premiere on March 3, 1943, was an overwhelming success, marred only by the fact that during the evening Berlin experienced its most severe bombing raid to date. Six weeks after the premiere, Leander left Germany, and the film was taken out of distribution.[75] Despite its short theatrical run, *Damals* was included in an unpublished list from November 13, 1944, of the most successful films produced in Nazi Germany.[76]

Damals engages in a popular discourse of disjunctive female identity brought into focus by the authority of language and law. Two opposing images of woman are anchored in the main protagonist Vera Meiners (alias Dr. Gloria O'Conner). The identity of this woman vacillates between a selfless mother and a deceitful, suspected murderess. This opposition represents an allegorical conflict between conformity and degeneracy based on the strict polarity between masculinity and femininity. The ideological work of the film is to criminalize female transgression against male authority while rewarding the suffering and sacrifice of "true" motherhood with the security of the nuclear family. Concurrently, the film assures the survival of the family by demanding that the father eventually acknowledge the value of motherhood. Woman's relation to law and language is characterized by deception and impotence. The male representatives of the law and social hierarchy narrate the complex, non-linear story, achieve narrative closure, administer justice, and restore order on both the narrative and social levels.

The film begins in South America, where Dr. Gloria O'Conner (Zarah Leander) is arrested for the murder of Frank Douglas (Karl Martell). When the authorities learn that Dr. O'Conner died at a quarantine station in Las Casas, the prisoner refuses to speak, even to reveal her true name, Vera Meiners. Seeking information on this unknown woman, District Attorney Mendoza publishes her photograph and arrest warrant in newspapers all over the world. Vera's story begins to unfold in a series of four flashbacks as friends and colleagues contact Mendoza with details about her past. In 1920s Lübeck, Vera lives happily with her husband, the attorney Jan Meiners (Hans Stüwe) and their two-year-old daughter Eva until she receives a letter from her former boyfriend Frank Douglas. Fearing her husband's jealousy, she secretly meets Douglas in Hamburg to end their relationship definitively. When Jan learns that Vera has lied to him about her clandestine rendezvous, he divorces her. Rebuilding her life in Switzerland, Vera becomes a doctor but is dismissed from her position for having performed an operation against the explicit orders of the hospital director, Professor Rigaud. Without economic means and deprived of her medical license, Vera becomes a variety singer in Lisbon and falls in love with the clown Pablo (Rossano Brazzi). Just as she is about to find some personal happiness, Frank Douglas appears again. He secures her a job as a nurse in South America, where she can be with her daughter, who has spent years in a boarding school. Vera renounces her love for Pablo through deceit in order to fulfill her maternal duties. At the quarantine station in Las Casas, Vera meets Dr. Gloria O'Conner, who is dying from typhus. Despite the violent protests of her fellow travelers, Vera informs the authorities about the infectious disease and is placed under stricter quarantine, thereby losing her nursing position. After months of unemployment, she assumes the identity of the deceased Dr. O'Conner and begins to practice medicine again. Returning to the present time frame, Jan Meiners arrives in South America to regain custody of his daughter. Jan discovers Vera has accepted imprisonment to protect Eva, who is likewise innocent of murder but equally guilty of poor judgment. The womanizer Frank Douglas was murdered by the father of a young woman who committed suicide after Douglas had seduced and abandoned her. At the conclusion, Vera is exonerated of murder, released from prison, and reunited with her daughter and former husband.

Damals contains all the elements of a successful filmscript that springs the boundaries of any single genre. It is a melodrama of a wife's defiance, a husband's jealousy, and the depths to which their bad judgment lead. It is also a crime story of murder, false imprisonment, and suicide. With its musical numbers by Zarah Leander and locales ranging from a bourgeois living room to a nightclub, from Lübeck to Lisbon and Las Casas, *Damals* was a calculated hit.

The film opens with the typical elements of the 1940s film noir or crime film. In a nightclub, a band plays a Latin American melody while a crowd forms on the dance floor. The rhythmic music follows the action to a hotel corridor as a woman wearing a black sequined dress with a lizard brooch on her lapel steals out of a hotel room and disappears into the rain-drenched night. Sailors come out of a dusty bar, a bus passes by, and the mysterious woman kicks the hotel key down the sewer just as a foghorn screeches and the sound of screaming crowds is heard. She enters the bar cast in the moving shadows of an overhead fan. Not reacting to the fact that the bar is closed, she orders an espresso in a deep voice and writes "Everything in order" on a note. Before her drink arrives, the elusive woman has vanished without a trace. The scene cuts to the same hotel room where a man is found shot to death.

The initial sequence sets the stage for the audience to understand the main protagonist as a criminal. The chiaroscuro lighting effects, "degenerate" music, exotic locations on the margin of proper society, and a murder all work to define Vera as deviant. The South American venue displaces the crime from any specifically German context and from self-directed social criticism. Travel to the exotic realm, as Siegfried Kracauer maintains, can serve as an escape from examining one's own social ills:

> Travel is one of the great possibilities of society to keep itself in a permanent state of absentmindedness, which protects it from a confrontation with itself. It helps imagination onto the wrong paths, it covers up the view with impressions, it contributes to the glories of the world so that

its ugliness is not noticed. (The increase in world knowledge it brings serves to transfigure the existing system in which it was acquired.)[77]

These unfamiliar images build on cultural constructs of National Socialism that posit the exotic as deadly. The beautiful and mysterious woman who inhabits this space, who frequents hotels, bars, and the harbor district at night, is likewise codified as a threat to normalcy and order. The dark imagery of crime is necessary for the audience's misrecognition of Vera as a murderer.

Vera's criminal status is reconfirmed when it becomes evident she has repeatedly lied to the district attorney and adopted a false identity. The mise en scène contributes to a definition of Vera as aberrant. The interrogation room with its honeycombed ceiling, venetian blinds, ceiling-level windows, fans, and sharp lighting contrasts that cast barred shadows on the walls visually imprison this strange woman. Vera, her body partially hidden in the shadows, thus suggesting the partial truths she espouses, obviously lies in her first interrogation. Her claim that she was never at the hotel contradicts what the audience has just witnessed. Confronted with evidence of her lies and false identity, Vera refuses to participate in the legal proceedings. Brought to her prison cell, she passes a woman screaming to be released from this insane asylum while another woman smokes, bares her legs, and plays a screeching blues song.[78] Grouped together with women who are portrayed as crazy and degenerate, Vera is located among the asocial.

According to the Reich and Prussian Ministry of the Interior in 1937: "Those to be considered asocial are persons who demonstrate through behavior towards the community, which may not in itself be criminal, that they will not adapt themselves to the community."[79] Individuals who deviate from prescribed social and sexual norms (alcoholics, prostitutes, the physically and mentally handicapped), and those who are "particularly unproductive and unrestrained, and who in the absence of a sense of responsibility do not conduct orderly domestic lives or raise their children to be useful racial comrades" were designated asocials.[80] "In the Nazis's view of the world, 'asocial' and criminal behavior was not determined by either individual choice or social environment, but was innate, and hence heritable."[81] Based on the genetic threat to the nation, criminal biologists demanded the exclusion of asocials and criminals from the community through preventative custody (*Vorbeugungshaft*), forced labor, or internment in concentration camps where they were marked with black triangles. More women than men were accused of asocial behavior and "social feeblemindedness," which often resulted in sterilization and inclusion in the euthanasia program.[82] Set within this discursive context, *Damals* posits aberrant femininity as a crime.

Vera appears as both a mysterious, lying, accused murderess and as a dedicated doctor who cares for her patients above everything. Before she is brought in for questioning, Vera is shown tending to her patients, combating not only disease but also the incompetence of her assistant. This dual image of Vera, the healer who devotes her life to others versus the asocial woman who transgresses moral and legal conventions, becomes the focus of the four flashbacks. These inner stories show how Vera's life is nearly destroyed each time she lies and defies male authority. The narrative works as much to determine the conclusive identity of this woman as to prove her guilt. Indeed, the film questions the extent to which her *being* is the criminal offence. Vera's disjunctive identity is based on her adherence to two opposing codes, the motherhood principle based on compassion, self-sacrifice, and devotion to others, and the fatherhood principle based on law, authority, and order. The first two flashbacks record the consequences of Vera's asocial behavior, namely her refusal to conform to patriarchal standards. The second two flashbacks illustrate how Vera's sense of compassion is eventually tempered by obedience to a higher order.

The first flashback to Lübeck establishes Vera's former idyllic status as a beloved wife and mother and a respected member of the community. The Meiners's spacious and elegant living room filled with well-dressed guests signals the economic security and prominent social status of the happy couple. Dressed in a modest black evening gown with a white lace collar and sleeves, a rose at her breast, her hair in tight curls, and lighted from above giving her a slight halo effect, Vera exudes contented domesticity. Surrounded by her husband and admiring guests, she is located at the center of the frame and becomes the focus of everyone's attention. Seated at the piano, her body conspicuously hidden, she sings a soft, slow lullaby, while looking up admiringly at her husband:

> Tonight, when the Night quiet and fine
> steps into my room here,
> I wrap myself up in her coat
> and say pleadingly to her:
> Dear Night, come, let me say to you,
> what I wish from the heart.
> No clock shall strike today
> and time shall stand still,
> and the world will not breathe!
> When he holds me in his arms![83]

Vera's song redefines the night in the context of socially sanctioned environs and institutions. The night, first introduced as a threat, a time of murder and intrigue in some distant land, becomes a blanket of security in the protective domain of the German family. The prosperity, security, and social integration linked to marriage, however, come at the expense of a woman's career and public life. Far from illustrating merely the private realm, the Meiners's home has become a public forum where the status of woman is debated:

> WOMAN GUEST: You men are such egoists. Say, why don't you let her become a singer?
>
> JAN: That would be the last straw. I am happy that she didn't become a doctor.
>
> DR. PETERSEN: Exactly. That's the way life goes. Finally God invents a creature who possesses every good talent. She can do something. She studies medicine, and besides that has a splendid voice, looks wonderful. And what happens? She falls in love with our good Meiners.
>
> JAN: Hey, you.
>
> DR. PETERSEN: Who is surely my best friend, but overnight, so to speak, all career plans are botched, and she's just a wife.
>
> VERA: Just? Can one be even more?
>
> WOMAN GUEST: No, not when you're happy.
>
> VERA: I'm happy![84]

Vera's identity centers on the ambiguous term *Frau*, denoting both wife and woman. Her acceptance of a self-definition that links a woman's social being to her biological functions necessitates that she relinquish a public role as doctor or singer in favor of a "natural" role as wife and mother. Conforming to her husband's vision of an ideal woman, Vera devotes her god-given talents to heal, nurture, and entertain her family and circle of friends. Meiner's insistence that his wife eschew an independent role in the limelight is deemed correct because both the women present concur that if a wife-woman is happy then that is all the identity she needs. The debate about female autonomy becomes superfluous when their adorable daughter Eva appears. All attention is directed to the child. As Vera lifts her to her lap, Jan bends down, and they form a tableau of the model family.

Vera endangers her idyllic home life by meeting Frank Douglas in Hamburg without her husband's knowledge. Although it is clear that Vera is a faithful wife and had rejected Frank long ago because he was not a suitable marriage partner, her reckless independence contributes to the dissolution of her marriage. She ventures away from home, defies her husband's authority, and lies to him. Jan learns of her deceit when the train to Copenhagen that she was supposed to be traveling on derails, a less than subtle visual image of male rage and impotency. Vera is punished for her transgression with banishment from paradise. Jan divorces her.

The flashback to Switzerland reveals how the contradictory nature of Vera's personality leads to disaster. She is shown to be a dedicated doctor who risks her professional life for the welfare of a young patient. Her compassion for others, however, is at variance with the established order.

Upon examining the young Paulette Gaspard, Professor Rigaud declares that nothing can be done at the moment since the girl's heart cannot withstand surgery. Vera breaks the news to the child's mother, Mrs. Gaspard, who appeals to Vera for help based on a "natural" bond between women, their common struggle to aid a child in need: "Doctor, you have to help me. The professor is certainly a good doctor, but he is only a man. What does such a man know about a mother, even if he's well educated. Even if he's a father. You're a woman. You must understand that. You can't simply say to me, your child's lost. We can't do anything."[85]

Corresponding to the popular sentiment in Nazi rhetoric that "being a woman means being a mother," the two women are defined by their shared motherly instinct.[86] The solidarity among women established in the dialogue correlates visually as the identities of the two women merge optically. When Vera dresses for surgery, her face is superimposed onto Mrs. Gaspard's face in a dissolve establishing a clear affinity between the two women. Featured often as comrades, photographed in the same frame, side by side in a medium shot, Vera and Mrs. Gaspard face their common destiny together.

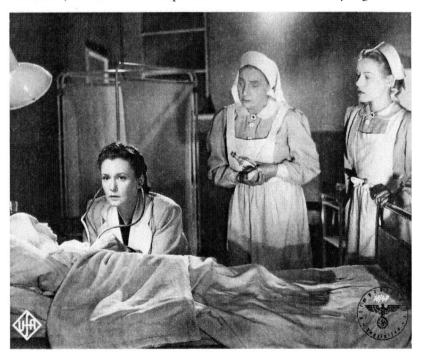

Women as caregivers: *Damals.*

The impassioned plea of a mother to save her daughter leads Vera to lie and disobey the professor's orders. Surrounded by a glass encasement with latticework resembling a barred cage, the child's mother on the one side, the invisible professor on the telephone occupying the other trajectory, Vera is literally caught between her passive role in the patriarchal order and the dictates of motherhood. The insignificance of women in the male order is confirmed when Professor Rigaud and his male colleague Dr. Lugeon revive the child to health and restore order. Vera then remarks to Mrs. Gaspard: "Now we are both completely superfluous here."[87]

The deadly consequences of self-assertion and disobedience are made clear by the head nurse, who remarks: "Where would we be, if every young doctor meddled with the treatment of his supervisor . . . if he did exactly the opposite of what was strictly ordered? Patients in the hospital would no longer be certain about their life."[88] Vera's transgression against male authority no longer affects merely the health of her immediate family as in Lübeck; her defiance now threatens the health of the entire community.

When asked why she risked her career and the patient's life, Vera shows a picture of herself with her daughter and harkens back to the motherhood principle: "Don't you understand that I would do whatever it took to save a child for its mother."[89] Vera's profound sense of motherly duty and selfless actions, while framed in a positive light, are abated by her misguided autonomy and sedition. The value of motherliness is juxtaposed to the law of the father. Although self-sacrifice is deemed an essential quality, one must conform to an established structure under the proper guidance of a "genuine" leader. Since Vera does not submit to the hierarchical system of power, she is again punished with banishment. She is fired and her medical license is revoked.

The flashback to Lisbon shifts the struggle in Vera's life to the level of personal desires versus motherly responsibility. The action begins in a crowded Lisbon nightclub where Vera is engaged as a singer. Her first performance suggests that she has adopted a new, more passionate identity. Her costume, song, gestures, and especially the staging of the gaze all contribute to the portrayal of an erotic woman within acceptable limits.

Vera is photographed alone on an elevated circular stage, the center of attention but disengaged from the protective realm of the *Volksgemeinschaft* she experienced in Lübeck. She is now an eroticized woman on display, surrounded by a demanding public audience. Dressed in a low cut, floor-length black gown with a mantilla, veil, huge dangling earrings, and a tambourine in her hand, and thus properly marked as foreign, she sings of her romantic longings:

> Who knows what secretly moves a woman's heart,
> for whom it blazes afire?
> Suddenly, you feel that it beats ardently for you

when it blissfully admits to you:
I can't say what I like about you so much.
Is it your laugh, your gaze?
I don't know, whether it's intoxication
or love that holds me,
I only feel — you would be my happiness . . .
I could love someone like you,
gentle but full of ardor;
to belong to someone like you completely
and to swear to him a thousand vows!
I could love someone like you
how good my heart would be for him . . .
I would like to give to someone like you
my soul and my life!
He will be everything for me,
my sun, my happiness, my world![90]

Vera's performance begins with a long shot of her on stage surrounded by viewers seated at tables, in slightly raised box seats, and standing in the balcony. Presented as an enticing, available woman singing of her desire to submit to a passionate man, Vera is the source of scopophilia not only for the onscreen audience and the clown Pablo but also for the cinematic audience. The mutual desire evolving between Vera and Pablo is marked by the dramatization of their gazes depicted in intercut tracking shots and close-ups, symmetrical camera movements, and continuity editing. In a medium shot, Vera turns towards Pablo and nods to him while the camera slowly moves in until she is in a close-up. With a cut to Pablo, the same tracking device reveals his yearning for her and grants the audience a privileged glimpse at the affection and intimacy developing between the two characters. However, after Vera looks at Pablo directly and smiles, she lowers her eyes coyly, mitigating the effect of her "unladylike" gaze. As if aware of the distance mandated by voyeuristic pleasure, Vera diverts her gaze from Pablo back to the onscreen audience; her adherence to the conventions of the spectacle is signaled by a long shot that re-establishes the distance between Vera and her audience. Conforming to the concept of women as the untouchable object of the erotic male gaze, Vera entices a spectator and then hits him with her tambourine when he tries to grab her.

Offstage Vera cautions Pablo that it would be "irrational" for him to love her, but he envisions a romantic future together: "My love is much greater than the greatest castle. Do you want to live in it?"[91] When offered a nursing position in South America, however, Vera is faced with a dilemma. She can opt for either personal happiness with her Latin lover or a life of service as a nurse and mother. She never even considers the possibility of combining the two roles; passion simply stands in the way of a better life. By rejecting Pablo, they can both pursue more "productive" lives. He can fulfill his dream of becoming a bicycle racer, and she can return to her vocation as a caretaker. Vera's only concern is for her daughter Eva: "It is definitely better for her. She will become much healthier, stronger. I'll have her with me again." As the purveyor of truth, the elderly clown recognizes the needs of the child are greater than those of the mother: "A child is much more important than a couple of months of happiness, or a couple of years."[92]

Convinced that she must allow Pablo to reject her, Vera adopts a vamp persona and ridicules his sentimentality. Her costume abounds in the accoutrements of the fetishized woman: a black floor-length sequined gown slit down the front with a deep decolletage, black feathers on her shoulders, and a black collar with a rose around her neck, while both wrists are bound by black straps originating at the genitals. Holding a glass of champagne, Vera staggers onto the stage while the old clown paints hearts on the young clown's face. She leans against a larger-than-life Neptune ship's figurehead and sings a "filthy song" of wanton lust:

> Every night a new fortune
> and new flirtations
> every night another mouth,
> that's the way it'll be for me:
> Don't talk about loyalty
> or feelings,
> I can only play with love!
> Today you and tomorrow you . . .
> there's no other way,
> there's no other way,
> that's the way it'll be for me:
> I'm not one of those women,
> who only do certain nice things
> very quietly and secretly
> because they don't dare to do anything in the light
> I don't care at all
> even if the whole world learns about it
> I am not a Miss after all
> with double standards.[93]

Playing the temptress, Vera slaps the Neptune figure in the face, wraps the tethers of her dress around her arm, and looks into the audience from left to right, toasting her new men. Pablo watches her from the side stage, resuming his position as the privileged voyeur, but now he is ensnared in an overhanging net. The camera movement and editing in this scene are largely the converse of those used in her last musical number and signal the changed state of affairs. They now suggest a closer, more causal relationship between Vera and her audience while denoting polarity between Vera and Pablo. In a reaction tilt shot the camera moves from the balcony down to Vera, emphasizing the cause and effect relationship between the audience and Vera's spectacle while connecting a lewd woman straddling the bars with her bare legs to the equally vulgar woman on stage. By contrast, sharp editing cuts separate Vera from Pablo. When she swaggers over to Pablo, walking directly toward the retreating camera, aggressive, menacing, an animal after her prey, Pablo pulls the net from in front of his eyes, as if he were seeing her unmasked for the first time, and flees from the spider woman. The sound of broken glass accompanies the final close-up of Vera's mournful countenance.

Leander's musical number is reminiscent of Marlene Dietrich's performance in *Der blaue Engel* (1930), from the seductive woman with a deep voice, vampish costumes, and provocative lyrics down to the maritime artifacts, clown motif, and male humiliation. But unlike the siren Lola Lola, Vera is clearly in disguise. Her deception is based on her selfless love for her daughter; she lies to her lover so that she can resume her parental role, adopting the masquerade of promiscuity and narcissistic self-absorption to achieve the status of respectable (meaning chaste) motherhood.[94] *Damals* participates in the discursive tradition that maintains the impossibility of combining female desire and motherhood. Juxtaposed to a life of entertainment and passion is hard work and virtuous suffering. Vera opts for the difficult life of motherhood with its duties, sacrificing her own happiness for the sake of her daughter. She rejects the "unacceptable" life in the nightclub and embraces the socially "acceptable" role of a woman who devotes her life to others.

The last flashback to the quarantine station in Las Casas establishes Vera's real identity. Confronted with the evidence of typhus and the possibility of mass contamination, Vera refuses to be dissuaded by the pleas of her fellow travelers and attempts to report the outbreak of infectious disease. Nearly trampled by the frantic, swarming masses, Vera sounds the alarm. Without considering how this action will have detrimental effects on her life (namely, unemployment and isolation in a foreign country), Vera finally conforms to social expectations. She subjugates her compassion for individuals to a greater authority for the good of the community, proving herself worthy of rehabilitation.

With its complex narrative structure consisting of four flashback sequences covering some twenty years and four countries interwoven into a present-day framework, *Damals* disrupts linear development and forces viewers to readjust their "reading" of Vera with each new narrator and time frame. The externalization of the storytelling process illustrates how patriarchal discourse tends to exclude and control women. *Damals*'s flashback technique neither questions the relationship between an individual's perspective and objective reality nor does it demonstrate primarily how each point of view is limited. Instead, it highlights who can articulate the story and who must remain silent.

Each flashback is initiated by a man from Vera's past, who assumes responsibility for the narrative in order to clarify and master the complicated events. The male voice is granted the author-ity to narrate a potentially subversive tale and much of his task will be to come to grips with an ideological conflict inherent in Vera's story. If the patriarchal symbolic order, and National Socialism in particular, dictate an active male and a passive female as necessary components for social harmony, how can a film about passive male figures telling the story of a noncompliant, active woman conform in the end to this dogma and simultaneously recuperate the characters? The flashback device in *Damals* requires viewers to re-evaluate events from a privileged point of view, but it does not encourage moviegoers to question the system of gender norms or to adopt a critical awareness of authoritarian structures. Instead the film directs this energy towards a re-evaluation of Vera as a person and her motivations. Vera is such a highly sympathetic figure played by a superstar that the audience seeks means to rehabilitate her. Since she never overtly rebels against the system and her refusal to conform causes her great suffering, the narrative framework provides a possible solution to her personal dilemma and the fundamental ideological contradiction. The men who narrate her story extinguish any trace of female sedition. The male act of narration denies Vera's agency while still allowing for her punishment. Vera is simultaneously penalized for her transgressions in the past and valorized in the present. The male narrators, especially Jan Meiners, determine that Vera's actions were most harmful to her and necessary for the welfare of others, therefore she is exonerated of any grievous wrongdoing.

The elimination of Vera Meiners's voice from the authorial point of view corresponds to her lack of authority in the social order. The contradictions inherent in her position are embodied in Zarah Leander's status as a cultural icon of sexual ambiguity signified in her legendary masculine voice and excessive feminine role as singer of erotic songs. Vera Meiners's unyielding insistence on adhering to the motherhood principle is equally incongruous with her strong assertion of the fatherhood principle. If she is to be rehabilitated, she can no longer convey this paradox. Within the discursive tradition that posits femininity as deficient, woman's normalcy is predicated on her silence. Laura Mulvey summarizes this practice:

> Either she must gracefully give way to the word, the name of the father and the law, or else struggle to keep her child down with her in the half-light of the imaginary. Woman then stands in patriarchal culture as a signifier for the male other, bound by a symbolic order in which man can live out his fantasies and obsessions through linguistic command by

imposing them on the silent image of woman still tied to her place as bearer, not maker, of meaning.[95]

Vera's distance from language is illustrated in her altercation with Jan in Lübeck. When Jan confronts Vera with her lies, she replies "If our entire life together until now is not an answer, I can't give you another one."[96] Vera's existence must speak for itself. Woman, defined as biology, as life itself, cannot reveal her truth through the cultural construct of language. After her identity is questioned, Vera refuses to speak, unable to convey the complexities of her position. Only after her "true" identity has been established in the fourth flashback does Vera speak for herself, narrating how she adopted the identity of Dr. Gloria O'Conner. Woman's distance from language and agency is encoded in the narrative framework in still a different way. Although men initiate the discursive act, the story unfolds without a voice-over narration and reveals information each man could not have known at the time the events transpired. Although it appears that the narrative point of view agrees with Vera's perspective, she is still bereft of agency since she must illustrate her life and give evidence with her physical presence and without the command of narration.

Whereas each flashback works to establish the identity and crimes of Vera Meiners, the present-day frame also explores the extent to which Jan Meiners is guilty. Characterized as a jealous, untrusting man, Jan first appears in Lübeck entrapped by his own coldness; slumped over a desk with his back to the cell-like windows, the howling wind is his only companion in this self-imposed prison. When Jan and Vera meet again in South America, they are both visually confined by prison bars, as if to imply that they are both guilty of transgressions: she for her defiance and deception, he for abandoning his daughter.

Although Vera is always aware of her obligations as a mother, Jan seems oblivious to the fact that fatherhood carries with it responsibilities. Vera can accept Jan's rejection of her but not his neglect of their child. She is especially angered by his refusal to accept a letter in which she pleaded with him to support Eva financially:

> We broke up. I was no longer your wife. So, what was I to you? But for me, even if you weren't my husband any more, for me, you were always the father of my child . . . until that moment, that "delivery refused." That was it. That was the end. Something happened in me. You don't exist for me any more. For me you are just a strange man. A strange man doesn't need to know where my daughter is. It is none of his business.[97]

Eva also chastises her father's behavior: "My father never cared about me, not me, not my mother."[98] Vera's defiance is a mild transgression compared to Jan's crime: he is guilty of deserting his family.

After reading the documents submitted in Vera's defense, sworn testimony gathered by an official of the law, Jan finally recognizes the value of the motherhood principle:

ATTORNEY: One gets to know a brave life there.

JAN: Yes, and always for others.

ATTORNEY: And she always hurt herself in doing so.[99]

Ironically, Jan, who refused to care for his family financially and emotionally, sits in judgment of Vera and pronounces her a fit mother.

Jan's verdict corresponds to the basic tenets of the National Socialist legal system: "dynamic law" and "intentional criminal law" (*Willensstrafrecht*). Dynamic law, as opposed to an abstract, rigid code of principles, is concerned with the ever-changing "welfare of 'the people' as conceived by the party rather than with the liberty of the individual."[100] Intentional criminal law is based on the notion that proof of criminal activity alone is not sufficient to administer justice. The motivation behind a criminal act is necessary to establish the gravity of an offense and suitable punishment. National Socialism propagates "the myth of a law that is uniquely capable of identifying and justly evaluating the authentic subjectivity of the offender, that which he 'really' is, and of meting out punishment accordingly."[101]

The charges of asocial behavior levied against Vera are set within the context of her identity as a mother. Although Vera defied authority (and was clearly punished with exclusion from society), she was motivated in each case by the welfare of others rather than individual gain. Most significantly, she has displayed personal and social responsibility in providing her child with an orderly domestic life. Eva provides the most convincing evidence that her mother is not guilty of asocial behavior: "But she can't be held innocently in prison any longer. She did nothing else her entire life but toil, worry, and sacrifice for me."[102] Conforming to the dictates of National Socialism, which posits motherhood in terms of suffering and self-sacrifice, Vera's identity as a good mother is confirmed.

The representatives of the law, District Attorney Mendoza, the lawyer Jan Meiners, and Vera's defense attorney, take control of the situation and discover the true murderer. Gathered at the nightclub, the three men identify the bass player as the offender and speculate on his motivations. Jan reveals that the bass player was the father of a young girl who committed suicide after a man (assumed to be Frank Douglas) seduced and abandoned her. Jan then speculates that when the bass player saw Douglas take another young girl, Eva, up to his hotel room, the musician shot Douglas to prevent a repetition of events. Murder, initially depicted as a crime of passion, is reevaluated as a harsh necessity to ensure the stability of future families. Since Frank Douglas seduced young girls and belittled women like Vera who were "honest, upright, with children," his death is presented as just punishment. The murderer is also transformed into an avenger with heroic dimensions: "It is terrible what he did, but he did it ultimately for his daughter's sake."[103] Confronted by the three attorneys, the bass player administers his own punishment by committing suicide. The solution to the mystery, the return to normalcy, and the implementation of justice are all carried out by men of the law. The system of law and order, briefly disturbed, is restored.

The final scene visualizes Vera's innocence and the reconstituting of the family. Accompanied by the earlier melody of "Request to the Night," which signified Vera's acknowledged and protected position in the bosom of her family and friends, Jan waits at the sun-drenched prison gate. Eva arrives with a bouquet of roses in her arms, looks at her father, and then quickly walks away from him. Vera is freed from her prison cell and walks from the darkness into the light. Her daughter and ex-husband are now filmed from behind the bars, giving us Vera's view of them as she leaves the prison, but also suggesting that the entire family has been imprisoned. When she sees her mother, Eva hugs her father in reconciliation. Again Vera walks out from the darkness into the shadows of bars, and finally into the bright light, symbolic of her filmic journey from guilt to innocence. Eva hugs her mother and then turns toward the camera. In a close-up the two women face the camera, Eva's eyes turned toward the left where her father is standing off, Vera's eyes lifted slightly toward the heavens in a gesture of looking forward into a common future. The press brochure for the film is less ambiguous: "Vera Meiners is free again. She recognizes the inner change in her husband, who was unjustly jealous back then, and begins a new life together with him."[104]

This reunion is not depicted, most likely because the happy ending is simply beyond belief. *Damals* demonstrates what Molly Haskel identifies as the rotten core of the 1940s woman's films: "in their sublimation or evasion of adult reality, they reveal, almost by accident, real attitudes toward marriage — disillusionment, frustration, and contempt — beneath the sunny-side-up philosophy congealed in the happy ending."[105]

The Double-Edged Sword

If, as Goebbels contended, film is a first-class pedagogical tool, what lessons can be drawn from these two motion pictures? Does *Opfergang* promote the sanctity of marriage because in the last moments the husband renounces his passionate mistress and recognizes his wife as a gentle and giving soul? By the same token, does *Damals* advocate reconciliation and respect for motherhood because the husband finally acknowledges his own failings and his wife's sacrifices for the good of their family and community? Or do these motion pictures vent the frustrations of cheerless, unfulfilled marriages and reveal a history of deceit, betrayal, and discontent? Ultimately, they tell both stories, one of happy endings and one of prolonged suffering.

The Nazi melodrama presents the audience with a world in which deviant behavior unfolds, and the longing to rebel against conventional morality (to commit adultery, to lie, to defy authority) is satisfied. By identifying with the fictional characters, the spectator can vicariously experience forbidden pleasures without the threat of actual punishment, thus freeing rebellious emotional energy and directing it towards fantasy and away from action. These motion pictures also serve a didactic function by revealing the consequences of such narratives. Since "abnormal" conduct is consistently punished within the filmic text (and in the fascist state), the spectator can conclude that genuine transgressions against societal norms will also be punished in reality. The emancipatory potential inherent in cinematic sedition is tempered by the specter of fictional and authentic retribution. With its double-edged narrative, the melodrama celebrates and punishes transgressions against societal norms. The genre enchants viewers with female suffering and sacrificial death, satisfying the emotional need for romance while sublimating fantasies of domination to the level of beautiful art.

Delving into hidden desires is only one side of the coin. The Nazi melodrama also presents a reality in which even the most serious problems are readily resolved. Despite abundant interpersonal conflicts, these films reestablish the social order and the nuclear family unit. This happy ending offers the promise of a better world in which a woman's sacrifice of self-identity and self-determination is rewarded with marital stability. Although the image of strong female protagonists might seem to work against prevalent gender stereotypes, it ultimately reconfirms the status quo. Woman may receive extensive attention in these films, but they do not determine the course of their family life. The male characters make the essential decisions about the future of the family and marriage. They decide if the marriage will survive, they judge the truth, and they make the critical choices. Contextualized within the totalitarian state where the majority of families are separated by war, these sentimental melodramas also provide an *Ersatz* emotional life. With their double-edged narratives, *Opfergang* and *Damals* teach moviegoers to embrace Nazi ideology in their everyday lives . . . and even in their dreams.

Notes

[1] See Stephen Lowry, *Pathos und Politik: Ideologie in Spielfilmen des Nationalsozialismus* (Tübingen: Max Niemeyer, 1991); and Dora Traudisch, *Mutterschaft mit Zuckerguß?: Frauenfeindliche Propaganda im NS-Spielfilm* (Pfaffenweiler: Centaurus, 1993). Lowry concentrates on the two most popular melodramas, *Die Goldene Stadt*

(*The Golden City*) and *Die große Liebe* (*True Love*). Traudisch provides an extensive study of five melodramas under the aspect of anti-natalism.

[2] "Mann und Frau sind von Anbeginn der Welt zwei verschiedene Wesen, mit ebenso verschiedenen Funktionen. Rein biologisch gesehen ist des Mannes Rolle zur Erhaltung des menschlichen Geschlechts eine relativ kurzfristige, die der Frau eine ungleich längere, opfervollere. Sie birgt viele Monate die Zukunft eines Volkes in ihrem Schoß — gebärt unter Schmerzen, behütet und bewahrt das Kommende mit allen Fasern ihres Herzens." Gertrud Scholtz-Klink, *Die Frau im Dritten Reich: Eine Dokumentation* (Tübingen: Grabert, 1978), 48–49.

[3] "Diese nicht wegzudiskutierende Grundwahrheit . . . ist der Ausgangspunkt für alle weitere Gestaltung eines Zusammenlebens und -arbeitens in jedem kultivierten Volk." Scholtz-Klink, *Die Frau im Dritten Reich*, 48.

[4] "Des Mannes Aufgabe in einem gesunden Volk wird primär stets die schöpferische Tat sein, die der Frau das Gestalten, Behüten, Erhalten, Bewahren. Diese natürlichen Wesenszüge der Frau bergen über ihr leibliches Muttertum in sich alle Anlagen seelischer und geistiger Mütterlichkeit." Scholtz-Klink, *Die Frau im Dritten Reich*, 49.

[5] "Ist sie eine rechte Mutter, so verliert sie sich selbst in ihrer Familienaufgabe. Aber wunderbar: gerade dadurch wird sie im tiefsten Sinn Frau und Mensch. Je selbstverständlicher sie sich aufgibt, desto mehr. Im Verlieren ihres Lebens findet sie sich, ihre wahre Würde, ihren eigensten Menschen. . . . Sie wird Mutter und damit Vollmensch auf dem Weg der Selbstverleugnung, nicht auf dem der Selbstbehauptung." Guida Diehl, *Die deutsche Frau und der Nationalsozialismus,* 3d ed. (Eisenach: Neuland, 1933), 92.

[6] Virginia Wright Wexman, *Creating the Couple: Love, Marriage, and Hollywood Performance* (Princeton: Princeton UP, 1993), 5.

[7] The Marriage Health Law was amended shortly before the outbreak of war to expedite marriages for soldiers, see Jill Stephenson, *Women in Nazi Society* (New York: Barnes & Noble, 1975), 44.

[8] After 1937 women could retain paid employment and still qualify for a marriage loan.

[9] See Michael Burleigh and Wolfgang Wippermann, *The Racial State: Germany 1933–1945* (New York: Cambridge UP, 1991), 140 and 250; and Gisela Bock, "Racism and Sexism in Nazi Germany: Motherhood, Compulsory Sterilization, and the State," in *When Biology Became Destiny: Women in Weimar and Nazi Germany*, eds. Renate Bridenthal, Atina Grossmann, and Marion Kaplan (New York: Monthly Review, 1984), 271–96. Angelika Ebbinghaus, ed., *Opfer und Täterinnen: Frauenbiographien des Nationalsozialismus* (Nördlingen: Greno, 1987) examines the role women played as social workers, nurses, doctors, and camp guards, and concludes that women were not just victims but also perpetrators in the Nazi system of racial selection, sterilization, experimentation, and extermination of human beings designated "unworthy of life" (lebensunwert).

[10] "Auch die Ehe kann nicht Selbstzweck sein, sondern muß dem einen größeren Ziele, der Vermehrung und Erhaltung der Art und Rasse, dienen. Nur das ist ihr Sinn und ihre Aufgabe." Adolf Hitler, *Mein Kampf* (Munich: Franz Eher, 1935), 1: 275–76.

[11] "Gedenke, daß du ein Deutscher bist!/ Du sollst Geist und Seele rein erhalten!/ Halte deinen Körper rein!/ Du sollst, wenn du erbgesund bist, nicht ehelos bleiben! Heirate nur aus Liebe!/ Wähle als Deutscher nur einen Gatten gleichen oder artverwandten Blutes!/ Bei der Wahl deines Gatten frage nach seinen Vorfahren!/ Gesundheit ist Voraussetzung auch für äußere Schönheit!/ Suche dir nicht einen Gespielen, sondern einen Gefährten für die Ehe!/ Du sollst dir möglichst viele Kinder wünschen!" Abridged from Hans Hagemeyer, ed., *Frau und Mutter: Lebensquell des Volkes*, 2d ed. (Munich: Hoheneichen, 1943), 290.

[12] Stephenson, *Women in Nazi Society*, 41.

[13] Laura Mulvey, "Notes on Sirk and Melodrama," in *Home is Where the Heart Is: Studies in Melodrama and the Woman's Film*, ed. Christine Gledhill (London: British Film Institute, 1987), 75.

[14] Mulvey, "Notes on Sirk and Melodrama," 75.

[15] "Die Idee des Männerbundes als Prinzip der Ordnung hat unser Volk vor dem Chaos des Bolschewismus gerettet. Aber auch das andere muß gesagt werden: die Übersteigerung dieser Idee, ihre Festlegung als alleiniger Maßstab aller Dinge zerreißt die Volksgemeinschaft." Lydia Gottschewski, *Männerbund und Frauenfrage: Die Frau im neuen Staat* (Munich: J. F. Lehmann, 1934), 9.

[16] David Bordwell, *Narration in the Fiction Film* (Madison: U of Wisconsin P, 1985), 72.

[17] Molly Haskell, *From Reverence to Rape: The Treatment of Women in the Movies* (New York: Holt, Rinehart, and Winston, 1973), 155.

[18] "Man hat kürzlich einmal festgestellt, daß siebzig Prozent aller Kinobesucher Frauen sind. . . . Warum die Frauen ins Kino gehen, ist klar: sie wollen Liebe sehen und Gefühle haben. Beides wird der Spielfilm, mit einem heiteren und einem nassen Auge, nicht müde, ihnen zu spenden. Auch lieben es ihre Gedanken, um menschliche Dinge zu kreisen und psychologischen Konflikten nachzuhängen. Hier ist ihnen den Film ein unaufhörlicher Übungsstoff für das Leben. Sie haben zudem von der Natur mehr Sinn für das Musische mitbekommen und auch mehr Neigung, sich Wunschträumen zu überlassen, und auch daran läßt es der Spielfilm nicht fehlen." Frank Maraun, "Das Erlebnis entscheidet: Der abendfüllende Kulturfilm — von verschiedenen Seiten gesehen," *Der deutsche Film* 2, no. 7 (January 1938): 189.

[19] "Ein unberechtigter Vorwurf: Ist der Film eine weibliche Kunst? Frauen und Männer sind sich einig in der Forderung nach dem künstlerischen, lebensnahen Film." *Film-Kurier* 128 (June 3, 1938).

[20] Binné considered women "aufnahmebereiter weit zugänglicher und aufgeschlossener als der Mann." Ingrid Binné, "Was erwartet die deutsche Frau vom Film," *Licht-Bild-Bühne* 135 (June 11, 1938). She argued further: "Die Frau schaut heute nicht mehr teilnahmslos den politischen Vorgängen im Reich und in der Welt zu. Sie steht lebendig miterlebend mitten im Geschehen unserer Zeit." Ingrid Binné, "Wie sieht die deutsche Frau den ausländischen Film?" *Licht-Bild-Bühne* 170 (July 22, 1938). See also Ingrid Binné, "Was sagt die Frau über Wochenschau und Kulturfilm?" *Licht-Bild-Bühne* 192 (August 17, 1938).

[21] "Wir sehen in der Frau die ewige Mutter unseres Volkes und die Lebens, Arbeits- und auch Kampfgefährtin des Mannes." Binné, "Was erwartet die deutsche Frau vom Film."

[22] Christine Großmann writes of women: "Sie haben mehr Phantassie, wenn man darunter die Fähigkeit zu träumen versteht, die Fähigkeit, mitzugehen mit dem Geschehen, das auf der Leinwand vor ihnen abrollt, und die Fähigkeit, sich selbst in diese Geschehnisse hineinzudenken." Christine Großmann "Worin besteht die Wirkung des Films auf die Frauen?" *Licht-Bild-Bühne* 78 (April 1, 1938).

[23] David Welch, *Propaganda and the German Cinema 1933–1945* (New York: Oxford UP, 1983), 217.

[24] Mary Ann Doane, *The Desire to Desire: The Woman's Film of the 1940s* (Bloomington: Indiana UP, 1987), 4.

[25] Stephenson, *Women in Nazi Society*, 101.

[26] Louis P. Lochner, ed., *The Goebbels Diaries 1942–1943* (New York: Doubleday), 230.

[27] Kristina Söderbaum, *Nichts bleibt immer so: Rückblenden auf ein Leben vor und hinter der Kamera*, 3rd ed. (Bayreuth: Hestia, 1984), 183–84.

[28] Gerd Albrecht, *Nationalsozialistische Filmpolitik: Eine soziologische Untersuchung über die Spielfilme des Dritten Reiches* (Stuttgart: Ferdinand Enke, 1969), 152.

[29] Although Vera Meiners's concern for her daughter Eva motivates her to sacrifice her own happiness repeatedly in *Damals*, the mother-daughter relationship is never fully developed on screen. *Kora Terry* (1940) features twin sisters who embody the archetypal split of whore and madonna. For an analysis of this film, see Traudisch, *Mutterschaft mit Zuckerguß*, 131–49.

[30] "Harlans spezifische Dienstleistungen fürs Dritte Reich waren seine schweren Melodramen . . . die alle insgesamt seismographisch die innen- und außenpolitische Entwicklung des NS widerspiegeln." Karsten Witte, "Der barocke Faschist: Veit Harlan und seine Filme," in *Intellektuelle im Bann des Nationalsozialismus*, ed. Karl Corino (Hamburg: Hoffmann und Campe, 1980), 150–51.

[31] Critical evaluations of *Opfergang's* artistic merit and ideological content vary widely. Friedemann Beyer considers *Opfergang* Harlan's masterpiece (*Die Ufa Stars im Dritten Reich: Frauen für Deutschland* [Munich: Heyne, 1991], 232); while Francis Courtade and Pierre Cadars term it "puerile romanticism" (*Geschichte des Films im Dritten Reich* [Munich: Hanser, 1975], 246). Richard Taylor sees it as indirect propaganda (*Film Propaganda: Soviet Russia and Nazi Germany* [New York: Harper & Row, 1979), 165–66). According to Siegfried Zielinski, by presenting an idealized portrait of marriage as a durable institution, *Opfergang* worked to pacify soldiers and their wives separated by the war (*Veit Harlan* [Frankfurt a. M.: Rita G. Fischer, 1981], 33). Bogusław Drewniak maintains that *Opfergang* enjoyed extraordinary success among the public during its premiere run and in its first month (December 8, 1944 to January 12, 1945) brought in the enormous sum of 10 million RM (*Der deutsche Film 1938–1945: Ein Gesamtüberblick* [Düsseldorf: Droste, 1987], 631–32, 675–78). Traudisch offers an excellent in-depth study of anti-natalism in *Opfergang* (*Mutterschaft mit Zuckerguß*, 150–86). For an earlier version of this chapter, see Mary-Elizabeth O'Brien, "Male Conquest of the Female Continent in Veit Harlan's *Opfergang* (1944)," *Monatshefte* 87, no. 4 (1995): 431–45.

[32] Veit Harlan, *Im Schatten meiner Filme* (Sigbert Mohn: Gütersloh, 1966), 168–69. Friedemann Beyer summarizes Goebbels's relationship to the film: "Rasch wurde

Opfergang zu einem seiner Lieblingsfilme, den er sich privat immer wieder ansah, um danach häufig über den Tod zu philosophieren. Freigeben wollte er den Film nicht." (*Die Ufa Stars*, 235) [*Opfergang* quickly became one of his favorite films, which he viewed privately again and again in order to philosophize about death afterwards. He did not want to release the film.]

[33] "Dabei wollen wir gar nicht verkennen, daß der Film natürlich als große und in die Tiefe dringende Massenkunst in stärkster Weise auch der Unterhaltung zu dienen hat. Aber in einer Zeit, in der der gesamten Nation so schwere Lasten und Sorgen aufgebürdet werden, ist auch die Unterhaltung staatspolitisch von besonderem Wert. . . . Darüber hinaus aber ist der Film in seiner modernen Entwicklung ein nationales Erziehungsmittel erster Klasse." Goebbels's speech from October 12, 1941, qtd. in Albrecht, *Nationalsozialistische Filmpolitik*, 480.

[34] For a discussion of how Nazi entertainment films work to sublimate and redirect socially unacceptable desires, see Traudisch; Lowry; and Heide Schlüpmann, "Faschistische Trugbilder weiblicher Autonomie," *Frauen und Film* 44/45 (October 1988): 44–66.

[35] "Nicht das ist die beste Propaganda, bei der die eigentlichen Elemente der Propaganda immer sichtbar zutage treten, sondern das ist die beste Propaganda, die sozusagen unsichtbar wirkt." See Goebbels's speech from February 15, 1941, qtd. in Albrecht, *Nationalsozialistische Filmpolitik*, 468.

[36] The discourse on femininity in *Opfergang* corresponds to strategies found in the classic film narrative. Annette Kuhn describes how the classic Hollywood cinema attempts to recuperate woman: "A woman character may be restored to the family by falling in love, by 'getting her man,' by getting married, or otherwise accepting a 'normative' female role. If not, she may be directly punished for her narrative and social transgression by exclusion, outlawing or even death," *Women's Pictures: Feminism and Cinema* (New York: Routledge & Kegan Paul, 1982), 34–35.

[37] I could find no historical reference to any group named German Colonial Union (*Deutscher Kolonialbund*). The closest equivalent is the *Kolonialverein*, a private organization founded in 1882 to help foster colonialism in Germany. See Woodruff Smith, *The German Colonial Empire* (Chapel Hill: U of North Carolina P, 1978); and Arthur J. Knoll and Lewis H. Gann, eds., *Germans in the Tropics: Essays in German Colonial History* (New York: Greenwood Press, 1987).

[38] The *Reichskolonialbund,* founded in 1933 and reorganized in 1936, monopolized colonial activity in Germany until early 1943. See Wolfe W. Schmokel, *Dream of Empire: German Colonialism, 1919–1945* (New Haven: Yale UP, 1964). According to Klaus Kreimeier, the Ufa board of directors considered colonialism an appropriate film topic for the 1933/34 production, but the material became politically sensitive when a few months later when the National Socialists expelled Hugenberg from the cabinet for his colonial aims (*Die Ufa Story: Geschichte eines Filmkonzerns* [Munich: Hanser, 1992], 247–48). By 1937 colonial topics were again embraced by the film community because Hitler openly supported the policy of reestablishing Germany's colonial empire in his Harvest Festival speech (*Die Ufa Story*, 307–8).

[39] Filming of *Opfergang* began in August of 1942, see Beyer, *Die Ufa Stars*, 228. Rommel's troops pushed the British back into Egypt in June 1942 and were within

fifty miles of Alexandria. By November 7–8, 1942, however, the Anglo-American troops landed at Algiers, Oran, and Casablanca. By May 1943 German troops surrendered and the desert campaign was essentially over.

[40] Kuan-yin, the Chinese translation of Avalokitesvara, "a bodhisattva especially associated with the principle of compassion . . . watches over all beings and heeds their cries of suffering and distress." See Raoul Birnbaum, "Avalokitesvara," in *The Encyclopedia of Religion*, ed. Mircea Eliade (New York: Macmillan, 1987), 2: 11–14.

[41] "Albrecht, Albrecht, du bist jetzt ein berühmter, würdevoller Mann, darfst dir solche Geschichten nicht mehr leisten. Stellung verpflichtet." All film dialogues are taken from the videocassette of *Opfergang* in commercial distribution. The censorcards contain no dialogue and no narrative summaries. Compare *Opfergang*, Censor-Card 59952, Bundesarchiv-Filmarchiv, Berlin.

[42] Sigmund Freud, "The Question of Lay Analysis: Conversations with an Impartial Person," in *The Standard Edition of the Complete Psychological Works of Sigmund Freud*, ed. and trans. James Strachey (London: Hogarth, 1953), 20: 212.

[43] A press advertisement for *Opfergang* summarizes the conflict as follows: "Es geht in diesem Film um die Entscheidung eines Mannes zwischen zwei Frauen, in denen er das rätselhafte Widerspiel des himmlisch Reinen [Octavia] und des irdischen Begehrens [Äls] zu erkennen glaubt. Fast erliegt er dem fremden Zauber der einen — bis er durch eine an Selbstaufopferung grenzende Tat der anderen und somit von der edlen Größe und tiefen Liebe dieser, seiner Frau zur Umkehr bestimmt wird." [This film is about a man's decision between two women, in whom he recognizes the puzzling reflection of heavenly purity (Octavia) and earthly desire (Äls). He almost succumbs to the strange magic of the one — until an act bordering on self-sacrifice by the other one convinces him of his wife's true nobility and deep love and determines his return home.] *Opfergang: Ein Ufa Farbfilm*, press package (Berlin: Werbedienst der Deutschen Filmvertrieb-Gesellschaft, n.d.), 3, *Opfergang* Document File 12480, Bundesarchiv-Filmarchiv Berlin.

[44] "Sie ist, was sie immer war." *Opfergang* film dialogue.

[45] Linda Schulte-Sasse, "The Jew as Other under National Socialism: Veit Harlan's *Jud Süß*," *German Quarterly* 61, no. 1 (1988): 28.

[46] "Einer dieser Stunden wird deine letzte sein." *Opfergang* film dialogue.

[47] "Wind und Wellen, Sonnenglut und Sonnenlust." *Opfergang* film dialogue.

[48] Beyer recognizes the fatal mother motif as common to all of Kristina Söderbaum's films in the Third Reich (*Die Ufa Story*, 233). There is an implication that Äls's mother also bore her child out of wedlock, since it is Äls's stepfather who bequeaths her the estate and not her biological father, who is never mentioned.

[49] Both Äls and her mother are described as "waghalsig," "leichtsinnig," and especially "unvernünftig." "Eine kranke Mutter? . . . Am meisten leidet doch das Kind darunter." *Opfergang* film dialogue.

[50] Traudisch, *Mutterschaft mit Zuckerguß?* 178–79.

[51] "Es hätte ja auch gar keinen Sinn. Kaum bist du da, da schließt du das Haus wieder ab und ziehst nach dem Süden oder nach dem Norden und dann muß es wieder raus,

das Kind. Das ist doch nichts für ein Kind. Oder willst du es überall mit hinschleppen? Ein Kind muß ein geordnetes Leben haben." *Opfergang* film dialogue.

[52] National Socialism exalted the nuclear family as the "germ cell of the nation," but it tolerated and during the later phases of the war propagated the idea of unwed motherhood for the Aryan select. See "Dem Führer ein Kind schenken: Mutterkult im Nationalsozialismus," in *Frauen unterm Hakenkreuz,* eds. Maruta Schmidt and Gabi Dietz (Berlin: Elefanten Press, 1983), 74–94. For a discussion of sterilization measures taken against women deemed "unfit," see Bock, "Racism and Sexism in Nazi Germany," 271–96.

[53] "Was der Mann an Opfern bringt im Ringen seines Volkes, bringt die Frau an Opfern im Ringen um die Erhaltung dieses Volkes in den einzelnen Fällen. Was der Mann einsetzt an Heldenmut auf dem Schlachtfeld, setzt die Frau ein in ewig geduldiger Hingabe, in ewig geduldigem Leid und Ertragen. Jedes Kind, das sie zur Welt bringt, ist eine Schlacht, die sie besteht für Sein oder Nichtsein ihres Volkes." Adolf Hitler's speech on September 8, 1934, in Nuremberg before the NS-Frauenschaft, in *Reden und Proklamationen 1932–1945,* ed. Max Domarus (Munich: Süddeutscher Verlag, 1965), 1. 1: 451. My emphasis.

[54] Äls lacks an individual identity; she is described as being the nature she inhabits: "Albrecht und Octavia reiten am Meer entlang. Im Anblick der Brandung denken beide an Äls, die Wind und Welle war" (*Opfergang, Illustrierte Film Bühne* 1943 [Munich: Verlag Film-Bühne, n.d.], my emphasis). [Albrecht and Octavia ride along the ocean. While looking at the surf both think about Äls, who was wind and waves.] Octavia voices this sentiment in the film with her remark to Albrecht: "wind and waves were her element. She is in wind and waves."

[55] From its premiere until today, film critics have termed the *Faschingsball* sequence in *Opfergang* superfluous. Ludwig Brunhuber, a contemporary critic of the film, writes in his film description: "Die Farbe, von Bruno Mondi an der Kamera mit schwelgerischer Lust und Freiheit gemischt, wird zum wesentlichen Ausdruck, steigert sich zu wahrem Farbenrausch, wie in dem Karnevalsfest, was auf Kosten des Atmosphärischen, der Filmdichtung geht" (*"Der Opfergang,"* [n.p., n.d.], *Opfergang* Document File 12480, Bundesarchiv-Filmarchiv Berlin) [The color, which Bruno Mondi mixes with luxurious delight and freedom in the camera, becomes a fundamental expression, intensifies to a true color-intoxication, like at the carnival festivities, which is achieved at the cost of the film's atmosphere and poetry]. Zielinski assesses the carnival sequence in much the same light: "Charakteristisch für den dramaturgischen Einsatz der Farbe ist zum Beispiel eine pompöse inszenierte Karnevals-Szene in *Opfergang,* die für den Handlungsverlauf völlig unbedeutend ist, dafür aber eine Fülle optischer Reize vermittelt" (*Veit Harlan,* 34) [Characteristic for the dramaturgic use of color is, for instance, a pompously staged carnival scene which is completely meaningless for the plot development but conveys a plethora of optical stimuli].

[56] The carnival is a central event in *Barcarole* (1935) and *Carnival of Love* (Karneval der Liebe, 1943).

[57] Mikhail Bakhtin, *Rabelais and His World,* trans. Helene Iswolsky (Cambridge, MA: MIT Press, 1968), 7 and 255.

[58] Mary Ann Doane, *Femmes Fatales: Feminism, Film Theory, Psychoanalysis* (New York: Routledge, 1991), 46.

[59] "Sie hat geschrien wie am Spieß." *Opfergang* film dialogue.

[60] "Man ist ihm immer nah, dem Tod. Und es ist ja auch ganz gut, wenn man ihm ab und zu ein bißchen zulächelt und sagt: du bist mein Freund. Du kommst, wenn ich nicht mehr kann." *Opfergang* film dialogue.

[61] Doane, *Desire to Desire*, 64–65.

[62] "Sterben müsse die an dem Ehebruch schuldige Frau und nicht der Ehemann. Die Ehe müsse vielmehr erhalten bleiben. Das wäre übrigens nicht nur für die Front, sondern auch für die Heimat im volkserzieherischen Sinne besser." Harlan, *Im Schatten meiner Filme*, 164.

[63] The aestheticizing of female pain is well illustrated in fascist melodramas such as *La Habanera* (1937), *Zu neuen Ufern* (1937), *Ich klage an* (1941), *Die Goldene Stadt* (1942), and *Damals* (1943).

[64] Äls: "So zu sterben, das wäre der schönste Tod." *Opfergang* film dialogue. Hanna: "Ich fühle mich so leicht, so glücklich, wie noch nie. Ich wünschte, es wäre der Tod." *Ich klage an* film dialogue. Karl Ludwig Rost writes: "Nicht die Angst vor dem Tode, sondern die Angst vor einsamen Sterben ohne den geliebten Mann [erscheint] als das eigentliche Grauen." Karl Ludwig Rost, *Medizin im Spielfilm des Nationalsozialismus*, ed. Udo Benzenhöfer and Wolfgang Eckart (Tecklenburg: Burgverlag, 1990), 46.

[65] See Saul Friedländer, *Reflections of Nazism: An Essay on Kitsch and Death*, trans. Thomas Weyr (New York: Harper & Row, 1984); Jay W. Baird, *To Die for Germany: Heroes in the Nazi Pantheon* (Bloomington: Indiana UP, 1990); Peter Reichel, *Der schöne Schein des Dritten Reiches: Faszination und Gewalt des Faschismus* (Munich: Hanser, 1991).

[66] The figure Don Pedro in Douglas Sirk's *La Habanera* (1937) represents a notable exception. He dies from a tropical fever, but his life could have been saved if he had not had the cure destroyed.

[67] Saul Friedländer, *Reflections of Nazism*, 43.

[68] "Das Ungestüm, jung sterben zu wollen, als elegante Windsbraut auf den Wellen zu reiten und auf dem Rücken der Pferde zu jagen, das Ungezähmte, Fieberhafte und Lebenssüchtige kommt durch Kristina Söderbaum sehr wirkungsvoll zum Ausdruck. Sie weiß mit dekorativer Anmut zu sterben." Richard Biedrzynski, "Liebe, Leid und Luxus," *Völkischer Beobachter*, Berlin ed. (December 31, 1944).

[69] Ariane Thomalla, *Die femme fragile: Ein literarischer Frauentypus der Jahrhundertwende* (Düsseldorf: Bertelsmann-Universitätsverlag, 1972).

[70] Octavia: "Aber wir können uns doch später so machen, wie wir wollen, oder vielmehr wie du es willst, Albrecht." Later, Octavia says: "Ich bin so glücklich, wie es Albrecht ist." *Opfergang* film dialogue.

[71] "Die Welt der Frau ist der Mann. An anderes denkt sie nur ab und zu." Henry Picker ed., *Hitlers Tischgespräche im Führerhauptquartier 1941–42* (Bonn: Athenäum, 1951), 326.

[72] "In ihrer durch Vornehmheit gekühlten Schönheit, in ihrer Größe, Gelassenheit und unachtsam gemessenen Haltung." Rudolf Binding, *Der Opfergang* (New York: Prentice Hall, 1934), 4.

[73] Leander contributed significantly to her own mythic status by portraying herself as an unwanted intruder in the German film world: "Goebbels war durchaus nicht begeistert davon gewesen, daß die Ufa ausgerechnet eine Ausländerin zur leading lady der eigenen Gesellschaft und wenn möglich des gesamten deutschen Films aufbauen wollte. Er betrachtete es als Armutszeugnis, daß das stolze dritte Reich nicht eine eigene Garbo produzieren konnte. Diese Schwedin paßte ihm einfach nicht, und dementsprechend behandelte man mich von oben wie Luft." Zarah Leander, *Es war so wunderbar! Mein Leben* (Hamburg: Hoffman und Campe, 1973), 170. [Goebbels was by no means enthusiastic that Ufa wanted to make a foreigner of all people the leading lady of its own company and, if possible, the entire German film industry. He considered it evidence of inadequacy that the proud Third Reich could not produce its own Garbo. This Swede simply did not suit him and one treated me accordingly as if I were invisible.] The conditions of her initial contract with Ufa (choice of screenplays, 200,000 RM a year, 53% of her wages to be paid in Swedish crowns directly to her Stockholm bank account) as well as her personal outings with Goebbels belie Leander's assessment of her treatment.

[74] In *Heimat* (1938) Magda does not marry the father of her illegitimate child (he commits suicide), but she is eventually accepted by her father and reintegrated into the family. In *Der Weg ins Freie* (1941) Antonia commits suicide to maintain her former husband's current marriage.

[75] See Cornelia Zumkeller, *Zarah Leander: Ihre Filme — ihr Leben* (Munich: Heyne, 1988), 133 and Kreimeier, *Die Ufa Story,* 354–55. Drewniak maintains that Leander's films continued to be shown in Germany after her departure, but numerous press releases about her were barred from publication (*Der deutsche Film,* 136).

[76] Drewniak, *Der deutsche Film,* 631. For contemporaneous accounts of *Damals* in the trade press, see Erno Ohlisch, "Mit den Augen des Architekten: Walter Haags Bauten zu dem neuen Zarah-Leander-Film der Ufa 'Damals,'" *Film-Kurier* 191 (August 17, 1942); Georg Speckner, "Dreimal mit Zarah Leander: Hans Stüwe in dem neuen Ufa-Film 'Damals,'" *Film-Kurier* 197 (August 24, 1942); Hermann Hacker, "Der Wechsel der Schauplätze: Blick auf den Zarah-Leander-Film 'Damals,'" *Film-Kurier* 282 (December 1, 1942); "'Ich habe Sie belogen!' Dramatische Szene mit Zarah Leander in dem Ufa-film 'Damals,'" *Film-Kurier* 262 (November 7, 1942); H. S., "In der Quarantäne-Station: Dramatische Szenen aus dem Ufafilm 'Damals,'" *Film-Kurier* 282 (December 1, 1942); and F. H. "Von der Führung des Schauspielers und ihren Voraussetzungen: Anmerkungen anläßlich der Arbeit Rolf Hansens an dem von ihm inszenierten Ufa-Film 'Damals,'" *Film-Kurier* 282 (January 14, 1943); "Wer kennt diese Frau?" *Filmwelt* 3/4 (January 20, 1943).

[77] "Das Reisen ist eine der großen Möglichkeiten der Gesellschaft, sich in einem dauernden Zustand von Geistesabwesenheit zu halten, der sie vor der Auseinandersetzung mit sich selber bewahrt. Es hilft der Phantasie auf die unrichtigen Wege, es deckt die Aussicht mit Eindrücken zu, es trägt zu den Herrlichkeiten der Welt, damit ihrer Häßlichkeit nicht geachtet werde. (Der Zuwachs an Weltkenntnis, den es bringt, dient zur Verklärung des bestehenden Systems, in dem er erworben wird.)" Siegfried Kracauer, *Das Ornament der Masse: Essays* (Frankfurt a. M.: Suhrkamp, 1977), 288.

[78] Michael Kater writes: "jazz's potential for being identified with ill-suffered minorities or pariahs of German society, the demimonde, the depraved, blacks, Jews, rendered it forever suspect in the eyes of social and racial bigots, even if they were privately tempted to relish the peculiar aesthetics of this music" (*Different Drummers: Jazz in the Culture of Nazi Germany* [New York: Oxford UP, 1992], 25). A public campaign against women smoking was launched as early as 1933. See "Frauen sollen nicht öffentlich rauchen," *Vossische Zeitung,* August 19, 1933, qtd. in Clifford Kirkpatrick, *Nazi Germany: Its Women and Family Life* (Indianapolis: Bobbs-Merril, 1938), 105.

[79] Burleigh, *The Racial State,* 173.

[80] The directive of the Reich Ministry of the Interior from 1940, qtd. in Burleigh, *The Racial State,* 182.

[81] Burleigh, *The Racial State,* 167.

[82] Burleigh, *The Racial State,* 168.

[83] "Heut,' wenn die Nacht ganz leise und fein/ tritt in mein Zimmer hier,/ hüllt' ich mich in ihren Mantel ein/ und sag' bittend zu ihr:// Liebe Nacht, komm,' laß dir sagen,/ was ich ganz von Herzen will./ Keine Uhr soll heute schlagen/ und die Zeit soll still stehen,/ und nicht atmen soll die Welt!/ Wenn er mich im Arme hält!" Text and music by Ralph Benatzky, *Damals, Das Program von heute* 1871 (Berlin: Das Program von heute, Zeitschrift für Film und Theater, n.d.). The same song is named "Bitte an die Nacht" in *Damals, Illustrierter Film-Kurier* 3309 (Berlin: Vereinigte Verlagsgesellschaften Franke & Co. KG., n.d.) but includes only the second stanza. When performing the song in this film, Leander changes "ihre Arme" in line three to "ihren Mantel" and transposes "stehen" and "still" in line eight.

[84] Alte Frau: "Was seid ihr doch für Egoisten, ihr Männer. Du auch. Sag mal, warum läßt du sie nicht Sängerin werden?" Jan: "Das fehlte noch. Ich bin froh, daß sie nicht Ärztin geworden ist." Sanitätsrat Petersen: "Ja, eben. So geht es im Leben. Endlich erfindet der liebe Gott ein Geschöpf, das alle guten Gaben besitzt. Sie kann was. Sie studiert Medizin, und außerdem eine herrliche Stimme, sieht wundervoll aus. Und was passiert? Sie verliebt sich in unseren guten Meiners." Jan: "Du." Sanitätsrat Petersen: "Der zwar mein bester Freund ist, aber übernacht sozusagen, sind alle Karrieren pfuscht, und sie ist nur noch Frau." Vera: "Nur noch. Kann man denn mehr sein?" Alte Frau: "Nein, wenn man glücklich ist." Vera: "Man ist sehr glücklich!" All film dialogues are taken from the videocassette of *Damals* available in commercial release. The censor cards include a narrative description but no film dialogue. Compare *Damals,* Censor-Card 58689, Bundesarchiv-Filmarchiv, Berlin.

[85] "Frau Doktor, Sie müssen mir helfen. Der Professor ist ja bestimmt ein guter Arzt, aber er ist doch nur ein Mann. Was weiß denn so ein Mann, auch wenn er noch so gelehrt ist, von einer Mutter. Selbst wenn er Vater ist. Aber Sie sind doch eine Frau. Sie müssen das doch verstehen. Sie können doch nicht einfach zu mir sagen, Ihr Kind ist verloren. Da kann man nichts machen." *Damals* film dialogue.

[86] "Frausein heißt Muttersein." Paula Siber von Groote, *Die Frauenfrage und ihre Lösung durch den Nationalsozialismus* (Berlin: Kallmeyer, 1933), 23.

[87] "Jetzt sind wir beide hier ganz überflüßig." *Damals* film dialogue.

[88] "Wo gehen wir denn dahin, wenn jeder junge Arzt dem Chef bei seiner Behandlungsweise dazwischen pfuscht . . . wenn er sogar bei strikter Einordnung gerade das Gegenteil tut? Die Kranken in der Klinik werden ihres Lebens nicht mehr sicher." *Damals* film dialogue.

[89] "Begreifen Sie nun, daß ich einer Mutter ihr Kind retten möchte, um welchen Preis auch immer." *Damals* film dialogue.

[90] "Wer weiß denn, was ein Frauenherz heimlich bewegt,/ für wen es lodernd entbrennt?!/ Doch plötzlich fühlst du, daß es für dich innig schlägt,/ wenn es dir selig bekennt:/ Ich kann nicht sagen, was mir an dir so gefällt,/ ist es dein Lächeln, dein Blick?/ Ich weiß nicht, ob ein Rausch, ob die Liebe mich hält,/ ich fühl nur, — du wärst mein Glück . . .// Refrain: Einen wie dich könnt' ich lieben,/ zärtlich und doch voller Glut;/ einem so wie dir ganz gehören/ und ihm tausend Schwüre schwüren!/ Einen wie dich könnte ich lieben,/ wie wär' mein Herz ihm so gut . . . / Einem so wie dir möcht' ich geben/ meine Seele und mein Leben!/ Er soll mir alles sein,/ meine Sonne, mein Glück, meine Welt!" Text by Bruno Balz with music by Lothar Brühne reproduced in *Damals, Das Program von heute* (1871), n.p.

[91] "Meine Liebe ist viel größer als das größte Schloß. Willst du darin wohnen?" *Damals* film dialogue.

[92] Vera recognized, "Für sie ist es bestimmt besser. Sie wird viel gesunder werden, kräftiger. Ich hab' sie wieder bei mir." The elderly clown agrees: "Ein Kind ist viel wichtiger als ein paar Monate glücklich sein, oder ein paar Jahre." *Damals* film dialogue.

[93] "Jede Nacht ein neues Glück/ und neue Liebelei'n/ jede Nacht ein andrer Mund,/ so soll es bei mir sein:/ Sprich nicht von Treue,/ nicht von Gefühlen,/ ich kann mit Liebe/ immer nur spielen!/ Heute dich und morgen dich . . ./ So und nicht anders,/ so und nicht anders,/ so soll es sein für mich!// Ich bin ja keine von den Frauen,/ die die gewissen netten Sachen/ weil sie bei Licht sich nichts getrauen,/ nur immer still und äußerst heimlich machen/ auch wenn's die ganze Welt erfährt/ das ist mir ganz egal/ Ich bin ja schließlich keine Miss/ mit doppelter Moral." Text by Bruno Balz with music by Lothar Brühne reproduced in *Damals, Das Program von heute* (1871), n.p.

[94] Linda Williams recognizes the same strategy in the Hollywood classic *Stella Dallas* (1937). See "'Something Else Besides a Mother': *Stella Dallas* and the Maternal Melodrama," in *Home is Where the Heart Is: Studies in Melodrama and the Woman's Film,* ed. Christine Gledhill (London: British Film Institute, 1987), 313.

[95] Laura Mulvey, *Visual and Other Pleasures,* 15.

[96] Vera maintains, "Wenn unser ganz bisheriges Leben keine Antwort ist, eine andere kann ich dir nicht geben." *Damals* film dialogue.

[97] Vera gives her husband an impassioned reckoning: "Wir haben ja Schluß gemacht. Ich war nicht mehr deine Frau. Also was ging ich dich an? Aber für mich, wenn du auch nicht mehr mein Mann warst, für mich warst du doch immer der Vater meines Kindes, bis zu diesem Augenblick, bis zu diesem 'Annahme verweigert.' Da war es aus. Da war es zu Ende. Da entstand in mir was. Du bist für mich nicht mehr auf der Welt. Du bist für mich ein fremder Mann. Ein fremder Mann braucht nicht zu wissen, wo meine Tochter ist. Es geht ihn nichts an." *Damals* film dialogue.

[98] Eva reiterates that her father abandoned them: "Mein Vater hat sich nie um mich gekümmert, um mich nicht, um meine Mutter nicht." *Damals* film dialogue.

[99] The attorney comments, "Ein tapferes Leben, das man da kennenlernt." Jan concedes, "Ja, und immer für andere." Whereupon the attotney concludes, "Und immer hat sie sich selbst dabei geschadet." *Damals* film dialogue.

[100] J. P. Stern, *Hitler: The Führer and the People* (Berkeley: U of California P, 1975), 120. For a discussion of women in the legal profession, see Stephenson, *Women in Nazi Society,* 170–73. In a letter to the Reich Minister of Justice dated August 24, 1936, Martin Bormann, Deputy of the Führer, conveyed Adolf Hitler's policy towards women lawyers and judges: "Er [der Führer] hat entschieden, daß Frauen weder Richter noch Anwalt werden sollen. Juristinnen können deshalb im Staatsdienst nur in der Verwaltung verwandt werden." Qtd. in Scholtz-Klink, *Die Frau im Dritten Reich,* 61. [He has decided that women shall neither be judges nor lawyers. Female jurists can therefore be employed as civil servants only in administration.]

[101] Stern, *Hitler: The Führer and the People,* 123.

[102] Eva argues, "Aber sie darf doch nicht länger unschuldig im Gefängnis. Sie hat ihr ganzes Leben lang nichts anders getan, als sich für mich geplagt, gequält und geopfert." *Damals* film dialogue.

[103] Vera recognized that Frank Douglas would never admire women who were "brav, bieder, mit Kind." Jan concludes, "Es ist schrecklich, was er getan hat, aber er hat es schließlich um der Tochter willens getan." *Damals* film dialogue.

[104] "Vera Meiners ist wieder frei. Sie erkennt die innere Umkehr ihres damals aus Eifersucht ungerechten Mannes und beginnt gemeinsam mit ihm ein neues Leben." *Damals, Das Program von heute* 1871.

[105] Molly Haskell, 156.

"Dream or Reality? The Public and Film Community Answer,"
Der deutsche Film (1939).

5: The Forbidden Desires of Everyday Life: The Problem Film

I N MAY 1939, *Der deutsche Film,* the official journal of the Reich Film Chamber, published a special issue devoted to the question of what the public wanted from cinema, "a dream world or reality?" Two mottos framed the discussion and imparted the highest authority in the Third Reich. The Führer was quoted first: "Theater, film, literature, press, radio, they all have to serve the maintenance of universal values living in the spirit of our folk."[1] The second motto stemmed from the propaganda minister: "Film should not escape from daily hardship and lose itself in a dreamland that only exists in the minds of starry-eyed directors and scriptwriters but nowhere else on earth."[2] This special issue also contained surveys and scholarly articles, in which moviegoers, actors, directors, and critics all agreed that the film industry should make exemplary films about contemporary life in Nazi Germany. Critics lamented that "problem films," serious dramas dealing with social issues, seldom graced the screen. What the German public needed, they argued, was riveting stories about ordinary people with typical conflicts. Audiences would recognize the universal values National Socialism strove to uphold by watching movies with sympathetic characters representing the needs of the entire community. Normal problems in everyday life were not supposed to be covered up with the fairy tales of pure fantasy or depressing stories drenched in hopelessness and despair. Viewers needed positive films about daily hardships to learn how to form realistic expectations and deal with disappointment. The consensus was clear: cinema should reflect reality.

It is surprising that the trade press would argue so adamantly in favor of the problem film because the genre demands an honest discussion of society's ills in a way that National Socialism routinely rejected. With its emphasis on how "the individual confronts social contradictions (class difference, moral conventions, poverty) beyond his/her control and/or comprehension," the problem film casts a critical look at the world as it is and explicitly calls for change.[3] Although the public wanted serious movies about contemporary life, the propaganda ministry required that these movies demonstrate optimism and conflict resolution at any price, a prescription contrary to the very definition of the problem film. Thus Hitler and Goebbels were often disappointed with the type of films they had originally promoted and were compelled to censor several important problem films because they depicted contemporary social and economic issues all too realistically. Unflattering films that scrutinized class relationships and social institutions were labeled "defeatist" and summarily banned. Massive state control of the motion picture industry made it extremely difficult for directors to make blatantly oppositional films and also insured that only about two dozen completed films were banned between 1933 and 1945.[4]

Three problem films stand out as well-made movies that expose social problems National Socialism did not want to address openly or could not solve satisfactorily: *Das Leben kann so schön sein* (Life can be so Wonderful, Rolf Hansen, 1938), *Der verzauberte Tag* (The Enchanted Day, Peter Pewas, 1944), and *Via Mala* (The Street of Evil, Josef von Baky, 1945). All three films were banned by the National Socialist regime for being defeatist and presenting the *Volksgemeinschaft* in an unfavorable light, but it is not their status as censored films per se that makes them so interesting. Rather it is their ability as problem films to capture the spirit of the time, reveal its dilemmas, and lend insights into how individuals dealt with social problems beyond their control. A common feature of these problem films is that they leave the viewer with haunting images of unfulfilled passions, senseless brutality, and dissatisfaction with the status quo. Attached to these stories of wasted lives is often an unconvincing happy ending. Whether an appeasement strategy for the censor or a cynical device to highlight unresolved social issues, this incongruity leaves a disturbing aftertaste and beckons the viewer to contemplate alternative endings. The characters in these films do not conform to Nazi expectations of heroic warriors and self-sacrificing mothers. Young men are often weak and passive; older men can be petty tyrants obsessed with order and hierarchy. Young women resolutely insist on meeting their sexual and economic needs; older women often remember their hopes despite years of compromise. Far from embodying party slogans, the characters voice discontent with everyday life and imagine a world where things are different. As Thomas Schärer has convincingly argued, these films "destroy illusions and identification and call norms and values into question, instead of reinforcing them, for example gender roles. They do not place viewers via identification opportunities uniformly in society like most films in the Nazi period did in order to neutralize potential calls for change."[5]

Das Leben kann so schön sein, Der verzauberte Tag, and *Via Mala* are stylistically innovative, provocative, and illustrate particularly well both the aspirations and the limitations of cinema in the Third Reich. All three films underwent state supervision and original approval, including pre-censorship of the treatment and script, careful oversight during the shooting, and an orchestrated pre-release advertising campaign before being completed and eventually banned. Considering the extensive resources utilized and the publicity invested in these films, they were expected to channel the discussion about contemporary society in a way that conformed to the state's ideological agenda. Unfortunately, *Das Leben kann so schön sein, Der verzauberte Tag*, and *Via Mala* are not available in commercial release in Germany or the United States and have not received sufficient scholarly attention. In this chapter I explore how these three films reflect a growing dissatisfaction with the status quo and the pressing need to find genuine solutions to social problems. These films are products of their time and chart a shift away from concrete economic issues to the more elusive areas of emotional and existential conflicts. *Das Leben kann so schön sein* bears the markings of 1938 Germany, a time when workers struggled to win the long-touted material success but were consumed by fears of an imminent catastrophe. *Der verzauberte Tag* echoes the harsher reality of 1943–1944, a post-Stalingrad war-weary society where women faced economic hardship alone and fantasized about love while violence entered into everyday life. *Via Mala* reflects the terror of 1944–1945 and the quandary of postwar Germany, the relentless violence inflicted upon innocent victims and the questions of collective guilt and an unmastered past.

Consumerist Fantasies: *Das Leben kann so schön sein* (1938)

Das Leben kann so schön sein is a serious drama about a young couple whose marriage is nearly destroyed by financial troubles and unrealistic expectations. Lighthearted moments and the casting of comedian Rudi Godden and girl-next-door Ilse Werner as the sympathetic couple helped to mitigate the film's critique of modern marriage, housing, and employment. The relatively young and inexperienced director Rolf Hansen encountered resistance early on and the film underwent several name changes, highlighting its problematic nature from the start.[6] The titles waver between a bleak portrait of economic hardship and a rosy picture of married life: *The Last Trading Day of the Month* became *A Person is born*, then *Happiness in Installments*, and finally *Life can be so Wonderful*.[7]

Das Leben kann so schön sein passed the censor in Berlin on December 20, 1938, and premiered at the Opernkino in Vienna three days later on December 23, 1938.[8] Goebbels normally viewed important films before their premiere and could censor any film he considered harmful to National Socialist sensibilities. In December 1938, Goebbels was preoccupied with his own personal life and spent little time overseeing film production or the propaganda ministry. Ordered by Hitler to forsake his mistress Lida Baarova and reconcile with his wife Magda, Goebbels's life at this point reads like a melodramatic filmscript. With the propaganda minister otherwise engaged, *Das Leben kann so schön sein* was shown directly to Adolf Hitler who broke off the screening and banned the film. Hitler was reportedly enraged by the depiction of a housing shortage and the overall tone of the film.[9] On January 3, 1939, the Ufa board of directors attributed the ban to the film's "potential to sabotage the government's population growth policies."[10] Despite Hansen's attempt to edit the film, Goebbels issued a press directive on January 5, 1939, stating: "The Ufa film *Das Leben kann so schön sein* has been banned. It contradicts National Socialist population growth policies and to some extent directly opposes them."[11] Hansen's film did not premiere in Germany proper until after the war.[12]

The film opens in a hospital, where the young insurance salesman Hannes Kolb (Rudi Godden) awaits word on the condition of his pregnant wife Nora (Ilse Werner) who fell down the stairs after a heated argument. In a series of flashbacks, Hannes recounts their courtship and troubled marriage. The young lovers dream of owning their own home on a quiet lake, a bright and cheerful place far from the watchful eyes of strangers. Visiting a new housing tract, they imagine a life together in this idyllic setting, but their hopes are shattered by economic reality. Hannes convinces Nora that they lack the financial security to marry, let alone buy a house. He eventually gathers the courage to propose, but he wants Nora to be a working wife and take a job as a seamstress in a clothing factory. Despite her wish for an apartment with simple modern furniture, he insists they rent a single furnished room in a boarding-house. The dark and dreary building, the close quarters with vexing neighbors, and the constant talk of financial problems put a strain on the marriage. When Nora tells Hannes she is pregnant, he becomes paralyzed with fear. Hoping she can calm his worries about their future, Nora eventually lies and says she made a mistake and is not expecting. Hannes is consumed with visions of disaster and neglects his wife. His passivity and jealousy drive her to action. She reveals that she is seven months pregnant and packs her bag to leave but falls down a flight of stairs. After the final flashback, Hannes admits his guilt and vows to start anew. He has decided that Nora will quit her job and stay home with the baby in a bright new apartment filled with her own furniture. After delivering a healthy boy, the couple silently reconciles. In the last frame, Nora comforts her husband saying: "Don't cry, Hannes. Now everything's going to be all right."[13]

In a series of interviews conducted in the fall of 1938, Rolf Hansen cautioned that *Das Leben kann so schön sein* would be a daring experiment in both form and content. The film would challenge viewers with its complex narrative told in flashbacks and with characters who were "people of our time, resembling us and occupied with our fate. Their problems and existential questions are not located in no man's land, but rather are experienced and suffered by us daily, hourly."[14] Hansen recognized that his film might be a hard sell because it did not offer the typical escapist fare found in many feature films: "It is always a problematic matter to show the public a film that leads them back into their own everyday life. And so plainly and realistically as we are planning to do. After all, people want to be distracted and find some illusions when they go to the movies in the evening."[15] The director hoped viewers would see themselves and their daily struggles honestly reflected on screen. Ultimately, the audience would need to accept the film on its own terms: "The success of this film, which does not gloss over or romanticize life, let alone trivialize it, can only depend on its realism and truthfulness."[16]

In striking contrast to other films made around this time, *Das Leben kann so schön sein* deals frankly with the controversial themes of married working women and the underemployment of men.[17] The main characters, a factory worker and a white-collar employee, are ordinary people with a typical problem: they do not know how to make ends meet. Their story represents the plight of many married couples in the 1930s. When the NSDAP came to power in 1933 at the height of the Great Depression, six million German workers were unemployed. In its first two years in office, the party launched a series of campaigns against married working women and promoting full employment of men.[18] The Law to Decrease Unemployment (June 1, 1933) called for "employment of female factory workers in households, as far as possible, in order to replace them with men in the factories."[19] The same law introduced marriage loans as a means to increase the number of marriages, raise the birth rate of racially pure Aryans, and fight against "double-earners," families with both spouses working. Interest-free marriage loans of 1,000 RM were granted to couples on the condition that the wife quit her job. The loan was not paid out in cash but in vouchers for household goods and furniture. One-fourth of the loan was automatically repaid with the birth of each child. Numerous private companies, factories, and banks joined the government in providing financial incentives (loans or severance pay) for married women to leave the workforce and return full-time to the "natural" role of wife and mother. By 1936 the government's hostility toward double-earners abated due to necessity. The country had reached full employment and even suffered a labor shortage in such key sectors as the armament industry. At the same time Hitler demanded that the economy prepare for war within the next four years. Married women were now considered essential to the labor force and encouraged to continue working. Accordingly, in 1937 the law was amended so that married women were not required to give up their job as a precondition for a marriage loan.

Nora's job as a seamstress in a clothing factory may seem like a minor detail, but it is highly representative of female employment patterns in peacetime Germany. Employed in the textile industry where women comprised about half the workforce, Nora shares the fate of many young wives in 1938. Like the majority of married working women, she only takes on a job because her husband's income is insufficient to cover living expenses.[20] Despite Nazi propaganda trumpeting motherhood, the number of married working women actually rose from 35% in 1933 to 41% in 1939, with the vast majority taking on low-paid factory work.[21] And even though married women were officially encouraged to join the workforce in 1938, the social stigma attached to being a "double-earner" remained strong. Hannes, for example, insists that Nora lie to everyone in the factory and pretend to be single because he fears that she will be fired if her boss finds out she is married. The movie's plotline illustrates the disparity between propaganda and embedded social values, the government's call to change attitudes based on the state's immediate needs and the people's inability to modify entrenched beliefs so quickly.

As an insurance salesman, Hannes is a white-collar employee without sufficient financial security to start a family. Since he is new to the job, he must prove himself by reaching a high sales quota before he will be granted his own sales district and a guaranteed monthly income. He estimates that he will initially have to write thirty policies a month to earn 150 RM but an apartment will run 50 RM and food 60 RM, so they will have only 40 RM for the rest of their living expenses.[22] Unfortunately Hannes is not able to meet his quota and his wages fall below those of the average worker and head of a four-member household who earned 157 RM monthly.[23] His frantic worries about how to make ends meet, while presented in a sympathetic and often humorous light to suggest he is overreacting, nonetheless reflect the real-life financial hardship facing many workers and white-collar employees. To ensure full employment and rearm the nation, the Nazi government instituted an economic policy that sought to freeze wages, set price controls, and limit overall consumer expenditures. Despite the government's efforts to maintain stable wages and prices, the cost of living index rose by 6% between 1933 and 1938.[24]

Along with its critical look at employment, *Das Leben kann so schön sein* addresses the problem of housing. The film describes two radically different social environments: a single-family home in a suburban settlement and a boarding-house in a downtown Berlin apartment building. The former is a cheerful private space beyond the economic means of the average office worker, while the latter is a dismal communal space where the lower middle class must abide. Although Hansen's film does not openly criticize the Nazi party or any government agency for the housing conditions, it implies that workers still suffer from economic hardship and that the government has not done enough to raise the standard of living. The question of suitable housing goes well beyond financial issues and evokes the deeper need for privacy. It also challenges the National Socialist government's ability to balance two apparently opposite domestic agendas, what Hans-Dieter Schäfer has called "the divided consciousness" of the Third Reich. On the one hand, National Socialism presented itself as a meticulously organized system that offered the masses a sense of wholeness through participation in communal rituals and threatened violent retribution against nonconformity. On the other hand, it promoted itself as an agent of continuity that guaranteed the masses a private sphere in which to enjoy some degree of individualism and a wide assortment of consumer goods and entertainment.

The model house on a beautiful lake is an unobtainable dream for the young seamstress and salesman. At Nora's urging, they pretend they are happily married and living in their own home. In a close-up of her glowing face resting on Hannes's shoulder, Nora voices her innermost desire for domestic bliss, "When we're married, then it has to be wonderful. As wonderful as one can ask from life. It has to be true happiness!"[25] Nora's dream includes not only a loving relationship but also a private sphere shielded against outsiders. Sitting at the breakfast table, the couple relishes the solitude: "This is the first time no one can disturb us, where we are truly alone!" They fantasize that they can lock the door and be completely insolated. Nora promises Hannes, "When we finally have our own home, I won't let anybody in! It has to belong to us alone!" In desperation and "with a wild expression of hunger on her face," Nora pleads, "When, Hannes, when?"[26]

Only in nature does the couple momentarily capture the feeling of being sheltered. Nestled together in a rowboat on a lake at sunset, Hannes and Nora find the privacy they desperately long for, but their contentment does not last long. Hannes starts counting pennies and worries about how they

Contentment in nature: *Das Leben kann so schön sein.*

can earn enough money to pay for living expenses. He tells Nora they will have to wait to marry until he can guarantee their financial security: "We have to think about the future. And we have to pay premiums on it as with any insurance. And if people like us don't have money for it . . ." Nora finishes the thought: "we pay for it with happiness."[27]

The stark reality is that the newlyweds cannot afford to own their own home. Instead they move into a dreary turn-of-the-century boarding-house with a dark paneled entryway, oriental rugs, and heavy curtains. The dimly lit rooms are cluttered with massive, old-fashioned furniture, and the thin walls let the neighboring tenants hear everything from the toilet flushing to a lover's quarrel. Characteristic of the oppressive air surrounding this place is the safety chain that always bars the front door. There is no private realm where the individual can develop, where one can have a private conversation in bed, make a cup of tea, have a fight, or cook a meal alone.

In an effort to alleviate the severe housing shortage, the Nazi government promoted privately funded construction and subsidized its own housing projects, but the supply never met the demand. By 1938 there was still a severe housing shortage.[28] The construction of single-family homes in model settlements like the one featured in *Das Leben kann so schön sein* was widely publicized but actually only comprised about one-tenth of all new housing.[29] The majority of new housing starts consisted of multiple-family homes and apartment buildings, but the regime continued to propagate the idea that it would provide more and more Germans with a detached house in a village setting. As cultural critic Peter Reichel has noted, the government routinely conjured up "images that suggested a low cost of living and high quality of life: health, self-sufficiency, family idyll, and tranquility in home sweet home."[30]

Settlement construction (*Siedlungsbau*), planned communities of single, double, and multiple family houses, began in the nineteenth century as a way to provide urban workers with low-cost housing and growing industries with a stable workforce. When the NSDAP seized power in 1933, it continued to support settlement construction as part of the overall strategy to combat massive unemployment and a severe housing shortage.[31] In this early stage, settlements were designed primarily for unemployed and low-income workers and emphasis was placed on self-sufficiency. By 1935 however, workers were required to be employed. The modest homes were often equipped with stalls for small farm animals, vegetable garden plots, and a tool shed. Officials recognized that creating a positive living environment was good for workers, industry, and the state. Workers could enjoy a comfortable and practical living space, a healthy lifestyle with outdoor activities, pride in ownership, privacy, and social status. Industries considered the most reliable and productive employees to be a settled workforce attached to the land with a vested interest in having a steady income. The state also benefited from its role as facilitator, providing a grateful citizenry with strong ties to the local community and industry. Workers who possessed a stable home environment and economic security were also more likely to have children and provide the state with new citizens.

The National Socialists were quick to promote the idea that settlement housing was part and parcel of their efforts to raise the average worker's social status, level class differences, and dislodge the long-standing prejudice against the urban poor and the unskilled laborer. In an article in the journal *Soziale Bauwirtschaft* from 1935, settlements were lauded as an indispensable means to create a harmonious, classless society:

> These settlement houses are not huts; they are a home of one's own, like the ones that previously could only be built by well-off burghers. The workers who move into these houses and live in these settlements are no longer proletarians. They join the ranks of farmers, artisans, and burghers. The worker is no longer a despised foreign body standing at the unemployment office, but instead a national comrade in the community of creators.[32]

The rehabilitation of the worker, his transformation from a contaminant invading the sacrosanct national body to a contributing member of a select fellowship, takes place in the same discursive tradition that National Socialism continually employed to define its citizens and its enemies. Settlement housing guaranteed not only the redistribution of wealth but also the redress of a social injustice by elevating the worker to his rightful position in the national community.

The widespread desire to own a home was not only a response to material necessity; it was also the need to retreat from a highly structured public sphere, a life centered on uniforms, party insignia, political organizations, social responsibilities, and the watchful eye of the Gestapo. While the Nazi regime refashioned German cities using massive architectural structures to reflect the state's hegemony and grandeur, private individuals increasingly chose to decorate their homes in nineteenth-century Biedermeier and traditional folk interior designs to gain a sense of homeliness and intimacy.[33] Historian Detlev Peukert explains the far-reaching effects of Nazi architecture on the ordinary citizen: "The monumental public spaces, resembling stage sets, reduced people into mere ornament; the individual was lost within huge perspectives that could be filled only if he was merged into a marching column. The desire to retreat into the private sphere, into comfortable and familiar small spaces, was therefore all the more pressing."[34] Viewed within this cultural context, Hannes's assertion that in 1938 he cannot afford the 15,000 RM settlement home contradicts Nazi propaganda and reflects a serious lack of faith in the government's ability to deliver on its promises.

An important aspect of the retreat into the family and home was the government's promise of affordable, high-quality household goods and a better standard of living.[35] National Socialism wanted to radically alter German society by establishing a racial state, but it also sought to guarantee its citizens stability, continuity, and "the sense that inside their own four walls their lives basically remained unchanged."[36] The government's racial and imperialist aims coexisted with an explicit assurance of a politically free zone filled with consumer products. Although one-fifth of the gross national product was devoted to the rearmament industry in 1938, the production of consumer goods that same year rose to its highest point since 1928.[37] The government took full credit for Germany's rapid recovery from the Great Depression (in 1936 Germany reached full employment and matched its industrial output of 1928/29) and continually publicized that German industries were manufacturing everything from washing machines and vacuum cleaners to electric stoves and coffee machines. Despite periodic shortages and the often prohibitively high price of many household appliances, the return to a pre-depression standard of living and the prospect of acquiring durable goods in the near future did much to bolster Hitler's popularity.[38]

Das Leben kann so schön sein prominently features both the promise and the limits of working class consumerism. Nora spends her days working in a factory sewing women's lingerie and dreaming about decorating her home. She takes her husband window-shopping because she longs for simple, well-made, modern household furnishings. In keeping with the fashion of the day, she chooses light and practical furniture made of German fir and ash.[39] Demonstrating that she will be an efficient housewife, Nora admires a highly functional kitchen cabinet and gushes, "if a man only knew what that means to a woman."[40] The furniture for the entire house is 750 RM and can be purchased with a marriage loan.[41] But this too is out of their reach, and Hannes convinces Nora that they must settle for less. Hannes refuses to take on any debt because he fears he cannot pay it back. He does not want a marriage loan, even though Nora does not have to quit her job to qualify and since she is pregnant one-fourth of the loan is automatically repaid, because he has no confidence in the future and fears a downward spiral into penury. His only concession is to give Nora a sewing box, a piece of furniture she considers a pure luxury but which symbolizes the domestication of her labor. Nora cherishes this gift because it represents her dream of being a wife and mother, sewing clothes for her family at home and not for strangers in a factory.

The Ufa studio proposed an advertising campaign that would tie in contemporary consumer culture with the movie's plot. The studio advised theater owners: "Looking for and buying furniture, those are things that play a big role in the life of everyone who wants to get married! An entire series of scenes in this film treat Hannes and Nora's plans, which continually revolve around exactly these things. Considering this fact, one could surely make a deal with a big furniture company to carry out an effective, reciprocal advertising campaign."[42] In this early form of product placement, the Ufa studio hoped that it could channel the public's consumerist fantasies into interest for its own product, *Das Leben kann so schön sein*. The studio even suggested that theater owners contact the local city hall to get the names and addresses of couples who had recently married so that they could mail an advertisement to this target group.

While consumerism might resonate with viewers as a contemporary issue, the characters seem outdated. The boarding-house occupants are a ragtag group of lost souls who resemble cliché figures from the hated *Systemzeit*. The downwardly mobile elderly couple, the bohemian musician, the flapper, the dandy, and the petty bureaucrat seem better suited to a film set in the 1920s than one that claims to be about contemporary German life in 1938. Screenwriter Jochen Huth admitted that his original play dealt with an earlier time period and a different set of social issues: "When this play came to the stage years ago it was very closely connected to the problem of unemployment. [. . .] Today this question is no longer relevant due to the fortunate change of circumstances."[43] Regardless of whether or not Huth was skilled enough to adapt his characters to a later time frame or choose to retain outdated figures as a way to mitigate criticism of the present by implying that they were stuck in the past, he did not provide the audience with positive role models. None of the characters is living out his dreams. Some have resolved to accept defeat and adapt to limitations; others firmly believe in future success. Despite their differences, they share a need for order and meaning in a chaotic world. All the characters adopt a life strategy to protect themselves and gain a sense of security.

Among the boarders, the postal official Meier is the most obsessed with order. Meier organizes everything from the use of the bathroom, kitchen, and telephone to the coat rack where each peg has an assigned name card. When one boarder stays in the shower longer than the allotted fifteen minutes and messes up the carefully planned schedule, Meier fears the loss of control will lead to "squabbles, quarrels, hostilities, anarchy, chaos!"[44] The manicurist Ellen adopts a different strategy; she looks for security in money and hopes to marry a rich man. The traveling salesman Dewitt finds comfort in the certainty that he can sell his wares to anyone and in his "bachelor's pad which naturally includes the unavoidable Turkish smoking table and countless photos of scantily clad young women with guaranteed flawless morals."[45] The middle-aged piano teacher Fräulein Grün takes refuge in astrology and believes that destiny is written in the stars. She relies on the steadfast rules of the horoscope to guide her and reads Hannes's destiny with amazing accuracy: "You are a Gemini. Uncertain, irresolute, whooping with joy, deadly sad. Prone to weakness, more cowardly than courageous. More head than heart. Very cautious. And on the whole, not born under a lucky star."[46] When Hannes asks what he can do about it, she replies with utmost certainty, "Nothing!"

The kind, old-fashioned landlady Sophie von Klützner functions as the voice of experience and encourages Nora to accept limitations as part of life.

When Sophie and her husband Eduard lost all their savings in the hyperin-
flation of 1923, they decided to rent out their home "so that one knows
where one belongs." Sophie continues, "It wasn't simple at first. We imagined things so differently. But everything turned out okay. You get used to
everything. Life isn't always easy, but love, you know, love helps you get
over so much. Then you can put up with a lot."[47] If the young girl is flexible
and lowers her material expectations, she can expect love and personal contentment as her reward. Sophie consoles Nora, "Everything comes with
time. You are still so young. The best things are ahead of you. And for a
happy, loving couple even the smallest hut has enough room."[48] Nora conforms to this rule and goes along with her husband's demand that they save
every penny, but Hannes does not fulfill his part of the bargain.

Hannes is so insecure and fearful that he does not know how to respond
to Nora's conjecture, "life could be so wonderful." Tired of his passivity, Nora
literally takes the rudder of their boat and tries to build up his ego. She pleads
with him, "Have more confidence in yourself. Have a little courage. It isn't
dangerous. You only have to take a chance, be brave, Hannes. . . . You have
to believe in yourself."[49] In the course of the film, Hannes never seems to learn
this lesson, to believe in himself (and by extension the government). His fears
are so deeply rooted, so convincing, that it is difficult to believe in his total
conversion at the end of the film. Nora's final comment that he should not cry
is hardly reassuring. This passive male character is the antithesis of the model
Nazi hero; he is "a person who has lost his nerve out of sheer worry, in the
end no longer believes in his own capacity for work and is almost destroyed by
his lack of courage to go on living."[50] While Hitler, Goebbels, and the Ufa
board of directors did not directly criticize the character of Hannes, their
censure of this film based on "population growth policies" is implicitly a
rejection of male impotency. Nazi cinema rarely if ever featured men lacking
self-control and determination as the protagonists of serious dramas.

Hannes's reaction to the news that he will soon be a father marks him
as a weakling. On the anniversary of their engagement and first sexual encounter, Nora tells Hannes she is pregnant. He stares at her silently until the
light goes out of his eyes, and his smile turns to stunned panic. The music
turns downbeat as Nora registers his disappointment and mirrors it. Hannes
does not conform to the expected behavior of a married man in a state where
procreation of racially fit Aryan babies was considered every healthy citizen's
primary duty. Hannes's failure as a father, his reluctance to accept Nora's
pregnancy and give her the support she needs as an expectant mother, goes
against one of the highest principles of National Socialism: the mother cult.

In the working world Hannes is equally weak and ineffective. In a flashback he meekly tells his boss that as a family man he needs a promotion and
a raise. The scene has a nightmarish quality. It opens with the general director
(Kurt Seifert) sitting at his desk surrounded by darkness, but the camera

tracks in quickly, the light behind the desk suddenly illuminates an immense stained glass window in the background, and a secretary walks into the room. As if waking from a dream into reality, the unnatural lighting and props shift to a more conventional setting. The oblique camera work, however, signals that this reality is as bizarre as any dream. The obese director, who bears a remarkable resemblance to a Georg Grosz caricature, is filmed at an extremely low angle making him look abnormally huge and domineering, while the slender Hannes is seated in an oversized armchair filmed at a high angle rendering him small and insignificant. As the scene ends, a low-angle camera moves into a close-up of the smiling director, so that his gigantic face fills the entire screen while the space surrounding him goes dark.

The director's condescending smirk fades to black, but it leaves a haunting afterimage accompanied by the shrill sounds of a piccolo. In a rapid series of shots, the siren-like music follows Hannes as he climbs up and down flights of stairs, runs down endless streets, and jumps in and out of trains, constantly moving in different directions. He frantically pleads with his potential customers: "Life today is so dangerous. Don't you read the newspapers? Just imagine all the things that can happen to you. And what can you do about it? Absolutely nothing. Accident and burglary, fire and sickness. On every corner bad luck is just waiting for you to come along. You could slip on a banana peel."[51] His sales pitch is accompanied by a montage of a woman falling on a banana peel, a dead man on the floor next to a butcher knife, a car crash, a thief breaking into a wall, a fire, a man carried on a stretcher, newspaper articles on natural catastrophes, floods, and a train crash. Laughter fills the last frames of Hannes's apocalyptic vision, and the flames slowly dissolve into the image of a cheerful old man tending sunflowers in his garden. In a heavy Berlin accent, the old man dismisses Hannes as a doomsayer, "No way. If I thought like you, then I'd never stop paying. And what would I get for my trouble? Nothin' but worry. I'm not afraid anymore. I know about life." Turning the tables, the old man asks Hannes, "Are you insured?," to which the insurance salesman must admit he is not.[52] In this scene, so rare in Nazi cinema because it shows the random violence of everyday life, two opposing worldviews clash; pessimism is contrasted with optimism, images of cataclysm with those of contentment, and a fearful youth with a secure older generation. And while mature characters like the elderly gardener, Sophie and Eduard von Klützner, and Nora's uncle espouse a confidently sanguine world outlook and playfully berate Hannes, it is the specter of youthful fear that lingers and is never convincingly resolved.

The depiction of a frightened young man, unable to accept financial or emotional responsibility for his wife and child, is a criticism that goes to the core of the carefully fashioned masculine identity in Nazi Germany. The triad hero image of the soldier-worker-farmer is a man of action and resolve. Hannes recognizes that he does not fit the mold. When the manicurist Ellen admits that living in the boarding-house in such close proximity has destroyed her illusions about men, Hannes retorts, "We men only exist in your illusions! If you need them, go to the movies."[53] In this striking moment of self-reflectivity, when a movie character criticizes the believability of a movie character, the audience is made aware of how the media disseminate unrealistic masculine images.

Nora is much better at conforming to the idealistic standards of female sacrifice and self-abnegation, but she cannot completely suppress her own wishes and individuality. When the demands become overwhelming she complains: "sometimes I get so fed up!" and later "Oh, sometimes I'd like to scream."[54] Nora is willing to accept a meager material existence but she needs her husband to protect and shield her emotionally from others. Unfortunately Hannes hides from trouble and lets Nora fight their battles. She protests: "But you always let me fight it out on my own. You never stand up for me Hannes. You always let me do everything alone."[55] Even at work she must bear an unfair emotional burden. Since Hannes fears Nora will lose her job if she admits to being married, he insists that she lie to everyone at work and pretend to be single. When her boss asks her out to coffee, she feels obligated to go. Hannes follows them into the coffee shop but never gathers the courage to confront the other man. At home he launches into a jealous rage. Nora is stunned and asks: "Why do you leave me so terribly alone to deal with everything?"[56] After Hannes kicks her sewing box, his gift symbolizing her dreams of luxury and domestic happiness as well as his willingness to compromise, she decides to leave him. This simple act of cruelty represents for Nora the last straw, a clear indication that Hannes will not invest in their marriage or their future as a family.

The film concludes with a happy ending so neat and clean that it stretches the limits of believability. When Hannes hears the news that Nora has given birth to a son, he becomes a changed man. Beaming with confidence and joy he marches off to see his wife and child accompanied by the swells of triumphant music as if to suggest the heralding of a king. The doctor remarks that this sudden transformation is typical: "With every birth two human beings are born! The child and the father!"[57] A close-up of the newborn contentedly sucking his thumb is followed by the smiles of the happy parents. The final shot is a close-up of Nora's tear-stained face as she comforts her husband with the words: "Don't cry Hannes, now everything will be alright." This happy ending echoes the assessment of the working class in Nazi Germany as noted in the secret reports of the outlawed Social Democratic Party (Sopade): "Strength through Joy seems to prove that the solution to social problems can be avoided, if one gives the worker more 'honor' instead of more wages, more 'joy' instead of more free time, more petty bourgeois self-esteem instead of better working and living conditions."[58]

Der verzauberte Tag

Female Desire and the Gaze:
Der verzauberte Tag (1943–1944)

Peter Pewas's first full-length feature film *Der verzauberte Tag* tells the story of a young girl who wants to break free from social and economic limitations and experience life to its fullest. The film, based on Franz Nabl's short story "Die Augen" (The Eyes), was shot at the Ufa studios in Babelsberg between June and October 1943, and after several delays a finished film was sent to the propaganda ministry on July 1, 1944. Pewas's film immediately came under scrutiny. In an unusual move, Goebbels arranged a viewing of the film on July 6, 1944 in the propaganda ministry's air-raid shelter, where it was widely criticized. From the summer of 1944 until January 1945, *Der verzauberte Tag* was repeatedly slated for changes, and while the film was never officially banned, it was also never edited to the propaganda ministry's satisfaction and did not premiere in Nazi Germany.[59]

Peter Pewas (pseudonym for Walter Schulz, 1904–1984) came to film with an extensive and varied artistic background. After an apprenticeship in metal work and a lengthy period wandering through Tyrol, he studied at the Bauhaus school in Weimar, working closely with Moholy-Nagy, Klee, and Kandinsky. He made a name for himself as a graphic artist designing film advertisements and was credited with developing the "filmic poster style" (filmischer Plakatstil), which used colors, forms, and photomontage in striking new ways. He joined the first students at the new German Film Academy in Babelsberg where he studied direction, screenwriting, acting, lighting, and photography. The director of the academy, Professor Wolfgang Liebeneiner, became his mentor and hired him as an assistant for the state-sponsored propaganda films *Bismarck* (1940) and *Ich klage an* (1941). Pewas was considered a talented newcomer who could develop an innovative visual style and treat contemporary issues with the realism Goebbels wanted from the problem film. The Ufa studio hoped Pewas could fulfill Goebbels's mandate by making a film that did "not escape from daily hardship and lose itself in a dreamland that only exists in the minds of starry-eyed directors and scriptwriters but nowhere else on earth."

In a series of interviews published in 1943, the young director discussed his eagerness to create a new type of film, one that would challenge viewers by demanding a critical distance reminiscent of Brechtian aesthetics. Pewas argued in favor of objective and analytical observation over the classical cinema's reliance on identification and its erasure of all evidence testifying to its status as constructed reality. He maintained: "This film does not show beautiful people but rather real human beings. *Der verzauberte Tag* should not distract but rather collect and stimulate."[60] Pewas saw his film as pioneering work: "We are creating a film here which in a certain sense will bring a new view to scenery and photography. We should avoid, and I want to emphasize this from the start, glamorous delusions and love play. I resolutely want to steer away from any superficiality. The plot, which is characterized by strong and healthy feelings, obliges me in my efforts. It is a matter of illustrating the actions of a young person who has to be transported out of a petty bourgeois atmosphere."[61]

Der verzauberte Tag begins in a hospital where the young Christine Schweiger (Winnie Markus) lies unconscious with the artist Albrecht Götz (Hans Stüwe) at her side. A narrator sets the stage for her story, which is told in a single flashback. Christine and her neighbor Anni work at a newspaper stand in the train station but dream of having a more exciting life, traveling, falling in love, finding romance and wealth. Spring is in the air and both girls yearn for change. Christine breaks off her engagement to the narrow-minded accountant Krummholz despite her mother's fears for her future. Anni has invented a fiancé named Maximilian and is thrilled when the handsome stranger Emil is willing to play the part of her fairy tale lover. After Anni learns that Emil is a con man wanted by the police, she turns to Stationmaster Wasner for comfort, and although both of them want someone else, they settle for each other. A mysterious stranger also changes Christine's life. One day she sees Albrecht Götz staring at her from a train, and their mutual gaze is so intense that Christine believes they are destined to fall in love. The next day she receives roses from an anonymous admirer and sees Götz again, so she agrees to drive out into the country with him. They spend an enchanted day together among the blossoming trees and make love that night. Christine is devastated to learn that Götz did not send her flowers nor did he see her that first day at the train station; he was actually reading the letters on the newsstand to gauge the extent of an eye injury. Believing that fate has played a cruel trick on her, she runs away. Alone on the street at night, she is accosted by a one-eyed man and then shot by Krummholz in a drunken, jealous rage. Returning to the present, Christine awakens in the hospital where Götz professes his love in a dramatic, if unconvincing, happy ending.

Startling images, remarkable photography and lighting, symbolic props, and the skillful use of space dominate this film and take precedent over plot and dialogue. The narrator's opening monologue, spoken by director Pewas in the slow and measured cadence of poetry, sets the mood:

> It is springtime. Overnight a warm rain fell and brought out the last blossoms. The trees stir, and the fountains are in high spirits, the birds are singing, and desire is everywhere. Through these panes it is quiet. Here lies a young person, Christine, wondrously transformed by spring and now destroyed. She is feverish. Her hands search for a letter that fell out of her coat pocket in the night of the misfortune, as people are calling it. The nurse found it long ago. The stranger takes it and is alarmed. Almost hesitantly he sees his address. He opens it. Sinking into another world he reads about a spring day when a disaster was brewing fatefully and silently like the shadow of a cloud.[62]

The ethereal quality of a cloud's shadow poignantly describes the vague dissatisfaction and restless yearning afflicting the characters in *Der verzauberte Tag*. The film is both a fairy tale of desire and a sober tale of harsh reality. The characters live in their own world and rarely, if ever, connect with their fellow human beings. Like the numerous train tracks pictured in this film, there are many parallel realities that seldom intersect. The men and women need from each other exactly what the other is not willing or able to give. One man wants a sweet and innocent virgin, another wants a passionate carefree lover, and a third wants a faithful servant, but they all want a woman who meets their needs without making any demands of her own. The women worry about money and how to make ends meet, but they also crave romance and passion. They waver between waiting for Prince Charming and settling for Mr. Right-Now with the prospects of a pension.

The two young salesgirls are caught in a restrictive social environment but yearn for freedom and adventure, which lie beyond the horizon. Contained in their newsstand but surrounded by the allure of travel, they watch the trains go by and dream of being whisked away to another realm. Christine and Anni use different strategies to escape from everyday life and find an outlet for their sexual desires. Anni uses fantasy, inventing a noble lover who will arrive any day now to take her away. She steadfastly refuses to accept her bleak existence: living in a modest rented room, forced to pawn her underwear, hungry for a piece of meat, starved for affection, and working in a job without much prospect for the future. The dark-haired Anni adopts a dark, erotic attitude and appearance, fashioning herself as a vamp in the hopes of seducing a rich man who will take care of her. At home she dons black lace slips, drapes herself in silk, feathers, and veils, and touches the lines of her figure as she admires her body in the mirror. At work she wears dresses with a provocative neckline, boasts about her make-believe boyfriend, and even sends herself flowers and letters to bolster her reputation as a desirable lover.

Anni and Christine at work in the newstand, *Der verzauberte Tag*.

The blond Christine represents the lighter model: healthy, natural, virginal. She lives with her widowed mother in a cramped apartment and gets up early to go swimming in the lake. Unlike Anni, Christine is not preoccupied with her appearance. Christine stands in her white slip with her back to the mirror and puts on a modest, high-collared dress for work. But she too is restless. When she brushes her hair and stretches, she seems like she could almost spring outside the confining walls and low ceiling of her tiny attic room. Whereas Anni has made up a wealthy lover, Christine is not exactly sure what she wants. She often daydreams, staring out into the empty space off-camera and voicing an indeterminate desire for a different life. Invariably, each time she projects her desire into the void, a train whistle pierces through the daily grind and beckons her to far-off places.

One day at the train station, Christine expresses her vague longing, "Anni, do you sometimes feel the same way? You think, with the train now pulling in, something is coming that you have been waiting for the entire time. You don't know what it is, you can't really describe it. But you only know . . . anyway, you know this much, there has to be something else."[63] The composition of this scene reiterates in visual terms that Christine is at a crossroads and must choose a path. Myriad lines cross the screen and suggest the open possibilities for movement in limitless directions. Christine stands in the right foreground facing the camera but looking off slightly to the left where no one is standing. Behind her an elevated metal walkway traverses the top horizontal plane and in the center of the frame a train approaches the platform on an inverted v-shaped track. Even the lines of Christine's clothes, a light colored suit in a diamond-shaped pattern with a contrasting dark plaid collar and cuffs, make the eye move in different directions. Christine and her darker mirror image Anni hope to find the path that will lead them to a life of excitement and intrigue, passion and sexual fulfillment. Anni naïvely believes, "If you wish for something from the bottom of your heart, it will come true."[64] Christine is equally certain that love is the key: "For me it was simply the discovery that someone belongs to me. My life will take a whole new path."[65]

Frau Schweiger hopes her daughter Christine will opt for financial security over romance and marry Rudolf Krummholz, a middle-aged accountant obsessed with order. Krummholz, whose name means crooked or bent piece of wood and alludes to male impotency, is a small man in both stature and attitude. Dressed in a prim three-piece suit complete with starched attached collar, bowler hat, and cane, his hair rigidly parted exactly down the middle, he is a caricature of the petty bureaucrat. At work he knows his proper place in the pecking order, dominating his underlings and kowtowing to his superiors. He tries to order his personal life in a similar manner by regulating his engagement to Christine in a business-like manner and even designing an hourly household work schedule for her to follow after they are married. Krummholz assures Christine that he does not need a wife who thinks, and he smugly observes to Frau Schweiger: "You can rear a young wife. You only have to help her settle into her duties as a housewife. By the way, nicely put, huh?"[66] Christine breaks off her engagement to Krummholz and places her hopes in the stranger Albrecht Götz, who can offer her the change she so desperately seeks.

Ironically, the artist Albrecht Götz is a man with distorted vision. He readily admits, "I see everything completely veiled."[67] His eyesight was nearly destroyed when a former lover threw acid in his face after he jilted her. However, Götz also suffers from a more general flawed vision in his sexual relationships. He views women as "speculators looking for the easiest life possible," and sees himself as "an object of desire," because he has made something out of his life.[68] Götz, whose name is derived from *Götze* meaning "idol," is the object of extreme devotion but also a man who operates under fallacies and fails to see his numerous lovers as individuals. He is drawn to women and needs to possess them both physically and as images, because "for an artist a woman is the most interesting object. She is like nature, unfathomable, unpredictable, and full of secrets."[69]

Considering the emphasis placed on flawed male vision and image making, it is not surprising that *Der verzauberte Tag* also problematizes the female gaze. In a highly significant exchange of glances between Götz and Christine, she upsets the traditional gender-specific roles in the visual economy structuring sexual desire. In classical narrative cinema, as Laura Mulvey has shown, "pleasure in looking has been split between active/male and passive/female. The determining male gaze projects its fantasy onto the female figure, which is styled accordingly. In their traditional exhibitionist role women are simultaneously looked at and displayed, with their appearance coded for strong visual and erotic impact so that they can be said to connote *to-be-looked-at-ness*."[70] Mary Ann Doane has demonstrated that when this order is reversed, when woman assumes agency of the look and its corresponding subjectivity, she "poses a threat to an entire system of representation." Doane maintains: "There is always a certain excessiveness, a difficulty associated with women who appropriate the gaze, who insist upon looking." Classical cinema often solves this dilemma by punishing the display of excessive female desire with violence and even death because "the woman as subject of the gaze is clearly an impossible sign."[71]

It is at the train station, a place where lives intersect and excessive female desire is repeatedly displayed, that Christine first sees Götz. In this scene Christine is transformed from the enthralled viewer of a romantic spectacle to the active pursuer of her own desire. After watching a couple kissing passionately on the platform, Christine notices that a man (Götz) is looking out of the train window in her direction. She misreads the situation and thinks he is staring at her. A series of shot/reverse shots from both characters' point of view show that they are looking at different things. When Christine perceives that Götz is watching her, she does not demurely look away. Instead, her face lights up with a smile, and she returns his unwavering gaze. However, several shots from Götz's point of view reveal that he does not see her at all and is actually trying to read the advertisement written on the kiosk. At the center of a shadowy black frame, the letters "Zeitschrift" (magazine) are slowly brought into focus and confirm that Götz is recovering from his eye injury. The next day, the scene is repeated and again gendered ways of seeing cause confusion. This time Götz sees Christine staring at him with longing and is so surprised by her active and fixed gaze that jumps from the departing train to meet this woman who is openly seducing him. However, his first remark, "Have you ever been painted before?" highlights that Christine represents an untenable position, the subject of the gaze and the object of desire, the spectator and the image.[72] Eventually disaster strikes because Christine fails to remain an image and insists upon giving her desire free reign. In essence, she refuses to acquiesce and accept her role as Fräulein Schweiger, or Miss Silent One as her name means in English.

The women in *Der verzauberte Tag* must make the difficult choice of either following their heart or ensuring that they are taken care of financially. Christine and Anni frequently worry about economic security, but they struggle against a system that forces them to marry a breadwinner instead of a lover. Both women refuse to be submissive and passively wait for a man to come along. Anni takes the initiative by consciously fashioning her public image as a desirable lover. Christine declines to marry a man she finds repugnant simply because he will provide her with a good standard of living, and she actively seduces Götz (albeit unwittingly). Ultimately both women will pay for their assertiveness and seductive poses by becoming the victims of a crime. When Anni tries to realize her ardent fantasy of being an alluring woman from a wealthy family, she is betrayed by Emil, who only romanced her in the hopes of stealing her money. After Christine tries to live out the dream of finding her soulmate in a chance encounter, she not only learns that Götz considers her merely a sexual adventure, she is also molested on the street, and finally shot by her spurned ex-fiancé.

Both women display an all-consuming passion that appears to be liberating but is mired in unrealistic ideals. While they uniformly refuse to conform and become passive, they also adhere to a highly sentimental view of love. Anni hopes to be swept off her feet by a fiery and dangerous stranger, while Christine believes that she is destined to meet the love of her life. These young women envision love in terms of a Harlequin romance, but as Anni's landlady remarks: "You can't live on perfect roses."[73] In the press package for *Der verzauberte Tag*, Christine is described as a self-absorbed young woman who invites disaster through her naïveté and refusal to accept reality: "[she] egotistically keeps on supplying nourishment to her daydreams from every possible incident in everyday life, until she no longer distinguishes between dream and reality and is drawn into an experience that almost takes a tragic end."[74] Much of these unrealistic expectations for love are linked to ideal images of femininity such as the one Anni encounters when she goes to a nightclub with "Maximilian" (Emil). Anni watches the stage as a ballerina holding a birdcage dances on a pedestal surrounded by mirrors. This silent and beautiful figure, lifted right out of a little girl's jewelry box, represents the lofty ideal of womanhood as captive spectacle. Put on a pedestal, imprisoned in a gilded cage, displayed as an image and a reflection, she is a lifeless and unobtainable ideal.

When Emil asks Anni why she has told everyone they are engaged and he is her "fairytale prince," her response is "because I want it so very much."[75] For the first time in the film, Anni is dressed in a modest black dress with a high-necked white collar and comes across as both vulnerable and honest. She drops her pretense, looks off into space, then closes her eyes and melts into Emil. Anni's illusions are destroyed when she discovers that Emil is a marriage swindler. However, unlike Christine, Anni recognizes that her fantasies will probably never come true, and she contemplates a marriage of convenience. Stationmaster Wasner confesses that he has given up hope of winning Christine's affection and has now fallen in love with Anni. When he proposes on their first date, Anni replies, "marriage? To be taken care of? It would be nice." She hesitates at first to settle for security because she worries about what would happen if one day a dangerous stranger like her fictional Maximilian actually walked into her life. Wasner assures her "by then there will probably be children, and you will be older and calmer."[76]

In contrast to Anni's sober assessment of marriage, Christine's first date with Götz reaffirms her sentimental view of love. The couple drives out into the country, a place of bright sunshine, empty roads, and open fields. They are alone to enjoy the solitude and have a picnic among the blooming trees. Yet even in this idyllic setting, social and economic limitations define Christine's existence. While Götz sketches her portrait and assures her he is listening, Christine talks about the lack of money and the need to work: "I've learned now from my mother what it means to be on your feet from morning till night and then worrying about the money needed."[77] She laments the feminine condition and asks, "Why am I not a man? As a man you have the chance to realize the greatest ideas."[78] Christine and Götz do not communicate with each other and seem to exist in parallel universes, but they dance together under the trees by moonlight in a scene of startling beauty that conveys sincere happiness and freedom.

Parallel to Christine's rise is Krummholz's fall. In a highly stylized scene, Krummholz is rejected and loses all sense of order. The original screenplay called for the scene to be staged in a realistic manner on the living room sofa, but Pewas transformed it into a cinematic tour de force with symbolic lighting, props, and optical effects. Pewas restaged the action to visualize the character's psychological turmoil and mounting rage. Frau Schweiger stands in the foreground in an almost completely dark kitchen except for a single light from the stove, while Krummholz waits for her in the brightly lighted living room visible through the archway in the background. He enters the darkness and bends down to tend the fire just as Frau Schweiger announces that Christine does not want to marry him. Harsh light floods his face, the glowing ambers of the fire are reflected in his eyeglasses, and snaking plumes of smoke rise from a large pot of boiling water as the mother tells him: "Maybe she wants something else."[79] Christine's refusal to marry throws Krummholz into a downward spiral;

he tries to drown his sorrow in alcohol and the company of loose women but eventually lashes out at the woman who rejected him.

In a series of crosscuts to three different events transpiring simultaneously, the audience is shown how Krummholz, Anni, and Christine come to grips with the problem of unobtainable idealized love. Krummholz laments the loss of his ideal woman as he sits alone at the lake near the firing range (*Schießplatz*), surrounded by the sounds of barking dogs and gunshots. In a frantic attempt to block out his humiliation and anger, he stages a wild party in his rented room, dancing to "degenerate" jazz music and getting drunk with prostitutes. At the same time, Anni goes to the lake for a romantic walk with Stationmaster Wasner, and while she too mourns the loss of ideal love, she decides to settle for financial security. Finally, Christine returns to Götz's home after a beautiful day in the countryside and is swept away by his polished seduction and even flattered when he remarks that she will be his first "Christine." They make love offscreen to the sound of her breathing while the camera pans over his numerous artworks idealizing love and feminine beauty until it stops at a broken blossom on the glass table in front of her limp wrist. Just as Christine is deflowered, Krummholz's forlorn image is suddenly reflected in the glass table, reminding the viewer that the fulfillment of one dream is the destruction of another. Afterwards Götz dangles a string over Christine and plays with her as if she were a cat. He is surprised she behaved so recklessly and became intimate with a man she hardly knew. Only now does Christine learn that Götz never saw her at the train station. He did not seek her out, send her flowers, and try to win her over. She is ashamed of herself because she now believes she behaved like a whore, seducing some unknown man with her unwavering gaze. She recognizes she was just an adventure for a man whose only concern is to finish the painting of his newest conquest.

Christine takes flight into the rainy night, but she cannot escape from her shame and disillusionment. The camera narrates her emotional turmoil with a montage of falling trees and roaring waves superimposed over her as she runs down the wet and deserted streets. She grasps a glistening chainlink fence just as the train whistle blows, bracing herself against the rush of emotions associated with this recurring piercing sound. Slowly she comes upon a bridge and stares out into the fog, while another montage of trains, tracks, smoke, and Götz's face is superimposed upon the bleak and nearly suicidal scene. Christine finally makes her way to a café, where she writes Götz a letter explaining her motivations: "It was like a miracle. I am not reckless. I believed in the rule of destiny as something holy. You will understand me. Fate made a fool of me, for which I am ashamed. We can never see each other again."[80]

As Christine leaves the café, a one-eyed man grabs her on the street. When she defends herself against his unsolicited advances, his vitriolic retort is: "If you hang out on the street here at night, then you have to know what a man wants from you."[81] Again marked a whore by a man with flawed vision, Christine frees herself from his grasp and runs home only to find a drunken Krummholz waiting for her and shouting triumphantly, "I came to get what's rightfully mine."[82] The scene takes on a nightmarish quality as the background suddenly turns black, the soundtrack goes silent, and Christine forcefully pushes him away. He orders her to stand still, and when she refuses to be a captive image, he shoots her. Krummholz staggers backwards and breaks a window, smashing the ornate portrait of a beautiful naked woman etched into the glass. Both Christine and the shattered image fall to the floor in ruins.

Krummholz attacks Christine: *Der verzauberte Tag.*

However, tragedy is averted and all the loose ends are resolved. While Christine lies unconscious in the hospital reliving her troubled memories and dreams in a montage superimposed over her feverish body, Krummholz is arrested and led off to prison. Götz rushes to Christine's side and reads her letter. He finally comes to his senses as Christine awakens. She looks at him and says: "the eyes," to which he replies: "Don't speak. I was blind, but now I see you as you are, as I love you."[83] Although the last shot shows the couple kissing, their relationship is still predicated on the controlling male gaze and the silent woman.

Unlike *Das Leben kann so schön sein, Der verzauberte Tag* does not portray everyday life with realistic details. Pewas's film does not cite exact wages,

prices, or consumer products, nor does it refer to specific government programs like marriage loans and settlement housing. The economic hardship
of working women so typical of life in 1944 Germany is presented in more
universal terms as part of the feminine condition. Christine learns from her
widowed mother what it means to be the working poor, but there is no
mention of such wartime burdens as ration stamps, shortages of food,
clothing, and fuel, or the conscription of women into the Reich Labor
Service (*Reichsarbeitsdienst*). Even Anni's need to pawn her lingerie and her
desperate pleas for meat seem to indicate her unrealistic material desires and
not necessarily abject poverty brought on by war, especially since she has
enough money to send herself flowers. *Der verzauberte Tag* depicts a different but equally valid reality: the problem of daydreaming and living with
unfulfilled desires. During the Second World War, a period of scarcity and
separation, people continued to have sexual and economic needs but few
outlets beyond daydreaming. As Karsten Witte has aptly stated: "*Der verzauberte Tag* expresses the bombed-out moviegoer's desire for warmth and
security after the military losses at Stalingrad and in Africa and offers them
a dreamlike preview of a future without prospects, the loss of the present,
and the sweep through the past."[84]

In its proposed advertising campaign, the Ufa studio emphasized that *Der
verzauberte Tag* presented ordinary people with ordinary problems but in a
way that made the familiar seem extraordinary. Günther Dietrich praised *Der
verzauberte Tag* because it portrayed "people of our time, with our joys and
troubles. And yet this film shows things that we do not see in everyday life.
Here the mask falls from the faces as it were. The most subtle psychological
stirrings are made visible and force us to participate in this destiny so gripping
exactly because it is so commonplace."[85] Critic Hermann Hacker, writing for
the same Ufa press package, asserted that Pewas's film could help contemporary viewers to come to terms with a pressing, if elusive, social problem:

> It is fine and useful that this film examines a problem whose occurrence
> cannot be denied simply because it does not appear visible in the every-
> day world. And it is equally fine that the young director Peter Pewas,
> who is presenting with *Der verzauberte Tag* his first major work, devel-
> ops the problem of dangerous daydreaming to the last consequence and
> generates the solution in a natural way through the power of real life.[86]

The question of how mass audiences might have reacted to this film in
1944 cannot be answered with any certainty, but the varied reactions from
the select viewers in the propaganda ministry's air-raid shelter suggest that
the film was too ambiguous for propaganda purposes. Reich Film Intendant
Hans Hinkel summarized the film's mixed reception in a letter to Goebbels:

The air-raid shelter association's opinion of the film was predominantly negative. Above all the male viewers sharply rejected the film, because they thought Christine's fiancé (Ernst Wladow) was depicted as too foolish and also Hans Stüwe as Prof. Götz was unconvincing. A number of female viewers accepted the film uncritically, while others rightly posed the question what this film actually wanted to express. They also were not certain about the plot development. Only a few coworkers in leading positions in various departments recognized the dangerous tendency behind this film. It arises from the prostitution milieu, the unpleasant depiction of the bourgeois official, the coquettish behavior of Anni (Eva-Maria Meinecke), and in general the very obvious direction.[87]

Hinkel never explained what he meant by the term "very obvious direction," but he seemed to be indicating that the problem lay in the film's tone rather than in its content. In an interview conducted in 1978, Peter Pewas maintained that *Der verzauberte Tag* was censored primarily because of his directorial style:

It was only the style, because the material was absolutely approved, supported from above. I always had the feeling that in those days when all the fronts were shaky people did not want a collapse on the cultural front. They did not want any formal experiments, any acoustical experiments. They wanted something tangible, people spoke of cultural bolshevism.[88]

Ironically, the sophisticated visual style Goebbels wanted and the trade press routinely promoted transformed an acceptable story with potential propaganda value into a multivalent and presumably subversive film that the National Socialists could not allow audiences to see.

Coming to Grips with the Past: *Via Mala* (1944–1945)

Via Mala is a *Heimatfilm* gone terribly wrong, a hellish vision of family life, physical and mental abuse, murder, and collective guilt. Directed by Josef von Baky and based on John Knittel's internationally acclaimed novel about a brutal drunkard who is killed under mysterious circumstances, the film underwent an amazing number of changes and delays over a four-year period. Thea von Harbou's screenplay was submitted to the censor on May 21, 1941, but only approved nine months later on February 28, 1942. Despite the high start-up costs including the purchase of copyrights from Switzerland, Goebbels stopped the project because the material was "too gloomy."[89] Over a year later, *Via Mala* was revived, and filming began on July 12, 1943 at the Ufa studios in Babelsberg and later on location in the Tyrolean village of Mayrhofen. After several further delays, Baky submitted a completed film to the Ufa board of directors on March 30, 1944, but on April 15 the propaganda ministry ordered Baky to reshoot the ending. The new version was submitted to the censor on January 15, 1945. Reich Film Intendant Hans Hinkel finally approved the film on March 9, 1945, but rescinded the order ten days later. On March 19, 1945, Hinkel issued the following statement: "The film department has already been informed that the film *Via Mala*, which in itself has been judged to be good, has to be rejected at this time due to its gloomy character. The film is only approved for foreign release."[90] According to writer Erich Kästner, *Via Mala* premiered in Mayrhofen on April 7, 1945, one month before Germany's unconditional surrender.[91]

Via Mala is set in an isolated sawmill on a rocky mountaintop next to a roaring waterfall, where the miller Jonas Lauretz (Karl Wery) terrorizes his extended family. On a stormy winter night, Lauretz sends his grown son Nikolaus (Malte Jäger) to town for alcohol but when he returns home empty-handed, the old man savagely whips him. The pious wife and her embittered daughter Hanna are powerless against this brute. Equally helpless are Lauretz's mistress Kuni, who lives with the family, and his lackey Jöry, whom the old man has crippled with his beatings. The angelic daughter Silvelie (Karin Hardt) tries to intercede on Nikolaus's behalf, but when Lauretz learns that she has convinced the innkeeper Bündner to refuse him liquor, he beats her too. That night Lauretz disappears and is never seen again. The town judge believes that he was murdered and begins to interrogate the family, but dies during the hearing. The family starts to prosper and heal its wounds, but the old man's evil spirit seems to haunt the sawmill. Everyone suspects the other of murder because they all had good reasons for wanting Lauretz dead. The new town judge Andreas von Richenau (Viktor Staal) falls in love with Silvelie, and when she tries to tell him about her father, he refuses to listen. Despite her repeated attempts to remember the past, Andi insists they forget it all and marry. After they are wed, Andi assumes his post as town judge and finally reads the Lauretz file. Certain that the old man was murdered, Andi feels obligated to serve justice and reopen the case. During the hearing at the sawmill, the innkeeper Bündner confesses that he killed Lauretz out of love for Silvelie. The entire family forgives him because Bündner only did what each of them wanted to do all along.

This fantasy of collective patricide features a brutal father figure resembling the monsters found in German expressionist horror films. Baky not only uses the horror film conventions of chiaroscuro lighting and irregular camera shots, he also creates suspense by drawing out the old man's entrance and by focusing on the other characters' fear of him as they await his arrival. Lauretz seems like an unstoppable force rather than a human being. He is frequently presented as a shadow, an isolated body part, or supplanted by the whip so closely associated with him. Filmed from behind at an extreme low angle that makes him appear immense and aggressive, Lauretz's unnaturally large and stiff body fills the screen and dominates the space. He moves with the awkward gait of the Golem or Frankenstein through a nearly barren room comparable to a prison cell with its low ceilings, thick walls, tiny windows, and sturdy doors. Lauretz's first appearance on screen is exemplary. In a prolonged, extreme close-up we see the doorknob slowly turn and a gigantic hand appear in the door jamb. The camera cuts to an enormous man shot from behind at a low angle as he walks to a small door on the other side of the room. He is so large that he has to bend down to avoid hitting the ceiling beams. He opens the heavy door to a howling storm, whistles into the dark, and closes the door. The camera cuts to two women paralyzed with fright and staring at the giant in silence. He turns around, and the audience gets its first look at his face as he takes a whip from the coat rack and leaves the house. The entire scene is shot without any dialogue. The incessant noise of the sawmill, the roaring waterfall, the raging storm, the piercing whistle, and the dull but steady shuffling of Lauretz's boots are contrasted to the women's silent terror. Lauretz is like a destructive force of nature from which no one can escape. When the women are finally alone, they agree, "That isn't a father, that's a beast."[92]

The monstrous patriarch Lauretz: *Via Mala*.

Lauretz faces little opposition. His wife and daughters are defenseless and cannot leave the miserable sawmill or his sphere of influence. Even his mistress Kuni cannot escape his cruel grasp: "Do you think I like being here? Do you think I wouldn't rather leave today than tomorrow? This God damned miller! [. . .] I ran away once. He brought me back. He'd find me anywhere. He'll never let go of me. Devil. Devil."[93] The men are also powerless to stop the relentless attacks. The lackey Jöry confronts the old man and tries to restrain him but is thrown to the floor like a rag doll. Lauretz's son Nikolaus is a weakling who cannot stand up to his cold-blooded father and bears the brunt of his wrath. When Nikolaus falls on the rocks and breaks the bottle of schnapps, he wants to run away but allows his mother and sister to carry him inside. Surrounded in a tableau of women tending his wounds, he is already broken in body and soul, but his father sadistically tortures him further. Lauretz chases him into his room and whips him behind locked doors as the women beg, pray, and grow numb with despair. For Nikolaus there is no escape from his tiny, claustrophobic room with its slanted roof and no escape from the cycle of fear and torment. Lying face down on his bed crying pitifully, his back a series of bleeding open wounds, Nikolaus refuses to forgive his father: "May the Lord forget me, if I forget this."[94]

The innkeeper Bündner offers a ray of hope as a rational and compassionate man who might be able to stop the abuse. The villagers respect Bündner as a business leader who has brought prosperity and a sense of well being to the entire community. They value him more than the mayor or the judge, because as one man explains: "You can't be voted into office or fired. You are simply here. And it is fortunate for the entire village that you are here. For everyone who has something on his heart."[95] Unbeknownst to the villagers, Bündner has made a deal with Lauretz. The innkeeper is secretly in love with Silvelie and has agreed to give the old man liquor whenever he wants in exchange for having Silvelie live and work in his inn. Silvelie begs Bündner to help her, "He is no longer human. He is going to kill us yet. You don't know what kind of a life they lead down there in the sawmill."[96] Now faced with Lauretz's ultimatum, "No schnapps, no Silvelie," Bündner refuses to give him any liquor, but he passively stands by as the old man beats his daughter. Instead of interfering, he goes to his office, pets his dog, drinks two shots of schnapps, and stares off into space. Bündner is unwilling or unable to confront the tyrant head on, and the entire community of men gathered at the inn allows Lauretz to commit a violent crime without any consequences. No moral or legal authority openly challenges this savage man, but Lauretz is never seen again after this night.

With the miller's mysterious disappearance, the sawmill is transformed and its occupants begin to flourish. It is spring, the trees are in bloom, and a cheerful melody fills the air. The house has taken on a feminine, harmonious ambience: light now streams in from the windows and open door, and flowers and plants decorate the formerly barren room. Most significantly, the old man's whip, rifle, and walking stick have been replaced by a woman's straw hat, apron, and spinning wheel. Nikolaus is now strong enough to chop wood, Hanna has found a useful occupation as a nurse, and Kuni has regained her self-respect. While to all appearances everyone is better off, they live in constant fear and suspect each other of murder. The trembling mother admits that her husband haunts her dreams, "He is always there as soon as it gets dark. He sits in the corner at the kitchen stove. He crouches by the woodpile. He walks behind me to the mill. He lurks at my bed. I am always so afraid."[97] Although Lauretz has been gone for six months, his evil presence is still deeply felt. The family leaves his chair empty and sets a place for him at the table. They even cut a piece of bread for him at lunch because his absence makes them feel just as uneasy and frightened as his presence ever did. They have been so psychologically wounded that Lauretz continues to color their existence. The family cannot stop performing these deeply ingrained subservient acts even after they have become senseless rituals.

In contrast to the earlier scenes of threatening cliffs and violent storms associated with Lauretz, peaceful snow-covered mountaintops in the distance and a lovely little town in the valley set the stage for Andreas von Richenau's arrival. Dressed in a modern suit, Andi arrives by a horse-drawn coach but decides to walk in the sunshine just as the church bells ring and Silvelie walks down the road. Their paths literally cross at the graveyard, and they start walking together, stealing glances and then demurely looking away. They hear folk music playing in the distance and agree to dance without exchanging a word. With the mountain in the background and surrounded by blossoming trees, Silvelie and Andi dance together in a scene of fluid movement, growing intimacy, freedom, and happiness. With her father's departure and Andi's arrival, Silvelie is introduced to another world, one in bloom, filled with carefree movement, collective joy, and love.

When Silvelie learns that this stranger is the new judge, she runs away and questions whether she is to blame for her father's death: "Maybe I am bad. Maybe my father's death is my . . . Who knows."[98] The judge's presence leads the entire family to wonder who is responsible for Lauretz's death. The mother suspects her son, Hanna thinks Kuni did it, Nikolaus believes Jöry saw something, but they all agree it could never have been Silvelie. This divinely pure woman, who brings out the best in everyone and is revered above all else, suffers from the buried secrets and tries to master the past. When Andi asks her to marry him, she laments that she cannot be his wife because she thinks about her father "day and night." Andi tries to convince her that she must forget everything that happened in the past: "I know. I spoke with Mr. Bündner. About you, your father, your family, your entire unfortunate past. That is all behind you, Silvelie. Even if your father had an accident or something. [. . .] You have nothing to do with him anymore. He lies down there. Forget it, forget everything. Think only of me." Silvelie is the voice of conscience and pronounces the simple moral imperative: "I cannot forget, I may not."[99] Although she repeatedly tries to bring up her father's death, Andi refuses to hear about it, because he does not want to know about anything so painful. Since Andi, a community leader who embodies moral and legal authority, refuses to delve into the past and assign guilt, Silvelie agrees to forget. She tells her family: "I want the past to finally be past. Make a clean break and try to start over."[100] At Silvelie's urging Andi takes her father's place at the table and assumes the role of family patriarch. He helps Nikolaus realize his dream of studying at a technical school, and he implicitly promises to take care of the family. Silvelie confides to her sister that Andi is the benevolent presence they all so desperately need: "He has ordered everything and made amends."[101]

It is only when Andi assumes his official post as town judge that he changes his mind and insists that the past is very much present. After he reads the Lauretz file, he is convinced that Silvelie's father did not die a natural death. When he confronts her, she refuses to talk about the matter: "My father is dead, for me, for everyone."[102] Earlier she had been willing to tell him the truth, but now she warns against digging too deeply into the circumstances surrounding her father's death: "Leave the past alone or it will bring misfortune to you and me!"[103] Now that Andi is a public official and not simply a husband, he feels obligated to seek justice "whatever the price," because "law must remain law."[104] He tells his wife that duty comes first because "We cannot live in an unclean world."[105] Silvelie is not convinced that law and justice are the same thing, and she fears that if Andi continues with an investigation, "Law will triumph and the people will be destroyed."[106]

The web of guilt and intrigue becomes more and more tangled as each member of the family confesses to the murder in order to save the others from harm. They all earnestly admit that they harbored ill will against Lauretz and considered killing him. From the onset, they realized that Lauretz's murder was not the act of an individual. Regardless of who actually killed the beast, they all wanted him dead. Even in their first interrogation with the old judge, they stressed how they belonged together and deserved the same fate. No one could be singled out because they all suffered the tyrant's wrath and therefore had to stick together until the bitter end. Hanna argues that the murder was a form of collective wish fulfillment and therefore no one can assign blame to any individual: "Mentally every one of us killed him. Mentally every one of us is guilty. If any one of us killed him, then he did our deed and is no more guilty than we are."[107]

In a surprise announcement, Bündner confesses that he killed Lauretz on that fateful night by pushing him off the bridge into the abyss. Unlike the family members, who were victims of abuse and wanted to kill their oppressor out of hatred, Bündner acted out of love for Silvelie. At first he wanted to believe that he was doing a selfless and valiant deed by rescuing her from a living hell, but he soon realized that the murder was motivated by his own egocentric need to keep Silvelie nearby. It is this injustice that gnaws at his conscience, the recognition that he acted out of selfishness, rather than the remorse over murder. Bündner is compelled to acknowledge his actions because: "Injustice tears into a person like the saw into the log."[108]

Because they all had imagined killing Lauretz, they believe they are all equally guilty of the crime. As if the real-life murder was merely the logical consequence of their collective imagination, the family accepts Bündner's act as necessary. Most striking in this higher justice is that they exonerate him of any wrongdoing and seem to accept that he will not be punished. Hanna states for the record, "If he is guilty, then we all are."[109] Frau Lauretz admits her own culpability and says, "God forgive him and us."[110] Even the judge agrees with his wife when she grants the murderer an acquittal (*Freispruch*), so that Bündner's final words seem rhetorical: "Then I can stand before any judge with a peaceful heart."[111]

Via Mala anticipates the central moral crisis of postwar Germany: collective guilt and coming to grips with the past (*Vergangenheitsbewältigung*). In *Via Mala* Baky has created a problem film that encapsulates the defining myth of German national identity as told in the ruins of the fallen Reich. The father figure in this parable of tyranny bears a remarkable resemblance to the image of Adolf Hitler that would emerge on the pages of history books years later. Like Jonas Lauretz, a monster who brutalizes the innocent in his mad drive for intoxication, Hitler would be characterized as a psychopathic god spreading the pathology of evil, a behemoth intent on destroying everything in its path on the quest for ecstatic power.[112] However, the fantasy of patricide and the overthrow of tyranny remained just that, a fantasy never actualized in the film or in reality.

While today's viewer with the benefit of hindsight may accept more easily the parallels between Baky's film and Germany's painful coming to grips with its dictatorial past, it is highly unlikely that the contemporary viewer in 1945 would have been oblivious to the self-referential aspects of *Via Mala*. The pervasive violence directed against those defined not only as weak and innocent but also as family members allowed the viewer to identify with the victims as "one of us." Nazi Germany valorized Adolf Hitler as more than just a statesman and national leader; the Führer was seen as an authoritarian father figure destined to protect the national family (*Volksgemeinschaft*). The cinema in particular fostered the image of Hitler and previous heads of state as the national patriarch in such films as *Triumph des Willens* (1935), *Ohm Krüger* (1941), and *Der große König* (1942). Moviegoers so familiar with symbolic father figures and the increasing horrors of Nazi dictatorship would not need to stretch their imaginations all too far to make a comparison between Lauretz and Hitler. The allegorical nature of *Via Mala,* the troubled family as a synecdoche for the German nation, is most clearly seen in the figure of Silvelie. With her crown of blond braids and pure heart, Silvelie is like Germania, the female personification of Germany rendered in antiquity as the sorrowful prisoner, in the middle ages as the venerated queen, and in the nineteenth century as the triumphant warrior. The family and community members feel obligated to protect this innocent young woman at all costs because she represents all that is good in each of them. She tames the beast, comforts the sorrowful, and restores honor to the downtrodden. Lauretz's fate is sealed when he beats Silvelie; the assault on Germania can never be pardoned.

The identity of the murderer, his motivation, and his punishment are essential to *Via Mala,* not only as mystery conventions but also as guideposts for the viewer to debate moral issues and consider the validity of behavioral models. The propaganda ministry recognized the importance of these questions because it ordered Baky to reshoot the film's ending. Baky's first version had already deviated from John Knittel's original 1934 novel in which the entire family except Silvelie conspired together to kill Lauretz. In Baky's first version, Bündner confessed to the murder and then threw himself from the same bridge where he had killed Lauretz, in effect taking on the roles of both judge and executioner.[113] The evildoer who commits suicide in a chivalrous act of self-sacrifice to grant his loved ones a free conscience and closure was not without precedence in Nazi cinema.[114] So why did the propaganda ministry insist on a new ending? By having Bündner tried not in a court of law but by the family, the film conforms to National Socialist concepts of a higher justice. According to this unwritten law, the individual must behave according to his beliefs and popular customs while the community decides whether he acted in good faith or not. Bündner confesses that he was motivated by self-interest, putting his own desires first and not considering the good of the whole. It is this crime, his failure to conform to the ideal of the *Volksgemeinschaft,* that the people's court exonerates. Hanna, Nikolaus, and their mother all agree that Bündner's murderous deed fulfilled the community's will and that he therefore deserves to be set free. Bündner's acquittal suggests that the end justifies the means. Murder is a legitimate action if the perpetrator believed in what he was doing and the community benefited from the elimination of an evil monster. This master narrative, in which the enemy was vilified as a non-human destructive force justifiably killed in order to serve the greater good, had a long and rich tradition in German cinema. In films ranging from *Der Golem, wie er in die Welt kam* (1920) and *Nosferatu: Eine Symphonie des Grauens* (1921) to *Jud Süß* (1940) and *Heimkehr* (1941), a parade of monsters who terrorized the homeland were defeated by innocence and self-sacrifice. This potent national narrative, used so effectively in 1940 to justify the murder of the Jewish racial enemy and in 1941 to warrant military aggression against the sub-human Eastern barbarian, was recycled in 1944–45 to call for the murder of an enemy within, the evil father intent on destroying all that the family holds dear.

Film critic Werner Sudendorf recently wrote that "with its intention to sweep under the table the question of collective guilt and an unmastered past, [*Via Mala*] is a permanent retraction of previously biased fundamental positions. [. . .] As such the film gets caught up in a web of contentions and principles."[115] Indeed, *Via Mala* seems to be caught between two time periods, and while it begins the discussion of a collective past, it is marked by the propaganda ministry's imprint. On the one hand, Baky's film exposes the physical and psychological scars that tyranny has left on its victims. Norbert Grob has suggested that *Via Mala* is "a film of aesthetic resistance," because it "presents an image of the rawest violence, an image of terror, and of the wounds and pain that this terror has caused in the people surrounding it."[116] On the other hand, the victims never actually enact their fantasy of tyrannicide, leaving the deed to an outsider. Most significantly, Baky's film provides a limited forum for a debate on the past because the happy ending demands closure without delving too deeply into the question of personal and collective responsibility.

Via Mala demonstrates what Alexander and Margarete Mitscherlich have described as Germany's "inability to mourn." In their psychological study, first published in 1967, the Mitscherlichs analyzed how postwar German society refused to accept collective responsibility for its immediate past and the genocide and world war perpetrated in the name of National Socialism. Germany, they argued, "did not succumb to melancholia; instead, as a group, those who had lost their 'ideal leader,' the representative of a commonly shared ego-ideal, managed to avoid self-devaluation by breaking all effective bridges to the immediate past." Germans as a group refused to mourn the loss of their national patriarch and assigned all guilt to this one omnipotent individual because "any minority, when everything that is evil and dangerous has been projected onto it, can be persecuted with impunity." Until the nation overcame "the instinctive and unconscious self-protective forces of forgetting, denying, projecting, and other similar defense mechanisms," it could never come to grips with its own past.[117] *Via Mala* mirrors this process of denying the past and collective guilt. Lauretz's murder is justified because he is a demonic monster: "Everything evil stems from him."[118] The moral imperative, "I cannot forget, I may not," is quickly replaced with the urgent warning to: "Leave the past alone or it will bring misfortune to you and me!" Whereas the Lauretz family admits psychological culpability ("Mentally every one of us killed him"), their deed nonetheless remains in the realm of thought, and therefore the guilt in their hearts must in the end be construed as innocence. The admission of collective guilt is immediately retracted when they grant Bündner (and themselves) an acquittal, because as Fritz Göttler has noted, "The coming generation will refuse to sit in judgment because otherwise it must condemn itself."[119]

Via Mala teaches the viewer that the horrible past, years of brutalization and hatred, can now be forgotten, because an outsider confessed to wrong-doing. Murder is stylized as an act of love rather than hate, regrettable but plainly the only recourse in a society ruled by a higher sense of justice but beset with ineffective moral and legal leadership. All evil stems from one mad and violent patriarch. The murderers are all victims and collective guilt is swept away to the dustbin of history. Everyone forgives everyone else their sins because they are all sinners at heart. The murderous past simply disappears.

A Happy Ending?

"What do you want to see in film: problems or entertainment without problems, destinies from real everyday life or from an improbable world in which all wishes are fulfilled, idle loafers in a rich milieu or working people in a working world?"[120] When faced with such a rigid either/or, reality or dream world, the vast majority of moviegoers, critics, filmmakers, and actors in 1939 voted for reality. The public wanted to see movies about contemporary life, engaging stories that shed light on the times, and also showed sympathetic characters dealing with problems they knew about from their own lives. Motion pictures need to engage the viewer and offer identification opportunities, because, according to director Carl Froelich: "The fate unfolding up there on the screen before us should and must be so strong that it simply forces us to feel that we are one with the performers, to make their experience our own."[121]

Moviegoers and critics generally agreed that great films were not made on the either/or principle; they needed equal parts of reality and fantasy. A faithful rendering of everyday circumstances without some measure of imagination could be journalism but never art. Popular actor Heinz Rühmann suggested an approach that offered a middle ground: "Reality as dream world! Film should show real life but in a more relaxed form."[122] One viewer summarized the prevailing outlook: "Film should not be a pale imitation of reality but rather should idealize everyday life, demonstrate the meaning of daily work, show our neighbors and ourselves in those moments in which we possess universal validity and become types. Accentuate stronger than reality does! Show our world very small and very great, heroism and brutality! But always our world: how it is and how it could be."[123]

While there was a general consensus that cinema should focus on reality, there was no consensus on what "reality" meant. Most writers wanted movies about the present, but they also demanded a highly optimistic approach to a difficult, if not grim, existence. For example, one viewer argued that the following story line reflected everyday reality in 1939 Germany: "An honest worker who earns his modest bread with daily hard labor is always satisfied and retires at seventy-five with an old-age pension of 60 RM. He is nevertheless thankful to God or fate and certainly does not need to be naïve but rather a philosopher of life, who is above wealth and the good life and is happy with what remains: forest, field, military, art, maybe even his laughter."[124]

The scenario of the happy worker struggling all his life to survive but content with his meager lot is a prescription for national socialist realism that would surely have gained favor from both Hitler and Goebbels. The Führer and the Propaganda Minister repeatedly called for films about the present, but they were by no means issuing an open invitation to filmmakers to criticize party ideology or social institutions. They wanted a selective form of realism that would include positive heroes, an optimistic portrayal of the working world, an innovative but easily understood style (*Volkstümlichkeit*), and films infused with the universal values inherent in Nazi politics (*Parteilichkeit*).[125] This formula for realism dominated the critical debate and also explains why the problem films under discussion failed to reach a mass audience in the Third Reich.

Das Leben kann so schön sein, Der verzauberte Tag, and *Via Mala* do not present positive role models and a rosy, optimistic world in which everyone is satisfied with their fate. Despite their different approaches and styles, all three films showcase ordinary people who dream of a better life but are left with so many unfulfilled wishes that succumb to defeatism. These films resolve conflicts with a happy ending, but the characters' sudden outbursts and small gestures convey more honesty than any contrived narrative closure. The forlorn voices of Nora, Anni, Christine, and Silvelie resonate long after the movies are over and encapsulate a pervasive desperation with everyday life. Nora's "Sometimes I get so fed up," Anni's, "We're not going to live very long anyway," Christine's "There has to be something else," and Silvelie's "Dear God, how are we supposed to endure this? I can't stand it any longer," defy the forced optimism and disingenuousness imposed on problem films to mitigate their social criticism.[126] It is difficult, if not impossible, to forget the image of Silvelie hugging the chimney in a world without human warmth or Nora gently rocking her sewing box hoping her husband will one day want their baby. These small gestures speak volumes about the acute need for love and simple acts of kindness.

The characters' emotional, economic, and existential conflicts are not resolved by any structural changes in society but by the sudden conversion of a single man who comes to his senses in the nick of time. In the last minute, Hannes recognizes his own foolishness and vows to start anew, Götz sees Christine as if for the first time and falls madly in love with her, and Bündner confesses to a crime everyone wanted to commit and is miraculously exonerated of any guilt. The resolution of conflicts via the "happy ending" contradicted the basic project of the problem film: to expose those areas of a failed social contract that required a far-reaching collective solution. The very concept of a happy ending was widely debated in the trade press and closely linked to the consumer-driven Hollywood film industry. Writing for *Licht-Bild-Bühne* in March 1939, Hans Joachim Neitzke summarized the dominant critical stance:

> The term originally comes from America where it developed in film production from a catch phrase for the cheap concession to public taste to a business principle. For the German public it became a measure of worth that contained a specific meaning: "happy end" at all costs, even if it demonstrates the absurdity in the inner logic of the film events: the optimism of "keep smiling," even if the theme is serious and tragic. [. . .] The German has never cherished a preference for such optimism, which transfigures everything in a rosy light, and today he is less likely to cherish it than ever before. Not because he is inherently a pessimist, but rather because he is actually an optimist. But an optimist based on a heart that remains intact, an unbroken vitality. He looks at things straight in the eye, not to make conciliatory compliments but to discuss them seriously. *He acknowledges the ethical battle conditions of life.*[127]

The critics wanted well-crafted stories and argued that a harmonious resolution had to evolve out of the circumstances rather than be tacked onto the end of the film. However, they seemed to agree with the propaganda ministry's censors that motion pictures should provide positive role models, so that viewers could develop further their innate steely optimism and triumph over the "ethical battle conditions of life." *Das Leben kann so schön sein, Der verzauberte Tag,* and *Via Mala* failed on both accounts. The happy endings attached to these films are so incongruous with the main plot that they actually call attention to unresolved problems. Moreover, these films display a deeply rooted pessimism and portray men and women who are all too human, weak, desperate, obsessed, and violent.

The female characters are ordinary young women who work in ordinary jobs: a seamstress, a salesgirl, and a hotel maid. But they display a restlessness and determination seldom seen in German motion pictures of the 1930s and 1940s. Above all their relentless quest for autonomy, economic independence, sexual pleasure, and spiritual comfort define them and capture the spirit of their times. Nora, Christine, Anni, and even Silvelie express desires that are most often left unspoken in the cinema because they contradict the notion of a nation gladly sacrificing individual fulfillment for the good of the whole. The young women in these problem films find it increasingly difficult to suppress their basic needs; they crave a space of their own and the right to roam unfettered. They struggle against the monotony, conformity, and violence of everyday life in Nazi Germany, a struggle that does not easily comply with the state's ideological agenda or the popular image of social harmony found in so many motion pictures.

The male characters also deviate from the standard gender role models found in feature films of the Third Reich. Rarely did viewers encounter young men like Hannes and Nikolaus who had lost all faith in the future and were paralyzed by the fear of arbitrary violence. These young men do not readily accept social responsibilities nor do they defend themselves, and yet they do not receive the typical punishment awaiting men found to be inadequate. Death is the fate for most weak male characters in Nazi cinema, but Hannes and Nikolaus continue to survive by depending on robust young women and capable older men for strength and guidance.[128] The middle-aged male characters fall equally short when measured against the unrealistic standards of masculinity prevalent in Nazi Germany. Like the young men, Bündner is a remarkably passive character. Although he secretly kills Lauretz, he is no man of action; he allows the woman he loves to be savagely beaten and never gathers enough courage to propose marriage until it is too late. Although men like the postal official Meier and the accountant Krummholz have established professional careers, they are so obsessed with order that they have no close personal relationships. These petty bureaucrats invest so much of their egos into a rigid world outlook that they lose all sense of who they are when reality intrudes upon their schedules and carefully laid plans. Meier remains a laughable stereotype, but Krummholz loses control completely and becomes a violent criminal. The drunkard Jonas Lauretz, by contrast, is no petty tyrant; he is a true tyrant who forces his own savage order on the weak and helpless. This violent man without any apparent redeeming qualities dies a violent death and will never be mourned. The positive male hero is conspicuously missing from the problem film. The one male character who comes closest to the ideal of honor and resolve is the judge Andreas von Richenau, but his status as an outsider who "has ordered everything and made amends" seems to indicate that in 1945 society needed an external solution to its internal problems.

All three films thematize memory and illustrate how the past continues to inform the present. In both *Das Leben kann so schön sein* and *Der verzauberte Tag* the process of remembering is depicted in omniscient flashbacks that allow the male characters to re-evaluate their lives. Hannes relives his first year of marriage and the very act of narration grants him the necessary distance to work through his fears. Memory is rendered in a way that empowers Hannes to see across time. Each memory sequence begins with an extreme close-up of Hannes's eyes as he conjures up a past that is then superimposed on his present. By visualizing the past and his role in it at the same time as he watches himself, Hannes can see where he went wrong and can imagine a different future. Götz also remembers the recent past in a single flashback, and through the process of recollection, embedding himself like a character in a movie while retaining his position as observer, he is finally able to see the world clearly and can picture a future with Christine. In *Via Mala,* by contrast, memory is repeatedly blocked. In Baky's film the past is over and done, it is never revisited through flashbacks, visual replay, or acoustic reminders. No one except Silvelie wants to recall what has happened; they all want to bury the past and start over with a clean slate. Silvelie's attempts to broach the topic are met with such resistance that she eventually gives up. When the past is momentarily made present it does not help the Lauretz family members to come to grips with their own actions. Only Andi, an outsider for whom the events hold no personal significance, witnesses Bündner's confession and walk through the crime scene. The other characters do not take part in this recollection process and do not see it as a means to re-evaluate their own past and change their present. The most striking difference between these three films is that *Das Leben kann so schön sein* and *Der verzauberte Tag* deal with a personal history and characters who want to learn from their past mistakes to change the way they think in the present, while *Via Mala* deals with a collective history and characters who seek redemption without remorse. Although *Via Mala* had the potential to initiate a healthy debate about the immediate past, it fails because it remained a product of its time, a project torn by too many conflicting agendas. Its linear narrative style stalls the active process of memory, which calls for critical distance, analysis, and reflection so that the past remains past.

The problem films discussed here reveal compelling social fantasies that were deemed too unruly to explore in their current form. In essence, they delivered the honest assessment of contemporary society that the genre promised. In 1938 the fear of the future and the overwhelming sense of impending disaster were overshadowed by an equally powerful belief that with sufficient economic resources the individual could protect himself and his family from the outside world. *Das Leben kann so schön sein* shows just how compelling National Socialism's promises were to the ordinary man. The dream of a good job, consumer goods, and a home on the outskirts of Berlin, a private sphere still located in the real world, was the price for conformity. In exchange for the ability to retreat inward, the ordinary citizen implicitly promised to retreat from political engagement. By 1944 the tangible effects of world war had left their mark on the cinematic imagination, but the pervasive sense of loss was still countered by a stubborn insistence on preserving hope for a better future. *Der verzauberte Tag* expresses the longing for a world beyond the here and now, a place where one can enjoy financial independence, freedom, and romance. This utopian fantasy is nearly devoid of any specific references to contemporary life in the bombed-out cities of war-torn Germany. The reality of 1944, days consumed with monotonous labor and nights spent worrying about loved ones, was so incongruous with this fantasy of hope that it appeared as a mere trace. The present seemed to hold so little promise that it could not be accommodated by anything less than an urban fairy tale, where destiny reigns and wishes come true. By 1945 the social fantasy has left the modern metropolis for the safety of the mountains, leaving behind the complex problems of everyday life in the cities to concentrate on the microcosm of mythic village life. *Via Mala* begins as a nightmare unfolding in a hellish world where a cruel father attacks his own children. By killing the oppressor, the survivors free themselves from the curse of the past and can live happily ever after in their own beautiful, isolated world. All of these films voice the ardent wish to retreat into a private sphere, and as contemporary problems impinged more and more on the lives of individuals, the social fantasies became less and less anchored in a specific reality. As German cities were bombed and its armies were retreating on all fronts, the cinema of the Third Reich encouraged viewers to conjure up their own private world. Heinz Rühmann's concluding remarks in *Die Feuerzangenbowle* (The Punch Bowl, 1944) encapsulate the successful formula for popular cinema and for survival as the National Socialist world crumbled: "Truth is only in the memories we carry with us, the dreams we spin, and the desires that drive us. Let us be content with that."[129]

Notes

[1] "Theater, Film, Literatur, Presse, Rundfunk, sie haben alle der Erhaltung der im Wesen unseres Volkstums lebenden Ewigkeitswerte zu dienen." Adolf Hitler, March 23, 1933, Motto, *Der deutsche Film* 3, no. 11 (May 1939): 305.

[2] "Der Film darf also nicht vor der Härte des Tages entweichen und sich in einem Traumland verlieren, das nur in den Gehirnen wirklichkeitsfremder Regisseure und Manuskriptschreiber, sonst aber nirgendwo in der Welt liegt." Joseph Goebbels, Motto, *Der deutsche Film* 3, no. 11 (May 1939): 305.

[3] Thomas Elsaesser and Michael Wedel, eds., *The BFI Companion to German Cinema* (London: British Film Institute, 1999), 120.

[4] Propaganda Minister Goebbels instituted a system of pre-censorship requiring the approval of treatments and scripts before shooting and careful oversight during the shooting and editing to avoid censorship after the completion of a film. These efforts, combined with post-censorship of the final product, a vigilant advertising campaign, and an orchestrated critical response insured that only about two dozen completed films were banned between 1933 and 1945. For an overview of censorship, see Felix Moeller, *Der Filmminister: Goebbels und der Film im Dritten Reich* (Berlin: Henschel, 1998); and Kraft Wetzel and Peter Hagemann, *Zensur: Verbotene deutsche Filme 1933–1945* (Berlin: Volker Spiess, 1978).

[5] "Sie zerstören Illusionen und Identifikationen und stellen Normen und Werte in Frage, statt sie zu bekräftigen, beispielsweise die Geschlechterrollen. Sie plazieren die Zuschauenden via Identifikationsangebote nicht durchgängig in der Gesellschaft, wie das die meisten Filme der NS-Zeit taten, um potentielle Veränderungswünsche

zu neutralisieren." Thomas Schärer, *Filmische Nonkonformität im NS-Staat: Eine Filmreihe 7.–15. April 1997* (Berlin: Freunde der deutschen Kinemathek, 1997), 1.

[6] Rolf Hansen (1904–1991) started his career as an actor in Munich and at the National Theater in Weimar before working as a film editor and directorial assistant for Carl Froelich at the Ufa studios. Hansen had already directed one full-length feature film, the comedy *Gabriele, eins, zwei, drei* (1937) starring Marriane Hoppe and Gustav Fröhlich. He would later gain fame as the director of Zarah Leander's blockbuster melodramas *Der Weg ins Freie* (1941), *Die große Liebe* (1942), and *Damals* (1943).

[7] The original German film titles were *Ultimo, Ein Mensch wird geboren, Glück auf Raten,* and finally *Das Leben kann so schön sein.* Jochen Huth wrote the screenplay based on his own play *Ultimo.*

[8] *Das Leben kann so schön sein,* Censor-Card 50115, Bundesarchiv-Filmarchiv, Berlin. These censor cards provide a description of each scene but not the dialogues. In a chart listing the premieres outside the capital of Berlin, *Licht-Bild-Bühne* notes that *Das Leben kann so schön sein* premiered in Vienna at the Opernkino on December 23, 1938, but it leaves a conspicuously empty space for the date of the Berlin premiere. See "Voranlauf in der Provinz: Erstes Halbjahr der Spielzeit 1938/39," *Licht-Bild-Bühne* 24 (January 28, 1939).

[9] Wetzel, *Zensur,* 90.

[10] "Weil er die Bevölkerungspolitik der Regierung zu sabotieren geeignet ist," qtd. in Wetzel, *Zensur,* 90.

[11] "Der Ufa-Film *Das Leben kann so schön sein* ist verboten worden. Er widerspricht bevölkerungspolitischen Grundsätzen des Nationalsozialismus und steht ihnen z.T. direkt entgegen," qtd. in Wetzel, *Zensur,* 91.

[12] Since Austria was annexed on March 13, 1938, the Austrian film industry and cinemas were already under the same strict censorship guidelines as in effect in Germany proper (*das Altreich*). In 1949 Hansen and Huth attempted to reconstruct the film, which premiered in Hamburg on February 9, 1950, under the title *Eine Frau fürs Leben* (A Wife for Life), but which has not been commercially released in video format. My analysis is based on the reconstructed version *Eine Frau fürs Leben,* available in videocassette at the Bundesarchiv-Filmarchiv, Berlin. All dialogues are taken from the original filmscript available at the Hochschule für Film und Fernsehen "Konrad Wolf" Potsdam-Babelsberg library. See Jochen Huth, *Ein Mensch wird geboren: Ein Film von Jochen Huth nach Motiven aus seiner Komödie des Alltags Ultimo!* (Filmscript, Berlin, [c. 1938] n. pag.).

[13] "Nicht weinen Hannes. Jetzt wird alles gut." Huth, *Ein Mensch wird geboren.*

[14] "Die Menschen, die [Jochen Huth] auf die Bühne stellt, sind Menschen unseres Schlages, unserer Zeit und mit unseren Schicksalsfragen beschäftigt. Ihre Probleme und Lebensfragen liegen nicht in Niemandsland, sondern werden täglich, stündlich von uns erlebt und erlitten." "Sprung von der Reichsautobahn nach Brasilien: Drei neue Filme — *Mann für Mann, Glück auf Raten, Kautschuk,*" *Filmwelt* 41 (October 7, 1938).

[15] "Es ist immer eine problematische Angelegenheit, dem Publikum einen Film zu zeigen, in dem es in seinen eigenen Alltag zurückgeführt wird. Und dann so deutlich und wirklichkeitsnah, wie wir es vorhaben. Schließlich wollen die Menschen abends im Kino abgelenkt werden und einige Illusionen vorfinden." "Ein Film über dich und mich: *Ultimo*," *Filmspiegel* 37 (September 9, 1938), 112–14.

[16] "[D]er wahre Erfolg eines solchen Films, der das Leben nicht beschönigt oder romantisiert, um nicht zu sagen verkitscht, [kann] nur von seiner Wirklichkeitsnähe und seiner Wahrhaftigkeit abhängen." "Sprung von der Reichsautobahn nach Brasilien."

[17] *Eine Frau wie du* (1939, Tourjansky), for example, features a factory social worker (Brigitte Horney) who with a few encouraging words can help workers and their families resolve conflicts. For a brief discussion of working women in German films after 1938, see Bogusław Drewniak, *Der deutsche Film 1938–1945: Ein Gesamtüberblick* (Düsseldorf: Droste, 1987), 261–66.

[18] See Jill Stephenson, *Women in Nazi Germany* (New York: Barnes & Noble, 1975), 84–89, 99–100.

[19] Qtd. in Annemarie Tröger, "The Creation of a Female Assembly-Line Proletariat," in *When Biology Became Destiny: Women in Weimar and Nazi Germany*, ed. Renate Bridenthal, Atina Grossmann, and Marion Kaplan (New York: Monthly Review Press, 1984), 241.

[20] Ian Kershaw notes that about half of the workers in the Bavarian textile industry were women and consumer goods industries in general employed a high percentage of female labor. In a large clothing factory in Upper Bavaria, seamstresses enjoyed a good wage, earning on the average 20–26 RM a week. See Ian Kershaw, *Popular Opinion and Political Dissent in the Third Reich: Bavaria 1933–1945* (Oxford: Oxford UP, 1983), 15–16, 92. See also Norbert Westennieder, *"Deutsche Frauen und Mädchen!" Vom Alltagsleben 1933–1945* (Dusseldorf: Droste, 1990), 66, 70.

[21] Westennieder, *"Deutsche Frauen und Mädchen!"* 71. Whereas by 1936 married women were encouraged to seek employment, in 1938 all single women under the age of twenty-five were required to fulfill a year of service in the agricultural sector or as domestic help. This year of duty (*Pflichtjahr*), instituted for men as early as 1935 and women after 1938, was administrated by the *Reichsarbeitsdienst*.

[22] Hannes: "Wenn ich dreissig Abschlüsse im Monat mache, kann das hundertfünfzig Mark bringen." Nora: "Du wirst mehr machen." Hannes: "Oder weniger. Es liegt nicht nur an mir. Eine Wohnung kostet fünfzig Mark. Essen für uns beide sechzig Mark, bleiben vierzig Mark." Huth, *Ein Mensch wird geboren*.

[23] Westennieder, *"Deutsche Frauen und Mädchen!"* 66.

[24] Avraham Barkai, *Nazi Economics: Ideology, Theory, and Policy*, trans. Ruth Hadass-Vashitz (New Haven: Yale UP, 1990), 256.

[25] "Wenn wir verheiratet sind, dann muß es so schön sein. So schön, wie man es nur verlangen kann vom Leben. Es muß das Glück sein!" Huth, *Ein Mensch wird geboren*.

[26] "Das erste Mal, wo uns keiner stören kann! Wo wir richtig allein sind — im eigenen Heim. . . . Das muss uns allein gehören! Wann, Hannes, wann!" The stage directions read, "Wieder bekommt ihr Gesicht diesen wilden Ausdruck des Hungers." Huth, *Ein Mensch wird geboren*.

[27] "'Und an die Zukunft müssen wir denken. Und da müssen wir eben Prämien bezahlen, wie für jede Versicherung. Und wenn man kein Geld dafür hat wie wir.' Nora greift heftig nach den Rudern: 'Dann zahlt man mit Glück.'" Huth, *Ein Mensch wird geboren.*

[28] In 1938–39 the housing shortage in Augsburg was estimated at 20% with similar shortages in Munich and Nuremberg. Kershaw, *Popular Opinion*, 99.

[29] Westenrieder, *"Deutsche Frauen und Mädchen!"* 63.

[30] "Bilder, die geringe Lebenshaltungskosten und hohe Lebensqualität suggerierten: Gesundheit, Selbstversorgung und Familienidylle und beschauliches 'Glück im Winkel.'" Peter Reichel, *Der schöne Schein des Dritten Reiches: Faszination und Gewalt des Faschismus* (Munich: Hanser, 1991), 309. For a discussion of the discrepancy between Nazi propaganda and the actual housing construction, see also Barbara Miller Lane, *Architecture and Politics in Germany, 1918–1934* (Cambridge, MA: Harvard UP, 1968), 205–12.

[31] For a detailed examination on National Socialist policy on settlements as well as extensive photographs and floorplans, see Ute Peltz-Dreckmann, *Nationalsozialistischer Siedlungsbau: Versuch einer Analyse der die Siedlungspolitik bestimmenden Faktoren am Beispiel des Nationalsozialismus* (Munich: Minerva, 1978).

[32] "Diese Siedlungshäuser sind keine Hütten, sie sind Eigenheime, wie sie früher nur von gutgestellten Bürgern errichtet werden konnten. Die Arbeiter, die in diese Häuser ziehen und in diesen Siedlungen leben werden, sind keine Proleten mehr. Sie rücken auf die Reihe der Bauern, Handwerker und Bürger. Nicht ein Fremdkörper ist der Arbeiter mehr, der verachtet an seiner Stempelstelle steht, sondern ein Volksgenosse in der Gemeinschaft der Schaffenden," qtd. in Sonja Günther, *Das deutsche Heim: Luxusinterieurs und Arbeitermöbel von der Gründerzeit bis zum Dritten Reich,* Werkbund-Archiv 12 (Giessen: Anabas, 1984), 115.

[33] Reichel, *Der schöne Schein*, 308–12.

[34] Detlev J. K. Peukert, *Inside Nazi Germany: Conformity, Opposition, and Racism in Everyday Life,* trans. Richard Deveson (New Haven: Yale UP, 1987), 190.

[35] "Der für das Dritte Reich charakteristische Rückzug in die Familie oder das eigene Haus war von Anfang an mit einem großen Interesse an neuartigen 'amerikanischen' Haushaltsgeräten und Zerstreuungsgütern verbunden." Hans Dieter Schäfer, *Das gespaltene Bewußtsein: Deutsche Kultur und Lebenswirklichkeit,* 3d ed. (Munich: Hanser, 1983), 122.

[36] Richard Grunberger, *The Twelve-Year Reich: A Social History of Nazi Germany, 1933–1945* (New York: Holt, Rinehart & Winston, 1971), qtd. in Schäfer, *Das gespaltene Bewußtsein,* 114.

[37] Michael Burleigh and Wolfgang Wippermann, *The Racial State 1933–1945* (Cambridge: Cambridge UP, 1991), 288; and David Schoenbaum, *Die braune Revolution: Eine Sozialgeschichte des Dritten Reiches,* trans. Tamara Schoenbaum-Holtermann (Berlin: Ullstein, 1999), 126.

[38] "Während die Diktatur die Arbeiterschaft vor allem durch Sicherheit und Aufstiegschancen überzeugte, band sie mittlere und gehobene Schichten außerdem mit einer breiten Konsumgüter-Produktion an sich." Schäfer, *Das gespaltene Bewußtsein,* 117.

[39] Reichel, *Der schöne Schein*, 316.

[40] "Wenn ein Mann nur wüsste, was das für eine Frau bedeutet." Huth, *Ein Mensch wird geboren*.

[41] "Nora: 'Und alles in allem nur siebenhundertfünfzig.' Chef [des Möbelgeschafts]: 'Und doch noch auf Ehestandsdarlehen, na? Macht Heiraten da nicht Spass?'" Huth, *Ein Mensch wird geboren*. The censor cards quote a higher price of 1350 RM but note that the furniture can be purchased with a marriage loan, compare *Das Leben kann so schön sein*, Censor-Card 50115.

[42] "Möbelbesichtigung und Möbelkauf — das sind Dinge, die im Leben aller Heiratslustigen eine große Rolle spielen! Der Film schildert in einer ganzen Reihe von Szenen die Pläne von Hannes und Nora, die immer wieder gerade um diese Dinge kreisen. Unter Berücksichtigung dieser Tatsache dürfte man mit einer großen Möbelfirma bestimmt eine wirkungsvolle Gegenseitigkeits-Werbung vereinbaren und durchführen können." "Praktische Werbe-Vorschläge," *Das Leben kann so schön sein*, advertising materials (Berlin: August Scherl Verlag, n.d.), 6, *Das Leben kann so schön sein*, Document File 9596, Bundesarchiv-Filmarchiv Berlin.

[43] "Als dieses Stück vor Jahren auf der Bühne erschien, war es in seiner Grundtendenz sehr eng mit dem Arbeitslosenproblem verknüpft. . . . Heute ist diese Frage durch die glückliche Wandlung der Umstände völlig außer Kraft getreten." "Sprung von der Reichsautobahn nach Brasilien." When *Das Leben kann so schön sein* was shown in the German Democratic Republic in 1962, the press noted the similarity between Huth's characters and stock figures from the Weimar Republic. Hannes Kolbe was described as a white-collar worker in the crisis period of the late Weimar Republic, who resembled the main character in Hans Fallada's *Kleiner Mann — was nun?*, a novel about an unemployed expectant father published in 1932. See *Das Leben kann so schön sein: Progress-Dienst für Presse und Werbung* (Berlin: VEB Progress Film-Vertrieb, July, 1962), *Das Leben kann so schön sein*, Document File 9596, Bundesarchiv-Filmarchiv, Berlin.

[44] "Zank, Streit, Feindschaft! Anarchie! Das Chaos!" Huth, *Ein Mensch wird geboren*.

[45] "Herr Dewitt, Reisender, wechselnder Branche, hat seine Bude auf Junggesellenart umgemodelt, es fehlen natürlich nicht der unvermeidliche türkische Rauchtisch und die zahlreichen Photos stark ausgezogener junger Damen garantiert einwandfreier Moral." "Der Architekt kann lachen: Stilleben aus Plüsch und Troddeln," *Das Leben kann so schön sein: Ufa Bild- und Textinformation* (Berlin: Ufa-Pressestelle, n.d.) n.p., *Das Leben kann so schön sein*, Document File 9596, Bundesarchiv-Filmarchiv, Berlin. The figure of Dewitt has been reduced significantly from the original screenplay, most likely a result of extensive editing after Hitler's ban. Compare Huth, *Ein Mensch wird geboren* and the videocassette copy *Eine Frau fürs Leben* at the Bundes-archiv-Filmarchiv, Berlin. Since Dewitt is described as "the most tolerable [boarder], an optimist and always cheerful" ["Der Reisende Dewitt ist noch am erträglichsten, er ist Optimist und immer vergnügt"], his scenes with Hannes were probably cut because Hannes confides his fears too openly to the traveling salesman. See *Das Leben kann so schön sein*, *Illustrierter Film-Kurier* 2905 (Berlin: August Scherl Verlag, n.d.).

[46] "Sie sind Zwilling. Unschüssig, schwankend, himmel hoch jauchzend, zu Tode betrübt. Schwächlich veranlagt, eher feige als mutig, mehr Kopf als Herz, sehr vorsichtig und im Ganzen kein Sonnenkind des Glücks." Huth, *Ein Mensch wird geboren.*

[47] "Damit man weiss, wo man hingehört. Es war ja nicht einfach die erste Zeit, wir hatten es uns so anders gedacht — Aber es geht alles. Man gewöhnt sich an alles. Das Leben ist nun mal nicht so leicht, und die Liebe sehen Sie, die Liebe hilft über so viel hinweg. Dann kann man eine Menge ertragen." Huth, *Ein Mensch wird geboren.*

[48] "Kommt alles. Sie sind ja noch so jung. Das Schöne haben Sie alles noch vor sich. Und Raum — ist in der kleinsten Hütte für ein glücklich liebend Paar." Huth, *Ein Mensch wird geboren.*

[49] "Das Leben könnte so schön sein. [. . .] Trau dir schon mehr zu. Hab doch ein bißchen Mut. Es ist nicht gefährlich, man muss nur etwas wagen, tapfer sein, Hannes. [. . .] Glauben muss du an dich." Huth, *Ein Mensch wird geboren.* Note that Nora's statement is in the subjunctive form, while the film's title is in the indicative form.

[50] "Ein Mensch, der vor lauter Sorgen jeglichen Mut verloren, zum Schluß keinen Glauben mehr an seine eigene Arbeitskraft hat und der an seinem mangelden Lebensmut fast zugrunde geht." "Spielleiter sucht Schauspieler," *Das Leben kann so schön sein: Ufa Bild- und Textinformation* (Berlin: Ufa-Pressestelle, n.d.), *Das Leben kann so schön sein,* Document File 9596, Bundesarchiv-Filmarchiv, Berlin.

[51] "Das Leben heutzutage ist so gefährlich. Lesen Sie keine Zeitungen? Stellen Sie sich doch bloss mal vor, was Ihnen alles passieren kann. Und was können Sie dagegen machen? Garnichts. Unfall und Einbruch, Feuer und Krankheit. An jeder Ecke wartet das Pech bloss drauf, dass sie kommen. Auf einer Bananenschale können Sie ausrutschen." Huth, *Ein Mensch wird geboren.*

[52] "Ach wat. Wenn ick so dächte wie Sie, dann käme ick aus dem Zahlen jarnicht mehr raus. Und wat hätte ick davon? Nischt, wie Angst. Mich machsense nicht mehr bange. Ich kenne det Leben. Sind Sie denn nu versichert?" Huth, *Ein Mensch wird geboren.*

[53] Ellen: "Mit euch Männern zusammenleben, ich danke. Die ganzen Illusionen gehen einem zu Teufel." Hannes: "Wir Männer bestehen überhaupt nur aus euren Illusionen! Wenn Sie die brauchen, gehen Sie doch ins Kino." Huth, *Ein Mensch wird geboren.*

[54] "Manchmal habe ich es so satt!" and later, "Ach, manchmal möchte ich schreien." Huth, *Ein Mensch wird geboren.*

[55] "Aber du lässt es mich alleine auskämpfen, nicht wahr? Du stehst nie vor mir, Hannes. Du lässt mich immer alles allein tun." Huth, *Ein Mensch wird geboren.*

[56] "Warum lässt du mich denn so furchtbar allein—mit allem?" Huth, *Ein Mensch wird geboren.*

[57] "Bei jeder Geburt werden zwei Menschen geboren! Das Kind und der Vater!" Huth, *Ein Mensch wird geboren.*

[58] "KdF scheint zu beweisen, daß die Lösung der sozialen Fragen umgangen werden kann, wenn man dem Arbeiter statt mehr Lohn mehr 'Ehre,' statt mehr Freizeit mehr 'Freude,' statt bessere Arbeits- und Lebensbedingungen mehr kleinbürgerliches Selbstgefühl verschafft," qtd. in Ralf Wolz, "Mobilmachung," in *Heimatfront: Kriegsalltag in Deutschland 1939–1945,* ed. Jürgen Engert (Berlin: Nicolai, 1999), 25.

59 *Der verzauberte Tag* premiered in Zurich in 1947 and was shown in a limited run in West Germany in 1951. It was also featured at the Berlin Film Festival retrospectives "Forbidden German Films, 1933–1945" (1978) and "The Director Peter Pewas" (1981), both organized by the Stiftung Deutsche Kinemathek, and at the film series "Filmic Nonconformity in the Nazi State" (1997), organized by the Freunde der Deutschen Kinemathek in Berlin.

60 "In diesem Film werden keine Schönlinge, sondern wirkliche Menschen gezeigt. *Der verzauberte Tag* soll nicht zerstreuen, sondern sammeln und anregen." W. B., "Eine Rechnung, die nicht aufgeht: Dreck oder Gold, sagt Peter Pewas zu seinem ersten Film." Newspaper article, 1943, Peter Pewas, Personal File, Bundesarchiv-Filmarchiv, Berlin.

61 "[Es] soll hier ein Film gestaltet werden, der in gewisser Hinsicht einen neuen Aufriß in der Szenerie und in der Fototechnik bringen wird. Vermieden werden soll — und das möchte ich vorweg betonen — gleisnerisches Gaukel- und Liebesspiel. Ich will gegen jegliche Verflachung energisch ansteuern; die Handlung selbst, die durch starkes und gesundes Empfinden ausgezeichnet ist, kommt mir bei meinen Bemühungen auch entgegen. Es gilt, die Handlung eines jungen Menschen aufzuzeigen, der einer spießbürgerlichen Atmosphäre entrückt werden muß." W. B., "Eine Rechnung, die nicht aufgeht."

62 "Es ist Frühlingszeit. Über Nacht ging ein warmer Regen nieder und brachte die letzten Blüten auf. Die Bäume regen sich, und übermutig sind die Brunnen, die Vögel singen, und Sehnsucht ist überall. Durch diese Scheiben ist Stille. Hier liegt ein junger Mensch, Christine, vom Frühling wundersam verwandelt und nun zerstört. Sie fiebert. Die Hände suchen einen Brief, der in der Nacht des Unglücks, so sagt man, aus ihrer Manteltasche fiel. Die Schwester hat ihn schon längst gefunden. Der Fremde nimmt ihn und erschrickt. Fast zögernd sieht er seine Anschrift. Er öffnet ihn. In eine andere Welt versinkend liest er von einem Frühlingstag, wo ein Verhängnis schicksalhaft und unhörbar heraufzieht wie der Schatten einer Wolke." All dialogues quoted here are taken from the 35-mm film print of *Der verzauberte Tag* available at Bundesarchiv-Filmarchiv, Berlin.

63 "Anni, geht's dir manchmal auch so? Du denkst, mit dem Zug, der jetzt einläuft, kommt etwas, worauf du die ganze Zeit gewartet hast. Du weißt nicht, was es ist, kannst es doch nicht beschreiben. Du weißt nur . . . jedenfalls soviel wie, es muß etwas anders geben als . . ." *Der verzauberte Tag* film dialogue.

64 "Wenn man etwas vom Herzen wünscht, geht es in Erfüllung." *Der verzauberte Tag* film dialogue.

65 "Für mich war es einfach die Erkenntnis, daß ein Mensch doch zu mir gehört. Mein Leben wird einen neuen Weg nehmen." *Der verzauberte Tag* film dialogue.

66 "Eine junge Frau kannst du dir ziehen, nicht. Man muß ihr nur helfen, sie in ihre Hausfrauenpflichten einzuleben. Übrigens, gut gesagt, huh?" *Der verzauberte Tag* film dialogue.

67 "Ich sehe alles einfach verschleiert." *Der verzauberte Tag* film dialogue.

68 Women are described as "Spekulanten auf ein möglichst bequemes Leben" and a successful man as "ein begehrtes Objekt." *Der verzauberte Tag* film dialogue.

[69] "Für den Künstler ist die Frau das interessanteste Objekt. Sie ist wie die Natur, unergründlich, unberechenbar und voller Geheimnisse." *Der verzauberte Tag* film dialogue.

[70] Laura Mulvey, *Visual and Other Pleasures* (Bloomington: Indiana UP, 1989), 19.

[71] Mary Ann Doane, "Film and the Masquerade: Theorizing the Female Spectator," in *Issues in Feminist Film Criticism,* ed. Patricia Erens (Bloomington: Indiana UP, 1990), 50 and 51.

[72] "Sind Sie mal gemalt worden?" *Der verzauberte Tag* film dialogue.

[73] "Von perfekten Rosen kann man nicht leben." *Der verzauberte Tag* film dialogue.

[74] "[Das Mädchen führt] seinem Wunschtraum aus allen möglichen Vorkommnissen des Alltags ichbezogen solange Nahrung zu, bis es nicht mehr zwischen Traum und Wirklichkeit unterscheidet und in ein Erlebnis hineingezogen wird, das beinahe einen tragischen Ausgang genommen hätte." Hermann Hacker, "Der gefährliche Wunschtraum: Zu dem Terra-Film *Der verzauberte Tag.*" *Der verzauberte Tag Presse-Heft* (Berlin: Inland-Pressedienst bei der deutschen Filmvertriebs-GmbH, n.d.), 11, *Der verzauberte Tag,* Document file 18397, Bundesarchiv-Filmarchiv, Berlin.

[75] Anni tells everyone she has a "Märchenprinzen," "weil ich es mir so sehr wünsche." *Der verzauberte Tag* film dialogue.

[76] Anni says: "Heiraten? Versorgt sein? Schön wäre es." Wasner encourages her, "dann sind vielleicht schon Kinder da, und du bist älter geworden und ruhiger." *Der verzauberte Tag* film dialogue.

[77] "Von meiner Mutter habe ich jetzt gelernt, was es heißt, von früh bis spät auf den Beinen zu sein und dann die Besorgnis um das nötige Geld." *Der verzauberte Tag* film dialogue.

[78] "Warum bin ich kein Mann? Als Mann hat man doch die Möglichkeit, die größten Ideen zu verwirklichen." *Der verzauberte Tag* film dialogue.

[79] "Vielleicht hat sie andere Wünsche." *Der verzauberte Tag* film dialogue.

[80] "Es war wie ein Wunder. Ich bin nicht leichtsinnig. Ich habe an das Walten des Schicksals geglaubt wie an etwas Heiliges." The final lines of her letter are revealed later: "Du wirst mich verstehen. Das Schicksal hat mich zum Narren gehalten, daß ich mich schäme. Wir dürfen uns nie wiedersehen." *Der verzauberte Tag* film dialogue.

[81] "Wenn du dich nachts hier auf der Straße herumtreibst, dann wirst du wohl auch wissen, was man von dir will." *Der verzauberte Tag* film dialogue.

[82] "Ich hole mir das, was mir zusteht." *Der verzauberte Tag* film dialogue.

[83] Christine: "Die Augen." Götz: "Nicht sprechen. Ich war blind, aber jetzt sehen sie dich so wie du bist, so wie ich dich liebe." *Der verzauberte Tag* film dialogue.

[84] "*Der verzauberte Tag* bekundet, nach der Kriegswende in Stalingrad und Afrika, den Wunsch nach Wärme, Geborgenheit der ausgebombten Kinogänger und bietet ihnen einen traumhaften Ausblick in die Zukunftslosigkeit, den Verlust der Gegenwart und das Überrollen durch Vergangenheit." Karsten Witte, *Frankfurter Rundschau* (March 26, 1978).

[85] "Menschen unserer Tage, mit unseren Freuden und Sorgen stehen vor uns. Und doch zeigt dieser Film Dinge, die wir im Alltag nicht sehen. Hier fällt gleichsam die Maske von den Gesichtern. Feinste seelische Regungen werden sichtbar und zwingen

zum Miterleben dieses in seiner Alltäglichkeit so ergreifenden Schicksals." Günther Dietrich, "Hinter der Wirklichkeit: Ein Film aus dem Alltag — kein alltäglicher Film," *Der verzauberte Tag Presse-Heft, 7.*

[86] "Es ist schön und nützlich, daß sich dieser Film mit einem Problem auseinandersetzt, dessen Vorkommen nicht damit abgestritten werden kann, daß es in der Welt des Alltags nicht sichtbar in Erscheinung trete. Und ebenso schön ist es, daß der junge Regisseur Peter Pewas, der mit dem "Verzauberten Tag" seine erste große Arbeit vorlegen wird, dies Problem des gefährlichen Wunschtraumes bis zur letzten Konsequenz entwickelt und die Lösung auf natürliche Weise durch die Macht des wirklichen Lebens herbeiführt." Hacker, "Der gefährliche Wunschtraum," 11.

[87] "Die Beurteilung des Films durch die Luftschutzgemeinschaft war überwiegend negativ. Vor allem die männlichen Besucher lehnten den Film scharf ab, weil ihnen der Verlobte der Christine (Ernst Wladow) zu trottelhaft gezeichnet war und auch Hans Stüwe als Prof. Götz nicht überzeugte. Eine Anzahl von weiblichen Besuchern hat diesen Film kritiklos hingenommen, während andere wiederum mit Recht die Frage stellten, was eigentlich mit diesem Film zum Ausdruck gebracht werden soll. Über den Handlungslauf seien sie auch nicht klar. Nur wenige Mitarbeiter des Hauses, die in Führungsaufgaben verschiedener Abteilungen stehen, erkannten die gefährliche Tendenz, die in diesem Film steckt. Sie ergibt sich aus dem Halbweltmilieu, der unerfreulichen Zeichnung des biederen Beamten, der koketten Führung der Anni (Eva-Maria Meinecke) und überhaupt der sehr eindeutig geführten Regie." Letter from Reich Film Intendant Hinkel to Goebbels, dated July 7, 1944, qtd. in Wetzel, *Zensur,* 138. See also Ulrich Kurowski and Andreas Meyer, eds., *Der Filmregisseur Peter Pewas: Materialien und Dokumente* (Berlin: Volker Spiess, 1981), 43, 74.

[88] "Es war nur die Machart, denn der Stoff war absolut genehmigt, war befürwortet worden von oben. Ich hatte immer das Gefühl, die Leute wollten seinerzeit, wo die ganzen Fronten ins Wanken geraten waren, keinen Einbruch an der Kulturfront. Sie wollten keine Formversuche, keine akustischen Versuche, sie wollten Handfestigkeit, da fiel auch das Wort Kulturbolschewismus." Interview with Peter Pewas on January 6, 1978, qtd. in Wetzel, *Zensur,* 40.

[89] "Auf Weisung des Herrn Reichsministers vorläufig zurückgestellt, weil der Stoff zu düster ist," qtd. in Wetzel, *Zensur,* 143.

[90] "Die Filmabteilung sei bereits unterrichtet worden, daß der Film *Via Mala,* der an sich gut beurteilt wurde, wegen seines düstern Charakters zur Zeit zurückgestellt werden muß. Der Film ist nur für das Ausland freigegeben worden," qtd. in Wetzel, *Zensur,* 144.

[91] Erich Kästner wrote in his diary on April 8, 1945: "Auch Harald Braun war nicht müßig. Gestern abend startete er im hiesigen Kino die Welturaufführung des Films *Via Mala,* et tout le village était présent. Denn die Außenaufnahmen wurden im Vorjahr in und bei Mayrhofen gedreht, und so mancher Einwohner hatte, gegen ein kleines Entgelt, als Komparse mitgewirkt. Nun war man gekommen, um das Dorf, die Gegend und sich selber auf der Leinwand wiederzusehen." Erich Kästner, *Notabene 45: Ein Tagebuch,* qtd. in Fritz Göttler, "Westdeutscher Nachkriegsfilm: Land der Väter," in *Geschichte des deutschen Films,* ed. Wolfgang Jacobsen, Anton Kaes, and Hans Helmut Prinzler (Stuttgart: Metzler, 1993), 171. Baky's film premiered under the new title *Via Mala: Die Straße des Bösen* in East Berlin on January 16, 1948.

[92] "Das ist kein Vater, das ist ein Vieh." All dialogues taken from the videocassette copy of *Via Mala* available at the Bundesarchiv-Filmarchiv, Berlin.

[93] "Glaubst du, ich bin gern hier? Glaubst du, ich gehe nicht lieber heute als morgen weg? Dieser Gott verflüchter Müller! — Dann geh doch. Wo soll ich denn hin? Wo soll ich denn hin? Auf die Straße, wo du hingehörst. Ich bin so einmal weggelaufen. Er hat mich wieder geholt. Er findet mich überall. Er läßt mich nicht los. Der Teufel. Der Teufel." *Via Mala* film dialogue.

[94] "Gott soll mich vergessen, wenn ich es ihm vergesse." *Via Mala* film dialogue.

[95] "Deshalb mehr als der Bürgermeister oder der Amtmann. Euch kann man nicht wählen oder absetzen. Ihr seid da. Und es ist ein Glück für das ganze Dorf, daß Ihr da seid. Für jeden, der etwas auf dem Herzen hat." *Via Mala* film dialogue.

[96] "Er ist kein Mensch mehr. Er bringt uns noch um. Sie wissen nicht, was sie da unten in der Mühle für ein Leben führen." *Via Mala* film dialogue.

[97] "Ich habe so Angst. . . . Aber er ist immer da, sobald es dunkelt. Er sitzt in der Ecke am Küchenherd. Er hockt auf dem Holzstapel. Er geht hinter mir zur Mühle. Er lauert an meinem Bett. Ich habe immer Angst." *Via Mala* film dialogue.

[98] "Vielleicht bin ich schlecht. Vielleicht bin ich für meinen Vater . . . Wer weiß es?" *Via Mala* film dialogue.

[99] "Andi: 'Nein, Silvi. Ich weiß, was Du willst. Du denkst an deinen Vater.' Silvelie: 'Ja, bei Tag und bei Nacht.' Andi: 'Ich weiß es. Ich habe mit Herrn Bündner gesprochen. Vor dir, von deinem Vater, von deiner Familie, von der ganzen unglückseligen Vergangenheit. Das liegt hinter dir Silvi. Auch wenn dein Vater verunglückt ist oder irgendwo . . . Du hast mit ihm nichts zu tun. Er liegt unten. Vergiß es, vergiß das alles. Denk nur an mich.' Silvelie: 'Ich kann nicht vergessen, ich darf nicht.'" *Via Mala* film dialogue.

[100] "Ich will, daß die Vergangenheit endlich vergangen ist. Macht einen Strich darunter und versucht von vorne an." *Via Mala* film dialogue.

[101] "Er hat alles geordnet and gutgemacht." *Via Mala* film dialogue.

[102] "Mein Vater is tod, für mich, für alle." *Via Mala* film dialogue.

[103] "Lass die Vergangenheit, oder es gibt ein Unglück für dich und für mich!" *Via Mala* film dialogue.

[104] "Recht muß Recht bleiben . . . um jeden Preis." *Via Mala* film dialogue.

[105] "Wir können nicht leben in einer unsauberen Welt." *Via Mala* film dialogue.

[106] "Das Recht wird siegen und die Menschen werden zugrunde gehen." *Via Mala* film dialogue. Bündner echoes this sentiment later when he speaks to Andi, highlighting that this view of justice takes precedence over Andi's unbending notion that "law must remain law."

[107] "Im Geist hat ihn jeder von uns umgebracht. Im Geist ist jeder von uns schuldig. Wenn irgendeiner ihn umgebracht hat, so hat er unsere Tat getan und dann ist er nicht schuldiger als wir." *Via Mala* film dialogue.

[108] "Ich dachte, sie aus der Hölle zu erlösen. Gewiß wollte ich sie erlösen, aber ich wollte Silvelie um mich haben. Das war das Unrecht. . . . Unrecht zerfrißt den Menschen wie die Säge den Baumstamm." *Via Mala* film dialogue.

[109] "Wenn er schuldig ist, dann sind wir das alle." *Via Mala* film dialogue.

[110] "Gott verzeih ihm und uns." *Via Mala* film dialogue.

[111] "Dann kann ich mich ruhigem Herzen jeden Richter stehen." *Via Mala* film dialogue.

[112] The following book titles illustrate the branch of history that explains Hitler's rise to power and genocidal plans in terms of monsters, sickness, or madness. See Franz L. Neumann, *Behemoth: The Structure and Practice of National Socialism, 1933–1944* (New York: Octagon Books, 1963); Robert G. L. Waite, *The Psychopathic God: Adolf Hitler* (New York: Basic Books, 1977); Edleff H. Schwaab, *Hitler's Mind: A Plunge into Madness* (New York: Praeger, 1992); George Victor, *Hitler: The Pathology of Evil* (Washington, DC: Brassey's, 1998); Fredrick C. Redlich, *Hitler: Diagnosis of a Destructive Prophet* (New York: Oxford UP, 1998). For an excellent outline of the historical debates surrounding Hitler, see Ian Kershaw, *The Nazi Dictatorship: Problems and Perspectives of Interpretation,* 3d ed. (New York: Routledge, Chapman & Hall, 1993).

[113] Bündner's suicide is described in *Via Mala, Das Program von heute* (Berlin: Das Program von heute, Zeitschrift für Film und Theater GmbH, n.d.) and *Via Mala, Illustrierter Film-Kurier* (Berlin: Vereinigte Verlagsgesellschaft Franke & Co., n.d.). While these film programs contain no dates, they were clearly printed in Nazi Germany because these publications were discontinued after World War II. The altered ending is featured in the video copy available at the Bundesarchiv-Filmarchiv, Berlin and described in *Via Mala: Die Straße des Bösen, Illustrierte Film-Bühne* 665 (Munich: Film-Bühne GmbH, n.d.). See *Via Mala,* Document File 18403, Bundesarchiv-Filmarchiv, Berlin.

[114] See *Zu neuen Ufer* (1937) and *Der Weg ins Freie* (1941).

[115] Werner Sudendorf wrote in 1990: "In seiner Absicht, die Frage der Kollektivschuld und der unbewältigten Vergangenheit unter den Tisch zu kehren, ist der Film ein dauernder Widerruf von vorher eingenommenen prinzipiellen Positionen . . . So verheddert sich der Film im Geflecht von Behauptungen und Prinzipien," qtd. in *Das Jahr 1945 und das Kino,* ed. Norbert Grob and Helma Schleif (Berlin: Stiftung deutsche Kinemathek, 1995), 159.

[116] "Er zeichnet ein Bild der rohesten Gewalt, ein Bild des Terrors — und der Wunden und Schmerzen, die dieser Terror in den Menschen drumherum anrichtet. . . . ein Film des ästhetischen Widerstands: auch ein Aufruf zum Tyrannenmord." Norbert Grob, "Die Vergangenheit, sie ruht aber nicht," in *Das Jahr 1945 und das Kino* (Berlin: Stiftung Deutsche Kinemathek, 1995), 32, 33.

[117] Alexander and Margarete Mitscherlich, *The Inability to Mourn: Principles of Collective Behavior,* trans. Beverley R. Placzek (New York: Grove Press, 1984), 26, 18, 15.

[118] "Alles, was schlecht ist, kommt vom ihm." *Via Mala* film dialogue.

[119] "Es wird eine Generation kommen, die sich weigert zum Richter zu werden, sonst müßte sie sich selber verurteilen." Göttler, "Westdeutscher Nachkriegsfilm," 173.

[120] "Was wollen Sie im Film sehen: Probleme oder problemlose Unterhaltung, Schicksale aus dem wirklichen Alltag oder aus einer unwahrscheinlichen, alle Wünsche erfüllenden Welt; Müßiggänger in einem reichen Milieu oder arbeitende Menschen in einer Welt der Arbeit?" Hans Spielhofer, "Wunschtraum oder Wirklichkeit:

Eine Betrachtung über Notwendigkeit und Problematik ihrer Abgrenzung," *Der deutsche Film* 3, no. 11 (May 1939): 317.

[121] "Das Schicksal, das da oben auf der Leinwand an uns vorüberzieht, soll und muß so stark sein, daß es uns einfach zwingt, uns mit den Handelnden eins zu fühlen — ihr Erleben zu dem unseren zu machen." Hete Nebel, "Künstler antworten uns: Professor Carl Froelich: Zeitnahe muß nicht gleichbedeutend mit Gegenwart sein!" *Der deutsche Film* 3, no. 11 (May 1939): 311.

[122] "Die Wirklichkeit als Wunschtraum! — der Film soll das wirkliche Leben zeigen, aber in einer aufgelockerten Form." Heinz Rühmann, "Kurz und bündig," *Der deutsche Film* 3, no. 11 (May 1939): 314.

[123] These viewer remarks were considered so significant that they were quoted twice in the same issue of *Der deutsche Film:* "Der Film soll kein Abklatsch der Wirklichkeit sein, sondern den Alltag idealisieren, den Sinn der täglichen Arbeit aufzeigen, unsere Nachbarn und uns selbst zeigen in Augenblicken, in denen wir Allgemeingültigkeit haben und Typen werden. Stärker akzentuieren also, als es die Wirklichkeit tut! Unsere Welt ganz klein zeigen und ganz groß, Heroismus und Brutalität! Aber immer unsere Welt: wie sie ist, wie sie sein könnte." Spielhofer, "Wunschtraum oder Wirklichkeit," 319; and also Frank Maraun, "Das Ergebnis: Wirklichkeit bevorzugt! Eine Untersuchung über den 'Publikumsgeschmack," *Der deutsche Film* 3, no. 11 (May 1939): 308.

[124] "[Ein Zuschauer] wünscht sich als Helden mal einen braven Arbeiter, der durch tägliche schwere Arbeit sein bescheidenes Brot verdient, immer zufrieden ist und mit 75 Jahren mit 60 RM Invalidenrente davon weiterlebt, trotzdem dankbar ist, Gott oder dem Schicksal, dabei durchaus nicht einfältig zu sein braucht, sondern ein Lebensphilosoph, der über Reichtum und Wohlleben erhaben ist und sich über das freut, was übrigbleibt: Wald, Feld, Militär, Kunst, vielleicht auch sein Lachen." Spielhofer, "Wunschtraum oder Wirklichkeit," 318.

[125] My term "national socialist realism" purposefully plays off the notion of "socialist realism," because they are remarkably similar prescriptive formulas.

[126] Nora: "Manchmal habe ich es so satt!" Huth, *Ein Mensch wird geboren.* Anni: "Wir leben sowieso nicht lange," and Christine: "Es muß etwas anders geben." *Der verzauberte Tag* film dialogue. Silvelie: "Lieber Gott, wie sollen wir das aushalten? Ich kann es nicht mehr ertragen." *Via Mala* film dialogue.

[127] "Aus Amerika übernommen, wo er einst durch die Filmproduktion vom Schlagwort für die billige Konzession an dem "Publikumsgeschmack" zum Geschäftsprinzip avancierte, wurde er beim deutschen Publikum zu einem Wertmesser, der eine bestimmte Bedeutung enthielt: "glückliches Ende" um jeden Preis, mochte es auch die innere Logik der Filmereignisse ad absurdum führen: Optimismus des "keep smiling," mochte die Thematik noch so ernst und tragisch sein. Der deutsche Mensch hat für einen solchen, alle Dinge rosarot verklärende Optimismus noch niemals eine Vorliebe gehegt, und er hegt sie heute weniger denn je. Nicht weil er im Grundzug ein Pessimist wäre, sondern weil er selbst — Optimist ist. Optimist aber aus heil gebliebenem Herzen, aus ungebrochener Lebenskraft. Er blickt den Dingen ins Auge, nicht um ihnen konziliante Komplimente zu machen, sondern um sich ernsthaft mit ihnen auseinanderzusetzen. *Er erkennt die ethischen Kampfbedingungen des Lebens an.*" Hans Joachim

Neitzke, "Rückzug vor der Entscheidung: Happy end — ja oder nein?" *Licht-Bild-Bühne* 65 (March 17, 1939), emphasis in original.

For further contemporaneous articles on the problem film and the happy end, see L. E. D. "Gibt der Film ein falsches Weltbild?" *Licht-Bild-Bühne* Beilage zur Nr. 25/26 (January 29, 1938); Walter Panofsky, "Was will das Publikum auf der Leinwand sehen?" *Film-Kurier* 224 (September 24, 1938); "Problem-Filme? Ja!" *Licht-Bild-Bühne* 24 (January 29, 1940); Theodor Riegler, "Traumbild und Wirklichkeit," *Filmwelt* 6 (February 9, 1940); Walter Panofsky, "Die Sache mit dem happy end: Historische Beispiele zu einem oftdiskutierten Thema," *Film-Kurier* 108 (May 11, 1942); and "Ein Grundproblem der Filmgestaltung: Über den harmonischen Ausklang eines Films," *Film-Kurier* 9 (January 12, 1943).

[128] The drunkard pilot Gaston Thibaut in *Kongo Express* (1939) redeems himself in death, while the artistic weakling Claus Werner drowns as punishment for his treason in *Kolberg* (1945).

[129] "Wahr sind nur die Erinnerungen, die wir mit uns tragen, die Träume, die wir spinnen und die Sehnsüchte, die uns treiben. Damit wollen wir uns bescheiden." *Die Feuerzangenbowle* (1944, Helmut Weiß), film dialogue.

Epilogue

GENRE FILMS APPEALED to mass audiences in the Third Reich and also to the propaganda ministry because they operated successfully on many different levels. These popular motion pictures featuring favorite stars as predictable characters in formulaic narratives were comforting in their familiarity and corresponded in large part to consumerist fantasies of an apolitical realm beyond the here and now. Genre films endorsed the pleasure of repetition and recognition, catering to the desire for stability and epistemological certainty through such mundane experiences as recalling familiar stories, characters, conflicts, and resolutions.

With its divided consciousness, constantly assuring the German people that things remained the same and just as vehemently arguing that a revolution had taken place, National Socialism could not effectively negotiate a logical synthesis of these opposing ideas and did not try to do so. Instead it allowed the competing notions to coexist in a tense fashion, mediated by such institutions as the cinema. With its dreamlike quality and ability to conjure up alternative realities, the cinema could theoretically bridge the gaps in ideology in a non-rational, visceral manner. In a world of changing circumstances and evolving social practices, when the Nazi regime was trying to reshape German society and embark upon imperial conquest, the familiarity of genre cinema was especially reassuring because it could be taken as evidence that the more things change the more they remain the same.

Propaganda Minister Goebbels was equally smitten by genre cinema because it was eminently profitable, reinforced the government's claim that a nonpartisan social arena continued to exist, and could promote a value system compatible with ordinary beliefs while still being conducive to the regime's political agenda. Focusing on heroes who possess traditionally positive personality traits such as loyalty, self-sacrifice, and obedience together with devotion to a higher ideal, hierarchical allegiance, and camaraderie, entertainment films delivered attractive role models. Equally attractive were aberrant characters who flaunt their difference and exist on the margins but typically motivate social cohesion and are justifiably reintegrated into the community or eliminated from it entirely. Such typed characters placed within a recognizable set of events were marketed in the hope that similar stories with similar outcomes could convey steadfast ideas and elicit predictable responses.

Perhaps even more useful than teaching evaluative norms, motion pictures could inspire viewers to adopt general attitudes to harmonize with the goals of

National Socialism. Foremost among these was the stance that personal happiness, when in accord with the needs of the community, could substitute for political empowerment or the relative well-being of those defined as others. Whether imagined as the quiet satisfaction of being alone in a rowboat in *Das Leben kann so schön sein,* the dream of living together in a castle of the heart in *Damals,* or finding temporary shelter in a surrogate family in *Verklungene Melodie,* popular narratives of the Third Reich consistently depict the desire to retreat into a protective shell and self-defined territory. The profound wish to escape the watchful eyes of strangers and the constraints of everyday life is only attainable in fleeting moments, for the spiritual home is like the cinema, a phantasmagoria that is ever-shifting and only recoverable through memory. However, if one recalls the lyrics from one of the most successful wartime musical revues, the feeling can be recaptured. As the song from the ice capade extravaganza *Der weiße Traum* (1943) instructs: "Buy yourself a colorful balloon, take it firmly in your hand, imagine it flying with you to a distant fairytale land — buy yourself a colorful balloon and with some fantasy you will fly to the land of illusion and be happy like never before."[1] Flights of fantasy could transport the willing viewer at any time back to the land of illusion and happiness as reconstituted in the mind's eye. The advice given in this blockbuster film illustrates poignantly that the moviegoer was not considered a passive somnambulist mesmerized and paralyzed by some inescapable trance. Instead it encouraged the audience to become active daydreamers, willingly choosing psychological fantasies to color their world, evoking the sounds and images experienced in the cinema to imagine a painful reality in a more pleasant manner.

Happiness defined as ecstasy expresses the belief in a higher purpose and is routinely linked to musical performances and collective identity. The zealous actor cum revolutionary whipping up the audience emotionally to ignite political passions in *Tanz auf dem Vulkan,* the young musician playing the church organ to lead his fellow soldiers to safety and commending himself to the raging fires of martyrdom in *Wunschkonzert,* and the celebrated singer motivating wounded soldiers to swing to the beat and recommit themselves to battle in *Die große Liebe,* each endorse a form of feverish happiness that rises above individual wishes to forge unity and communal desire.

Finally, *Schadenfreude* or finding joy in other people's pain is an effective strategy to demarcate the lines between us and them and conversely to take delight in erasing those boundaries, if only momentarily. The pleasure in seeing enemies endure ridicule and loss in *Robert und Bertram,* the exquisite beauty of watching a passionate woman dying in *Opfergang,* and the enjoyment of such forbidden pleasures as miscegenation and deviant sexuality in *Kautschuk* or *Frauen für Golden Hill,* encourage viewers to accept and even welcome suffering that is framed as just and ultimately seductive. The marginalization of Jews, asocials, and biological inferiors and their inevitable punishment in popular narratives make suffering, exclusion, and elimination seem like the natural course of events and socially acceptable. Likewise, the pain of redeemable and admirable characters is made meaningful in alluring ways. Routinely, genre films support the view that heroic death in battle for a higher purpose is inherently attractive and commands euphoric adherents because it exalts the common loss of life to the level of the sacred. Consuming other people's pain may be a human preoccupation as old as storytelling itself, but in Nazi Germany it supported institutional violence of untoward dimensions.

Helmut Käutner, generally considered the closest thing Nazi cinema had to an oppositional director, populated his melancholy films with vaguely dissatisfied characters in narratives that constantly go against the grain. In his melodrama *Romanze in Moll* (1943), Käutner gives voice to a skepticism that casts doubt on the very essence of genre cinema in the Third Reich and its claim on happiness. His tragic lovelorn heroine Madeleine poses the trenchant question, "Do we really have a right to happiness?"[2] If happiness is defined as the individual's right to choose affiliations, the freedom to form elective affinities, then a cursory look at Madeleine's life delivers a resounding no. Forced to endure the caged environment of her loveless petty bourgeois marriage, the brutal sexual advances of her husband's employer, and a potentially liberating affair that must nonetheless be rendered in a minor key, her suicidal response in the film's opening scene renders the question moot. In Nazi Germany happiness was not a right but a political tool.

Genre films played a significant role in advancing a mindset that encouraged viewers to filter reality in an agreeable fashion, focusing less attention on the outcome of events than on their emotional content. The historical musical, for example, transforms political and economic discord into social harmony, liberating feelings of frustration and injustice and channeling them into resolutions that restore the status quo. The blockage of social happiness, be it the lack of a genuine leader or the surreptitious influence of the Jew, is surmounted through stirring song and dance routines that advocate emotional succor rather than social change. In a similar manner, home-front films reconstitute war as a battle for culture rather than resources, shifting remote international conflict and violence to the intimate sphere of family and communal entertainment. This genre encourages feverish commitment to a higher ideal as the price for social cohesion and personal fulfillment, frames death and loss in meaningful ways, and tries to assure audiences that universal values continue to exist. Both the historical musical and the home-front film use music to elicit a binding belief and affective connection to events and ideas that transcend rational explanation.

Conversely, various genres center on disturbing pleasures and largely intolerable forms of happiness that threaten to destroy the tenuous social fabric and must be constrained. The adventure film, for instance, casts a rare glimpse at difference, focusing attention on alluring foreign bodies and distant realms. However, the voyeuristic pleasure afforded by the adventure genre is routinely located within moralistic narratives that permit or even wallow in deviance ephemerally, only to discipline and repudiate such delights in the end. As if to disavow foreign temptation, the hero in adventure films typically disenfranchises others, laying claim to their riches and incorporating their distinctiveness into his own. Alien people and places function largely as a compass in both senses of the word, as a device to navigate one's way and as a roundabout journey to the original starting point. Exploration abroad re-establishes the centrality of home and similitude. Likewise, the melodrama depicts the eruption of unacceptable desire within the established order in a highly ambivalent manner, by drawing considerable attention to dissatisfaction and demonstrating the need for alternative lifestyles only to deny their validity later on in categorical terms. Although it dwells on transgression against patriarchal authority, when all is said and done, the melodrama works to reconfirm the stability of the nuclear family and home.

With its prescribed mission to highlight social issues beyond the individual's control and plead for systemic changes, it is ironic that the Propaganda Ministry ever endorsed the problem film and understandable that examples of the genre rarely garnered enough official support to reach the big screen. Like the fewer than two dozen science fiction films that appeared in movie theaters during the Third Reich, the problem film remained a small and challenging genre. Similar to the science fiction genre, which convinces viewers to imagine the world in radical terms, casting off the known and embracing completely different paradigms of the truth, the problem film was potentially too drastic in its call for an alternate reality and thus too subversive. Both the hyper-fantasy of science fiction and the hyper-reality of the problem film would allow the carefully crafted self-image of the National Socialist world to collapse. The limitations of individual genres are emblematic of the limitation of cinema in general. As long as viewers see the reality outside the movie theater as incompatible with the communal fantasies projected onto the screen, then watching motion pictures cannot hope to be a transformative experience.

Nazi cinema shares much with its Hollywood counterpart: a reliance on genre films with mass appeal, highly structured narratives, audience identification and strong emotional attachment, a star system, studio advertising campaigns and a trade press, and most of all, a sensitivity to market forces in order to create and sell products the public wanted to buy. What makes the motion picture industry in the Third Reich unique is that its practitioners were profoundly aware that cinema's ideological potential was not a veneer but at its core, not a hidden agenda but its very essence. It is the coordinated attempt by the Nazi government to control and steer audience reactions, to achieve specific, transparent goals that separates this institution most clearly from the equally profit-driven, consumerist, popular cinema in the United States at the time. The Nazis wanted much more from the cinema than just profit, they hoped for a nearly religious ritual experience that could influence and satisfy the masses in an unprecedented, almost mystical transformation.

Joseph Goebbels did not merely want the cinema to animate entertaining stories to entice the public with appealing fantasies; he also saw cinema as a heuristic tool to cast the world itself as a meaningful story. Under Goebbel's tutelage, the film industry hoped to demonstrate that going to the cinema reveals the moral truth beneath the surface of things and recharges life with the significance, legitimacy, and urgency needed to believe that reality is a coherent and ordered system. It was their keen aspiration to prove that the act of watching motion pictures could inform the viewer's response to reality. However, despite broad oversight of the film industry, the Propaganda Ministry could not guarantee that viewers would receive films according to any preordained schemata. National Socialism's project of enchanting reality through motion pictures and mass culture resonated with the public at various levels, but the cinema could not sustain the broad-based following or absolute universal devotion necessary for a new pseudo-religion. As Max Weber warned in visionary fashion, "If one tries intellectually to construe new religions without a new and genuine prophecy, then . . . [one] will create only fanatical sects but never a genuine community."[3] National Socialism's attempts to re-enchant the world were not foolproof political strategies. Although the cinema in the Third Reich provided outlets for emotional needs, it could not transmit a uniformly acceptable political philosophy and forge a spiritual cohesion necessary to construct and maintain a genuine national community.

Coming to grips with the past, especially a past as destructive as that of Nazi Germany, has important lessons for the present. Goebbels argued often that the best propaganda is invisible and hides its intentions from the audience. At the heart of my book has been an effort to make the machine visible, to illustrate how the art of seduction practiced in movie theaters throughout the German Reich helped maintain the fascist state. It is my hope that this study contributes to an important area of scholarly work by making readers more aware of the powerful ideas behind cultural products often taken for granted as mere entertainment.

Notes

[1] "Kauf' dir einen bunten Luftballon, nimm' ihn fest in deine Hand, stell' dir vor er fliegt mit dir davon in ein fernes Märchenland — kauf' dir einen bunten Luftballon, und mit etwas Phantasie fliegst du in das Land der Illusion und bist glücklich wie noch nie." *Der weiße Traum* (1943, Geza von Cziffra).

[2] "Haben wir wirklich einen Anspruch auf Glück?" *Romanze in Moll* (1940, Helmut Käutner).

[3] Max Weber, "Science as a Vocation," *From Max Weber: Essays in Sociology,* ed. and trans. H. H. Gerth and C. Wright Mills (London: Routledge & K. Paul, 1948), 155.

Works Cited

"Abenteurlicher Kampf um das 'elastische Gold': Zu dem Film *Kautschuk*." *Filmwelt* 45, November 4, 1938.

Albrecht, Gerd. *Nationalsozialistische Filmpolitik: Eine soziologische Untersuchung über die Spielfilme des Dritten Reiches.* Stuttgart: Ferdinand Enke, 1969.

Altman, Rick. *The American Film Musical.* Bloomington: Indiana UP, 1987.

Anders, Franz E. [Franz Eichhorn]. *In der grünen Hölle: Kurbelfahrten durch Brasilien.* Berlin: Scherl, 1937.

Auerbach, Hellmuth. "Der Trommler." In *Das Dritte Reich: Ein Lesebuch zur deutschen Geschichte 1933–1945,* ed. Christoph Studt, 16–18. Munich: C. H. Beck, 1997.

Ayaß, Wolfgang. *"Asoziale" im Nationalsozialismus.* Stuttgart: Klett-Cotta, 1995.

B., W. "Eine Rechnung, die nicht aufgeht: Dreck oder Gold, sagt Peter Pewas zu seinem ersten Film." n.t., n.p., 1943, Peter Pewas Personal File, Bundesarchiv-Filmarchiv, Berlin.

Baird, Jay. *The Mythical World of Nazi Propaganda 1939–1945.* Minneapolis: U of Minnesota P, 1974.

———. *To Die for Germany: Heroes in the Nazi Pantheon.* Bloomington: Indiana UP, 1990.

Baker, Josephine, and Jo Bouillon. *Josephine.* Trans. Mariana Fitzpatrick. New York: Paragon House, 1988.

Bakhtin, Mikhail. *Rabelais and His World.* Trans. Helene Iswolsky. Cambridge, MA: MIT Press, 1968.

Bandmann, Christa, and Joe Hembus. *Klassiker des deutschen Tonfilms, 1930–1960.* Munich: Goldmann, 1980.

Barkai, Avraham. *Nazi Economics: Ideology, Theory, and Policy.* Trans. Ruth Hadass-Vashitz. New Haven: Yale UP, 1990.

Bathrick, David. "Radio und Film für ein modernes Deutschland: Das NS-Wunschkonzert." In *Dschungel Großstadt: Kino und Modernisierung,* ed. Irmbert Schenk. 112–31. Marburg: Schüren, 1999.

Becker, Wolfgang. *Film und Herrschaft.* Berlin: Spiess, 1973.

Belling, Kurt. "Der Film im Fronteinsatz." *Film-Illustrierte,* December 10, 1939.

Benjamin, Walter. *Das Kunstwerk im Zeitalter seiner technischen Reproduzierbarkeit.* Frankfurt a. M.: Suhrkamp, 1963.

———. *Das Passagen-Werk.* Vol. 5 of *Gesammelte Schriften,* ed. Rolf Tiedemann. 2d ed. Frankfurt a. M.: Suhrkamp, 1998.

———. "The Work of Art in the Age of Mechanical Reproduction." In *Illuminations: Essays and Reflections,* ed. Hannah Arendt, trans. Harry Zohn, 217–51. New York: Schocken, 1968.

Beradt, Charlotte. *Das Dritte Reich des Traums.* Frankfurt a. M.: Suhrkamp, 1981.

Berghaus, Günter, ed. *Fascism and Theatre: Comparative Studies on the Aesthetics and Politics of Performance in Europe, 1925–1945.* Providence: Berghahn, 1996.

"Berlins November Uraufführungen." *Licht-Bild-Bühne* 287, December 7, 1938.

Berndt, Alfred-Ingemar. Foreword to *Wir beginnen das Wunschkonzert für die Wehrmacht,* by Heinz Goedecke and Wilhelm Krug. Berlin: Nibelungen, 1940.

Bertram, Hans. *Flug in die Hölle: Bericht von der Bertram-Atlantis Expedition.* Berlin: Drei Masken, 1933.

Beyer, Friedemann. *Die Ufa Stars im Dritten Reich: Frauen für Deutschland.* Munich: Heyne, 1991.

Biedrzynski, Richard. "Liebe, Leid und Luxus." *Völkischer Beobachter,* December 31, 1944, Berlin edition.

Binding, Rudolf. *Der Opfergang.* New York: Prentice Hall, 1934.

Binné, Ingrid. "Was erwartet die deutsche Frau vom Film." *Licht-Bild-Bühne* 135, June 11, 1938.

———. "Was sagt die Frau über Wochenschau und Kulturfilm?" *Licht-Bild-Bühne* 192, August 17, 1938.

———. "Wie sieht die deutsche Frau den ausländischen Film?" *Licht-Bild-Bühne* 170, July 22, 1938.

Birgel, Franz A. "Luis Trenker: A Rebel in the Third Reich?" In *Cultural History through a National Socialist Lens: Essays on the Cinema of the Third Reich,* ed. Robert C. Reimer, 37–64. Rochester, NY: Camden House, 2000.

Birnbaum, Raoul. "Avalokitesvara." Vol. 1 in *The Encyclopedia of Religion,* ed. Mircea Eliade. New York: Macmillan, 1987.

Bloch, Ernst. *Erbschaft dieser Zeit.* Vol. 4 of *Werkausgabe.* Frankurt a. M.: Suhrkamp, 1992.

———. *Heritage of Our Times.* Trans. Neville and Stephen Plaice. Berkeley: U of California P, 1991.

Boberach, Heinz, ed. *Meldungen aus dem Reich: Auswahl geheimen Lageberichten des Sicherheitsdientes der SS 1939–1944,* 17 vols. Berlin: Pawlak Verlag Herrsching, 1965.

Bock, Gisela. "Racism and Sexism in Nazi Germany: Motherhood, Compulsory Sterilization, and the State." In *When Biology Became Destiny: Women in Weimar and Nazi Germany,* ed. Renate Bridenthal, Atina Grossmann, and Marion Kaplan, 271–96. New York: Monthly Review, 1984.

Bono, Francesco. "Glücklich ist, wer vergißt . . . Operette und Film: Analyse einer Beziehung." In *Musik Spektakel Film: Musiktheater und Tanzkultur im deutschen Film 1922–1937,* ed. Katja Uhlenbrok, 29–45. Munich: edition text + kritik, 1998.

Bordwell, David. *Narration in the Fiction Film.* Madison: U of Wisconsin P, 1985.

Bornemann, Hanns. "Der Kampf um *Kautschuk:* Gefahren und Abenteuer miterlebt im Ufa-Palast am Zoo." n.p., n.d. *Kautschuk,* Document File 8701, Bundesarchiv-Filmarchiv, Berlin.

Bredow, Wilfried von, and Rolf Zurek, eds. *Film und Gesellschaft in Deutschland: Dokumente und Materialien.* Hamburg: Hoffmann und Campe, 1975.

Breitenfellner, Kirstin. "Der 'jüdische Fuß' und die 'jüdische Nase': Physiognomik, Medizingeschichte und Antisemitismus im 19. und 20. Jahrhundert." In *Wie ein Monster entsteht: Zur Konstruktion des anderen in Rassismus und Antisemitismus,* eds. Kirsten Breitenfellner and Charlotte Kohn-Ley, 103–20. Bodenheim: Philo, 1998.

Brown, Frederick. *Theater and Revolution: The Culture of the French Stage.* New York: Viking Press, 1980.

Brunhuber, Ludwig. *"Der Opfergang."* n.p., n.d. *Opfergang,* Document File 12480, Bundesarchiv-Filmarchiv Berlin.

Burleigh, Michael, and Wolfgang Wippermann. *The Racial State: Germany 1933–1945.* Cambridge: Cambridge UP, 1991.

Claus, Horst. "Von Gilbert zu Goebbels: Hans Steinhoff zwischen Operette und Tonfilm mit Musik." In *Als die Filme singen lernten: Innovation und Tradition im Musikfilm 1928–1938,* ed. Malte Hagener and Jan Hans, 105–20. Munich: edition text + kritik, 1999.

Clifford Kirkpatrick, *Nazi Germany: Its Women and Family Life.* Indianapolis: Bobbs-Merril, 1938.

Courtade, Francis, and Pierre Cadars. *Geschichte des Films im Dritten Reich.* Munich: Hanser, 1975.

Crew, David F. Introduction to Klaus-Michael Mallmann and Gerhard Paul, "Omniscient, Omnipotent, Omnipresent? Gestapo, Society and Resistance." In *Nazism and German Society, 1933–1945,* ed. David F. Crew, 166. New York: Rutledge, 1994.

D., L. E. "Gibt der Film ein falsches Weltbild?" Beilage zur *Licht-Bild-Bühne* 25/26, January 29, 1938.

Damals, Censor-Card 58689, Bundesarchiv-Filmarchiv, Berlin.

Damals, Illustrierter Film-Kurier 3309. Berlin: Vereinigte Verlagsgesellschaften Franke & Co. KG., n.d.

Damals, Das Program von heute 1871. Berlin: Das Program von heute, Zeitschrift für Film und Theater, n.d.

Damals: Ein Ufa Farbfilm. Berlin: Werbedienst der Deutschen Filmvertrieb-Gesellschaft, n.d. *Damals,* Document File 2525, Bundesarchiv-Filmarchiv Berlin.

Daniel, Jamie Owen. "Reclaiming the 'Terrain of Fantasy': Speculations on Ernst Bloch, Memory, and the Resurgence of Nationalism." In *Not Yet: Reconsidering Ernst Bloch,* ed. Jamie Owen Daniel and Tom Moylan, 53–62. London: Verso, 1997.

Die Degenhardts, Censor-Card 60153, Bundesarchiv-Filmarchiv, Berlin.

Dennis, David B. *Beethoven in German Politics 1870–1989.* New Haven: Yale UP, 1996.

"Das deutsche Filmwesen während des Kriegszustandes." *Der deutsche Film* 4, no. 4 (October 1939): 94–95.

Diehl, Guida. *Die deutsche Frau und der Nationalsozialismus.* 3d ed. Eisenach: Neuland, 1933.

Dietrich, Günther. "Hinter der Wirklichkeit: Ein Film aus dem Alltag — kein alltäglicher Film." *Der verzauberte Tag: Presse-Heft.* Berlin: Inland-Pressedienst bei der deutschen Filmvertriebs-GmbH, n.d. *Der verzauberte Tag,* Document File 18397, Bundesarchiv-Filmarchiv, Berlin.

Doane, Mary Ann. *The Desire to Desire: The Woman's Film of the 1940s.* Bloomington: Indiana UP, 1987.

———. *Femmes Fatales: Feminism, Film Theory, Psychoanalysis.* New York: Routledge, 1991.

———. "Film and the Masquerade: Theorizing the Female Spectator." In *Issues in Feminist Film Criticism,* ed. Patricia Erens, 41–57. Bloomington: Indiana UP, 1990.

Drechsler, Nanny. *Die Funktion der Musik im deutschen Runkfunk, 1933–1945.* Pfaffenweiler: Centaurus, 1988.

Drewniak, Bogusław. *Der deutsche Film 1938–1945: Ein Gesamtüberblick.* Dusseldorf: Droste, 1987.

Dyer, Richard. *Only Entertainment.* New York: Routledge, 1992.

é. "Begegnung mit dem Jenseits: Filmarbeit über die Wüste, das wunderbare Erlebnis des Kameramanns." n.p., n.d. *Verklungene Melodie,* Document File 18268, Bundesarchiv-Filmarchiv, Berlin.

Ebbinghaus, Angelika, ed. *Opfer und Täterinnen: Frauenbiographien des Nationalsozialismus.* Nördlingen: Greno, 1987.

Eberlein, Ludwig. "*Verklungene Melodie:* Ein Tourjansky-Film im Gloria Palast." *Berliner Morgenpost,* n.d. *Verklungene Melodie,* Document File 18268, Bundesarchiv-Filmarchiv, Berlin.

Eichhorn, Franz. "Das große Abenteuer: Kamerabeute am Amazonas." *Licht-Bild-Bühne* 278, November 26, 1938.

Elsaesser Thomas, and Michael Wedel, eds. *The BFI Companion to German Cinema.* London: British Film Institute, 1999.

F., E. "Deutscher Film am Amazonas, Kampf mit Schlangen und Pyranhas, Abenteuer um die Gummimilch." *Licht-Bild-Bühne* 262, November 7, 1938.

Feuer, Jane. *The Hollywood Musical.* 2d ed. Bloomington: Indiana UP, 1993.

———. "The Self-Reflexive Musical and the Myth of Entertainment." In *Film Genre Reader,* ed. Barry Keith Grant, 329–43. Austin: U of Texas P, 1986.

Fiedler, Hans-Ottmar. "Tempo, Spannung, Atmosphäre: Der Spielleiter Eduard v. Borsody und seine Filme." *Filmwelt* 34, August 23, 1940.

Fiedler, Werner. *Deutsche Allgemeine Zeitung,* December 17, 1938, Ausgabe Groß-Berlin.

"Ein Film über dich und mich: *Ultimo.*" *Filmspiegel* 37, September 9, 1938, 112–14.

"Film und Zeitgeschehen: Zu dem Terra-Film *Fronttheater.*" *Der deutsche Film* 7, no. 1 (July 1942): 8–9.

"Der Film in Kriegszeiten: Neue Aufgaben und neue Pläne." *Licht-Bild-Bühne* 245, October 20, 1939.

Film-Kurier 267, November 14, 1938.

Film-Kurier 24, January 28, 1939.

Film-Kurier 28, February 2, 1939.

Film-Kurier 147, June 28, 1939.

"Filme des Monats." *Der deutsche Film* 3, no. 6 (December 1938): 163–64.

"Filme des Monats." *Der deutsche Film* 4, no. 2 (August 1939): 55.

"Filmmusik auf Schallplatten." *Der deutsche Film* 3, no. 12 (June 1939): 360.

Fischer, Hans Erasmus. "Filme, die wir sahen: *Kautschuk.*" *Filmwelt* 48, November 25, 1938.

Foucault, Michel. *Discipline and Punish: The Birth of the Prision.* Trans. Alan Sheridan. New York: Vintage Books, 1979.

Frauen für Golden Hill, Censor-Card 50106, Bundesarchiv-Filmarchiv, Berlin.

Frauen für Golden Hill, Illustrierter Film-Kurier 2907. Berlin: Vereinigte Verlagsgesellschaften Franke & Co., 1938.

Frauen für Golden Hill, Das Programm von heute 326. Berlin: Das Programm von heute: Zeitschrift für Film und Theater, GmbH, 1938.

"Frauen ziehen durch die Wüste: Anmerkungen zu dem Film *Frauen für Golden Hill*." *Filmwelt* 43, October 21, 1938.

Freud, Sigmund. "The Question of Lay Analysis: Conversations with an Impartial Person." Vol. 20 in *The Standard Edition of the Complete Psychological Works of Sigmund Freud*. Ed. and trans. James Strachey. London: Hogarth, 1953.

Freytag, Hartmut, ed. *Der Totentanz der Marienkirche in Lübeck und der Niko-laikirche in Reval (Tallinn)*. Niederdeutsche Studien 39. Cologne: Böhlau, 1993.

Friedländer, Saul. *Reflections of Nazism: An Essay on Kitsch and Death*. Trans. Thomas Weyr. New York: Harper & Row, 1984.

Fürstenau, Theo. *"Die Degenhardts."* *Deutsche Allgemeine Zeitung*, August 13, 1944.

Gay, Peter. *Weimar Culture: The Outsider as Insider*. New York: Harper & Row, 1968.

Gellately, Robert. *The Gestapo and German Society: Enforcing Racial Policy, 1933–1945*. New York: Oxford UP, 1990.

Gilman, Sander. *The Jew's Body*. New York: Routledge, 1991.

Goebbels, Joseph. "Das Kulturleben im Kriege." In *Die Zeit ohne Beispiel: Reden und Aufsätze aus den Jahren 1939/40/41*. Munich: Franz Eher, 1941.

———. Motto, *Der deutsche Film* 3, no. 11 (May 1939): 305.

———. *Reden*. 2 vols. Ed. Helmut Heiber. Dusseldorf: Droste, 1971.

———. *Die Tagebüücher von Joseph Goebbels*. Ed. Elke Fröhlich. Part I: Auf-zeichnungen 1923–1942, 9 vols. Munich: K. G. Saur, 1987–2000.

———. *Die Tagebücher von Joseph Goebbels*. Ed. Elke Fröhlich. Part II: Diktate 1941–1945, 15 vols. Munich: K. G. Saur, 1987–2000.

Goertz, Heinrich. *Gustaf Gründgens*. Reinbek bei Hamburg: Rowohlt, 1982.

Goethe, Johann Wolfgang von. *Wahlverwandtschaften*. Ed. Hans-J. Weitz. Frankfurt a. M.: Insel, 1972.

Gordon, Mel. *Voluptuous Panic: The Erotic World of Weimar Berlin*. Venice, CA: Feral House, 2000.

Göttler, Fritz. "Westdeutscher Nachkriegsfilm: Land der Väter." In *Geschichte des deutschen Films*, ed. Wolfgang Jacobsen, Anton Kaes, and Hans Helmut Prinzler, 171–210. Stuttgart: Metzler, 1993.

Gottschewski, Lydia. *Männerbund und Frauenfrage: Die Frau im neuen Staat*. Munich: J. F. Lehmann, 1934.

Graham, Cooper C. *Leni Riefenstahl and* Olympia. Metuchen, N. J.: Scarecrow Press, 1986.

Graml, Hermann. *Reichskristallnacht: Antisemitismus und Judenverfolgung im Dritten Reich.* 3d ed. Munich: dtv, 1998

Grant, Barry Keith. "Experience and Meaning in Genre Films," *Film Genre Reader,* ed. Barry Keith Grant, 114–28. Austin: U of Texas P, 1986.

Gressieker, Hermann. "Die Parole des deutschen Films." *Der deutsche Film* 4, no. 3 (September 1939): 63–67.

Grob, Norbert, and Helma Schleif, eds. *Das Jahr 1945 und das Kino.* Berlin: Stiftung Deutsche Kinemathek, 1995.

Groote, Paula Siber von. *Die Frauenfrage und ihre Lösung durch den Nationalsozialismus.* Berlin: Kallmeyer, 1933.

"Große Dekoration für Zarah Leander: Bei den Aufnahmen zu dem Ufa-Film *Die große Liebe.*" *Film-Kurier* 30, February 6, 1942.

Die große Liebe, Censor-Card 57295, Bundesarchiv-Filmarchiv, Berlin.

"*Die große Liebe:* Zarah Leander und Paul Hörbiger in einem neuen Film." *Filmwelt* 47/48, November 26, 1941.

Großmann, Christine. "Worin besteht die Wirkung des Films auf die Frauen?" *Licht-Bild-Bühne* 78, April 1, 1938.

Gruchmann, Lothar. *Totaler Krieg: Vom Blitzkrieg zur bedingungsloser Kapitulation.* Munich: dtv, 1991.

Grunberger, Richard. *The Twelve-Year Reich: A Social History of Nazi Germany, 1933–1945.* New York: Holt, Rinehart & Winston, 1971.

"Gründgens im Gespräch." *B.Z. am Mittag,* June 20, 1938.

"Ein Grundproblem der Filmgestaltung: Über den harmonischen Ausklang eines Films." *Film-Kurier* 9, January 12, 1943.

Günther, Sonja. *Das deutsche Heim: Luxusinterieurs und Arbeitermöbel von der Gründerzeit bis zum Dritten Reich.* Werkbund-Archiv 12. Giessen: Anabas, 1984.

Gürtler, Egon. "Weshalb gehen Sie in einen Film?" *Der deutsche Film* 3, no. 11 (May 1939): 316–17 and 325–26.

H., F. "Von der Führung des Schauspielers und ihren Voraussetzungen: Anmerkungen anläßlich der Arbeit Rolf Hansens an dem von ihm inszenierten Ufa-Film 'Damals.'" *Film-Kurier* 282, January 14, 1943.

H., G. "Mit dem Film *Mitternachtswalzer* am Rande der Sahara." *Filmwelt* 49, December 5, 1937.

Hackbarth, Wilhelm. "Das Lied der Hanna Holberg." *Filmwelt* 7/8, February 18, 1942.

Hacker, Hermann. "Der gefährliche Wunschtraum: Zu dem Terra-Film *Der verzauberte Tag.*" *Der verzauberte Tag: Presse-Heft.* Berlin: Inland-Pressedienst bei der deutschen Filmvertriebs-GmbH, n.d. *Der verzauberte Tag,* Document File 18397, Bundesarchiv-Filmarchiv, Berlin.

———. "Der Wechsel der Schauplätze: Blick auf den Zarah-Leander-Film 'Damals.'" *Film-Kurier* 282, December 1, 1942.

Hagemeyer, Hans, ed. *Frau und Mutter: Lebensquell des Volkes.* 2d ed. Munich: Hoheneichen, 1943.

Hahn, H. J. "Auf die Feinheit kommt es an: Kleinigkeit um eine Filmszene." *Filmwoche* 6, February 8, 1939, 174.

Hake, Sabine. *Popular Cinema of the Third Reich.* Austin: U of Texas P, 2001.

Harlan, Veit. *Im Schatten meiner Filme.* Gütersloh: Sigbert Mohn, 1966.

Harmssen, Hennig. "Flucht in die Unterhaltung: Verbote und Unverbindliches bestimmten den deutschen Film im Zweiten Weltkrieg." *Filmspiegel,* June 2, 1985.

Hart-Davis, Duff. *Hitler's Games: The 1936 Olympics.* London: Century, 1986.

Harvester, M. "Wer war Debureau?" *Licht-Bild-Bühne* 296, December 17, 1938.

Haskell, Molly. *From Reverence to Rape: The Treatment of Women in the Movies.* New York: Holt, Rinehart, and Winston, 1973.

Hauschild, Thomas, ed. *Lebenslust und Fremdenfurcht: Enthnologie im Dritten Reich.* Frankfurt a. M.: Suhrkamp, 1995.

Heil de Brentani, Mario. "Über den Volksfilm *Robert und Bertram.*" *Licht-Bild-Bühne* 161, July 14, 1939.

Henseleit, Felix. "*Die Degenhardts.*" *Film-Kurier,* August 15, 1944.

———. "*Frauen für Golden Hill.*" *Licht-Bild-Bühne* 5, January 6, 1939.

———. "Gemeinschaftserlebnis im Film." *Licht-Bild-Bühne* 14, May 18, 1940.

———. "*Kautschuk.*" *Licht-Bild-Bühne* 264, November 9, 1938.

———. "Szene zwischen Zeitaltern: Nachtaufnahmen in Johannisthal für den Gründgens-Film *Tanz auf dem Vulkan.*" *Licht-Bild-Bühne* 186, August 10, 1938.

Herf, Jeffrey. *Reactionary Modernism: Technology, Culture and Politics in Weimar and the Third Reich.* Cambridge: Cambridge UP, 1984.

Herzberg, Georg. "*Robert und Bertram.*" Beiblatt zum *Filmkurier* 162, July 15, 1939.

———. "*Verklungene Melodie/*Gloria-Palast." *Film-Kurier* 48, February 26, 1938.

Himmel, Konrad. "Eine Tat, die die Weltwirtschaft umformte." *Licht-Bild-Bühne* 207, September 3, 1938.

Hinkel, Hans. "Der Einsatz unserer Kunst im Krieg." *Der deutsche Film* 5, no. 11/12 (May/June 1941): 214–17.

Hippler, Fritz. *Betrachtungen zum Filmschaffen*. 5th rev. ed. Berlin: Max Hesses, 1943.

———. *Die Verstrickung*. Dusseldorf: Mehr Wissen, 1981.

Hitler, Adolf. *Mein Kampf*. Trans. Ralph Manheim. Boston: Houghton Mifflin, 1971.

———. *Mein Kampf*, 2 vols. Munich: Franz Eher, 1935.

———. Motto, *Der deutsche Film* 3, no. 11 (May 1939): 305.

———. *Reden und Proklamationen 1932–1945*. Ed. Max Domarus. 2.2 vols. Munich: Süddeutscher Verlag, 1965.

Hofer, Walter, ed. *Der Nationalsozialismus: Dokumente 1933–1945*. Frankfurt a. M.: Fischer, 1959.

Hoffmann, Hilmar. *"Und die Fahne führt uns in die Ewigkeit": Propaganda im NS-Film*. Frankfurt a. M.: Fischer, 1988.

Hollstein, Dorothea. *"Jud Süß" und die Deutschen: Antisemitische Vorurteile im nationalsozialistischen Spielfilm*. Frankfurt a. M.: Ullstein, 1971.

Holz, Elisabeth. "Festliche Hamburger Uraufführung von *Kautschuk*." *Licht-Bild-Bühne* 258, November 2, 1938.

Hömberg, Hans. "*Kautschuk* Premiere im Ufa-Palast am Zoo." n.p., n.d. *Kautschuk*, Document File 8701, Bundesarchiv-Filmarchiv, Berlin.

Horak, Jan-Christopher. "Luis Trenker's *The Kaiser of California:* How the West was Won, Nazi Style." *Historical Journal of Film, Radio, and Television* 6.2 (1986): 181–88.

Hu, Ha. "Hans H. Zerlett dreht die Geschichte von den zwei Vagabunden, die trotzdem in den Himmel kamen!" *Filmwelt* 3, January 20, 1939.

Hufszky, Hans. "Im Scheinwerfer: Gustaf Gründgens als Debureau." Beilage zur *Filmwelt* 50, December 9, 1938.

Hull, David Stewart. *Film in the Third Reich*. Berkeley: U of California P, 1969.

Huth, Jochen. *Ein Mensch wird geboren: Ein Film von Jochen Huth nach Motiven aus seiner Komödie des Alltags* Ultimo! Filmscript, Berlin, [c. 1938,] n.p. Hochschule für Film und Fernsehen "Konrad Wolf" Library, Potsdam-Babelsberg.

"'Ich habe Sie belogen!' Dramatische Szene mit Zarah Leander in dem Ufa-film 'Damals.'" *Film-Kurier* 262, November 7, 1942.

"Im Scheinwerfer: Das Künstlerehepaar Gustav Diessl-Maria Cebotari." Beilage zur *Filmwelt* 44, Oktober 28, 1938.

"Im Scheinwerfer: Staatsschauspieler Willy Birgel — der Künstler und Mensch." Beilage zur *Filmwelt* 52, December 23, 1938.

Iris, "Das Lokalstück: Die menschliche Komödie." n.p., n.d. *Robert und Bertram,* Document File 13931, Bundesarchiv-Filmarchiv, Berlin.

j., e. "Debureau spielt Louis Philippe: Nachtaufnahmen zu *Tanz auf dem Vulkan.*" *Filmwelt* 35, August 26, 1938.

Jary, Micaela. *Ich weiß, es wird einmal ein Wunder gescheh'n: Die große Liebe der Zarah Leander.* Berlin: edition q, 1993.

Jelavich, Peter. *Berlin Cabaret.* Cambridge, MA: Harvard UP, 1993.

Kaes, Anton. *From Hitler to Heimat: The Return of History as Film.* Cambridge, MA: Harvard UP, 1989.

———. "Mass Culture and Modernity: Notes Toward a Social History of Early American and German Cinema." In *America and the Germans: An Assessment of a Three-Hundred-Year History,* eds. Franz Trommler and Joseph McVeigh, Vol. 2: 317–32. Philadelphia: U of Pennsylvania P, 1985.

Kaes, Anton, Martin Jay, and Edward Dimendberg, eds. *The Weimar Republic Sourcebook.* Berkeley: U of California P, 1994.

"Kampf um die Frau in Australiens Wüste: Kirsten Heibergs erste Hauptrolle. *Frauen für Golden Hill* und Kameradentreue." n.p., n.d. *Frauen für Golden Hill,* Document File 5697, Bundesarchiv-Filmarchiv, Berlin.

Kanzog, Klaus. *"Staatspolitisch besonders wertvoll": Ein Handbuch zu 30 deutschen Spielfilmen der Jahre 1934 bis 1945.* Munich: diskurs film, 1994.

Kästner, Erich. *Notabene 45: Ein Tagebuch,* Zurich: Altrium, 1961.

Kater, Michael. *Different Drummers: Jazz in the Culture of Nazi Germany.* New York: Oxford UP, 1992.

Kautschuk, Censor-Card 49615, Bundesarchiv-Filmarchiv, Berlin.

Kautschuk, Illustrierter Film-Kurier 2879. Berlin: Vereinigte Verlagsgesellschaften Franke & Co., n.d.

Kershaw, Ian. *The Nazi Dictatorship: Problems and Perspectives of Interpretation.* 3d ed. New York: Routledge, Chapman & Hall, 1993.

———. *Popular Opinion and Political Dissent in the Third Reich: Bavaria, 1933–1945.* Oxford: Oxford UP, 1983.

Keyserling, Graf Hermann. *Das Reisetagebuch eines Philosophen.* 8th ed. Stuttgart: Deutsche Verlags-Anstalt, 1932.

Kindler, Helmut. "Star als Genre." *Der deutsche Film* 3, no. 12 (June 1939): 339–41.

Klein, Adolf. *Köln im Dritten Reich: Stadtgeschichte der Jahre 1933–1945.* Cologne: Greven, 1983.

Klockmann, Martin. "Kampf um gesellschaftliche Rechte: Zum Film *Tanz auf dem Vulkan.*" n.p., n.d. *Tanz auf dem Vulkan,* Document File 16695, Bundesarchiv-Filmarchiv, Berlin.

Klotz, Marcia. "Epistemological Ambiguity and the Fascist Text: *Jew Süss, Carl Peters,* and *Ohm Krüger.*" *New German Critique* 74 (Spring-Summer 1998): 91–124.

Knoll, Arthur J., and Lewis H. Gann, eds. *Germans in the Tropics: Essays in German Colonial History.* New York: Greenwood Press, 1987.

Koepnick, Lutz. *The Dark Mirror: German Cinema between Hitler and Hollywood.* Berkeley: U of California P, 2002.

———. "Unsettling America: German Westerns and Modernity." *Modernism/ Modernity* 2.3 (1995): 1–22.

Kongo-Express, Illustrierter Film-Kurier 3051. Berlin: Vereinigte Verlagsgesellschaften Franke & Co., n.d.

Kracauer, Siegfried. *From Caligari to Hitler: A Psychological History of the German Film.* Princeton: Princeton UP, 1947.

———. *Das Ornament der Masse: Essays.* Frankfurt a. M.: Suhrkamp, 1977.

———. "Vom Erleben des Krieges." In *Schriften.* Ed. Inka Mülder-Bach. Vol. 5.1. Frankfurt a. M.: Suhrkamp, 1990.

Kreimeier, Klaus. "Mechanik, Waffen und Haudegen überall: Expeditionsfilme: das bewaffnete Auge des Ethnografen." In *Triviale Tropen: Exotische Reise- und Abenteuerfilme aus Deutschland 1919–1945,* ed. Jörg Schöning, 47–61. Munich: edition text + kritik, 1997.

———. *Die Ufa-Story: Geschichte eines Filmkonzerns.* Munich: Hanser, 1992.

———. "Von Henny Porten zu Zarah Leander: Filmgenres und Genrefilm in der Weimarer Republik und im Nationalsozialismus." *Montage/Av: Zeitschrift für Theorie & Geschichte audiovisueller Kommunikation* 3.2 (1994): 41–54.

Krüger, Bernhard. *Das Abenteuer lockt: Filmexpeditionen, Expeditionsfilme, Ein Taschenbericht.* Berlin: Karl Curtis, 1940.

Kuhn, Annette. *Women's Pictures: Feminism and Cinema.* New York: Routledge & Kegan Paul, 1982.

Kühn, Volker. "'Man muß das Leben nehmen, wie es eben ist . . .' Anmerkungen zum Schlager und seiner Fähigkeit, mit der Zeit zu gehen." In *Musik und Musikpolitik im faschistischen Deutschland,* ed. Hanns Werner Heister and Hans-Günter Klein, 213–26. Frankfurt a. M.: Fischer, 1984.

Kurowski, Ulrich, and Andreas Meyer, eds. *Der Filmregisseur Peter Pewas: Materialien und Dokumente.* Berlin: Volker Spiess, 1981.

L. E. D. "Gibt der Film ein falsches Weltbild?" Beilage zur *Licht-Bild-Bühne* 25/26, January 29, 1938.

Lane, Barbara Miller. *Architecture and Politics in Germany, 1918–1934.* Cambridge, MA: Harvard UP, 1968.

Latour, Conrad F. "Goebbels 'Außerordentliche Rundfunkmaßnahmen' 1939– 1942." *Vierteljahrshefte für Zeitgeschichte* 11 (1963): 418–35.

Leander, Zarah. *Es war so wunderbar! Mein Leben.* Hamburg: Hoffman und Campe, 1973.

Das Leben kann so schön sein, Censor-Card 50115, Bundesarchiv-Filmarchiv, Berlin.

Das Leben kann so schön sein, Illustrierter Film-Kurier 2905. Berlin: August Scherl Verlag, n.d.

Das Leben kann so schön sein: Progress-Dienst für Presse und Werbung. Berlin: VEB Progress Film-Vertrieb, July, 1962.

Das Leben kann so schön sein: Ufa Bild- und Textinformation. Berlin: Ufa-Pressestelle, n.d. *Das Leben kann so schön sein,* Document File 9596, Bundesarchiv-Filmarchiv, Berlin.

Leiser, Erwin. *Nazi Cinema.* Trans. Gertrud Mander and David Wilson. New York: Collier, 1975.

Licht-Bild-Bühne 206, September 5, 1939.

Lochner, Louis P., ed. *The Goebbels Diaries 1942–1943.* New York: Doubleday, 1948.

Loiperdinger, Martin. *Rituale der Mobilmachung: Der Parteitagsfilm* Triumph des Willens *von Leni Riefenstahl.* Opladen: Leske & Budrich, 1987.

Loiperdinger, Martin, and Klaus Schönekäs. "*Die große Liebe:* Propaganda im Unterhaltungsfilm." In *Bilder schreiben Geschichte: Der Historiker im Kino,* ed. Rainer Rother, 143–53. Berlin: Wagenbach, 1991.

Lowry, Stephen. *Pathos und Politik: Ideologie im Spielfilm des Nationalsozialismus.* Tübingen: Niemeyer, 1991.

Luft, Friedrich. "Gründgens und der Film." In *Gründgens: Schauspieler, Regisseur, Theaterleiter,* ed. Henning Rischbieter, 29–37. Velber bei Hannover: Erhard Friedrich, 1963.

Lydor, Waldemar. "Gesprochene Tänze: Besuch bei Theo Mackeben." n.p., n.d. *Tanz auf dem Vulkan,* Document File 16695, Bundesarchiv-Filmarchiv, Berlin.

M., B. "Gauner in der Posse." *Robert und Bertram: Presseheft.* Leipzig: Tobis Filmkunst GmbH Pressedienst, n.d. *Robert und Bertram,* Document File 13931, Bundesarchiv-Filmarchiv, Berlin.

Ma. "Brigitte Horney." *Der deutsche Film* 3, no. 6 (December 1938): 156–59.

Maiwald, Stefan, and Gerd Mischler. *Sexualität unter dem Hakenkreuz: Manipulation und Vernichtung der Intimsphäre im NS-Staat.* Hamburg: Europa Verlag, 1999.

Mallmann, Klaus-Michael, and Gerhard Paul, "Omniscient, Omnipotent, Omnipresent? Gestapo, Society and Resistence." In *Nazism and German Society,* 1933–1945, ed. David Crew, 166–96. New York: Rutledge, 1994.

Mandell, Richard. *The Nazi Olympics.* New York: Macmillian, 1971.

Mannheim, Karl. *Ideology and Utopia: An Introduction to the Sociology of Knowledge.* Trans. Louis Wirth and Edward Shils. New York: Harcourt, Brace, and Co., 1936.

Maraun, Frank. "Das Ergebnis: Wirklichkeitsnähe bevorzugt!: Eine Untersuchung über den 'Publikumsgeschmack." *Der deutsche Film* 3, no. 11 (May 1939): 306–11.

———. "Das Erlebnis entscheidet: Der abendfüllende Kulturfilm — von verschiedenen Seiten gesehen." *Der deutsche Film* 2, no. 7 (January 1938): 187–89.

———. "Unsere Wehrmacht im Film." *Der deutsche Film* 4, no. 12 (June 1940): 227–32.

Messenger, Charles. *"Bomber" Harris and the Strategic Bombing Offensive, 1939–1945*. New York: St. Martin's Press, 1984.

Mitscherlich, Alexander, and Margarete Mitscherlich. *The Inability to Mourn: Principles of Collective Behavior*. Trans. Beverley R. Placzek. New York: Grove Press, 1984.

Moeller, Felix. *Der Filmminister: Goebbels und der Film im Dritten Reich*. Berlin: Henschel, 1998.

Monaco, James. *How To Read a Film*. Oxford: Oxford UP, 1981.

Morrison, Wilber H. *Fortress Without a Roof: The Allied Bombing of the Third Reich*. New York: St. Martin's Press, 1982.

Mosse, George. "Two World Wars and the Myth of the War Experience." *Journal of Contemporary History* 21 (October 1986): 491–514.

Mulvey, Laura. "Notes on Sirk and Melodrama." In *Home is Where the Heart Is: Studies in Melodrama and the Woman's Film,* ed. Christine Gledhill, 75–82. London: British Film Institute, 1987.

———. *Visual and Other Pleasures*. Bloomington: Indiana UP, 1989.

N., H. "Dic Birnc." *Filmwoche* 29, July 15, 1938.

Neale, Stephen. *Genre*. London: British Film Institute, 1980.

Nebel, Hete. "Die Gräfin und der Komödiant: Zwei Szenen aus *Tanz auf dem Vulkan*." *Filmwelt* 27, July 1, 1938.

———. "Künstler antworten uns: Professor Carl Froelich: Zeitnahe muß nicht gleichbedeutend mit Gegenwart sein!" *Der deutsche Film* 3, no. 11 (May 1939): 311.

Neitzke, Hans Joachim. "Rückzug vor der Entscheidung: Happy end — ja oder nein?" *Licht-Bild-Bühne* 65, March 17, 1939.

Nenno, Nancy. "Femininity, the Primitive, and Modern Urban Space: Josephine Baker in Berlin." In *Women in the Metropolis: Gender and Modernity in Weimar Culture,* ed. Katharina von Ankum, 145–61. Berkeley: U of California P, 1997.

Neumann, Franz L. *Behemoth: The Structure and Practice of National Socialism, 1933–1944*. New York: Octagon Books, 1963.

O'Brien, Mary-Elizabeth. "Aestheticizing War: Eduard von Borsody's *Wunschkonzert* (1940)." *Seminar* 33, no. 1 (1997): 36–49.

———. "The Celluloid War: Packaging War for Sale in Nazi Home-Front Films." In *Art, Culture, and Media under the Third Reich,* ed. Richard Etlin, 158–80. Chicago: U of Chicago P, 2002.

———. "Male Conquest of the Female Continent in Veit Harlan's *Opfergang* (1944)." *Monatshefte* 87, no. 4 (1995): 431–45.

———. "The Spectacle of War in *Die große Liebe.*" In *Cultural History through a National Socialist Lens: Essays on the Cinema of the Third Reich,* ed. Robert C. Reimer, 197–213. Rochester, NY: Camden House, 2000.

Ohlisch, Erno. "Mit den Augen des Architekten: Walter Haags Bauten zu dem neuen Zarah-Leander-Film der Ufa 'Damals.'" *Film-Kurier* 191, August 17, 1942.

Opfergang, Censor-Card 59952, Bundesarchiv-Filmarchiv, Berlin.

Opfergang: Ein Ufa Farbfilm. Berlin: Werbedienst der Deutschen Filmvertrieb-Gesellschaft, n.d. *Opfergang,* Document File 12480, Bundesarchiv-Filmarchiv Berlin.

Opfergang, Illustrierte Film Bühne 1943. Munich: Verlag Film-Bühne, n.d.

Otto, Paul. "Ein Monopol wird gebrochen: *Kautschuk* im Ufa-Palast am Zoo." n.p., n.d. *Kautschuk,* Document File 8701, Bundesarchiv-Filmarchiv, Berlin.

P., W. "Der 'falsche Lacher': Betrachtungen über die Psychologie des Publikums." *Film-Kurier* 155, July 6, 1938.

Panofsky, Walter. "Die Sache mit dem happy end: Historische Beispiele zu einem oftdiskutierten Thema." *Film-Kurier* 108, May 11, 1942.

———. "Was will das Publikum auf der Leinwand sehen?" *Film-Kurier* 224, September 24, 1938.

Papke, Lothar. "Familienroman von heute: *Die Degenhardts.*" *Völkischer Beobachter,* August 13, 1944, Berlin edition.

Paul, Wolfgang. *Der Heimatkrieg 1939 bis 1945.* Esslingen am Neckar: Bechtle, 1980.

Peltz-Dreckmann, Ute. *Nationalsozialistischer Siedlungsbau: Versuch einer Analyse der die Siedlungspolitik bestimmenden Faktoren am Beispiel des Nationalsozialismus.* Munich: Minerva, 1978.

Petley, Julian. *Capital and Culture: German Cinema 1933–1945.* London: British Film Institute, 1979.

Peukert, Detlev J. K. *Inside Nazi Germany: Conformity, Opposition, and Racism in Everyday Life.* Trans. Richard Deveson. New Haven: Yale UP, 1987.

Phillips, Richard. *Mapping Men and Empire: A Geography of Adventure.* New York: Routledge, 1997.

Picker, Henry, ed. *Hitlers Tischgespräche im Führerhauptquartier 1941–42*. Bonn: Athenäum, 1951.

Plambeck, James A. "United States Synthetic Rubber Program, 1939–1945." Industrial Organic Chemistry, Synthetic Rubber. http://www.chem.ualberta.ca/ ~plambeck/che/p265/p06184.htm. U of Alberta: copyright 1996.

Plant, Richard. *The Pink Triangle: The Nazi War against Homosexuals*. New York: H. Holt, 1986.

"Praktische Werbe-Vorschläge." *Das Leben kann so schön sein* [advertising materials]. Berlin: August Scherl Verlag, n.d. *Das Leben kann so schön sein*, Document File 9596, Bundesarchiv-Filmarchiv Berlin.

"Problem-Filme? Ja!" *Licht-Bild-Bühne* 24, January 29, 1940.

Redlich, Fredrick C. *Hitler: Diagnosis of a Destructive Prophet*. New York: Oxford UP, 1998.

Rehberg, Hans, Hans Steinhoff, and Peter Hagen. *Wenn Debureau spielt . . . Arbeitstitel*. Filmscript, Majestic Film: Berlin, n.d. Hochschule für Film und Fernsehen "Konrad Wolf" Library, Potsdam-Babelsberg.

Reichel, Peter. *Der schöne Schein des Dritten Reiches: Faszination und Gewalt des Faschismus*. Munich: Hanser, 1991.

"René Deltgen: Weg von der Landarbeit zur Bühne und zum Film." *Filmwelt* 43, October 21, 1938.

Rentschler, Eric. *The Ministry of Illusion: Nazi Cinema and its Afterlife*. Cambridge, MA: Harvard UP, 1996.

Rhode, Carla. "Leuchtende Sterne?" In *Wir tanzen um die Welt: Deutsche Revuefilme 1933–1945*, ed. Helga Belach, 119–38. Munich: Hanser, 1979.

Riegler, Theodor. "Im Scheinwerfer: Willy Birgel." Beilage zur *Filmwelt* 16, April 19, 1940.

———. "*Traumbild und Wirklichkeit*." *Filmwelt* 6, February 9, 1940.

Riess, Curt. *Das gab's nur einmal: Das Buch der schönsten Filme unseres Lebens*. 2d rev. ed. Hamburg: Verlag der Sternbücher, 1956.

Rikli, Martin. *Ich filmte für Millonen: Fahrten, Abenteuer und Erinnerungen eines Filmberichters*. Berlin: Schützen, 1942.

Robert und Bertram, Censor-Card 19914, Bundesarchiv-Filmarchiv, Berlin.

Robert und Bertram, Censor-Card 51648, Bundesarchiv-Filmarchiv, Berlin.

Robert und Bertram, Censor-Card 58867, Bundesarchiv-Filmarchiv, Berlin.

Robert und Bertram, Das Programm von heute 385. Berlin: Das Programm von heute, Zeitschrift für Film und Theater GmbH, 1938.

Robert und Bertram, Illustrierter Film-Kurier 2946. Berlin: Franke & Co, n.d.

Robert und Bertram, Lockende Leinwand 23. Berlin: Deutscher Verlag, July 31 — August 3, [1939].

Robert und Bertram oder die lustigen Vagabunden, Censor-Card 1337, Bundesarchiv-Filmarchiv, Berlin.

Robert und Bertram: Reklame-Ratschläge. Berlin: Tobis Filmkunst GmbH Werbedienst, n.d. *Robert und Bertram,* Document File 13931, Bundesarchiv-Filmarchiv, Berlin.

Robert und Bertram: Tobis Presseheft. Leipzig: Tobis Filmkunst GmbH Pressedienst, n.d. *Robert und Bertram,* Document File 13931, Bundesarchiv-Filmarchiv, Berlin.

Rony, Fatimah Tobing. *The Third Eye: Race, Cinema and Ethnographic Spectacle.* Durham: Duke UP, 1996.

Rose, Phyllis. *Jazz Cleopatra: Josephine Baker in Her Time.* New York: Doubleday, 1989.

Rost, Karl Ludwig. *Medizin im Spielfilm des Nationalsozialismus.* Eds. Udo Benzenhöfer and Wolfgang Eckart. Tecklenburg: Burgverlag, 1990.

Rühmann, Heinz. "Kurz und bündig." *Der deutsche Film* 3, no. 11 (May 1939): 314.

Rundell, Richard J. "Literary Nazis? Adapting Nineteenth-Century German Novellas for the Screen: *Der Schimmelreiter, Kleider machen Leute,* and *Immensee.*" In *Cultural History through a National Socialist Lens: Essays on the Cinema of the Third Reich,* ed. Robert C., 176–96. Reimer. Rochester, NY: Camden House, 2000.

S., H. "In der Quarantäne-Station: Dramatische Szenen aus dem Ufafilm 'Damals.'" *Film-Kurier* 282, December 1, 1942.

Schäfer, Hans Dieter. *Das gespaltene Bewußtsein: Deutsche Kultur und Lebenswirklichkeit 1933–1945.* 3d ed. Munich: Hanser, 1983.

Schärer, Thomas. *Filmische Nonkonformität im NS-Staat: Eine Filmreihe 7.–15. April 1997.* Berlin: Freunde der deutschen Kinemathek, 1997.

Schatz, Thomas H. *Hollywood Genres: Formula, Film Making, and the Studio System.* New York: Random House, 1981.

Schiller, Friedrich. *Sämtliche Werke.* Ed. Gerhard Fricke and Herbert G. Göpfert. Munich: Hanser, 1959.

Schlamp, Hans-Joachim. *Brigitte Horney.* Künstler-Biographien 1. Berlin: Verlag Robert Mölich, n.d.

Schluchter, Wolfgang. *Paradoxes of Modernity: Culture and Conduct in the Theory of Max Weber.* Trans. Neil Solomon. Stanford: Stanford UP, 1996.

Schlüpmann, Heidi. "Faschistische Trugbilder weiblicher Autonomie." *Frauen und Film* 44/45 (October 1988): 44–66.

Schmidt, Maruta, and Gabi Dietz, eds. *Frauen unterm Hakenkreuz*. Berlin: Elefanten Press, 1983.

Schmokel, Wolfe W. *Dream of Empire: German Colonialism, 1919–1945*. New Haven: Yale UP, 1964.

Schneider, Albert. *"Robert und Bertram." Licht-Bild-Bühne* 162, July 15, 1939.

———. *"Tanz auf dem Vulkan." Licht-Bild-Bühne* 296, December 17, 1938.

———. *" Verklungene Melodie:* Ein Ufa-Film, Gloria-Palast.*" Licht-Bild-Bühne* 49, February 26, 1938.

Schoenbaum, David. *Die braune Revolution: Eine Sozialgeschichte des Dritten Reiches*. Trans. Tamara Schoenbaum-Holtermann. Berlin: Ullstein, 1999.

Scholtz-Klink, Gertrud. *Die Frau im Dritten Reich: Eine Dokumentation*. Tübingen: Grabert, 1978.

Schomburgk, Hans. *Mein Afrika: Erlebtes und Erlauschtes aus dem Innern Afrikas*. 2d ed. Leipzig: Deutsche Buchwerkstätten, 1930.

Schöning, Jörg, ed. *Trivale Tropen: Exotische Reise- und Abenteuerfilme aus Deutschland 1919–1939*. Munich: edition text + kritik, 1997.

Schulte-Sasse, Linda. *Entertaining the Third Reich: Illusions of Wholeness in Nazi Cinema*. Durham: Duke UP, 1996.

———. "The Jew as Other under National Socialism: Veit Harlan's *Jud Süß.*" *German Quarterly* 61, no. 1 (1988): 22–49.

Schulz-Kampfhenkel, Otto. *Im afrikanischen Dschungel als Tierfänger und Urwaldjäger*. Berlin: Deutscher Verlag, 1937.

Schwaab, Edleff H. *Hitler's Mind: A Plunge into Madness*. New York: Praeger, 1992.

Schwark, Günther. *"Frauen für Golden Hill." Film-Kurier* 5, January 6, 1939.

———. *"Kautschuk:* Ufa-Palast am Zoo.*" Film-Kurier* 263, November 9, 1938.

———. *"Tanz auf dem Vulkan." Film-Kurier* 295, December 17, 1938.

Sengle, Friedrich. "Wunschbild Land und Schreckbild Stadt: Zu einem zentralen Thema der neuen deutschen Literatur." *Studium-Generale* 16 (1963): 619–31.

Silberman, Marc. *German Cinema: Texts in Context*. Detroit: Wayne State UP, 1995.

Smith, Woodruff. *The German Colonial Empire*. Chapel Hill: U of North Carolina P, 1978.

Söderbaum, Kristina. *Nichts bleibt immer so: Rückblenden auf ein Leben vor und hinter der Kamera*. 3rd ed. Bayreuth: Hestia, 1984.

"Sonderreklame — die notwendig ist! Werbung durch Musik!" *Tanz auf dem Vulkan: Reklame-Ratschläge*. Berlin: Tobis Filmkunst GmbH, n.d. *Tanz auf dem Vulkan*, Document File 16695, Bundesarchiv-Filmarchiv, Berlin.

Speckner, Georg. "Dreimal mit Zarah Leander: Hans Stüwe in dem neuen Ufa-Film 'Damals.'" *Film-Kurier* 197, August 24, 1942.

Speer, Albert. *Inside the Third Reich*. Trans. Richard and Clara Winston. New York: Macmillan, 1970.

Spieker, Markus. *Hollywood unterm Hakenkreuz: Der amerikanische Spielfilm im Dritten Reich*. Trier: Wissenschaftlicher Verlag, 1999.

Spielhofer, Hans. "Der Filmschauspieler: Eine typenkundliche Betrachtung," *Der deutsche Film* 2, no. 2 (June 1938): 326–28.

———. "Der wichtigste Film des Monats." *Der deutsche Film* 2, no. 10 (April 1938): 288–89.

———. "Wunschtraum oder Wirklichkeit? Eine Betrachtung über Notwendigkeit und Problematik ihrer Abgrenzung." *Der deutsche Film* 3, no. 11 (May 1939): 317–22.

"Spielleiter sucht Schauspieler." *Das Leben kann so schön sein: Ufa Bild- und Textinformation*. Berlin: Ufa-Pressestelle, n.d. *Das Leben kann so schön sein*, Document File 9596, Bundesarchiv-Filmarchiv Berlin.

"Sprung von der Reichsautobahn nach Brasilien: Drei neue Filme — *Mann für Mann, Glück auf Raten, Kautschuk*." *Filmwelt* 41, October 7, 1938.

Steinart, Marlis G. *Hitler's War and the Germans: Public Mood and Attitude during the Second World War*. Trans. Thomas E. J. de Witt. Athens, Ohio: Ohio UP, 1977.

Steinhoff, Hans. "Meine Filmarbeit mit Gustaf Gründgens." *Licht-Bild-Bühne* 188, August 12, 1938.

Stephenson, Jill. *Women in Nazi Society*. New York: Barnes & Noble, 1975.

Stern, J. P. *Hitler: The Führer and the People*. Berkeley: U of California P, 1975.

Struck, Wolfgang. "'Afrika zu unsern Füßen': Kinematographische Lufthohheiten über einem dunklen Kontinent." In *Geschichte(n): NS-Film — NS-Spuren heute*, ed. Hans Krah, 65–74. Kiel: Ludwig, 1999.

Suchen, Hans. *"Die große Liebe."* *Filmwelt* 23/24, June 24, 1942.

Tanz auf dem Vulkan, Censor-Card 49884, Bundesarchiv-Filmarchiv, Berlin.

Tanz auf dem Vulkan, Illustrierter Film Kurier 2862. Berlin: Franke & Co, 1938.

Tanz auf dem Vulkan: Presseheft. Tobis: Berlin, n.d. *Tanz auf dem Vulkan*, Document File 16695, Bundesarchiv-Filmarchiv, Berlin.

Tanz auf dem Vulkan, Das Programm von heute 298. Berlin: Das Programm von heute: Zeitschrift für Film und Theater, GmbH, 1937.

Tanz auf dem Vulkan: Reklame-Ratschläge. Berlin: Tobis Filmkunst GmbH, n.d. *Tanz auf dem Vulkan*, Document File 16695, Bundesarchiv-Filmarchiv, Berlin.

"Tauge-nichts und Tu-nicht-gut." n.p., n.d. *Robert und Bertram*, Document File 13931, Bundesarchiv-Filmarchiv, Berlin.

Taylor, Richard. *Film Propaganda: Soviet Russia and Nazi Germany.* New York: Harper & Row, 1979.

Thomalla, Ariane. *Die femme fragile: Ein literarischer Frauentypus der Jahrhundertwende.* Dusseldorf: Bertelsmann-Universitätsverlag, 1972.

Torgovnick, Marianna. *Gone Primitive: Savage Intellects, Modern Lives.* Chicago: U of Chicago P, 1990.

Töteberg, Michael. "Gustaf Gründgens." In *Cinegraph: Lexikon zum deutschsprachigen Film,* ed. Hans Michael Bock, E1–E8. Munich: edition text + kritik, 1984ff.

Traudisch, Dora. *Mutterschaft mit Zuckerguß?: Frauenfeindliche Propaganda im NS-Spielfilm.* Pfaffenweiler: Centaurus, 1993.

Trimmel, Gerald. *Heimkehr: Strategien eines nationalsozialistischen Films.* Vienna: Werner Eichbauer, 1998.

Tröger, Annemarie. "The Creation of a Female Assembly-Line Proletariat." In *When Biology Became Destiny: Women in Weimar and Nazi Germany,* ed. Renate Bridenthal, Atina Grossmann, and Marion Kaplan, 237–70. New York: Monthly Review Press, 1984.

"Ein unberechtigter Vorwurf: Ist der Film eine Weibliche Kunst? Frauen und Männer sind sich einig in der Forderung nach dem künstlerischen, lebensnahen Film." *Film-Kurier* 128, June 3, 1938.

"Veit Harlan zum Thema 'Falsche Lacher': Ein Regisseur tritt für das Publikum an." *Film-Kurier* 157, July 8, 1938.

Verklungene Melodie, Censor-Card 47669, Bundesarchiv-Filmarchiv, Berlin.

Verklungene Melodie, Illustrierter Film-Kurier 2772. Berlin: Vereinigte Verlagsgesellschaften Franke & Co., n.d.

Via Mala, Illustrierter Film-Kurier. Berlin: Vereinigte Verlagsgesellschaft Franke & Co., n.d.

Via Mala, Das Program von heute. Berlin: Das Program von heute, Zeitschrift für Film und Theater GmbH, n.d.

Via Mala: Die Straße des Bösen, Illustrierte Film-Bühne 665. Munich: Film-Bühne GmbH, n.d. *Via Mala,* Document File 18403, Bundesarchiv-Filmarchiv, Berlin.

Victor, George. *Hitler: The Pathology of Evil.* Washington, DC: Brassey's, 1998.

Virilio, Paul. *War and Cinema: The Logistics of Perception.* Trans. Patrick Camiller. London: Verso, 1989.

"Voranlauf in der Provinz: Erstes Halbjahr der Spielzeit 1938/39." *Licht-Bild-Bühne* 24, January 28, 1939.

W., H. "Im Scheinwerfer: René Deltgen." Beilage zur *Filmwelt* 55, n.d. *Kautschuk,* Document File 8701, Bundesarchiv-Filmarchiv, Berlin.

W. B. "Eine Rechnung, die nicht aufgeht: Dreck oder Gold, sagt Peter Pewas zu seinem ersten Film." n.t., n.p., 1943, Peter Pewas Personal File, Bundesar-chiv-Filmarchiv, Berlin.

Waas, Maria. n.t., n.p., n.d. *Die große Liebe,* Document File 6214, Bundesarchiv-Filmarchiv, Berlin.

Waite, Robert G. L. *The Psychopathic God: Adolf Hitler.* New York: Basic Books, 1977.

Weber, Max. *Economy and Society.* Eds. Guenther Roth and Claus Wittich. Trans. Ephraim Fischoff. Berkeley: U of California P, 1978.

———. "Science as a Vocation." In *From Max Weber: Essays in Sociology,* eds. and trans. H. H. Gerth and C. Wright Mills, 129–56. London: Routledge & K. Paul, 1948.

Wehner, Ilse. "Filme des Monats." *Der deutsche Film* 3, no. 7 (January 1939): 195–97.

———. "Filme des Monats." *Der deutsche Film* 3, no. 8 (February 1939): 228–29.

Welch, David. *Propaganda and the German Cinema 1933–1945.* New York: Oxford UP, 1983.

———. *The Third Reich: Politics and Propaganda.* New York: Routledge, 1993.

"Wer kennt diese Frau?" *Filmwelt* 3/4, January 20, 1943.

Westecker, Wilhelm. "Filmepos einer deutschen Familie: *Die Degenhardts* im Tauentzienpalast." *Berliner Börsen-Zeitung,* August 12, 1944.

Westennieder, Norbert. *"Deutsche Frauen und Mädchen!" Vom Alltagsleben 1933–1945.* Dusseldorf: Droste, 1990.

Wetzel, Kraft, and Peter A. Hagemann. *Zensur: Verbotene deutsche Filme 1933–1945.* Berlin: Volker Spiess, 1978.

Wexman, Virginia Wright. *Creating the Couple: Love, Marriage, and Hollywood Performance.* Princeton: Princeton UP, 1993.

White, Hayden. "Historiography and Historiophoty." *American Historical Review* 93:5 (December 1988): 1193.

Williams, Linda. "'Something Else Besides a Mother': *Stella Dallas* and the Maternal Melodrama." In *Home is Where the Heart Is: Studies in Melodrama and the Woman's Film,* ed. Christine Gledhill, 299–325. London: British Film Institute, 1987.

Witte, Karsten. "Der barocke Faschist: Veit Harlan und seine Filme." In *Intellek-tuelle im Bann des Nationalsozialismus,* ed. Karl Corino. Hamburg: Hoffmann und Campe, 1980.

———. *"Der verzauberte Tag." Frankfurter Rundschau,* March 26, 1978.

———. "Visual Pleasure Inhibited: Aspects of the German Revue Film." Trans. J. D. Steakley and Gabriele Hoover. *New German Critique* 24–25 (Fall/Winter 1981–82): 238–63.

Wolffram, Knud. *Tanzdielen und Vergnügungspaläste: Berliner Nachtleben in den dreißiger und vierziger Jahren.* 3d ed. Berlin: Edition Hentrich, 1992.

Wolschke-Bulmahn, Joachim, and Gert Gröning. "The National Socialist Garden and Landscape Ideal: Bodenständigkeit (Rootedness in the Soil)." In *Art, Culture, and Media under the Third Reich,* ed. Richard Etlin, 73–97. Chicago: Chicago UP, 2002.

Wolz, Ralf. "Mobilmachung." In *Heimatfront: Kriegsalltag in Deutschland 1939–1945,* ed. Jürgen Engert, 12–43. Berlin: Nicolai, 1999.

Wunschkonzert, Illustrierter Film-Kurier 3166. Berlin: Franke & Co, 1940.

Zielinski, Siegfried. *Veit Harlan.* Frankfurt a. M.: Rita G. Fischer, 1981.

Zumkeller, Cornelia. *Zarah Leander: Ihre Filme — ihr Leben.* Munich: Heyne, 1988.

Index